Red & Black in Haiti

MATTHEW J. SMITH

Red & Black in
Haiti

RADICALISM, CONFLICT, AND

POLITICAL CHANGE, 1934–1957

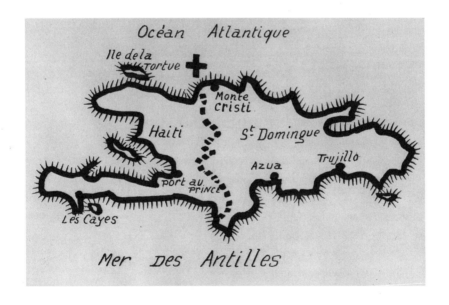

The University of North Carolina Press   *Chapel Hill*

Designed by Michelle Coppedge
Set in Whitman by Keystone Typesetting, Inc.

Part of this book has been reprinted with permission in
revised form from "Vive 1804!: The Haitian Revolution and
the Revolutionary Generation of 1946," *Caribbean Quarterly*
50, no. 4 (December 2004): 25–41.

The paper in this book meets the guidelines for permanence
and durability of the Committee on Production Guidelines for
Book Longevity of the Council on Library Resources.

The University of North Carolina Press has been a member
of the Green Press Initiative since 2003.

Library of Congress Cataloging-in-Publication Data
Smith, Matthew J., Ph.D.
Red and black in Haiti : radicalism, conflict, and political change,
1934–1957 / Matthew J. Smith. — 1st ed.
p. cm.
Includes bibliographical references and index.
ISBN 978-0-8078-3265-3 (cloth : alk. paper)
ISBN 978-0-8078-5937-7 (pbk. : alk. paper)
1. Haiti—Politics and government—1934–1971. 2. Communism—
Haiti—History—20th century. 3. Black nationalism—Haiti—History—
20th century. 4. Radicalism—Haiti—History—20th century. I. Title.
F1927.S656 2009
972.94'06—dc22   2008047298

cloth   13 12 11 10 09   5 4 3 2 1
paper   13 12 11 10 09   5 4 3 2 1

For Haiti

CONTENTS

Acknowledgments *ix*

Abbreviations *xi*

Introduction *1*

CHAPTER 1
The Postoccupation Dilemma: Ideology and Contention
    in the Vincent Years, 1934–1941 *13*

CHAPTER 2
Brown Power, Black Protest: The Lescot Regime and the Culture
    of Resistance, 1941–1945 *39*

CHAPTER 3
The Haitian Revolution of 1946 *71*

CHAPTER 4
Now Both Sides of the Hand Have a Chance: *Noirisme* and Opposition
    under Estimé, 1946–1950 *103*

CHAPTER 5
Blacks without Color: Military Rule and Radicalism in Transition,
    1950–1957 *149*

Conclusion *187*

Notes *197*

Bibliography *243*

Index *261*

ILLUSTRATIONS

The last U.S. flag is lowered and the Haitian flag is raised at a ceremony at
Cap Haïtien marking the end of the U.S. occupation, 6 August 1934 *10*

President Sténio Vincent, Foreign Minister Élie Lescot, and members of
the Garde d'Haïti High Command celebrate Haitian Independence Day,
1 January 1934 *14*

Max Hudicourt *18*

Jacques Roumain *18*

A Haitian-drawn map of Hispaniola made in November 1937 *34*

President Élie Lescot explains SHADA to Haitian peasant farmers, 1942 *45*

Daniel Fignolé *64*

Crowds gather in front of the National Palace during the January revolt,
1946 *79*

Members of *La Ruche* celebrate Lescot's overthrow, 11 January 1946 *81*

Masthead of the first issue of *Combat*, organ of the Haitian Communist
Party, 6 February 1946 *84*

President Dumarsais Estimé, Paul E. Magloire, Franck Lavaud, and Antoine
Levelt at a ceremony marking Estimé's assumption of executive powers,
16 August 1946 *111*

Daniel Fignolé addresses a crowd of supporters at Institut Mopique,
1947 *125*

A Socialist Party meeting at party headquarters, 1947 *131*

President Paul E. Magloire leads the military parade at the Haitian Flag Day
celebration at Champs de Mars, Port-au-Prince, 18 May 1954 *154*

François Duvalier and members of the army during the 1957 presidential
campaign *184*

ACKNOWLEDGMENTS

I am grateful to the numerous individuals and institutions that over the course of many years assisted in the completion of this book. My greatest thanks are to the several people I interviewed for the book. Their oral testimonies shed light on areas only partially revealed in the written sources. I regret that some have not lived to see the final product of a project they had a hand in creating. I can only hope that I have done justice to the life experiences and memories they so willingly shared.

In the earliest stages of the project at the University of Florida, David Geggus provided mentorship, careful supervision, expertise, and, most important, a fine example of exemplary scholarship. Murdo Macleod, Jeffrey Needell, Robert Zieger, Mark Thurner, and Gerald Murray offered encouragement and helpful advice on the preliminary draft of the manuscript.

Many of the arguments contained in the pages that follow benefited immensely from challenging discussions, insightful comments, and the unfailing support of various scholars, writers, activists, and thinkers of Haiti. Among those who warrant special mention are Léopold and Maxime Roumer, Alice Backer, Georges Corvington (who graciously supplied images for the book), Patrick Bellegarde-Smith, Carolle Charles, Thomas Dudley Fennell, Gage Averill, Pierre Buteau, Damien François (who also shared invaluable primary documents), Bryant Freeman, Thor Burnham, Roger Gaillard, Ermitte St. Jacques, Georges Michel, Marie-José Nzengou-Tayo, Richard Turits, Gérard Pierre-Charles, Millery Polyné, Chantalle Verna, Frantz Voltaire, Danielle F. Benjamin, and Ronald St. Jean. Early on I received crucial advice from Michael Dash. Much later, Michel Hector's critique of my findings and excitement for the subject inspired me through the final stages of research. Several people have commented on drafts of the book in part or in whole. I thank in particular John D. French, Roy Augier, and two anonymous readers for insightful comments and useful suggestions. While these comments and conversations have deepened my understanding of Haitian politics and history, I alone must bear responsibility for whatever faults the book may contain. I am also grateful to the staff of the University of North Carolina Press, especially Elaine Maisner and Paula Wald for their guidance and enthusiasm for the project. A special thanks to Eric Schramm, whose expert copyediting and careful attention to details greatly improved the quality of the book.

Funding for research and writing was made possible by the gracious assistance of several institutions. I thank the J. William Fulbright Foundation and the Institute of International Education; the University of Florida Department of History; The Harry S. Truman Library and Institute; The Center for Latin American Studies at the University of Florida for an A. Curtis Wilgus Travel Grant; and the University of Florida's College of Liberal Arts and Sciences for a Threadgill Dissertation Fellowship. The book was completed while I was an Andrew Mellon Visiting Professor at the Center for Latin American and Caribbean Studies at Duke University. I thank the center's staff and my colleagues in Durham for providing a warm and stimulating environment. My colleagues in the Department of History and Archaeology at the University of the West Indies, Mona, have my great appreciation for their continued support.

Financial assistance from these institutions made possible research travel, and I am most appreciative of the services provided by the librarians and archivists who assisted me during my visits. In Port-au-Prince, I would like to thank the staff of the Archives Nationales d'Haïti, especially Mme. G. Flaubert. Frère Ernst Even of the Institut St. Louis de Gonzague, Madame Françoise Thybulle, Nadège Constant, and the staff of the Bibliothèque National d'Haïti were always ready to assist. I owe a special debt of gratitude to the librarians and directors of the Bibliothèque Haïtienne des Peres du Saint-Esprit, who have labored against the odds to build and preserve an impressive collection. In the United States, the staff of the Latin American collection at the University of Florida, particularly Richard Phillips and Paul Losch, gave considerable assistance, as did Holly Ackerman at Duke. The staffs at the United States National Archives at College Park; the Manuscript Division of the Library of Congress; the Franklin D. Roosevelt, Harry S. Truman, and Dwight D. Eisenhower presidential libraries; and the Moorland-Spingarn Collection at Howard University provided expert help. At the Schomburg Center for Research in Black Culture of the New York Public Library, André Elizée pointed me to useful sources that I otherwise might have overlooked.

The friends and family who provided hospitality, financial support, accommodation, and transportation during my research trips have my gratitude. I am especially indebted to Johanne, Léo, and Gladys for more than I can mention. My family, Peter, Patsy, Iggy, Samantha, and Xavier, have my deepest love and respect for their years of patient understanding.

ABBREVIATIONS

The following abbreviations are used throughout the book.

ADEM   Association des Étudiants en Médicine, Pharmacie,
            et Art Dentaire
CDN   Comité de Défense Nationale
CEG   Conseil Exécutif Gouvernement
CEM   Comité Exécutif Militaire
CMG   Conseil Militaire de Gouvernement
CPUSA   Communist Party of the United States
FDU   Front Démocratique Unifié
FHT   Fédération Haïtienne des Travailleurs
FRH   Front Révolutionnaire Haïtien
FTH   Fédération des Travailleurs Haïtien
HASCO   Haitian American Sugar Company
ISI   Import Substitution Industrialization
JPDH   Jeunesse Progressive d'Haïti
JPP   Jeunesse Progressiste de Port-au-Prince
MOP   Mouvement Ouvrier Paysan (1946–56); Mouvement
            Organisation du Pays (1956–57)
NAACP   National Association for the Advancement of Colored People
PCH   Parti Communiste Haïtien
PDPJH   Parti Démocratique Populaire de la Jeunesse Haïtienne
PEP   Parti d'Entente Populaire
POPH   Parti Ouvrier Progressiste Haïtien
PPLN   Parti Populaire de Libération Nationale
PPN   Parti Populaire Nationale
PPSC   Parti Populaire Social Chrétien
PSH   Parti Socialiste Haïtien
PSP   Parti Socialiste Populaire
RD   Réaction Démocratique
SCISP   Service Coopératif Inter-Américain de la Santé Publique
SHADA   Société Haïtiano-Américaine de Développement Agricole
SOT   Syndicats d'Ouvriers et Travailleurs

Red & Black in Haiti

INTRODUCTION

The national colors shall be black and red.

—1805 HAITIAN CONSTITUTION

On the first of January 1934, the republic of Haiti celebrated its 130th anniversary as an independent nation. In a country born from a slave revolt, embittered by a history of regional, color, and class divisions, New Year's Day holds great meaning for Haitians. Yet despite a proud legacy of independence and several decades of attempts to shield their country from aggressive foreign penetration, on the first of January 1934 most Haitians did not consider themselves free. At the central square Champs de Mars, in the capital Port-au-Prince, the United States' red, white, and blue flag flew high, a visual reminder that the Caribbean's first sovereign nation was still in the throes of U.S. marine occupation. On the first of January 1934, independent Haiti resembled a colonized state.

In a few months, however, all this would change. After nearly two decades of U.S. occupation that witnessed popular and intellectual resistance, and a vigorous reevaluation of Haitian national discourse, the occupation was finally nearing its end. Nineteen thirty-four was, according to President Sténio Vincent in his New Year's state of the nation address, "the year of [Haiti's] Second Independence."[1] But if 1934 marked an end to the struggle for *désoccupation*, it was the beginning of a long and intense ideological and political conflict that would ultimately lead, in 1957, to one of the most brutal dictatorships the Caribbean has ever experienced: the regime of François "Papa Doc" Duvalier. It is the story of this conflict that is the subject of this book.

This book is about radical political movements in Haiti and their struggles in the period following the U.S. occupation until the creation of the Duvalierist state. It seeks to remedy a significant absence in the historiography on modern Haiti by investigating the turbulent politics of the postoccupation era, 1934–1957. The saga of the Haitian postoccupation presents a fascinating case of a small Caribbean nation with profound historical connections with the rest of the Americas, confronting the challenges and

1

legacies of recent foreign control while engulfed in the swirl of World War II and the cold war. Haiti's long history of resistance and independence distinguished the country from colonized Africa and its regional neighbors. Yet the postoccupation predicament, in which radicals with contrasting views of black power, radical nationalism, and Marxism fought for political space, suggests a situation not unlike the postcolonial struggles elsewhere in the world later in the twentieth century.

The postoccupation experience was modern Haiti's greatest moment of political promise. At its outset, black consciousness and an intense cross-class nationalism produced a rare opportunity for lasting political change. These years witnessed the establishment of a popular labor movement; the rise of political parties; a bitter and vibrant ideological struggle; and a shift toward an assertive brand of Haitian black nationalism, *noirisme*, that not only defined the future of Haitian politics, but also prefigured similar developments elsewhere in the Caribbean region. The postoccupation turning point came with the revolution of 1946, which sought to reverse the abuses in Haitian politics laid by the dominant political classes since independence, and continued by the country's rulers in the decade after 1934. However, the revolutionary movement quickly splintered and in its fragmentation created the roots of contemporary political tensions in Haiti.

Although these years involved dramatic and enduring shifts in Haitian political and social life, much of this history is remarkably understudied. At least two factors account for this lacuna. First, the complicated political history that marked the epoch from 1934 to 1957 has quite often discouraged scholars from engaging in serious study of the period. Scholars who have considered the full span of Haiti's political history often regard the post-occupation as merely a continuation of a cyclical pattern of turmoil no different from nineteenth-century contests or more recent upheavals.[2] Few writers have attempted to search the archival sources to unravel the knotted threads of the chronology. Even fewer have explored the broader implications of the various political movements of the era for the history of the region.

Second, historians of twentieth-century Haiti continue to be fascinated with the events, history, and issues associated with both the U.S. occupation and the Duvalierist state (1957–1986), demonstrated in the sizable literature generated on these periods. Most scholars of Haitian politics have tended to compress the interregnum into one or two general chapters that form the postscript or prelude to studies of the occupation or Duvalier.[3]

Departing significantly from these approaches, this book attempts a more complete political study of these overlooked years in Haitian history. It draws on extensive archival research, previously unused sources, interviews with various political and cultural figures of the era, and a close reading of contemporary accounts and the secondary literature to present a richer and more complicated picture of the interplay among political forces than is suggested in the existing scholarship. More specifically, the book explores the ways in which postoccupation radicalism emerged from being a largely unified elite-led movement in the 1930s to become a wider urban-based popular movement in the 1940s and 1950s that would draft the blueprint for current forms of social protest in Haiti. By exposing these cultural and political complexities and their articulations among radical groups, this study contributes to a broader discussion on the reasons for conflict and crisis in Haiti.

In reconstructing the postoccupation past, the book traces the ideas, activities, and organization of leading radicals. In so doing, it challenges common assumptions of Haitian politics during the period by emphasizing far-reaching ideological, regional, interclass, and social conflicts among groups competing for state control. It also emphasizes the connections between the Haitian experience and similar movements elsewhere in the region by placing Haitian radicalism within a broad context, and illuminating important links that served to invigorate its resistance.

The book's central thesis is that various radical movements issued a powerful challenge to the country's political traditions and transformed its political culture. This impact, however, changed over time, as did the attitudes and struggles of the radicals themselves. Often change was the result of pressure from the dominant social institutions fighting to preserve their threatened hegemony. On the other hand, much of the political conflict that marked the era emerged from internecine rivalries among radical groups that purported to be striving for the same goals. As the following chapters reveal, contingency frequently overshadowed ideological commitment in the formation of political allegiances.

A focus on domestic rivalries alone cannot completely explain this history. One of the crucial points this book stresses is that postoccupation Haiti unfolded in the shadow of sweeping social, cultural, and diplomatic changes in the region, which significantly affected the tone, nature, and prospects of political struggle. As with most other Latin American and Caribbean countries, the specter of U.S. anticommunism loomed large over the island. In Haiti, however, the problem was more complicated, as the strong focus on race, class, and color consciousness by radicals was often blurred in the perceptions of U.S. officials who were only too willing to label all opposition movements "communist." This factor greatly affected the relationship between the state and its opponents. The result was a divided opposition that over the two decades increasingly employed violence in its campaign for state power.

Haitian Color Politics

In order to explain the nature of political competition in Haiti, the roles race and color play in Haitian life must be briefly considered. It is important to distinguish between the two. Since independence in 1804, race has long been intricately bound up in the concept of Haitian national identity. Haitians of all social classes take great pride in their country's place as the first black republic in the western hemisphere. In Haiti, according to Gordon Lewis, "there are, certainly, superior cultures but not superior races," and this "superior culture exists not because of inherent superiority but because of fortunate circumstances."[4] This is not to suggest that racial problems do not exist in Haiti. At certain historical moments non-black groups, particularly Arab-Haitians, have been victimized because of racial or ethnic differences.[5] In general, however, social relations tend toward a division between an elite that is *milat*[6] and black, and a dark-skinned black majority.

This cleavage has a long history. In the immediate postindependence years a bitter color dynamic evolved in Haitian politics, marked by a division between the predominantly black-controlled north and the *milat*-controlled south. By the middle of the nineteenth century, *milat* politicians avoiding the question of social divisions cultivated an argument of superiority by claiming that their power was determined by a greater degree of competence. This sentiment was crystallized in Liberal Party ideologue Edmond Paul's slogan "power for those most capable." This dictum not only justified *milat* elite control of the state apparatus but also established a political order in which color and class would be closely intertwined.[7] The Liberal ideas of capability and competence collided with those of the National Party, which was largely led by a powerful landed black elite. The Nationalist clarion, "the greatest good for the greatest number," was used to justify state control by the non-*milat* sectors.

Haitian intellectuals since the nineteenth century have drawn attention to these rivalries and the ways they have infused political life.[8] It was, however, the work of James Leyburn in 1941 that brought the issue into full view and provided an opportunity for a larger academic debate on color divisions.[9] In his classic study *The Haitian People*, Leyburn argued that social divisions more closely resembled a caste system in which "the two castes are the élite and the masses. They are as different as day from night, as nobleman from peasant; and they as separate as oil and water."[10] The serious problems of applying a bipartite model of social division to the study of Latin America and Caribbean societies are obvious. Leyburn's perspective also resulted in severe criticism and led him to draw the regrettable conclusion, four years before the revolution of 1946, that "in the near future it is safe to say that there will be no more black non-élite presidents."[11] Yet he was correct in emphasizing the close relationship between class and color in Haiti.

David Nicholls, whose book *From Dessalines to Duvalier* is the leading and most influential work on the subject of political ideology and social conflict in Haiti, modified Leyburn's thesis by stressing the important role of the black middle class, according to Nicholls, which emerged during the occupation and forms an intermediary between the peasants and the light-skinned elite. In his tour-de-force study, which is particularly strong in examining the historical influences on the black middle class, Nicholls argued that color divisions supersede virtually all other issues, particularly class interests, and concluded that "divisions connected with colour have been one of the principal reasons why Haiti has failed to maintain an effective independence."[12]

A fundamental aspect of Nicholls's thesis is that the social polarization in Haiti determines the political groups they form. Thus each group supports political elites of a similar class and color background, largely on the expectation that their group interests will be secured. Although one can arguably find such a division operative in nineteenth-century politics, it is an inadequate explanation of twentieth-century political conflict. One of the major shortcomings of this perspective is its failure to properly explain the incongruity between the stated ideological positions of certain political groups, particularly those based on color, and their actions during moments of crisis. To be sure, Nicholls concedes at various points that political rivalries are not always reducible to color and that the "color question" itself is largely the preoccupation of elites with the majority of the nation left out. Still, color remains a central problematic for Nicholls as it does for analyses of Haitian politics. Nicholls's work, exceptional as it is, also offers little explanation of the agency of non-elite actors in shaping the terms of political debate.[13]

Michel-Rolph Trouillot has offered a thoughtful corrective to some of these problems by arguing that color has several functions in Haitian society. It is misleading, he argues, to view it as the basis of all social divisions. In order to understand its crucial role one must recognize that color assumes different meanings in cultural, social, and political arenas. These meanings have shifted markedly since independence, much like the "color line" itself, which has resulted in "darker and darker people" being included among the *milat* elite since the nineteenth century.[14] According to Trouillot, "beliefs and practices that Haitian urbanites refer to as the 'color question' do not operate in a social vacuum to the exclusion of all else. Instead color-cum-social categories operate in various spheres of urban life as part of different strategies of competition and struggle."[15]

This is not to suggest that a focus on color consciousness has little significance in explaining Haiti's political reality. Nicholls's insistence that color issues are so embedded in Haitian politics, that even critics of "the color question" are forced to confront it is perceptive. Nevertheless, an analytical framework that focuses solely on color consciousness provides a limited understanding of Haitian politics generally and the history of resistance movements in particular. By separating political actors in groups according to color, scholars have obscured the fact that quite often political contests were guided by factors that went beyond obvious color tensions. This was especially pronounced in the postoccupation period, which witnessed rapid and serious rearrangements of the political order locally and occurred against the backdrop of a global ideological battle. As the evidence and analysis presented in this book suggests, the reactions of political actors were not solely dominated by motives related to color but more accurately grew out of responses to various ideological and political dilemmas. If the frequent discussion of color differences emerged at times of political crisis, it was quite often a surface problem. Concerns over U.S. economic penetration, dictatorship, class issues, and, above all, a bitter competition for control of the state were also important.

The underlying weakness in arguments that emphasize color divisions as most important is the implicit suggestion that political ideology remained unaffected by the series of upheavals that characterized Haiti in the 1930s through the 1950s. One of the central arguments this book advances is that radicalism in postoccupation Haiti was much more fractured and heterodox than scholars have appreciated. Political allegiances among radicals, despite the frequent references to color in political discourse, were not necessarily based on ideological sympathies or color consciousness. Access to state power was quite often the central objective. During the height of Haitian black power in the Estimé years (1946–50), the dominant anti-*milat* rhetoric supported by the regime was weakened by political affiliations between *noiristes* who imposed Estimé and conservative members of the military who eventually overthrew him. It is this intense contest for political power that not only dashed the hopes of the radical movements during the mid-fifties, but also partially explains the ease with which Duvalier was able to marshal support from rival political forces while maintaining a *noiriste* position in 1957.

This book therefore presents an alternative approach to the study of postoccupation Haiti that moves beyond analyses of color consciousness and Marxist class-based interpretations to include a more rigorous examination of the period, the various political groups, and the social contexts from which they emerged.

Protest under the Occupation

The rise of radicalism in the postoccupation period was in large measure an evolution of various forms of resistance in the occupation years. The U.S. occupation provided ample inspiration for the development of a nationalist movement in the country. Launched in 1915 ostensibly for the collection of loans and to restore civil order—there were five presidents in the previous four years assassinated or forced out of office by coups—the occupation fast exposed its imperialistic character. U.S. control of the customs houses and the institutional racism of the occupiers manifest in the reinstitution of the slavish nineteenth-century *corvée* work system gave rise to popular resistance. In 1919 a rural guerrilla peasant movement of the cacos, led by Charlemagne Péralte, was violently quashed by the marines and its principal leaders executed.[16] In Port-au-Prince, however, less direct forms of protest continued. Among the *génération de l'occupation*, a strong sentiment of nationalism emerged and elites, both black and *milat*, resentful of the U.S. presence, pursued other avenues of resistance.

They were aided by developments in public education. The late-nineteenth-century reforms of President Lysius Salomon (1879–88) created greater access to education for many Haitians. For the first time, members of non-elite black families were afforded secondary school training that had largely been the province of the light-skinned elite. The beneficiaries of Salomon's reforms ensured the continuity of this practice in the twentieth century. By 1919 the numbers of students enrolled in urban schools had more than doubled turn-of-the-century figures.[17] To this must be added the increasing centralization of the capital. Although a small number of black professionals had lived in Port-au-Prince since independence, these two changes guaranteed greater access for non-elites to the professional ranks.

This was extended with the creation of vocational schools. To maintain control of these developments, the occupiers manipulated Haitian color politics appointing members of the bourgeoisie to high-ranking government and army posts. Such a policy made tense the social order in a city already swelling with the pressures of urbanization and increased professionalization.

Most significant of the changes in this period were the activities of a new generation of writers, scholars, and poets who exploited the educational opportunities and achieved prominent places among the intellectual elite. Several young members of the elite, *milat* and black, returned to Port-au-Prince after years of study in Europe, where they were exposed to the developments in black consciousness and radical ideas. Concerned with the state of affairs they found in their occupied homeland under the repressive Louis Borno, and excited by current European interest in black culture as well as the Harlem Renaissance, these young writers began to express their views in several journals and discussion groups. By 1925 they formed La Nouvelle Ronde, the principal aim of which was to resuscitate the turn-of-the-century nationalist movement by drawing attention to the literary innovations of Harlem and French writers and applying them to the Haitian situation.[18]

In July 1927 most of the members of La Nouvelle Ronde founded the journal *La Revue Indigène*. Although the journal ran for only six months, it proved extraordinarily influential among the Haitian intelligentsia. Its collaborators, who included Max Hudicourt, Jacques Roumain, Normil Sylvain, J. C. Dorsainvil, Emile Roumer, Étienne Charlier, Arthur Holly, and Jean Price-Mars, called for a new national program that explicitly rejected French cultural values and promoted the acceptance of Haitian ones. They stressed the significance of Haiti's African heritage and promoted its inclusion in the development of a uniquely Haitian literature.

In 1928 this movement was solidified with the publication of Price-Mars's seminal *Ainsi parla l'oncle* (So Spoke the Uncle). Taking peasant culture as his focus, Price-Mars's book was one of the first to deal specifically with Haitian vodou and religious customs in a scientific manner. As he concluded, his work was an attempt "to integrate popular Haitian thought into the discipline of traditional ethnography."[19] He chastised the elite for denigrating Haitian peasant culture and values. "Let us no longer scorn our ancestral heritage. Let us love it, let us consider it as an intangible whole."[20] Price-Mars, to be sure, glossed over much of the reality of peasant life and initiated a romanticization of Haiti's African heritage that would long continue in the work of his heirs. Yet his call for a cultural nationalism that was truly inclusive was both original and potent. It is this factor, above all, that would prove most inspiring to a succeeding generation of ardent nationalists.

The loose coalition of nationalist writers associated with *La Revue Indigène* was ephemeral. Several of its members remained unsatisfied with the cultural war against the elite that the review launched and yearned for more active protest against the perceived common enemy, the marines. Jacques Roumain, who at twenty-three was incarcerated twice in 1928 for alleged seditious activity, felt that the literary thrust of the review was far too indirect to effect real political change. Energized by the broad appeal of anti-occupation sentiment in the city, he began to express his consciousness in other ways. With the young journalist Georges Petit he formed the Ligue de la Jeunesse Patriote Haïtienne, the organ of which was *Le Petit Impartial*, a political paper that Petit had established in 1927. More political than the literary movement, the Ligue was one of the first organized attempts to mobilize youth from diverse social backgrounds.[21]

At the same time, militant political activism against the occupation re-emerged. At the end of 1929 a student strike at the Haitian-U.S. agricultural school in the town of Damien escalated into a large urban strike. Anti-U.S. attitudes were further heightened when marines fired into a demonstration of discontent peasants in the southern town of Marchaterre.

In the aftermath of these incidents and with reactions against the occupation growing in the United States, Washington sent a commission to Haiti in early 1930 to investigate the state of the occupation and suggest a new policy. Greeted everywhere they traveled by large excited crowds carrying paper Haitian flags of blue and red, the commissioners were asked bluntly by a Haitian journalist in Port-au-Prince: "[When] will you give us back our government?"[22] Following the Forbes commission's report, U.S. President Herbert Hoover decided on a gradual withdrawal of U.S. presence in Haiti, and an election of a new Haitian head of state.[23]

The significance of these events for the advance of the nationalist movement is difficult to exaggerate. The election of 1930 ushered in a wave of revolutionary nationalism and resulted in the arrival of Sténio Joseph Vincent as Borno's successor. Vincent was a *milat* intellectual who grew up without many of the privileges of others in his class. He demonstrated his intellectual capacity by graduating with a law degree at eighteen. He was also a liberal nationalist whose challenge to U.S. control was a sharp contrast to the accommodation of the previous two regimes. Positioning himself as an anti-occupationist, he won much support. Vincent was keenly aware of social tensions in Haiti and skillfully retained backing throughout the first

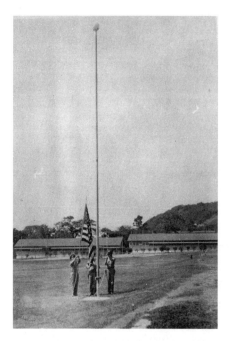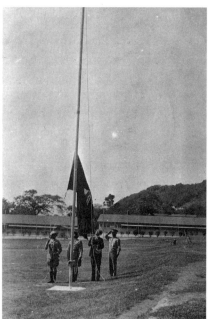

The last U.S. flag is lowered (left) and the Haitian flag is raised (right) at a ceremony at Cap Haïtien marking the end of the U.S. occupation, 6 August 1934. Courtesy of U.S. National Archives, USMC Collection.

half of his administration by appointing officials from both sides of the class and color divide.[24] By the mid-thirties his promise of a nationalist government was welcomed by several members of the indigenous movement.[25]

Eleven months after his celebrated New Year's Day message in 1934, Vincent validated his nationalist credentials by holding a state funeral in the northern city of Cap Haïtien for the leader of the caco resistance, Charlemagne Péralte. In that city not long before, the last U.S. flag was lowered. In its place, the blue and red Haitian flag, the premier symbol of the nation's independence, was unfurled and hoisted in a dramatic celebration of the marines' exit. As we shall see, such displays of political theater could not conceal the fissures in the nationalist movement; by 1934 the stage was set for greater conflict.

Outline of the Book

The chapters in this book are chronologically organized to chart the gradual evolution of postoccupation radicalism. Chapter 1 examines in detail the nature of the Vincent regime and the competing ideologies of *noirisme* and Marxism. Where previous histories have treated the era as one of quiescence on the part of urban radicals, this chapter argues that political activism against Vincent was constant. The chapter also discusses the changes in U.S. policy toward Haiti during the era of the Good Neighbor Policy and the first political crisis of the period, the massacre of 1937.

Chapter 2 continues this political narrative with an examination of the regime of Vincent's successor, Élie Lescot. Despite his nationalist rhetoric, Lescot sought, through calculated political maneuvers, to permanently silence opposition forces and consolidate light-skinned elite dominance of the Haitian polity. Of significant importance was the regime's relationship with the United States. During the Lescot years, U.S. foreign policy toward the country shifted once more as wartime demands propelled the Roosevelt administration to embark on a program of rubber cultivation in Haiti. A costly and ill-fated venture, the economic loss the country sustained strengthened the opposition against Lescot. The chapter treats these issues and gives particular attention to the activities of the anti-Lescot forces and the development of black consciousness among the popular classes.

Chapter 3 is a largely narrative account of the revolutionary movement of 1946. Relying on interviews with participants and a wealth of previously unused archival material, this account untangles the chronology of the revolt and sheds new light on the organization and debates within the Haitian Left. It also departs from established analyses by emphasizing the crucial role Marxism and labor played in shaping the democratic struggle, and it challenges common views that the election of Dumarsais Estimé was a result of the concerted effort of *noiriste* politicians by uncovering the central influence of the United States and the military in the months prior to the election.

Chapter 4 provides a detailed examination of the Estimé years, the most politically charged period in the pre-Duvalier era. These years of black power provided new opportunities for the politicians that took office in 1946 to develop an agenda of black nationalism. However, political rivalry and increasing intervention of the United States in local affairs overpowered their economic and political plans. Special treatment is given to the impact of *noirisme* on the social life of the country; the activities of the labor unions; military and civilian opposition to the regime; and the various factors that resulted in the overthrow of Estimé in 1950.

Chapter 5 is chiefly concerned with shifts in the tactics and approaches of radicalism and the general political and economic climate under the military rule of Paul Magloire. It depicts the Magloire years as a period defined by great economic strife and increased state repression. New sources are brought to bear on the controversial election campaign of 1956–1957, which signaled the end of this period of radicalism. The conclusion discusses the shortcomings of the political movements and considers the importance of the Haitian experience to the wider Caribbean.

It is hoped that by shedding much-needed light on this important period, this book helps to fill one of several major gaps in Haitian history and, in some small measure, contributes to a broader appreciation of a transformative era in the history of the modern Caribbean.

CHAPTER 1

The Postoccupation Dilemma
Ideology and Contention in the Vincent Years, 1934–1941

†

> Since a little over half a century, the country has
> been the victim of the same practices of small, clannish,
> ambitious leaders, who . . . do not understand the real
> Haitian problem. Foreign intervention could not alleviate
> this situation. Now the country should live under new laws.
> —*Manifeste de la Réaction Démocratique*, 1934

Haiti faced a series of new challenges with the end of the U.S.
occupation. Compared with the tumult of the years preceding
1915, the 1930s was a decade of relative political stability despite
the absence of major political or economic reforms. Equally important were
the strengthening of a semi-professional Haitian army, the Garde d'Haïti,
the creation of vocational schools, and the affirmation of Port-au-Prince as
the center of political power. President Vincent committed himself publicly
to a new era of reformism akin to Roosevelt's New Deal, and sought to
deepen ties with the United States and Haiti's powerful eastern neighbor,
the Dominican Republic. There were, however, few changes in the economic and social structures. The elites continued to dominate the financial
sector, and by virtue of this power were able to indirectly control the government. After 1934, the United States became Haiti's leading trading partner,
importing more than half of its annual coffee yield and carefully maintained
influence of Haitian finance.

These developments favored the interests of urban elites and offered little
benefits for the peasantry or urban workers. When the marines left, Vincent
fast assumed a more authoritarian leadership style, especially after his reelection in 1936. Having cut his teeth as a fierce opponent of the occupation,

13

President Sténio Vincent (at the head of the table), Foreign Minister Élie Lescot (seated at Vincent's right), and members of the Garde d'Haïti High Command celebrate Haitian Independence Day, 1 January 1934. Courtesy of U.S. National Archives, USMC Records.

the president was considered by mid-decade "one of the staunchest pro-Americans in the hemisphere."[1] He used the Garde d'Haïti to effectively silence his opposition with threat and imprisonment. Against this backdrop the political consciousness of the Haitian nationalists of the twenties assumed more radical forms.

This chapter explores the ideological and sociopolitical context of the radical movements of the thirties, their internal debates, the challenges they posed to the state, and the international environment that shaped interwar radicalism.

Color Is Nothing, Class Is Everything: The Marxist Vision of Haiti

The dismantling of marine control coincided with the fragmentation of the nationalist movement in the early thirties. The widespread repercussions of the Damien revolt provided enormous inspiration for the generation that came of age during the occupation. If the fervor created by the protest against the occupation in 1929–30 was to bear lasting fruit, a drastic restructuring of Haitian society was considered essential. While many of the nationalists of the late twenties acquiesced in their newfound political positions under Vincent, the more radical among them began to explore other political alternatives. In the 1930s the global appeal of Marxism among young radicals found resonance in Haiti.

Though Marxism had attracted the attention of some of the collaborators of *La Revue Indigène*, it never commanded any organized following. Nevertheless, this early interest was not lost on the country's occupiers who, still reeling from the rise in black militancy and the Red Scare in the United States, deemed the social divisions in Haiti a suitable condition for Bolshevik influence.[2] Widespread communist infiltration, in fact, had been cited by the U.S. Commandant of the Garde d'Haïti, R. P. Williams, as a principal cause of the Damien strike in 1929. In a somewhat paranoid report on the student strike submitted to the American High commissioner, Williams explained that "the recently formed young mens' organizations which are in full control of the radicals . . . are working up interest among the school children in their demands for legislative elections and early withdrawal." He added, "At Cape Haitian it is reported that children no longer salute the national colors at morning ceremonies, and are openly disrespectful to their teachers. At Jacmel . . . in the school children parade, the only colors carried was [sic] one flag of red with a green serpent."[3]

Such claims were doubtless exaggerated and reflective of U.S. hysteria and the marines misunderstanding of nationalism and anti-occupationism. However, it also suggested that Marxist ideas were starting to capture the sympathy of several outstanding Haitian intellectuals who participated in the strike. This was a concern for the dominant forces in Haiti.

By 1931 Jacques Roumain, the most radical of the militants of the twenties, had detached himself from the nationalist movement. From the late twenties his writings, especially those in *Le Petit Impartial* written under the pseudonym Ibrahim, began to stress class-related problems as the most central issues in local politics.[4] This was unsurprising given his background. Jacques Roumain was born on 4 June 1907 in Port-au-Prince to a well-respected family. On both sides, Roumain had connections with prominent Haitian statesmen, including his maternal grandfather, Tancrède Auguste, who briefly served as president (1912–13).[5] Roumain attended the best schools in Haiti before traveling to Switzerland and Spain, where he studied agronomy.

On his return to Haiti in 1927, the young Roumain developed a reputation not only for his talents as a writer and poet, but also for his activism and commitment to social justice.[6] For Roumain the early thirties were a period of intense personal transformation. He was inspired by the triumph and progress of the Bolshevik Revolution and envisioned similar achievements in his homeland. He saw firsthand the potential of popular protest to effect political change in 1930, something that the indigenous movement for all its cultural nationalism could not accomplish. Already an aggressive opponent of bourgeois standards, religious traditions, and imperialism, Roumain argued that, since the nationalist movement was born in the suffering of the majority, a political philosophy that sought to liberate them was the only acceptable model for Haiti. He gave an indication of this political awakening in a letter written to French writer Tristan Rémy in early 1932. "I have revised completely my political conceptions. . . . I am a Communist. At the moment I am not militant because the cadres for a political struggle do not yet exist in Haiti. The son of owners of extensive land holdings, I have renounced my bourgeois origins."[7]

For the next few years Jacques Roumain, one of the country's most gifted writers, would almost completely abandon his literary writings to devote his life to communist mobilization. He found support with two other radicals in their early twenties closely associated with the indigenous movement: Christian Beaulieu and the influential Louis Diaquoi, who briefly flirted with communism.[8] Beaulieu and Roumain, intent on forming a communist party in Haiti, traveled to New York in the spring of 1932 with the hope of obtaining financial aid from the Communist Party of the United States (CPUSA).[9] With the promise of support, contingent on the formation of an underground party, the two returned to Haiti, where they began to meet with students and organize clandestinely in the popular areas of La Saline and Bel-Air.[10]

It is not known exactly how many participants supported the movement or attended the meetings. The scant evidence on the early mobilization activities of the communists suggests that the following was very small and strongest among more privileged students primarily drawn to Marxist ideas out of curiosity. This is understandable given the socioeconomic conditions in Haiti in the thirties. Labor unionism was still gestating and the global effects of the Great Depression made many urban workers grateful for employment and less willing to organize. Moreover, Vincent's rhetoric of liberation was strong competition for Marxist radicals.

Whatever the real strength of communism in 1932, there was an undeniable worry among the elite of its potential growth. Once in power Vincent, fearing that the spread of radical ideas posed a potential challenge to his regime's nationalist allure, commented in private that when the "Americans have gone the government will . . . have to rely on force to maintain itself in power."[11] Vincent made good on this promise, placing the country in a state of siege shortly after taking office and instituting martial law at various points throughout his rule. His trusted minister of the interior, Élie Lescot (1930–34), was a vigilant combatant of communism, expelling various foreign nationals suspected of being linked to regional movements.

The rationale for such drastic measures may be explained by the political nature of the battle between communism and nationalism in Latin America in the thirties. Across the region, communists were perceived as anarchists, the antithesis of what nationalism stood for. In most cases forceful repression was officially endorsed as a deterrent. Vincent justified this approach once he learned of the connections between Haitian Marxists and agents of the CPUSA. In late 1932 correspondence between Roumain and communists in New York was intercepted by Haitian authorities and taken as evidence of an attempt to organize an active movement in the country. The government charged that Roumain and his associates were planning a general strike for the second week of January intended to hasten U.S. withdrawal and overthrow the regime. The funding for this grand scheme, they maintained, was provided by the New York chapter of the CPUSA and orchestrated by a Cuban communist living in Haiti, Dr. Omar Lind. At the same time the supposed plot was unearthed, the Haitian minister in Paris reported that Haitian radicals in the Latin Quarter were circulating news of active communist cells organizing in Haiti.[12]

Implicated in the Haitian red scare of the early thirties was another veteran of the indigenous movement, Max Hudicourt. Hudicourt was born on 25 June 1907 to a light-skinned elite family in the southern province of Jérémie. He moved to Port-au-Prince at a young age and became politically involved during the 1920s. Hudicourt, like Roumain, regarded Marxism a political ideology applicable to the Haitian situation. For him, Vincent's policies were antidemocratic and the president had betrayed the nationalist movement by being far too compliant with the United States. In contrast to his communist peers, however, Hudicourt was less fervent in his devotion to Marxism. Still, his background as a prominent member of the intelligentsia, his remarkable oratorical skills, and his connections with radicals in the city and the southern provinces, as well as outside Haiti, made him an influential figure.

Hudicourt was the leader of the radical organization La Réaction Démocratique (RD), formed in 1932, that included leaders of the student strike such as J. D. Sam, Georges Rigaud, and Jean Brierre. The group expressed their protest in the antigovernment paper Hudicourt edited, *Le Centre*,

Max Hudicourt   Jacques Roumain

which featured open admiration for state control of the means of production. Though communist language was intentionally avoided, he was accused of disseminating communist ideas. As with the Roumain case, letters between Hudicourt and a known communist in New York were found and used as evidence of his participation in a plot to overthrow the government.[13]

Based on these spurious claims, the two leading figures of the Haitian Left, Hudicourt and Roumain, were arrested, tried, and imprisoned for three months at the beginning of 1933.[14] Foreigners linked with both men, including Lind and H. Peguerro, a Dominican radical accused of attempting to stir up a strike of workers at the Haitian American Sugar Company (HASCO), were deported. The marines, anxious to rid the country of Marxist influences before leaving, launched a widespread campaign for the "Suppression of Bolshevist Activities" in Haiti, which they argued were "being organized and spread among the working class."[15] The sentencing of these high-profile leftists attracted much coverage in the local and international press and provoked criticism from labor organizations in New York, which lobbied for their release.[16]

It also exposed crucial differences in the political approach of both men that would bear significantly on the future of Haitian Marxism. After the trial, Hudicourt categorically declared, "I am not a communist. I believe in the fundamental principles of the doctrine but find it too ideological for our national well-being."[17] Roumain, for his part, defiantly held firm to his communist position as a statement written from his cell in the National Penitentiary attests: "My devotion is to the workers and to find a scientific solution of the Haitian problem . . . and not even the name Lescot or the *mulâtre* bourgeois leaders of exploitation and accomplices of American imperialism can ever discourage me."[18]

The attention from abroad, coupled with a hunger strike Roumain and Hudicourt began in early February, led to the release of both men after only four weeks in prison.[19] The thorough canvassing of the residences of suspected communists in the capital and the south convinced the government that the anticommunist campaign was successful in preventing the spread of the nascent communist movement in the country.

Despite the Garde's best intentions, incarceration left the young radicals undeterred. No sooner was he released than Roumain, along with Beaulieu, resumed his communist activities, secretly meeting with dockworkers and distributing antigovernment handbills around Port-au-Prince. During this period, the core of the movement expanded to include Étienne Charlier, a brilliant young member of the indigenous movement who was introduced to Marxism while pursuing a doctorate in Paris, Anthony Lespès, a Columbia University graduate and orthodox Marxist, Phito Marcelin, Saint-Juste Zamor, Saturnin François, Marcellus Sajous, Georges Petit, and Dorléans Juste Constant, a young pastor from Arcahaie.[20] This group would meet and discuss strategies in which Marxist philosophy could be applied to Haitian politics. The euphoria that accompanied the marines' withdrawal, highlighted by the symbolic removal of the U.S. flag, was for the communists an opportune moment to emerge. By the summer of 1934, they officially formed the Parti Communiste Haïtien (PCH), which replaced the Ligue Anti-Imperialiste that Roumain started with Petit a few months earlier.[21]

In June the Central Committee of the PCH released the party's program, *L'Analyse schématique 32–34*. Written jointly by Roumain and Charlier, *L'Analyse schématique* was the first Marxist critique of Haitian society. To a large degree, it was a response to a manifesto issued by La Réaction Démocratique, a few months before calling for greater state intervention in Haiti.[22] As a result, much of its tone was argumentative. Nonetheless, the party's position is distilled in two articulate sections penned by Roumain that introduce the work.

In the first Roumain dispels what he calls the "nationalist myth," arguing that "the arrival to power of the Nationalists began the process of decomposition of nationalism."[23] He viewed the nationalist movement as being corrupted by its inherent class contradictions that worsened once political power was attained. Explaining this in Marxist terms Roumain concluded: "The nationalist movement was incapable of fulfilling its promises because these nationalist promises collided with the nationalist bourgeoisie. . . . The large majority of the working class now understand the lies of the nationalist bourgeoisie. . . . The fight against imperialism is a fight against capitalism, foreign and local, and the excess of the Haitian bourgeoisie and the bourgeois politicians, valets of imperialism and cruel exploiters of the workers and peasants."[24]

If the first section was a critique of political developments since 1930, the second proved more revealing for its treatment of one of the more troubling issues in Haitian politics, the color question. From a Marxist viewpoint, Haitian color prejudice, while a historical reality, was more importantly a "sentimental expression of the opposition of class struggle."[25] Using Marxian dialectics, Roumain demonstrated that Haitian social relations were comprised of a black proletariat and a black petit-bourgeoisie "proletarianized" by international industrialization, and oppressed by a small bourgeoisie that happened to be mostly *milat*.[26] Thus color by itself had no significant bearing on the social order. To the extent that color held relevance at all it was only because it was "used as a mask by black politicians and *mulâtre* politicians to hide the true problem of class struggle."[27] For him, nationalists intentionally obscured this reality in order to gain political and social power. "The duty of the PCH, which is 98% black because it is a workers' party . . . is to put the proletariat on guard against the black politicians who would like to exploit to their profit their justifiable anger."[28]

In closing, Roumain called for a "Unique Proletarian Front without distinction of color" to "fight the solidarity of the capitalist bourgeoisie, black, *mulâtre*, and white," that would rally around the PCH's slogan: "Color is nothing, class is everything."[29]

The dissemination of *L'Analyse Schématique* and the surfacing of the PCH revived government opposition toward the left. In August, following a police raid on his house, Roumain was again arrested and court-martialed for treason when correspondence with a Haitian communist living in New York was discovered by the police. The authorities based their charges on the contents of one letter in particular, in which Roumain asked for "matériel" to be sent to Haiti. This was deliberately interpreted as a request for explosives to launch a communist overthrow. In reality, Roumain had been supporting a New York organization for the release of the nine black youths convicted in the Scottsboro case in Alabama and was merely asking for literature he purchased in that regard to be sent to him.[30] Nevertheless, in the much-publicized trial the government presented as key witnesses several officers from Vincent's secret police that had followed Roumain closely for several months. They testified that he received communist literature regularly on the wharves, and would frequently hold secret meetings with dockworkers inciting them to strike. The most damning evidence used against Roumain was *L'Analyse schématique*, which was considered as an admission of his communist leanings.[31]

Roumain's trial was the most prominent in a series of arrests of leftists that took place in August. All radical organs were forcibly closed and important activists, including Georges Petit and the popular Joseph Jolibois *fils*, head of the ephemeral Confédération Nationaliste des Ouvriers et Paysans d'Haïti, were jailed on manufactured charges.[32] Jolibois *fils* was especially targeted, having spent some time in Mexico where he allegedly worked with the Anti-Imperialist League of Mexico in 1927–28.[33] Hudicourt and the leaders of Réaction Démocratique were also pursued and imprisoned. Many of these men were signatories of an anti-Vincent declaration that appeared in the French black workers organ, *Le cri des nègres*, in the summer of 1934 that was smuggled into Haiti and distributed in the rural areas.[34] In the trial that followed the arrests, Roumain insisted that brochures were not explosives and a "communist was not a terrorist."[35] Such pleas fell on deaf ears and all of the accused were sentenced to three years in the national penitentiary.[36]

The harsh verdict handed down to Roumain sparked a repeat outcry against the Haitian government, particularly among U.S. black intellectuals with whom he enjoyed close friendships. Langston Hughes, who visited Roumain in Haiti in 1931, participated in a "Committee for the Release of Jacques Roumain," and in the international black press appeals were made for readers to lobby against the Haitian government and push for his release.[37]

While the trial and sentencing of the leading radicals accord with the government's alarmist reaction to the spread of communist ideology, it also served the immediate purpose of removing local opposition and thus paving the way for Vincent's reelection. Vincent had been maneuvering for a second term since at least 1933. A desire to maintain legitimacy and a belief that the country would collapse without his strong rule guided his decision. In 1935 he dissolved the legislature and replaced it with sworn supporters. Two proposals, for the abolition of the separation of powers outlined in the 1932 constitution and for executive control of the appointment of senators, passed a popular referendum the following year, enabling him to run virtually unopposed in the farcical elections on 15 May.[38]

With the security of another four-year term and faced with international opposition from radical organizations in the United States, Vincent saw fit to grant full pardons to Roumain, Petit, and the other radicals; they were released in the summer of 1936. The two years of confinement proved physically debilitating for several of these men. Roumain contracted malaria and Jolibois *fils* died from unexplained circumstances early in the year.[39] With weakened health and under constant police surveillance, Roumain left Haiti on 15 August, embarking on a five-year exile in Europe. From abroad Roumain worked to bring the repression in Haiti to the attention of the international left. Writing in the *Negro Worker* in 1937, he denounced Vincent's "police dictatorship" for its adoption of the "most brutal forms of terror and repression," and its "shameless exploitation of the mass anti-imperialist movement" of 1930.[40]

Although the PCH languished after Roumain's release and exile, there is evidence that younger members of the party continued the work of indoctrination. In 1936, the party launched a short-lived journal called *Vigie* under the direction of Antonio Fethière, Fritz Bourjolly, and Franck Legendre. With other communist sympathizers, they attempted to form cells in the provinces, particularly in Les Cayes and Gonaïves.[41] Even amidst the harsh government repression, communist sympathizers attempted to start a labor union of bus operators in 1936 and early 1937 that was immediately suppressed.[42] Government propaganda associated virtually all demonstrations with communist motives.[43] Whether these minor disturbances were actually influenced by communists or merely created by the government for political distraction, they did lead Vincent to issue an executive decree in November to combat the "violent" and "anarchistic" communist doctrines that were "dangers to the Haitian social order." The second article of the law was most explicit: "Any profession of communist faith, oral or written, public or private, will be punishable by an imprisonment of six months to one year and by a fine."[44] This reaction against perceived communist infiltration found universal support in the pro-government press, which surprisingly advocated a fascist type of dictatorship as necessary to combat communism. According to an editorial in the journal *Le Réveil*, "The nation must be like a guard at the door, blocking the passage of *la peste rouge*."[45]

The harsh response of the state seemed unnecessary given the limited capacity of the Marxists. Still, the overreaction toward the weakened communist movement in 1936 reflected the antagonism toward antigovernment protest during the mid-thirties. Vincent's manipulation of the nationalist movement to justify dictatorship proved successful in lessening the appeal of radical activism. Even with such constraints, it is wrong to conclude that Marxism was unimportant in Haiti during the thirties. David Nicholls has suggested that Haitian Marxists of the thirties may have been "wildly unrealistic in their assessment of the possibilities for social revolution."[46] He further noted that most "wrote from the comfortable homes of Pétionville and the Bois Verna, [elite suburbs] and their practical knowledge of the workers was restricted to a nodding acquaintance with their servants and with the tenants on their country estate."[47] The crusade against communism in the press was, however, illustrative of the fear and interest it commanded. Marxism was also a vital part of the ideological admixture that informed liberal-democratic protests, and thus destined to become an appealing ideology of resistance once the abuses of dictatorship became more concrete. The Marxists introduced a new critique of the Haitian social order that would remain a theoretical foil to other radical ideas. In other words, Haitian politics in the thirties was radicalized by the restricted efforts and loose organization of the Marxists. Finally, the presence of dynamic and intellectually capable personalities such as Roumain and Hudicourt, willing to eschew their elite origins to combat the local manifestations of imperialism, would greatly inspire radical elite youth to social action for years to come. This is a significant point to consider, as the Marxists of the thirties were the only radical groups with experience, albeit ephemeral and weak, in political organization.

Yet this form of active protest was not the only approach adopted by radicals in the repressive Vincent years. Within the black intellectual milieu existed another group that found much profit in the social critique and racial assertiveness of the movements of the twenties and that would use this admiration to elaborate on its black consciousness.

The Political Thought of the Griots

The indigénistes found their most important progeny among a small group of non-elite intellectuals in Port-au-Prince. As early as 1929 three young men who referred to themselves as Les Trois D met regularly in a rented house on Rue Fronts-Forts in downtown Port-au-Prince to discuss the significance of Price-Mars's work and the ethnological movement for the emerging black middle class.[48] The group included Lorimer Denis, a lawyer from Cap Haïtien, Louis Diaquoi, Roumain's associate and a journalist from

Gonaïves, and François Duvalier, from the capital who was then studying medicine at the Medical School in Port-au-Prince. All three first met at the Lycée Pétion, where they had been students in the mid-twenties under Price-Mars. The gatherings, held at Denis's house, christened the "Berceau de L'École historico-culturelle des Griots" by an associate, fast became a site for informal cultural and literary discussions.[49] In 1932, shortly before his death, Diaquoi suggested the name Griots for the group and for a journal they were planning.[50] Inspired by the name of the traditional African story-teller, the Griots perceived the intellectuals and the artists as the conduit through which folk history and culture is transmitted. According to Carl Brouard, one of the principal founders of *La Revue Indigène*, "Over there in the mysterious country of Africa when the Griots pass, men and women spit as a sign of disgust because the Griots are poets and sorcerers, and people are always scared of mystery."[51] Coming of age in the late occupation years, the Griot intellectuals formed an important core of the mid-thirties generation who identified themselves as "nouveaux Haitians," whose thought and approach regarding history, politics, and culture pointed the way forward for Haiti. The failings of the "anciens Haitians" of the preoccupation years had, by contrast, created the circumstances for the occupation.[52] For most of the thirties, the Griot collective refined their ideas through discussion and writings in several Port-au-Prince dailies, particularly *Le Petit Impartial*, of which Diaquoi was an editor, *L'Action National*, and Réné Piquion's *L'Assaut*.

In October 1938, following a failed attempt to start a daily, the quarterly *Les Griots* was formed with Duvalier, Denis, and the poets Clément Magloire *fils* (later Magloire St. Aude) and Carl Brouard as directors.[53] Their aim was to "continue the work of *La Revue Indigène*" and "assure the integration of [their] movement into national literature."[54] More scientific than literary, or for that matter political, the journal was largely devoted to articles on the psychological and biological distinctiveness of African and African-descended peoples. Duvalier, who in company with Denis wrote the majority of the essays in the review, adopted the racial theories of Arthur de Gobineau and Haitian theorist Arthur Holly, asserting that psychological and socio-cultural characteristics differed considerably between European and African peoples.[55] The basic problem in Haiti they argued was that the assimilation of French values had impaired the proper development of Haitian society. According to Duvalier, "Above all, the Haitian problem is a cultural problem and the solution can only be a profound reform of the Haitian mentality."[56] With an echo of Gobineau, they argued that this mentality was "unconsciously governed by [Haitians'] African heredity."[57]

In outlining this argument of Haitian identity, the Griots went further than their predecessors in emphasizing racial differences and offering an analysis of the vexing question of Haitian racial and color divisions. Drawing on their ethnographic research, they demanded a greater incorporation of folk practices, especially vodou, in national life. It is from the peasantry, the Griots argued, that Haitian culture derives. "The Haitian community is essentially rural," Duvalier and Denis stated, and vodou as the spiritual expression of the Haitian majority should be "embraced by all Haitians."[58] This call for the expression of the country's African heritage in music, literature, and religion represented a significant continuity with the indigenous argument.

A crucial aspect of Griot discourse was a focus on Haitian history and the rehabilitation of what David Nicholls has termed "a black legend" of the past.[59] Following in the footsteps of the nineteenth-century nationalists such as Louis Janvier, they argued that the country's most basic problem existed since independence: the constant exploitation of the majority of the black inhabitants by a small privileged *milat* elite. No systematic attempt had been made to redress the colonial predicament. The year 1804 was, in Duvalier's words, "more of an evolution than a REVOLUTION."[60] The true heroes of Haiti were the black leaders Toussaint, Dessalines, and Salomon. Their efforts to enforce lasting reforms beneficial to the majority were thwarted by the hegemonic control of a light-skinned elite. It was in discussing the nature of Haitian history that they refined the argument of authenticity. They argued that cultural authenticity defined all other aspects of social life. They maintained that there was a strong correlation between the color of Haiti's leadership and its underdevelopment. The Europhile outlook of the *milat* elite precluded them from appreciating the needs of a black country and thus made them ill-suited to chart the proper course of nationhood. It was only the more *authentique* blacks that could comprehend and meet these demands. Such a proposition clearly supported the aspirations of the black intellectuals, and also assumed a false stasis in Haitian color relations.

The insistence of the Griots on race and the vehemence with which they supported their sociocultural ideas encouraged them to formulate a political ideology at the heart of which lay racial authenticity. If the construction of a truly inclusive Haitian society warranted the repudiation of Francophone values, then the dissolution of a European-based democratic structure was equally necessary. Gobineau's idea that Africans by nature were inclined to a "paternalistic" and "despotic" government was instructive.[61] *Noiristes* argued that appropriation of French culture included a belief that European political institutions were essential to a civilized nation. In African political structures they found a more appropriate model for Haitian governance. Duvalier and Denis contended that the polities of modern Africa were based on communitarianism, and that the individualism inherent in Haitian politics was a consequence of the importation of French political systems during colonization.[62] Like their turn-of-the-century forebears, they argued that the *milat* hierarchy maintained such a system.

In the context of postoccupation Haiti the abuse of this system on the basis of color appeared most crude. For the Griot collective the Haitian elites, including the young communists, had erred by applying foreign models to the Haitian reality. The only hope for a change in this system was the conscious inclusion of Haitian customs and culture in all aspects of political and social life. On this point Duvalier and Denis were most direct: "The ultimate hope of our generation is to see that the movement that we have started in the literature of the country is expanded to all diverse manifestations of our social order. . . . Above all it is the conservation of our spiritual structure that can guarantee our originality and assure the continuity of our Race."[63]

The process by which this expansion could be realized was not, at the moment, well defined. Nor was the necessity of a black directorate considered as urgent. Indeed several members of the group subscribed to Vincent's rhetoric that he was Haiti's "Second Liberator" and praised him and Salomon as, in Brouard's words, "the two greatest leaders of the proletariat."[64] A *noiriste* political discourse, as the next chapter will argue, did not assume a precise articulation until the following decade.

Still, it is possible to discern the fundamental character of the Haitian variant of black power from the thinkers of the thirties. Though unformed at the time, at the base of *noirisme* was a strong anti-liberal component including the implementation of an authoritarian and exclusive state.[65] Diaqoui argued that liberal democracy in a country rife with color prejudice promised further divisions among blacks of different social classes to the benefit of the *milat* elite, who would always retain control.[66]

With the Italian invasion of Ethiopia in 1935, however, the *noiristes*, like most other black intellectuals in the region, supported Haile Selassie and the Abyssinians and strongly criticized Mussolini.[67] Thus, by the time World War II began, the Griots had outlined the framework of a black radical discourse.

The *noiriste* writers found no relevance in Marxism for the Haitian situation and generally distanced themselves from the Marxist intelligentsia.

Brouard, who had been close to Roumain during the twenties, parted company with his friend on this issue. "Communism," he said, "is far from being the best solution for the masses."[68] Duvalier was equally dismissive of Marxism, arguing that materialism held no relevance for Haitians.[69]

The heightened radicalism among the young intellectuals also created a generational struggle. Older nationalists of the indigenous movement viewed the discourse of authenticity and its essentialism with much ambivalence. Jean Price-Mars, the idol of the Griots, supported the ethnological movement and later the cultural radicalism associated with the *négritude* movement, but consistently criticized *noirisme*. He firmly objected to the movement on the grounds that it advocated greater social cleavages rather than national unity.[70] He recognized that a politically radical black consciousness could ultimately lead to despotism.

More conservative *milat* intellectuals like François Dalencour and Dantès Bellegarde dismissed the *noiriste* movement. Bellegarde found more utility in western cultural models as a framework for Haitian nationalism. The true problem for Haitians to overcome, he maintained, was their dependence on the United States. *Noirisme* threatened any cohesive struggle against U.S. domination, as the focus on culture and psychology lacked any program for economic development. Moreover, Bellegarde argued that *noirisme* promoted a racism that was akin to Nazism. He insisted that "all Haitians are of the same origin" and the emphasis on color differences was "not only false but criminal."[71] In his view, vodou was a hindrance to national progress. The promotion of vodou rituals and lore by *noiristes* was a demonstration of their desire to keep non-elite Haitians uneducated and depoliticized. It is to France, he argued, that Haiti owes its cultural debt, not Africa. He also drew attention to the obvious contradiction of a young intelligentsia influenced by the Parisian academy while advocating the acceptance of African traditions over Western ones: "In the center of the Americas a Dahomean island with a Bantu culture and a Dahomean religion for the amusement of the Yankee tourists."[72] Like most conservatives, Bellegarde advocated a liberal-democratic political structure, which would include members of all social groups.[73]

For the most part, the Griot argument for an African-based political system in postoccupation Haiti and their debate with the communists remained fixed in an intellectual setting during the thirties. Elites who were well aware of its postulations paid little attention to the movement, and it was never perceived as a serious threat to their dominance. It is telling that, unlike the Marxists, no members of the Griot movement were arrested or forced into exile. Though celebratory of the power of the peasantry and working-class, they only made a marginal impact on that constituency. The movement remained solely the preoccupation of a few black intellectuals.

By 1940 the review closed down once again due to a lack of funds, and in 1944 Duvalier left Haiti on a two-year course of study at the School of Public Health at the University of Michigan in Ann Arbor. Denis, who had published several articles on vodou with Duvalier in various journals between 1941 and 1944, devoted most of his time to research and teaching. In the late thirties Carl Brouard, the most radical of the poets in the Griot collective, converted to vodou and lived a bohemian existence outside the capital, scarcely writing. He long suffered from bouts of depression, his mental condition deteriorated, and by 1942 he publicly denounced vodou and the Griot movement, becoming a devout Catholic until his death in 1965.[74] But if it appeared, at least superficially, that the fervor of black nationalism would subside with the splintering of the Griot vanguard, the relevance of its meaning during the forties guaranteed its growth. During the next decade Haitian political consciousness would undergo a profound transformation and *noirisme* would find powerful interpretation in other places.

Good and Bad Neighbors: The Massacre of 1937 and Its Aftermath

The foregoing discussion emphasized the way in which the postoccupation predicament shaped urban radicalism by creating an atmosphere in which contrasting radical discourses could emerge. It must be borne in mind, however, that *désoccupation* took place amidst shifting U.S. foreign policy strategies. That *Vincentisme* could continue for over a decade in the autocratic fashion it did owes much to this factor. This external context determined the political conditions of governance in Haiti and contributed to the renewal of social tensions and conflicts. Thus in order to completely understand the political nature of activism in the thirties and beyond, a discussion of the impact of U.S. hemispheric policy as regards Haiti is necessary.

The gradual disengagement of U.S. control of Haiti was part and parcel of the abandonment of turn-of-the-century Big Stick policy initiatives and the move toward Herbert Hoover's contrasting Good Neighbor Policy.[75] Events such as the nationalist resistance in Haiti and the global suffering endured following the Wall Street crash of 1929 precipitated this evolution. Roosevelt's pledge of nonintervention in the domestic affairs of American states formed the overarching tenet of this new vision of Pan-Americanism.[76] In spite of its rhetoric of regional cooperation, the Good Neighbor Policy did not attempt to reduce U.S. economic control of Latin American and Caribbean countries. On the contrary, by influencing resource development in the region, Roosevelt effectively strengthened U.S. power and influence and increased the susceptibility of these poorer economies to the ebbs and flows of the U.S. economy. In the Haitian case, the United States remained the country's leading trading partner. The preponderance of U.S. trade was epitomized in 1935 with the granting of a twenty-five-year contract to Standard Fruit and Steamship Company for the development of the Haitian banana industry.

By the same token, nonintervention in political affairs facilitated the emergence of authoritarian regimes. The commitment of these regimes to work on the side of the United States in the geopolitical contest against the doctrines of communism, fascism, and Nazism won them considerable support. The net result was a spate of dictators, from Nicaragua to Cuba, intent on manipulating U.S. noninterference to strengthen personal power.

In the Caribbean few dictators were more adept at manipulating this policy than the two who came to power in Hispaniola in 1930: Vincent and Generalíssimo Rafael Leonidas Trujillo Molina in the Dominican Republic. With the degrees of political freedom afforded by the Good Neighbor Policy, both these men gained North American recognition while expunging their country's fragile democratic structures. They were able to flagrantly violate the very notions of liberal democracy enshrined in the rhetoric of Pan-Americanism and, especially in the case of Trujillo, use extreme violence to advance their own political programs. The abuse of this system was most brutally evinced in the genocide exacted on Haitians living on the Dominican border in 1937, a singular event that not only stands as one of the most traumatic episodes in modern Caribbean history but is also of import to the political development of Haiti during these years.[77]

The deep roots of the massacre can be traced to the twenty-year Haitian occupation of the Dominican Republic (1822–1842) under President Jean-Pierre Boyer and two invasions by Emperor Faustin Soulouque in the mid-nineteenth century. These experiences created the seeds for a virulent racialized anti-Haitian discourse in the Dominican Republic.[78] Less than a year after being sworn into office, Trujillo launched a minor attack on Haitians on the border, ostensibly over tax violations. Intermittent clashes erupted thereafter and proved to be a troubling concern for the Haitian government. In February 1936, after much negotiation on both sides and with U.S. arbitration, Vincent and Trujillo agreed on a treaty that attempted to solve the territorial dispute. Hailed as a triumph by all parties concerned, both countries agreed that a portion of the land near Dajabón be ceded to Haiti in return for a clear delineation of the Dominican side on the map.[79] Indeed, the relations between the two countries appeared to improve, judging by the fanfare and publicity that accompanied visits by Trujillo to Haiti and, in March 1937, a visit by Vincent to the first Intellectual Haitian-Dominican Congress, in Ciudad Trujillo.[80]

These measures effectively clarified the geographic boundaries of both countries occupying Hispaniola and strengthened diplomatic cordiality, but did little to address the question of the constant stream of Haitians and Dominicans that moved back and forth across the frontier. The massive deportation of Haitian and Jamaican sugarworkers from Cuba by Fulgencio Batista in the summer of 1937 put a strain on an already overburdened labor situation. Many of these returning workers found their way to the border where the promise of work was great. In an effort to realize his policy of *dominicanización* of the frontier, Trujillo imposed a series of quotas on the numbers of foreign workers allowed to work on the sugar plantations.[81] At the same time, he petitioned for "purer" "near white" Puerto Rican workers to settle in the border towns and supplant the Haitian colonies.[82] Dominican officials promoting strong anti-Haitianism in the local press justified these harsh new regulations as a response to the unceasing depredations of Haitian bandits and cattle herders, and the spread of vodou customs considered "anti-Christian" in the Cibao region.[83] The increasing mobility between the two countries and the restrictions on employment in the border towns led to a degradation in the living conditions for both Haitians and Dominicans.

Large numbers of Haitians were arrested for minor violations and placed in overcrowded jails where, on the orders of Trujillo's minister of justice, Julio Ortega Frier, many were killed.[84] Following reports in June 1937 of Dominican police denying Haitian tourists entry and several Haitian workers being brutally beaten by police, the Haitian minister in Ciudad Trujillo made urgent appeals to Minister of the Interior Georges Léger to strengthen the Garde patrol on the border as a "measure of prevention" against future occurrences.[85] These warnings went unheeded and the situation fast deteriorated.

After completing a month-long tour of the frontier in September, Trujillo publicly announced on 2 October that he had found a definitive solution to the border problem. Five days later, the United States resident Inspector in Cap Haïtien called the minister in Port-au-Prince to report that over eight hundred wounded Haitians had crossed the frontier with news of mass murders taking place in the northwest.[86] In short order similar reports were received from elsewhere confirming the minister's worst fears.

Although Trujillo's motives remain ambiguous, the grisly details indicate that the pogrom was carefully planned and orchestrated. According to eyewitnesses interviewed by the U.S. investigating officer in the Dominican Republic, on successive nights hundreds of Haitians were rounded up and taken to the immigration offices at Dajabón and MonteCristi with the understanding that they were to be deported. Once their visas were stamped, they were taken en masse to the docks where they were beaten with clubs and hacked to death with machetes and their bodies thrown in the sea. In Montecristi they were taken behind the fortress, shot, and buried there. "As a result of this campaign," the U.S. minister concluded, "the entire northwest frontier on the Dajabón side is absolutely devoid of Haitians."[87] Since most of the bodies were disposed of, U.S. officials were uncertain of the extent of the slaughter and the foreign press, receiving scant reports from Caribbean bureaus, insinuated that news of mass murders were exaggerated.[88] In the following weeks, however, reports of staggering numbers of killings in San Francisco de Macorís, Ouanaminthe in Haiti, and sixty-two other towns poured into the foreign ministries in both countries, prompting Norweb to conclude that "the incident had been much worse than previously thought. Neither sex or age were respected. . . . Haitians were apparently killed to the last person."[89] With diplomatic attention raised, Trujillo ordered the killings stopped. By that time, over 15,000 Haitians and Dominicans were dead.[90]

In a press statement in the Dominican paper *Listín Diario*, written by future president Joaquín Balaguer, the Trujillo administration accepted no blame for the massacre that they called "exaggerated commentaries."[91] Later the government would cite Vincent's failure to comply with Dominican requests that political exiles be extradited as a precipitating factor. While Dominican officials publicly evaded culpability, in private they freely boasted about the deed. At a dinner with Norweb, Ortega Frier, who was placed in charge of the Dominican investigation, insisted that the massacre was "imperative" as the continued immigration of Haitians to the region would have made the frontier "black within three generations."[92]

In Haiti, news of the massacre provoked contrasting reactions. At the state level, Vincent was surprisingly slow in issuing a response, which led the U.S. minister to assume that he either "is unaware of the extent of the killings or is deliberately minimizing the situation."[93] Vincent was very much aware of the murders as reports came into Port-au-Prince very early.[94] On the president's instigation, the local press refrained from extensive coverage of the event. This initial attitude of calm is typically explained as a fear of the possibility of war should the stronger Dominican army launch a counterattack against his regime.[95] It is true that Vincent deemed formal retaliation by a comparatively weaker Haitian army as an invitation for Trujillo (with possible assistance from other Hispanophone neighbors) to intervene. It was not just a matter of military weakness, however; as Thomas Fieherer has pointed out, there were sufficient numbers of officers in the Garde to patrol the border and prevent the slaughter.[96] A high-ranking officer in the Garde in the subsequent months noted that "for some time [he] thought there should be a stronger concentration of forces on the frontier and not in the capital where the security and stability of the government were never in danger."[97]

Vincent's response can be explained by other factors. Most obvious was his insistence that political attention be focused on the capital, where he believed the greatest threat to his regime would emerge. As a result, the government remained disconnected from provincial peasant life. The neglected calls for a stronger Garde presence from Haitian diplomats indicate the low priority Vincentists placed on the peasantry. Ultimately, Vincent was aware that launching a counterattack would only worsen matters and might possibly force the United States to reoccupy Haiti and erode the veneer of nationalism he spent nearly a decade constructing. Vincent, who in 1937 had every intention of running for a third term, knew that such an outcome would damage his public image. Vincent and his cabinet also benefited considerably from Trujillo's largesse and were not prepared to jeopardize their relationships with El Benefactor. Thus, a combination of fear, political conceit, and a desire to maintain a major source of personal capital dissuaded the Haitian government from reacting strongly. For these reasons the president elected to solve the debacle through international accord.

While Vincent exercised caution with Trujillo, news of the massacre was broadcast around the region. A handful of U.S. journalists in Ciudad Trujillo and Port-au-Prince covered the events in the U.S. press. Under pressure from his minister of foreign affairs, Georges Léger, Vincent finally decided to make an appeal to the United States. In mid-November, Vincent, in a cable to Roosevelt, complained that the Dominican investigation was "dragging out," thereby creating a situation "of irritation and tension to the greatest prejudice of the present interests of the two peoples and harmony of their future relations."[98] Vincent pressed for an Inter-American Conciliatory Committee to include delegates from Mexico, Cuba, and the United States. For his part, Roosevelt, despite offering his "profound regret," regarding the unfortunate "controversy," was hesitant to agree to Vincent's wishes, although there was growing attention to the massacre in the U.S. press.[99] For the Roosevelt administration it was the first real test of the efficacy of the Good Neighbor Policy. Rising German, Italian, and Japanese aggression made it necessary that the United States exercise caution in its foreign policy. The fact that Haiti's new foreign minister in Washington and former ambassador to the Dominican Republic, Élie Lescot, did little to pressure the State Department to intervene did not help.

Despite Vincent's best efforts, news of the massacre could not be contained locally. While he used diplomacy to resolve the conflict, popular protest returned to the streets of Port-au-Prince after nearly two years of relative quiet. Less than a week after the event an underground party called the Partie Révolutionnaire Haïtienne surfaced and began distributing pamphlets in the streets. Composed in the main of former associates of Jolibois *fils* and senators purged in the 1935 dissolution, its pamphlets called for a march on Santo Domingo and the overthrow of Vincent, whose quiescence was taken as proof of his collusion with Trujillo.[100] Vincent was labeled a cynical "Negrophobe" who ignored Trujillo's brutality on the border and wasted limited resources for the purchase of weapons and the maintenance of spies in the capital. Other pro-democracy groups that waged an intensive propaganda campaign in the city followed this pattern.

Among the most prominent agitators were Antoine Pierre-Paul, president of the very small Haitian Labor Union, and a former *caco* leader S. Thezan, both of whom galvanized small groups and threatened to launch a revolt.[101] There was also independent popular reaction as protesters staged small disturbances around the capital, defacing the recently named Avenue Trujillo (formerly Grande Rue) sign downtown and holding a large requiem mass for the victims.[102] The students at the Medical Faculty of the National University left classes for a week and organized small protests around the city.[103] Their stance was clear: "Last October thousands of our brothers were slaughtered across the border. In the face of that reality, our government has adopted a profound indignation. The country cannot remain solemn! . . . This is an offense to us all. We protest as blacks and as Haitians . . . we must defend our dead."[104]

That these actions were of serious concern to Vincent is revealed in his cable to Roosevelt in which he expressed his fear that without U.S. intervention, the "super-excitation of minds" in the capital could "give rise to new and more dangerous complications."[105] The situation in Port-au-Prince grew so tense that the security around the palace was more than doubled in November, a decision that aroused much criticism from the officer corps

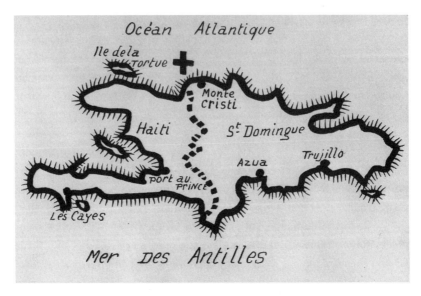

A Haitian-drawn map of Hispaniola made in November 1937. The cross at the top of the Dominican border is in commemoration of the victims of the 1937 massacre. Courtesy of U.S. National Archives, USMC Records.

who demanded greater deployment of forces in the border towns to prevent a repeat of the October killings.[106] The Garde promptly dealt with several small demonstrations near the Palace. They also inspired a spate of small-scale protests that would erupt periodically for the remainder of the presidency.[107] Despite the fact that these initial reactions were small, limited, and easily quelled, the government did perceive them as a portent of things to come and increased repression of all radical groups. The pro-government press described most of these demonstrations as Marxist inspired.[108]

The extent to which the moribund communist movement influenced this unrest is difficult to determine. The handbills used provocative terms in lambasting the "traitor" Vincent, "the real enemy of the Haitian people."[109] Yet this was hardly sufficient evidence of communist agitation. The U.S. minister, Frederick Mayer, in a report on the state of communist activities in the island, defined the protests of 1937 as "quasicommunist," lacking the size or level of organization found in other Latin American countries.[110] Lack of organized left-wing protest did not mean, however, that Marxist leaders of the RD and PCH remained unresponsive to the massacre. In Paris, Jacques Roumain wrote a scathing critique of both Vincent and Trujillo called "La Tragédie Haïtienne" in the journal *Regards* in November 1937. He was most harsh in his treatment of Vincent's dictatorship, which he blamed for the economic misery of the peasantry forced to leave their country in order to earn a meager living. He likened the labor situation between the two countries to a modern slave trade with Vincent serving as the trader. His comments on Trujillo as a Caribbean fascist stirred reaction from the Dominican minister in Paris, who petitioned the French government to arrest and fine Roumain for his "violent and virulent" attack against a foreign power.[111]

Ironically, it was among the forces entrusted with the security of the state that the most organized protest formed. Scarcely one month after the massacre, sixteen junior officers were accused of plotting to assassinate Vincent and topple his regime. These lower-ranking, mainly black officers, many of whom lost relatives in the massacre, were irritated by the regime's flaccid response. As one of the accused plotters confessed in his deposition, "The Dominicans had already massacred thousands of my brothers and I in my military uniform was forced to sit down and do nothing."[112] They were most angered by the moves of the head of the Palace Guard and Vincent's confidant Durcé Armand, who, fearful of the antigovernment threats, was responsible for the increase in the forces around the Palace. The plot's origins, however, lay with Armand. Various reports claim that Armand conspired with former Minister of the Interior Frédéric Duvigneaud to exploit the administration's weakened position and the sympathy many of the officers shared for their slain countrymen.[113] Once Vincent was overthrown, Duvigneaud would be installed as president and Armand as head of the Garde. The Commandant of the Garde and Armand's rival, Colonel Démosthènes P. Calixte, who forewarned the president of the plot, betrayed the conspiracy.[114] According to Calixte, Vincent removed Duvigneaud from the cabinet but only admonished Armand. When a cadre of Calixte's subordinates sought to protect their leader by attempting to assassinate Armand, Calixte was immediately incriminated.[115] The attempted murder of the head of the Palace Guard signaled just how far the crisis had reached. Facing charges of treason, Calixte fled the country, settling in France and later the Dominican Republic, where he would form a close relationship with the Trujillo government.

Vincent's tight control of the state was threatening to unravel. The political enemies he accumulated over the course of his rule regrouped. Sensing the vulnerability of the regime, a coalition of senators unsuccessfully approached aging ex-president Borno to persuade him to take over the government. Borno pleaded with U.S. officials to force Vincent's resignation, as the panic that followed the popular unrest could intensify.[116] By the time the Haitian-Dominican controversy was hastily settled in January 1938 (Trujillo offered Vincent, who accepted, an indemnity of $750,000 to be paid to the families of the victims in return for a cancellation of the independent investigation), confidence in the government was severely crippled.[117]

In 1938, Armand foiled another potential coup and several of the guilty officers were summarily executed. So volatile was the situation that the president briefly considered resignation.[118] Instead he sought to protect his regime by completely revamping the Garde hierarchy, removing potential enemies and replacing them with his favorites, thereby establishing a pattern that would be repeated by future dictators.[119] By undermining the power of the Garde he was able to strengthen his control of the country. In a speech at Les Cayes in December, Vincent extemporized on the current situation and blatantly declared his regime a dictatorship. Arguing that the "education of the people has not attained the level which would permit them to choose a chief of state," and that the Haitian majority had a "mentality so arrested that it hardly appears to be of this century," Vincent formally dispensed with parliamentary democracy.[120]

This move met with immediate resistance. The previous month five senators who vocally objected to Vincent were removed from office and arrested for alleged subversive activities.[121] Leftists capitalizing on the popular upset reemerged to form a unified front against the regime. Since the anticommunist law stipulated that members of the Communist Party were subject to immediate imprisonment, Marxists organized with other non-Marxist groups. Max Hudicourt's La Réaction Démocratique joined forces with the Parti Populaire Démocratique, a small party led by Beaulieu and Michel Roumain, and two other groups to form a coalition against the Vincent dictatorship. The group organized a large antigovernment demonstration in 1938 that provoked severe retaliation by the government. Most of the leaders were arrested and jailed. Hudicourt narrowly escaped arrest by fleeing Haiti and seeking exile in New York.[122]

In the face of government retaliation members of the intelligentsia wrote frantic appeals to the State Department pleading for the United States not to intervene but to urge Vincent to step down. They chastised the Roosevelt administration for lending support to the fight against European dictators and allowing Trujillo and Vincent to continue to rule in the Caribbean.[123] U.S. blacks also lent support to the radicals. Once Roosevelt agreed to U.S. participation in the Haitian-Dominican settlement, Walter White of the NAACP pleaded in vain with Secretary of State Cordell Hull that former diplomat and NAACP official James Weldon Johnson be sent to negotiate.[124] Likewise, Francine Bradley, head of the New York–based "Friends of the

Haitian People," which protested the communist trials in 1934, rendered harsh judgment on the failure of U.S. foreign policy to arrive at a solution to the crisis in Haiti.[125]

The open declaration of a dictatorship, the continued repression of political dissidents from the left and right, and the execution of Garde officers, some of whom came from influential families, exposed the disarray of internal politics. In a dispatch to the State Department, the U.S. foreign minister, Frederick Mayer, reported with dismay on the "Hitlerian fashion" with which Vincent dealt with his opponents in the wake of the massacre. In a letter to Cordell Hull, he offered a veiled plea for U.S. revocation of the principles of the Good Neighbor Policy to help bring order to the country. "If we maintain a policy of 'hands off' internal politics and permit the constitution to be flouted, we may well find the situation developing into a state of anarchy with all its attendant disadvantages and embarrassments."[126]

Vincent was able to avert disaster through political strategy. The next election was fast approaching and with declining popularity and greater opposition, the president, whose weary appearance reflected the heavy toll of the past three years, made it known that after a decade as the country's leader he was going to step down. He thus set in motion the mechanism for a smooth transition of executive power.

Conclusion

There are several points to consider in assessing this first crucial phase in the trajectory of postoccupation politics. Radical nationalists who believed in the rhetoric of a "Second Independence" could no longer do so after witnessing the reaction to the devastating events of 1937–38. It is worth pointing out that the Griot vindication of Haiti's African heritage reached full flower in the two years following the massacre. Although Vincent managed to successfully safeguard his regime through dictatorship, it was clear that he would be unable to sustain a third term. The predominantly light-skinned political elite that supported his regime knew too well that another term would invite unfortunate consequences. They were also aware that the mélange of radical ideas circulating among elite urban youth added to popular resentment and, if unchecked, could threaten the very fabric of elite control. No less important was the changing attitude of U.S. officials, who were beginning to make clear their concern over the unbending nature of the dictatorship.[127] Finally, the political elite knew that in order to maintain the power that *Vincentisme* assured, his successor had to be a man with enough political clout to negotiate with the forces—Trujillo, the United States, the Marxists, and the Garde—that had tested the mettle of the regime. The next president, more important, had to have a thirst for power so insatiable he would guarantee the preservation of the Haitian status quo. In 1940 no other politician proved better suited for such a task than Élie Lescot. It is to his administration that we now turn.

CHAPTER 2

Brown Power, Black Protest

The Lescot Regime and the Culture
of Resistance, 1941–1945

†

> When you consider the domestic economic and
> social problems of my country, it is a danger bordering
> on tragedy to establish a racial and racist line in Haiti. . . .
> In Haiti the white man has gradually extended his economic
> influence to the detriment of the native element, and our
> political instability has aided this white exploitation.
> —MAX HUDICOURT, *Jim Crow Menaces Haiti*, 1944

D uring the five years Élie Lescot governed Haiti, the country experienced notable transformations in its political and social life. The disenchantment with Vincent's rule provided an unfavorable start for his close associate Lescot, whose conservative administration was unable to contain the spread of radical impulses. More important, the silencing of the opposition at the end of the thirties ensured that any resurgence in political consciousness would prove a serious threat to political stability. Lescot sought to circumvent this danger by strengthening the power of the state and deepening political and economic ties with the United States. Nonetheless, his efforts achieved only short-lived success as the ideological ferment created by the Second World War reverberated loudly in Haiti.

This chapter analyzes the progress of Haitian society and economy during the war years, the increasing radicalization of the urban populace, and the series of challenges that the regime faced. Two major themes are addressed. The first is the nature of the Lescot regime and the ways in which internal and external factors served to shape its rule. Where previous accounts emphasize the prejudice of the administration, it is argued that the accentuation of color divisions, while indeed a defining characteristic, was more accurately a result of class and economic tensions worsened by wartime demands, the hostility of the traditional power structures, especially the French clergy, and the ambivalence of U.S. foreign policy.

The second part of the chapter examines the developments in Haitian Marxism, culture, color consciousness, and the military during these years. The Marxist Left underwent a series of changes in the latter stages of the war that bore heavily on its post-Lescot career. The growing division between the socialists and the communists over the direction of the left, however, weakened its ability to challenge the state. The black consciousness of the thirties also reemerged with new vigor and with new interpretations during these years. Both movements served to create a culture of resistance that expanded the acceptance of *noirisme* among the non-elite sectors of the urban population and contributed to the development of a radical political culture. These transitions also affected the Haitian Garde, which became increasingly politicized after the massacre of 1937. Together, these factors precipitated the regime's demise after World War II.

Elite Rule, Religion, and Rubber: Haiti in the War Years

On 15 May 1941, Élie Lescot became president of the republic. Lescot was born on 9 December 1883 in the northern town of St. Louis du Nord to a middle-class family. His family ties were strong in the north. Lescot's mother was reputedly once a lady-in-waiting to the court of Empress Adelina, wife of the infamous president and emperor, Faustin Soulouque (1847–1859).[1] After receiving his secondary education in Cap Haïtien, Lescot went to Port-au-Prince to pursue studies in pharmacy. Three years later, he returned to the north, settling in Port-de-Paix and worked with a relative in an export-import business. After his first wife died in 1911, Lescot began his ascendance in Haitian political life. In 1913 he was elected to the Chamber of Deputies. Seeing his political fortunes decline during the early years of the occupation, he migrated to France with his family in 1922 and lived there for four years. On his return, he managed to secure a judiciary post in Port-de-Paix and then became a minister of education under the Borno regime. By the time Vincent assumed power, Lescot was named minister of the interior. Four years later he served a three-year term as ambassador to the Dominican Republic, where he forged an important alliance with Trujillo that at first served him well in his political career. Between 1937 and 1941 he was Haiti's foreign minister in Washington.

After 1934 Lescot steadily built a strong international network of support strengthened during his years of Foreign Service in the United States. Apart from his close association with Trujillo, he was well known in Washington, where he fraternized with important senators and gained assurances of political and economic support months prior to the election. Confident of victory, Lescot promised Vincent "moral and material tranquility" in return for his endorsement.[2]

Although he was thought to be the most favored candidate, Lescot's nomination did not receive overwhelming support in the legislature. Political desire and disgust for his connections with Trujillo and the Port-au-Prince bourgeoisie angered the black members of the lower chamber. The challenge came from four prominent deputies, Jean Price-Mars, Frédéric Duvigneaud, the editor of Le Nouvelliste, Amilcar Duval, and Dumarsais Estimé, a young deputy from Verettes, all of whom argued that the country needed a black president.[3] This position did not reflect color consciousness. All these men were, in fact, close to Vincent and benefited greatly from his regime. Rather, their opposition grew from a fear of unchecked abuses of power among the light-skinned elite that a Lescot win promised. Individually, these men alerted U.S. authorities in Haiti of their grave fear of the consequences of a Lescot presidency, who, according to Price-Mars, was "steeped in the Hitlerian idea."[4] In the pages of Le Nouvelliste Duvigneaud pointed to Lescot's associations with Trujillo as a sign of his lack of patriotism. Despite their opposition, these candidates found little encouragement from their fellow legislators, the public, or the U.S. Legation, which continued to extend support to Lescot despite U.S. Minister J. C. White's repeated statements to the contrary.

There was also a great outpouring of support for Lescot in the local press, including the independent paper Le Matin, which openly endorsed his worldliness and contacts as valuable assets for the country. Le Mouvement responded to the objections of his challengers in the Senate by defending Lescot as "a man of history" who is "the protector and pride of his race." L'Action Radicale celebrated his international experience and influence as "necessary qualities to lead the country in this period of uncertainty caused by the war."[5]

Even with public approval in the press, Lescot left nothing to chance. Pressure was placed on all of his opponents. In an effort to further weaken the legitimacy of the opposition and to win even greater favor in the eyes of the United States, Lescot supporters circulated a rumor that German and Italian merchants in Port-au-Prince secured Axis funds through Panama to support their anti-Lescot campaign. Although these rumors were never substantiated and in fact denied by Vincent, who still harbored ideas of remaining in power, they did achieve the purpose of consolidating greater U.S. support for a Lescot presidency.[6]

Opposition to Lescot emerged in other quarters. At the beginning of the year rumors circulated of a possible Garde uprising led by Vincent's trusted Colonel Armand of the Palace Garde should Lescot take office.[7] Lescot nonetheless was confident of U.S. support for his candidacy. Moreover, he wielded his influence to gain, at least temporarily, the support of the upper echelons of the Garde. Lescot cunningly waited until twelve days before the election to declare his candidacy in an effort to limit the reformation of the weakened opposition.[8] The election gave Lescot a unanimous victory with fifty-six out of fifty-eight votes cast in his favor—a high margin, which then deputy Max Hudicourt later claimed was arrived at only after intimidation and the beating of some legislators before the election.[9]

After his inauguration the new president consolidated his power by reforming the key institutions in the country. In June he issued a decree naming himself the head of the Garde and controlled all appointments and military affairs. Lacking the political acuity of his predecessor, he appointed white and light-skinned members of the elite to major government posts, including his own sons Gérard as Head of the Cabinet and Roger as acting Lieutenant Colonel of the Palace Guard. Critics balked at Lescot's appointment of a Frenchman, Abel Lacroix, to the important post of finance minister. Lacroix and several other high-ranking cabinet members formed a small clique, often personally connected to the president and one another through family and business affairs.[10]

This entrenched policy of nepotism and light-skinned elite patronage did not mean that Lescot was oblivious to Haiti's black nationalist past. Contrary to common analyses of him, Lescot was in fact well aware of the importance of Haitian racial identity and occasionally acknowledged it as justification for his presidency. In his presidential address at the annual Flag Day celebration in May 1943, he directly attacked the French Catholic church as agents of European exploiters, and obliquely referred to their part in manipulating internal color prejudice: "Let us work toward a future so that all may enjoy a greater social justice and that the enslavement of the Negro by the white man be ended, may these cease in this land—land of liberty and heroism— the exploitation of the Negro by the Negro."[11] A year later at the same event he was more direct: "Young people, when you look upon this flag you should contemplate it with the emotion our ancestors felt that morning of 1803. . . . I command you to hate, to hate with all your soul those who insult your race and your country which these glorious and sublime blue and red colors symbolize."[12] This seeming contradiction in Lescot's political actions and public rhetoric can be explained by his vision of Haitian politics. Black nationalism for Lescot, as with other Haitian presidents, was a political device used at key moments to win popular support. The celebration of race and avoidance of color was a hallmark of the political discourse of light-skinned politicians since the nineteenth century.[13] More important, it was a defense against charges of color prejudice and abuse by the government.

Nonetheless, Lescot's position on race could not conceal the grave problems with his presidency, most clearly revealed in its economic policy. Lescot quickly made good on his campaign promise to cooperate with the United States in the war effort. Immediately following the Japanese bombing at Pearl Harbor on 7 December 1941 and before Roosevelt's celebrated declaration of war, Lescot announced war on the Axis powers, promising to send all necessary Haitian forces.[14] Although members of the Garde never participated in the war, Lescot was able to demonstrate his commitment in other ways. The Haitian government supported the war refugee effort by offering the placement of European Jews in Haiti, a program developed by Trujillo with moderate success in Sosúa in the North of the Dominican Republic.[15] Lescot's enthusiasm for the short-lived project later drew international criticism as an effort to "whiten" Haiti.[16] A program for the deployment of Haitian laborers in Florida and other Latin American nations working for the U.S. war effort was introduced briefly and abandoned.[17] Lescot's support of the Allied cause emerged from a desire to gain international notice and military and financial aid from the United States, and also to strengthen the power of the local oligarchy. He took full advantage of these special circumstances by suspending the constitution in 1942 and having the parliament confer him with unlimited executive powers.

Wartime expedience created an economic venture of considerable importance to the regime. When the Axis blockade of the South Atlantic cut off traditional rubber supplies from Malaya and the Dutch East Indies, the United States looked for other possible sites for rubber cultivation. It was long known that the cryptostegia vine (commonly referred to by its Haitian name, *korne kabrit*) that grew profusely in rural Haiti had a high latex content that could be exploited. Although wartime production had proved disastrous in the past, as illustrated by a failed logwood scheme during World War I, Haitian officials did not see any risks involved in rubber cultivation. Attempts to develop rubber in Haiti first began in 1903 during the era of the rubber boom in Brazil with two Belgian brothers. However, the real push for development arose in the late Vincent years when studies were conducted in Haiti regarding the viability of rubber cultivation there. The U.S. Department of Agriculture sent Harley Harris Bartlett, a professor of botany at the University of Michigan, to the Philippines in late 1940 to select high yield *hevea* plants and transport them to Haiti to supplement the cryptostegia plants. The U.S. plan for the cultivation of rubber won support from Lescot and Agricultural Minister Maurice Dartigue, who hoped that large-scale rubber production in Haiti would aid the war effort and stimulate the local economy.[18]

The Export-Import Bank in Washington granted $5 million in the fall of 1941 (later supplemented by U.S. credit of $7 million in November the following year) to develop rubber plants in Haiti. This money financed the development of the Société Haïtiano-Américaine de Développement Agricole (SHADA) with U.S. agronomist Thomas A. Fennell as general manager and Dartigue as vice-president. Fennell was in his third year as agricultural advisor in Haiti, having been appointed during the Vincent presidency to assist in agricultural development and in a public works project.[19]

The contract negotiated with the U.S. government in 1941 gave the company free rein in its activities and provided it with ample military support. That same year SHADA commenced production in Haiti, settling on large tracts of land in the northern countryside then eventually spreading across the country. By 1943, an estimated 47,177 acres were cleared to make way for the planting of cryptostegia. Eventually SHADA would claim jurisdiction over 100,000 hectares of land. A team of U.S. technicians worked with Fennell, and the large labor force mostly comprised peasant farmers lured from food crop cultivation to meet increasing rubber demands.[20]

Lescot was excited about the project, which he saw as an opportunity to demonstrate his support for Pan-Americanism and cooperation with the Allied cause.[21] He campaigned energetically throughout the five departments, convincing local delegates that the program was not a move by the U.S. private sector for control of the Haitian economy, but a government-sponsored organization that provided a "big push for Haitian agricultural development," and that the annual profits from the program would be "put aside for the amortization of the national debt and development of needed resources."[22] He clearly believed that SHADA was a step toward the modernization of Haiti in the postwar world.[23] A report in the government paper, *Le Continental*, shared the president's optimism: "Our present collaboration with the USA is for the best of the country because it is America that we must look to in our search for the secret of democracy."[24]

President Élie Lescot explains SHADA *to Haitian peasant farmers, 1942. Courtesy of Thomas Dudley Fennell.*

For its part, the United States initiated a massive public relations campaign to promote the project, including an international newsletter, in English and French, that often featured glowing reports on the progress of the company, elaborate projections of massive revenues, and photographs of a smiling Lescot inspecting the SHADA sites.[25]

Despite these expectations, the process of rubber cultivation proved troublesome from the beginning. In order to get access to Haiti's most arable land, peasant families were forcibly removed.[26] The company invested a considerable amount of its funds trying to get rubber from the *hevea* trees, an attempt that produced fewer yields than was originally hoped. The destruction that accompanied the project raised considerable resentment among government officials. Dartigue, while maintaining a public image of vigorous support, was alarmed at the measures taken, particularly in Jérémie, where nearly a million fruit-bearing trees had been cut down and the houses of peasants either invaded or razed.[27] He implored Fennell to recognize that if SHADA was to succeed in its venture it had to understand "the mentality and legitimate interests of the Haitian peasant and city dwellers"; failure to do so would foster greater hostility toward the company. The government, he argued, was willing to do what was necessary to guarantee the success of the project, "but only after all methods of persuasion had been exhausted."[28] To this end, Dartigue submitted a lengthy twelve-point proposal for the acquisition of land and the relocation of the peasants.[29]

By May 1944 all sides agreed that the rubber project was a failure. Rubber was never produced in significant numbers for large export. The production problem was further aggravated by a severe drought in 1943–1944 that resulted in a bad harvest and low yields. Equally problematic was the increasing pressure in the U.S. Congress from oil interests lobbying for petroleum-based synthetic rubber. The Allied victory in France in June 1944 raised confidence that the war would soon end and forced a reevaluation of all wartime programs. A U.S. military attaché, following a survey of rubber production in the north, concluded: "The worst thing that can be said of SHADA is that they are doing [their operations] at a considerable expense to the American taxpayer and in a manner that does not command respect of the Haitian people."[30] This sentiment was reiterated in a 1944 report sponsored by the Rubber Development Corporation, EX-IM Bank, and the State Department, which suggested the project's immediate termination and the gradual return of displaced lands to the peasants.[31] Fennell left for Puerto Rico to work with the Puerto Rican Agricultural Company, and processing in all but a few experimental plants in Gonaïves was discontinued, though some sisal manufacturing, for ropemaking, remained operative under the direction of J. W. McQueen.[32]

Realizing that the cancellation of the program would create massive unemployment and damage his prestige, Lescot desperately urged the Rubber Development Corporation to consider a slow reduction of the program and its continuation for at least the remainder of the war. When this was refused, he prompted Dartigue to make a request to the State Department for $1 million to compensate the Haitian government and finance a rehabilitation program. He later withdrew the request out of fear it might engender "controversy . . . between the two governments."[33]

To offset the imminent economic disaster, the government created in June 1945 an ambitious Five Year Plan for economic development that projected a substantial amount for the creation of highways, encouragement of local food crops such as coffee, cocoa, and cotton, and expansion of public works. Lescot pushed for work on the plan to begin immediately in order to reap benefits for the fiscal year 1945–46. It was apparent that his political career hinged on the success of this venture. Yet the government was bankrupt and ravaged by the disappointment of SHADA. With continuing restrictions on shipping, the perishable banana industry, still maintained by United Fruit, suffered. Coffee exports dropped steadily following the loss of the Western European market during the war and the glut in the U.S. market.

The plan, moreover, suggested little for the immediate relief of the thousands of peasants still suffering from displacement and a low crop yield from the previous year, a point that was not lost on an agitated public bitter over the expense of SHADA. Urgent demands from the State Department for a payment of $700,000 on amortized loans from the 1922 and 1923 agreements did not help. Lescot unsuccessfully campaigned for a twenty-five-year extension of payment on the debt for the treasury funds to be put to the service of the Five Year Plan.[34] With revenues dwindling, lack of skilled personnel in the ministries, and only marginal increases in agricultural expenditures since Vincent, the country's economic crisis deepened at the moment its president expected the economy to be flourishing.[35]

Perhaps the only real beneficiaries of Haiti's wartime economic policy were the urban bourgeoisie. Chief among them was O. J. Brandt, an elite Jamaican entrepreneur who relocated to Haiti in 1911. Brandt made his fortune working with the Haitian Canadian bank in the thirties. It was during the war years, however, that he became most powerful. When war was declared on the Axis powers, the state confiscated all property and assets owned by nationals from the Axis nations. At the time, Reinbold and Company, the leading import-export firm in Haiti, which controlled the coffee, cotton, and oil trade, was owned by a second-generation German family long established in the country.[36] The owners were arrested, tried as Nazis, and imprisoned, and their property was sold to the established elite, much of it landing in the hands of Brandt. With his new acquisition of coffee-processing plants, factories, and a specialized staff of foreigners, Brandt quickly rose to become one of the wealthiest men in the country. The government named a medical laboratory after him and gave Brandt the national order of honor and merit. Later he would attempt to build a shipping line in Haiti.[37] The seemingly unchecked rise of Haiti's wealthy elite facilitated by government corruption enlarged the already profound socioeconomic divisions in the country.

The disgrace of economic failure was but one challenge that wracked the regime. Equally damaging was the anti-superstition campaign launched by the Catholic church against vodou in 1942. The surface motive for the campaign was the eradication of superstitious tendencies perpetuated by vodou practitioners that, according to the French clergy, kept Haiti in a retrograde state. The open clash between the clergy and vodou practitioners dates back to 1896, when a prominent bishop in Cap Haïtien led a series of gatherings and meetings under the banner "League Against Voodoo" in the north, which unsuccessfully sought to win widespread support against vodou.[38] In 1935 the church found support from the Vincent administration when it outlawed superstitious practices.

Early in 1941, when small protests against vodou were reignited in the rural village of Hinche, the French clergy capitalized on the furor and launched a systematic campaign throughout the rural districts.[39] In the provinces *hounfòs* (vodou temples) were destroyed, vodou *tambous* (drums) were burnt, and practitioners were forced to renounce their devotion to "superstition." Although there was clear historical precedent for the campaign, the systematic way in which it was launched indicated more urgent tensions.

The rise in black consciousness, discussed below, and the percolating struggle between the ethnologists who championed vodou's recognition in national culture and the Catholic institutions suggest a more political impetus for the raids. Already a source of considerable controversy, vodou became a contested site during the early forties. A cultural factor worth considering was the impact of negative stereotypes of Haitian vodou in the United States. Since the Great Depression, a spate of travel books and horror films released in the United States served to popularize exotic and horrific images of Haitian vodou. That this angered Haitian intellectuals is evidenced by the writings of Price-Mars and other eminent scholars during the time. It also presented a notable problem to the government, which was then greatly concerned with U.S. impressions of Haiti. As early as 1934, following the release of lurid films set in Haiti such as *White Zombie*, the government placed restrictions on foreigners entering the country with movie cameras, as U.S. anthropologist Melville Herskovits found out on a research trip to Haiti.[40] Kate Ramsey has suggested that Vincent's 1935 law was issued in part to distinguish between national forms of Haitian dance and folklore and the rituals of vodou practices among the peasantry.[41] Conservatives in Haiti, especially the French clergy, praised state sanctions against vodou practices in the late thirties. The harsh language of the white priests who referred to vodou practitioners in pejorative terms only underlined the racial aspect of the campaign.[42]

Although these factors were important, the immediate factor was a religious dispute between the French clergy and U.S. Protestant groups, particularly Baptists and Methodists, then establishing colonies in the countryside. Protestantism in Haiti began growing among the peasants during the occupation. In the countryside, Lescot also supported the brief practice of appointing Protestants as *chefs de section* in the more Catholic regions such as the Marbial valley near Jacmel in the south, in an effort to break the hold of the Catholic church there.[43] The French clergy rejected Protestantism's emerging strength, which jeopardized the hegemony of the Catholic church. The clergy forced *rejetés* to recite an anti-superstition manifesto issued in Kreyòl, which included a clear anti-Protestant component.[44] By December, the campaign extended to the urban centers. In several neighborhoods, Catholic priests ordered the public burning of vodou masks, artifacts, and paraphernalia in the churchyards.[45] Violent harassment was most acute in the South, where a French *curé* reportedly led nearly three thousand *rejetés* in the Cayes-Jacmel district to burn all animals considered possessed by *lougawous* (werewolves). Included in the list, according to the report, was an Episcopalian priest, recently appointed by the president, who managed to escape before the campaign. Similar occurrences were repeated in Mirebalais and Verettes.[46] In all cases police intervention prevented the eruption of large-scale violence. The campaign aroused widespread opposition in the press and in the capital when a group of protestors fired shots in a chapel in the middle-class district of Delmas on 22 February 1942 during a morning mass presided by the Vicar of the Cathedral, Rémy Augustin. The Catholic newspaper *La Phalange* reported over two hundred shots were fired by police officers dressed as peasants in an effort to embarrass the church.[47]

Nevertheless, the incident showed the government's disavowal of the campaign and strengthened the anti-Catholic attacks in the press. In *Le Soir*, Jean Magloire wrote that the Catholic church had incited a civil war that had to be met with force.[48] The papal Nuncio Monsignor Silvani, attending Independence Day celebrations in Santo Domingo, decided to remain there and ordered the clergy to halt the campaign. In the Dominican Republic, the newspaper *Listín Diario* interviewed him. In the interview, he criticized the Haitians for their "barbarous" superstitions, describing the country as one that knew very little Christianity. Lescot responded by immediately declaring Silvani persona non grata.[49]

With little evidence, scholars have long claimed that Lescot lent full support to the anti-superstition campaign, yet there is clear proof that he had only minimal involvement in its organization and execution.[50] A point often overlooked in most accounts is that the launch of the campaign preceded Lescot's election by two months. That he was aware of the campaign early on is evidenced by a letter he wrote in June 1941 to Father Carl Edward Peters, a Catholic bishop in Port-de-Paix, in which he ordered the military "not to use any violence" in supporting Peters's program of combating superstitions through the promotion of Catholic masses in Kreyòl.[51] Yet this is insufficient proof of support. Lescot never made any public statements backing the clergy's assault and seems to have perceived the campaign as a small isolated occurrence. In a later reflection on the events, Lecot insisted that he was "in the most complete ignorance" of Father Peters's ultimate intention when he wrote the letter.[52]

By alleging that Lescot gave support to the campaign, historians implicitly suggest that he was on good terms with the French priests. On the contrary, despite claiming that his was a "Catholic government,"[53] Lescot was embroiled in a struggle with the French clergy that he deemed Haiti's "main source of dissidence" well before he took office.[54] With the conflict between state and church gaining strength in the early forties, Lescot read the abuses of the clergy as an attempt to embarrass and destabilize his administration.[55] A participant at an official reception for SHADA representatives in May 1941 noted that Lescot was "surprised speechless" at the "fascist salute" French priests and Catholic schoolboys gave him in the presence of U.S. officials.[56]

Given his penchant for placating his opposition by offering support, his letter to Peters was most likely an attempt to reduce the potential of Catholic hostility to his regime and demonstrate his new powers as commander-in-chief of the Garde. It may have also been a shrewdly calculated maneuver to give apparent support to the French clergy at the same time that he was slowly supplanting French priests with U.S. bishops in the rural districts as part of his program of Americanization. Once the crusade escalated, Lescot threatened to court-martial members of the Garde who assisted the priests. He also backed the campaign against the clergy in the press, which he ordered to stop only after the Archbishop of Port-au-Prince, Monsignor Le Gouâze, made peace with him.[57]

Even after the campaign ended, widespread reaction against it continued among the intelligentsia. The nonsectarian Jacques Roumain wrote a series of articles in Le Nouvelliste on the event, arguing that what the country needed was "not a campaign against superstitions, but a campaign against poverty."[58] Although contemporary critics of the campaign seldom singled out Lescot, the fact that it occurred under his watch was further cause for resentment.

Marxist Dissent and Division

If the Nazis, real or imagined, faced strict persecution during wartime Haiti, then the archenemies of the state, the communists and radical nationalists, would expectedly receive harsh treatment. Yet the communist movement underwent crucial changes during the Lescot years that diminished its role as a significant threat to the state. After leaving Europe and New York, its leader, Jacques Roumain, returned to the Caribbean in 1940 and once again became politically active. Roumain spent several months in Havana from the end of the year to early 1941 through the invitation of fellow poet and communist Nicolás Guillén, with whom he formed a close friendship in Spain and France in 1937.[59] While in Havana he worked closely with the Cuban communists and occasionally contributed to the Socialist Party paper, *Noticias de Hoy*, of which Guillén was an editor.[60] Encouraged by Lescot's campaign promise to pardon Vincent's opponents, Roumain returned to Haiti on 17 May.[61]

His encounter with active and well-organized communists in Cuba encouraged Roumain, who immediately set about reforming the PCH with a view of challenging the pro-U.S. Lescot government. Around the same time, Roumain's associate Max Hudicourt returned to Haiti after two years in exile, indicating that he had formed an alliance with the CPUSA.[62] Among the other radicals of the thirties brought together by both men were Roumain's brother Michel, Marc Lafontant, Étienne Charlier, Antonio Vieux, and Christian Beaulieu. The group met secretly at Charlier's downtown law offices. For the returning radicals, it was a time to renew bonds sundered by forced exile and share their experiences with intellectuals and movements in the United States, the Caribbean, and Europe.

With the return of Roumain and Hudicourt, the Port-au-Prince police immediately put the radicals under constant surveillance and spies followed their activities. Police reports alleged that Roumain was promised a monthly salary of $300 from Cuban leftists to develop a communist movement in Haiti. It was also claimed that he planned to encourage a sergeants' revolt in an effort to overthrow the government and meet the "urgent need of a communist government."[63]

Although these reports may be exaggerated, Roumain was, at least initially, committed to opposing the regime. A crucial split in the PCH vanguard in June thwarted any hopes of realizing it. Roumain's call to action found little support from other Marxists such as Hudicourt, Charlier, and Vieux, who took very seriously Lescot's reforms of the Garde and his subsequent order to arrest all dissidents. Roumain would eventually appreciate the risk of agitating against Lescot and had the foresight to realize the threat military reform would pose to the government. He stated as much in a conversation recorded by an undercover police officer: "These [new] measures are a danger not only to [the communists] but also to Lescot himself because he is a man who has no idea of what it means to be the Chef Militaire."[64] Ironically, Roumain, who became the only member of the PCH to hold a government post under Lescot, parted company with his compatriots on this point. Roumain would say of Hudicourt and Charlier, "[They] are my friends but we do not share the same political ideas. [They] are socialists and I am a communist."[65] The tensions between the socialist and communist tendencies among the PCH members played an important role in undermining the strength of the Marxist Left.

The schism in the movement, his alienation from Port-au-Prince workers due to his five-year exile, and the continuing imprisonment of his strongest ally Georges Petit left Roumain with few options to foment a strong opposition force. Moreover, in August, when the police seized and confiscated communist literature he ordered, he feared reimprisonment and gave up on the idea of reorganizing the PCH.[66] He thus began to focus his energies elsewhere. He was most anxious to apply the anthropological training he had learned while in exile in New York to the study of Haitian folklore.

Concerned with Roumain's political agitation and no doubt aware that the persecution of a radical with as grand an international stature could have unfavorable implications for his government, Lescot created a position for the communist leader. In August, Lescot offered Roumain the directorship of Lycée Pétion, which he accepted.[67] Not long thereafter, Roumain began to work on developing an idea for an ethnological school as an extension of the movement he started more than a decade earlier with Price-Mars. Lescot approved the idea and on October officially established it as a government institution naming Roumain the director. With government support Price-Mars also started an Institut d'Ethnologie, as a school for the training of ethnologists where Roumain taught pre-Colombian archaeology. The Bureau concerned itself mainly with the classification and excavation of archeological sites.[68] Roumain was enthusiastic about the project, supervising several minor excavations around Port-au-Prince as well as on the islands of La Tortue and La Gonâve, and establishing an ethnological museum in the capital. During his directorship of the Bureau, Roumain did very little political or literary writing, publishing instead a series of technical ethnological studies.[69] As part of his activities, he maintained a high profile in his public life and often chaperoned visiting intellectuals such as Guillén, who was in Haiti in 1942.

Much to the surprise of his contemporaries, Roumain accepted a prestigious post as *chargé d'affaires* in Mexico in October 1942, for which he was widely criticized.[70] Michael Dash has suggested that Roumain's decision was "influenced by the Communist Party which saw it as a good strategy at the time to have prominent Marxists placed in important public positions."[71] Roumain, however, appears to have developed a fraternity with Lescot since he assumed the post as director of the Bureau. His acceptance of the position in Mexico had much to do with the common ground he found with the strongly anti-Nazi Lescot regime and the president's open support for the Soviet Red Cross. The appointment was a victory for Lescot, who had grown worried about having the country's most renowned *communiste rouge* working so closely with the peasantry through his activities with the Bureau. With Roumain posted in a foreign country, the government clearly expected that the communists would remain disorganized.

Indeed, the fragmentation of the movement rendered any large-scale organization of communist militants more unlikely. It did not mean, however, a reduction in the fervor of the socialists. Charlier and Hudicourt fast grew disenchanted with Lescot's policies and vision of "Americanizing" Haiti. By June 1941, Hudicourt was making public his position that "the language of Lescot is the language of Vincent and [the country] cannot accept another ten years of bluff."[72] In the congressional elections of 1941, Hudicourt ran for a seat in the Assembly. During his campaign he was critical of the police chief, Captain A. N. Merceron. As a result, Hudicourt was physically beaten by the police and forced to seek refuge in the Dominican Republic and later New York.[73] He reentered Haiti in 1942 and, after one year of negotiations, was permitted to start a daily newspaper, *La Nation*, which first appeared on 5 April 1943.[74] Hudicourt assumed the role of director and financed the paper himself with funds from Aux Alliés, a small Pétionville moviehouse he co-owned with other socialist sympathizers, Dr. Georges Rigaud and Marcel Bauduy.[75]

The editor of *La Nation* was Max D. Sam, a young black Marxist close to the Roumain brothers and grandson of former president T. A. Simon Sam (1896–1902). Sam was born in Port-au-Prince in 1912 and became involved with activism when he participated with his brother Justin in the Damien strike. His radicalism grew more fervent in the late thirties when he worked with Michel Roumain as a writer for *Le Nouvelliste*.[76]

In its debut issue, the editors stated unequivocally that the paper was a political and social organ aimed at the liberation of the masses from the "avarice and discrimination of capitalist governments and foreign powers."[77] During the Lescot presidency, *La Nation* was the leading voice of the Marxist Left and ultimately became the longest running Marxist paper in Haitian history. It significantly influenced the young intelligentsia and was widely circulated among literate urban workers.[78] Most articles gave considerable attention to the war, with special concern over the progress of the Red Army on the eastern front. Speeches from Latin American Marxists in Mexico, Argentina, and Cuba were translated and printed in their entirety. There were also a series of theoretical articles on socialism and culture and the role of the USSR in the struggle for autonomy in Algeria.

Although its reportage was mainly devoted to international events, *La Nation* covered local stories and often suffered as a result. In July 1943, the paper ran an article criticizing police chief Merceron's brother, who, in a drunken brawl, shot four bystanders. In response the police chief threatened to kill his rival, Hudicourt, before Lescot intervened.[79] Following this incident the paper refrained from reporting government activities. This did not mean, however, that the directors of *La Nation* gave up their protest against the government. Hudicourt, for example, fearing that impending legislative elections in 1944 would provide an occasion for the government to extend its powers, continued to draw international attention to the administration's failures. In a letter to Cordell Hull, he discussed these issues and pointed to the "share of responsibility" borne by the United States since the occupation in creating the current crisis in Haiti. It was thus the duty of the "guilty" U.S. government to intervene and force Lescot to respect the provisions of the Atlantic Charter.[80]

In March 1944 Hudicourt was named juridical counselor of the Haitian delegation sent to the Conference of International Workers Organizations in Philadelphia. Though suspicious of Lescot's intentions, Hudicourt saw it as an opportunity to work toward the improvement of the conditions of urban workers and accepted the post. During his absence, however, Lescot, beleaguered by the SHADA debacle and the threat it posed to his control, announced the extension of his term of office for seven years, a revision of the constitution, and the suspension of congressional elections until after the war.[81] Hudicourt responded strongly by refusing to serve at the conference on behalf of Haiti and issued public statements to that effect in Philadelphia. Lescot was incensed. In his inaugural address on 15 May 1944, he referred to Hudicourt specifically by stating that the "injurious and malicious" campaign against the administration by young "pseudo-defenders of the proletariat" would not be tolerated.[82] Lescot made good on this threat by issuing two decree laws in late May, stating that anyone given a foreign mission and refusing to fulfill it would be guilty of treason and liable to court-martial. The decrees were made retroactive for a year so that Hudicourt would be held accountable.[83] Accordingly, the government revoked his passport and, under an extradition treaty with the United States, demanded his immediate return to Haiti.

With the assistance of the American Civil Liberties Union, Hudicourt secured refugee status from the U.S. government and left Philadelphia to settle in New York, where he remained in exile for the remainder of the Lescot presidency.[84] There he worked with another political exile, Henri Rosemond, building an underground network of radicals sympathetic to the Haitian cause and developing L'Association Démocratique Haïtienne. As in 1940, he was successful in gaining support from U.S. black intellectuals in Harlem and published in 1945 *Haiti Faces Tomorrow's Peace*, a pamphlet detailing the abuses of the Haitian government and U.S. policy in the country, prefaced by Columbia University professor of anthropology Regina "Gene" Weltfish.[85]

A month after Hudicourt left, *La Nation*, along with *Le Réveil*, was shut down by the government for "raising questions that sought to divide the citizens against each other," for "sowing hate and fomenting trouble," and for their attempt to "make Haiti a ground of disorders."[86] The paper was also implicated in a sergeants' revolt against Lescot, discussed in detail below.

Far removed from these events, Jacques Roumain conducted his diplomatic functions in Mexico in fine fashion. He represented Haiti at the First Inter-American Congress on Demography, and as founding secretary was instrumental in establishing the International Institute of Afro-American Studies, which included international luminaries Fernando Ortiz, Melville Herskovits, and Alain Locke.[87] His tenure in Mexico marked a return to literary writing, and in late 1943 he completed a manuscript that would become his *chef d'œuvre* and a hallmark of Caribbean literature, *Gouverneurs de la Rosée* (Masters of the Dew). His health, however, deteriorated rapidly during these years. The malaria he contracted during his incarceration, from which he never fully recovered, coupled with health problems related to alcoholism, weakened him. When Lescot extended his term of office and postponed legislative elections, Roumain considered challenging him and returned to Haiti on 7 August.[88] Fellow communists, the numbers of which were growing among the youth during the final stages of the war, expected him to repudiate his allegiance to the government and seriously reorganize the PCH as a legitimate party. For party members this was even more urgent as the PCH's other founding member, Christian Beaulieu, had died suddenly in 1943.[89] His plans were dashed, however, when cirrhosis of the liver claimed his life on 18 August. Roumain's unexpected death at an early age was received with shock in Haiti and around the world. *Cahiers d'Haïti* published a lengthy tribute issue to Roumain in which the contributors expressed deep disappointment at the loss of one of Haiti's most talented intellectuals.[90]

The deaths of Roumain and Beaulieu, the closure of *La Nation*, and Hudicourt's continuing exile during these uneasy years dealt a severe blow to the hopes of a revival of the Marxist Left in Haiti. There was cause for concern on the part of the government when a group of leading intellectuals mainly from the southern province of Jérémie, including Michel Roumain, Jean Brierre, Anthony Lespès, Max Sam, Emile Roumer, Roussan Camille, and Jules Blanchet, arranged a meeting shortly before Roumain's funeral.[91] Lescot seized this opportunity to win support from the radicals. He ordered the Haitian Air Force to fly them from Jérémie to the capital to attend the funeral as special guests of the government. That evening, after a dinner at the palace in their honor, the leftists had a five-hour session with Lescot in which they discussed literature, politics, and the future of the country. For Lescot it was a contrived display of admiration for radical intellectuals long shunned by the bourgeoisie. Most of the participants saw through the transparency of his gesture.[92] Nonetheless, there were few members willing to lead the movement in the face of government repression and especially with FBI agents and the Port-au-Prince police keeping close tabs on their activities.[93]

While the first generation of Haitian communists were forced to remain silent in the latter stages of the war, Marxism blossomed among a cadre of young, intensely radical students who would eventually lead the charge in its explosion on the political scene. The success of their challenge, however, was possible only because of the phenomenal expansion of black consciousness during the war years when the ideas of the *noiristes* of the thirties found powerful expression among the popular classes.

Black Consciousness in the Forties

Global changes occasioned by the war invigorated Haitian black consciousness. The spread of the *négritude* movement in the early forties was heralded by the Griot writers of the thirties as a confirmation of their arguments. It also brought the Haitian movement into a pan-African orbit. The *négritude* movement, which began in France in the thirties among French colonial students, drew on many of the currents in global black consciousness. In this regard, it closely resembled Haitian *indigénisme*. The crucial difference was in its reach. Where *indigénisme* attempted to reconstruct the Haitian cultural space, *négritude* aimed at defining a theory of cultural difference applicable to the entire black world.[94] For the Griots of the thirties, this meant a validation of the fundamental racial and psychological differences between blacks and whites. Notwithstanding the fact that *négritude* never explicitly acknowledged the biological argument, nor the strong anti-*milat* tendencies of *noirisme*, the similarities were indeed significant. Most important was the fact that the early *négritude* writers, like many of the writers from the Harlem Renaissance a generation earlier, found in Haitian history the roots of an independent black culture. Aimé Césaire, following a visit to the island in 1945, noted that Haiti was where *négritude* began. For the *noiriste* writers of the period, *négritude* provided the international solidarity they long sought.[95]

Haitian black nationalism also resonated strongly with black intellectuals in the United States. This intellectual relationship expanded greatly during the first half of the forties when Haiti remained foremost in the U.S. black view of global black politics.[96] Black intellectuals in the United States, such as Langston Hughes and Howard University professor Rayford Logan, formed close associations with Haitian intellectuals. Faced with their own civil rights struggles in the United States and the global crisis of World War II, many U.S. black intellectuals found in Haiti a strong example of racial pride and revolutionary change. The effects of U.S. imperialism on the island upset them. On a trip to Haiti in 1942, Logan was surprised to see that poverty was worse since his previous visit in the early thirties and that Port-au-Prince was "still poor and black" and "more American than 1934."[97] Other leading black intellectuals in the United States who paid considerable attention to Haitian affairs shared such consternation. Zora Neale Hurston, Langston Hughes, and Arna Bontemps published books on Haitian history, and NAACP secretary Walter White became a tireless advocate for the improvement of the stereotyped image of Haiti in North America.

There was a simultaneous development among Anglophone Caribbean black intellectuals such as Trinidadians C. L. R. James and George Padmore. The former's monumental work on the Haitian Revolution, *The Black Jacobins*, presented a racialized perspective of the revolution within a traditional Marxist framework as a model for Third World nationalism, and was an important part of a general reappraisal of Haitian history in the African Diaspora. Black discourse on Haiti in the United States and the Caribbean, though less specific on the question of color, had parallels with the Griot interpretation of history.

The net effect of these developments was greater support for a race-based political ideology. Although the Griots ceased to exist as a collective movement at this point, several of its adherents were excited by the role that Haiti played in black consciousness movements elsewhere. But international developments only partially explain the transitory state of *noirisme* in the forties. To understand its popular evolution it is necessary to examine the social and cultural changes in Haitian life under Lescot.

Since government prohibitions on public meetings extended primarily to Marxists, black intellectuals had a certain degree of freedom in which they could hold meetings. A series of clubs formed during this period, creating a vibrant atmosphere for debate. These so-called *clubs de dimanche* were held once a week. Groups of students and various members of the black intelligentsia would meet and discuss literature, history, art, and social science, including the writings of nineteenth-century nationalists and the ethnological work of the Griot writers.

The meetings took place in the popular neighborhoods of Port-au-Prince, such as Bel Air and Bas-Peu-De-Chose, and had a cross-class attendance. At these meetings much of the ideas of *noirisme* were debated. The condition of blacks at the time and the arrogance of the Lescot administration toward color prejudice was a frequent topic of discussion. Emile St. Lôt, a politically ambitious lawyer who was a regular at the *clubs de dimanche*, also formed his own discussion group, L'Amicale, in 1944, which prioritized blacks from the middle and popular classes as members. Le Cénacle d'Études, led by Dr. René Salomon, grandson of former president Lysius Salomon, also emerged during this time.[98]

There were other contexts shaping *noiriste* discourse in the forties. Changes in Haitian popular culture and social life played a crucial role in the diffusion of black consciousness. In the wake of the anti-superstition campaign, Price-Mars and Roumain launched a vibrant movement for the defense of vodou as central to Haitian folklore. Furthermore, the regional shift in attitudes toward national folklore in Latin America struck a responsive chord among certain sectors of the Haitian elite who claimed newfound pride in their African ancestry. In September 1942, a performance at the Rex Theater entitled *L'Heure d'Art Haïtien*, which featured vodou-inspired dances, poems, and songs, drew a capacity crowd and received favorable reviews in the press.[99] This rebirth was manifest strongly in the phenomenal evolution of the Haitian arts movement.

Beginning in the mid-thirties Haiti began to expand its cultural relations with the rest of the world in an effort to develop its nascent tourist industry.[100] U.S. artists such as DeWitt Peters and Selden Rodman traveled to Haiti and, in the case of the former, assisted in the establishment of a Centre d'Art in 1944, with considerable support from Lescot.[101] Surprised at the level of untapped talent he found in Haiti, Peters, a former teacher with the English school, promoted artists from the peasantry who had long produced art reflective of indigenous culture. Most of the paintings produced during this period were stirring visual records of peasant life, vodou iconography, and traumatic episodes in the history of the country's long independence. The positive response to the Haitian art movement was immediate and enduring. Haitian artists were acclaimed for their works overseas, and the appreciation of indigenous art locally was strengthened.

The expansion in Haitian art was matched by the development of a vibrant folkloric dance movement. Chicago dancer Katherine Dunham went to Haiti to study traditional dances that she later used in her repertoire. Lescot himself supported the folklore movement by sending a troupe led by Lina Mathion Blanchet to Washington to participate in a Pan-African Conference in 1941 that aroused considerable praise in the U.S. press.[102] This troupe featured singer and dancer Emerante de Pradines, whose father, Kandjo, had been a renowned turn-of-the-century composer. On returning to Haiti, de Pradines, along with Martha Jean-Claude, performed a regular concert series at the Rex Theater, where they often sang renditions of traditional vodou songs, then a novelty in Haitian social life.[103]

Neither the folklore nor the art movements ever took an opposition stance during these years. In fact, folklore found tacit support from the bourgeoisie, who religiously attended folkloric performances at popular Port-au-Prince nightclubs such as Cabanne Choucounne and the Voodoo Club on the weekends.[104] Though celebrating Haiti's African past, like the ideas of the Griots during the previous decade, these movements were never a threat to *milat* political hegemony. What they illustrate, however, is a deepening of racial pride and a redefinition of notions of Haitian identity.

It was among the popular classes that the potential of this movement was most radically interpreted through the development of a proto-commercial Haitian music. Jazz, introduced to Haiti in the 1920s by the marines, became popular among the youth in the mid-thirties. The Haitian derivative of U.S. jazz (commonly spelled *djazz*) incorporated Cuban and Dominican styles with the traditional U.S. format. The formation of the popular dance band, Jazz des Jeunes, in 1942 was an important development in the diffusion of *noiriste* ideas to the urban populace. With members coming from the new black middle class, the ten-piece group fast became sympathetic to the black political movement. The group responded strongly to the call of *indigénisme* dressing in "folkloric garb" and integrating traditional vodou rhythms into their musical structure.[105] In Caribbean countries, music often assumes what Gérard Béhague has called "counterhegemonic strategies toward the elimination of political and economic subordination."[106] In Haiti, music had long existed as a means of expressing nationalism and political discontent. During the 1929 strikes, Haitian band leader and composer Occide Jeanty, for example, played his revolutionary piece *1804* on the Champ de Mars as an act of protest.[107] It is therefore not surprising that this tradition of resistance expression in Haitian music would grow more forceful with the advent of proto-commercial music.

Together with the other leading band of the time, Orchestre Saïeh (whose leader incorporated vodou performance and songs into his American styled music), Jazz des Jeunes made popular the *vodou-djazz* form of Haitian music.[108] In content and form, they strayed from the traditional French styles and explicitly championed Haitian cultural authenticity. Jazz des Jeunes also frequently used Kreyòl expressions and proverbs to cast bitter comment on the social cleavages in the country and issue subtle invectives against the light-skinned elite. A line from the chorus of "Natif Natal" illustrates this: "Moun ki natifnatal, ki vreman nasyonal" (People who are native-born are truly national).[109] In a later song, "Anciens jeunes," they offered the following self-assessment: "Jazz des Jeunes is the Haitian people's treasured child. Their pride, their dignity, is to eat their own food. Living from their Garden, they love being ancient. By extolling the foreign, you betray only yourself."[110]

Haitian commercial music therefore amplified Haitian black consciousness and became an important vehicle for its dissemination. It was, according to ethnomusicologist Gage Averill, "in short an advertisement for black power."[111]

The dissemination of black consciousness through music and performance was assisted by the expansion of Haitian radio. Like jazz, radio was introduced to Haiti by the U.S. marines in 1926. In 1935 Ricardo Widmaïer launched the first commercial radio station in the country, HH3W. By 1948 there were seven radio stations operating in Port-au-Prince.[112] In the next decade, radio would play a critical role in Haitian political life, bringing Haitians in closer contact with international events and providing a forum through which political figures could reach the largely illiterate populace. In its early phase, however, radio was an important outlet for the expression of ideas through music and discussion. Intellectuals such as Dantès Bellegarde and Félix Magloire would have debates on HH3W every Tuesday evening.[113]

During the war, import shortages resulted in a decline in the supply of French and American records at the same time audience demands on radio increased.[114] To alleviate this problem, entertainment-oriented stations expanded the practice of in-studio concerts of groups such as Jazz des Jeunes. Since there was no fully developed recording industry in the country, these performances were very popular. These public expressions of black consciousness infused *noirisme* with greater force by extending its reach from the porches and drawing rooms of the black intelligentsia to the popular classes.

Daniel Fignolé: "The Moses of Port-au-Prince"

Where developments in the Haitian arts, intellectual life, and communications brought *noiriste* ideas to popular conscience, it was the progress of the labor movement that assured its full penetration. The Haitian labor movement, which had been small and unorganized for most of the century, began to form during these years. Joseph Jolibois *fils* formed a small union of artisans and peasants in 1930, the PCH, and other nationalist groups attempted to form syndicates under Vincent. However, the lack of any sustained organization or leadership stunted the growth of Haitian labor in the latter stages of the occupation. In addition, the Vincent regime's strict censure of opposition forces and careful monitoring of labor activities successfully subdued mass organization in Haiti. Restraints on labor were, to be sure, carried through by the Lescot regime. A government law insisted on the presence of a police officer at all meetings of workers associations.[115] This did not, however, assume the rigidity of the previous regime. Thus prior to the early forties, there was extremely limited potential for the development of a meaningful labor movement in Haiti.

Added to this was the important demographic shift that had been occurring in Port-au-Prince during these years. The promise of greater employment in the urban centers from the late occupation years produced an intra-island drift from the provinces to the capital. By the end of the forties, the total population of Port-au-Prince had increased to approximately 142,100, nearly half being born outside the capital.[116] As a consequence, the working population expanded with an estimated 80,000 urban dwellers over the age

PRINCIPAL ACTIVITIES OF THE POPULATION OF PORT-AU-PRINCE,
AGES TWELVE AND UP, 1949

Activity	Men	Women	Total
Economically Active	34,882	43,233	78,115
Workers	25,254	27,949	53,203
Unemployed	9,628	15,284	24,912
Economically Inactive	7,894	17,198	25,092
Housewives	—	9,148	9,148
Students	7,046	5,654	12,700
Disabled	198	283	481
Elderly	294	1,760	2,054
Others	356	353	709
No information	1,421	2,765	4,186
Total	44,197	63,196	107,393

Source: Recensement de la ville de Port-au-Prince, 24 January 1949, table 8.

of sixteen among the economically active population, both employed and unemployed.[117] This increase established a formative base for labor organization. By 1942, Le Peuple, a newspaper devoted exclusively to workers' issues, was launched, though it would only last for a year.

The communist movement made tentative steps to form a working-class base in Port-au-Prince during the early years of the PCH. Its weakened position in the mid-forties, however, prohibited any successful impact. Radicals from the elite, despite their championing of workers' causes, were also popularly viewed as beneficiaries of Lescot's color politics and most likely seen by some as less committed to changing the status quo. Noirisme, on the other hand, forcefully appealed for the creation of a political class truly representative of the black majority. Urban workers thus looked to representatives of the black middle class, with strong familial ties in the working class to lead them. The new labor leaders of the forties stood in stark contrast to those of previous decades in that they had achieved reputable social standing through education and reflected the aspirations of the popular classes.

No other political personality more epitomized the burgeoning philosophy of the labor movement, nor had as monumental an effect on its course, than Pierre-Eustache Daniel Fignolé. At a young age, the charismatic Fignolé rose to become one of the most influential figures in pre-Duvalier Haiti. More than any other political leader, Fignolé had the majority support of urban workers and thus proved to be a threat to every government of the era.

Fignolé was born in the small southern coastal town of Pestel. Although poor, his family had some political experience, as his grandfather, J. N. Fignolé, represented Pestel as senator in the late nineteenth century. The young Daniel migrated to Port-au-Prince in 1927 at the age of fourteen, following the death of his father. Raised by his paternal uncle, Job, Fignolé did well in his subjects and won a place at one of Port-au-Prince's most prestigious schools, Lycée Pétion. His poor health, caused by chronic malnutrition, and the need to supplement his mother's income forced Fignolé to seek employment while still completing his education at Lycée Pétion. Fignolé found a job as a private mathematics tutor for his more privileged classmates, often holding classes in the salons of the elite. Fignolé enrolled in law school in 1938 but had to withdraw due to his family's growing dependence on his income and a serious bout of tuberculosis in 1940 for which he was twice hospitalized.[118] With the death of his mother later that year, Fignolé went into teaching full-time, becoming a mathematics professor at Lycée Pétion, Petit Séminaire Collège St-Martial, and Collège Odéide.

Fignolé's initial radicalization, like that of many of his generation, accelerated with the global changes created by the war. His ideological sympathies, as far as he expressed them during these years, were a rough combination of the democratic ideals of Roosevelt, the socialist thinking of Léon Blum, and the writings of Haitian ideologues Louis Joseph Janvier and Jean Price-Mars. What most influenced Fignolé's political ideas were the discussions on *noirisme* in which he regularly participated. Fignolé frequented the *clubs de dimanche*, where he relished engaging in debates with light-skinned intellectuals. He often had the support of his students, many of who would turn up just to hear him.[119]

In 1941 Fignolé, then in his mid-twenties, began what was to become a prolific career as a political writer with the small journal *Le Réveil*. After a brief stint with *Le Réveil*, Fignolé, along with Joseph Déjean, Amilcar Lamy, Kléber Georges Jacob, and Mesmin Gabriel, launched their own newspaper, *Chantiers*, in 1942. The ideological tone of the paper was often vague and shrouded in the current language of democracy and liberalism. In its debut issue the editorial committee noted that the goal of the paper was to "establish in [Haiti] true democracy in the freedom, equality, and culture of the nation."[120] In early issues, Fignolé gave considerable focus to the

*Daniel Fignolé. From
Chantiers, 1946. Courtesy
of Bibliothèque Nationale
d'Haïti.*

government's social policies. He was not, at the time, concerned principally
with labor issues, devoting many of his articles to the need for education
reform. In a typical article, Fignolé warned that Lescot would not be successful in dealing with Haiti's economic malaise if he did not properly address
education. Fignolé called for an increase in primary schools across the
country to meet the ever-increasing number of school-age children. In explaining the fundamental problems of social inequity in Haiti, Fignolé and
the contributors to the paper adopted a *noiriste* perspective of Haitian history, evident in their harsh critique of the light-skinned elites. "The lazy,
selfish, egotistical, and sectarian bourgeois way of life is an insult to the
poverty of the peasant . . . who works for the pleasure of a class swollen with
prejudice; . . . the descendants of Toussaint and Dessalines are abandoned in
filth and ignorance." The solution to this predicament, he argued, was an
affirmation of Haiti's proud revolutionary heritage guided by strong and
capable black leaders: "Haitian society is very sick and in its collective
aberration, loses all sense of national and racial solidarity! Against that
perilous tendency and for the continuity of the nation it is time that all
conscious Haitians raise their voices. . . . We are black and we will stay black,
proud of our origins and proud of our glorious past."[121]

Given the repressive nature of the times, Fignolé's critique of Lescot was indeed bold. Unlike other radical papers of the period that were purposefully vague in their reference to the government, Fignolé was more direct. He argued that if Haiti was to take its place in the postwar world, it was necessary that it had a leadership concerned with the underprivileged. "Mr. Lescot," he warned, "the hour of the people is at hand."[122] Lescot retaliated to these charges by forcibly closing down *Chantiers*, terminating Fignolé's post as instructor in the government schools and keeping him under strict police surveillance.[123]

Despite the repression, Fignolé continued to write for other papers, sharpening his critique of the elite. Writing for *Le Réveil* under the pseudonym Jean Sadors, Fignolé commented in 1943 that "it is a universally known fact that in the countries where the bourgeoisie dupe the people, the conditions under which these two classes evolve will naturally be totally different." It was, Fignolé argued, "the enlightened men of the masses" who could be expected to develop a "proletarian consciousness" in Haiti.[124]

With limited income and no steady occupation, Fignolé devoted himself more fervently to political activism. It was during this time that Fignolé became prominent in labor issues. A confident and dramatic speaker, Fignolé believed in the power of the popular classes and often held impromptu meetings in downtown Port-au-Prince. Fignolé's passionate fast-paced public addresses were delivered in Kreyòl and punctuated by modulations in his voice that oscillated between a deep timbre and a sharp squeal, which he deployed for greater effect. His command over the laborers, domestics, and unemployed urbanites fast became legend. Fignolé's mastery of political symbolism and extraordinary capacity to sway his followers was emphasized by his insistence that he be referred to as "le professeur," a powerful gesture in a country where basic education remains a luxury.[125]

Though attracted to socialist philosophies, Fignolé had no interest in communism or the Marxism of the young radicals, many of whom numbered among his students.[126] As his early writings make clear, Fignolé was an ardent black nationalist who, more than his *noiriste* counterparts, reduced Haitian politics and history to a struggle between black and *milat*. This fundamental color struggle, he averred, was the fuel that ignited the class inequities that plagued Haiti. His black power ideas were less developed than the *noiristes*, as Fignolé avoided discussions of biological superiority and preferred to define the social struggle as one between the haves and have-nots. Again, writing as Sadors he noted, "[Here in Haiti] the bourgeoisie is claiming to be liberal at a time when liberalism is sweeping across

England. We see it for what it is. It is opportunist. It is the character of every bourgeoisie to prevent a social revolution of the poor."[127]

These views made Fignolé attractive to *noiriste* intellectuals. Before it closed down, *Chantiers* counted *noiriste* writers and members of the Griot clique such as Lorimer Denis, Love Léger, and François Duvalier among its writers. The roster of contributors included several black intellectuals who would play key roles in the political transformations of the next decade. In Fignolé, Duvalier and Denis found a leader who could bring their social ideas to the popular classes, a task neither of them achieved in the thirties. In 1945 they began work on their grand treatise, *Le problème des classes à travers l'histoire d'Haïti*, the most radical formulation of the *noiriste* thesis. Though later published as a book, it first appeared the following year in serial form in *Chantiers* and was dedicated to "the popular leader Daniel Fignolé, symbol of the aspirations and traditions of all classes of men."[128]

The Military Challenge

The political and social fragmentation that characterized Haitian society and governance was in large measure reflected in the Garde d'Haïti. Indeed, the Haitian army in the mid-forties was a microcosm of the contentious civil society. As we have seen, the military during the Vincent years had retained its staunchly pro-U.S. character, and the support of powerful politicians was always privileged over national interests. The first dramatic change in this feature occurred under Lescot, who more than his predecessor recognized the growing importance of the armed forces. He not only declared himself supreme commander of the Garde but also expanded the institution significantly by integrating the civilian corps des pompiers (firemen), developing greater centralization of the bureaucracy, and professionalizing high-ranking military positions, many of which acquired law degrees in the early forties. The addition of the previously independent Gardes côtes (coast guard) and corps d'aviation (air force) complemented the government's goals of modernization. These developments increased the numbers of officers and expanded the structure of the Haitian armed forces, which, according to a 1942 U.S. Joint Chiefs of Staffs report, totaled 154,322.[129]

Nevertheless, by giving greater prestige to the armed forces, these transformations served to deepen the entrenched system of corruption created under Vincent. Higher-ranking officers, mostly white and light-skinned, capitalized on their new powers and graft became common at all levels of the military structure. Problems were worse in the rural districts where the post of the rural police chief, the *chef de section*, was often sold by the head of the military department, sometimes for as much as $4,000, and bequeathed from father to son through as many as four generations. Once in control, a *chef* (commonly called by his preoccupation title, *Komandan*) became the only visible and accessible government official in the rural communities, typically ruling his jurisdiction with force and intimidation.[130]

The machinations of these newly trained professional officers raised much contention among their darker-skinned charges, who, in the heightened era of black consciousness, began to push for greater representation. Having to conduct raids on civilian vodouists in the provinces during the anti-superstition campaign was, not surprisingly, the source of much resentment among the lower-ranking officers. Robert Bazile, a black officer from a Catholic background who would play a role in the military intervention in the late forties, recalled the personal trauma of having to destroy sacred altars, trees, and a host of pre-Columbian artifacts, many of which were stolen and later sold to foreign museums.[131] Black consciousness was not the only ideology that influenced officers. A few young light-skinned members of the army, most notably Paul Laraque, who graduated with Bazile in July 1941, were fired by socialism, remained close to their radical peers, and resented elite control of the economy.[132]

Other leading black officers satisfied themselves by ruthlessly manipulating the venal system that characterized the regime and used it to establish a footing in the political sphere. One such person was Major Paul Eugène Magloire, the young son of a general from Cap Haïtien. Since graduating from the military school in 1930, Magloire rose steadily through the ranks and presented himself as one of Lescot's most trusted aides. He wielded the power his position afforded to build a strong cadre of support within the military and civilian ranks that he would later exploit.

The tensions among the lower-ranking blacks reached a boiling point in 1944. On 23 May sergeants in the Palace district of the Garde staged a minor revolt over the limited privileges and pay they were receiving.[133] The leaders of the conspiracy seem to have had every intention of fomenting a national rebellion and installing a new president. The suggested candidates supported by the soldiers were Colonel Armand, chief of the Palace Garde, and Jean Price-Mars.[134] The conspiracy was betrayed, however, when a machine gun was discovered stolen from the barracks. Of the forty-seven guards who conspired in the plot, seven were executed without court-martial and the remainder imprisoned. The glorification of the military overthrows elsewhere in Latin America in the pages of *La Nation* was cited as an inspiration for the plot and contributed to the closure of the socialist paper on 27 June.[135]

Military attempts to overthrow Lescot did not end with this plot. Another presumed plot was discovered in October.[136] Fifteen persons including two women were arrested and charged with complicity to assassinate the president. It was further discovered that the accused had a cache of revolvers enclosed in two diplomatic envelopes sent to the Dominican Consul at Belladère, Fernando Gómez.

Though troubled by the conspiracy, Lescot sought to use the incident to earn popular support for his flagging regime. He notified the press of the incident and implored the nation to unite against Trujillo's attacks. His attempt to paint himself as a victim of Dominican maliciousness had little effect as the wealth and high standard of living of his ministers became increasingly conspicuous. More important, however, was the fact that support from the Dominican Republic had started to wane as Lescot included Trujillo in the plot to overthrow the regime, although the reasons for this were never ascertained.[137] One explanation for the plot that received much attention in Port-au-Prince was that Lescot, after having been ushered into power with financial support from Trujillo, had become a megalomaniac and reneged on many of the promises he had initially made to Trujillo. Trujillo therefore responded by ordering Lescot's assassination. Such a view was no doubt instigated by the potentially tense situation between the two republics occasioned by Lescot's signing of an anti-tyranny resolution in Caracas during a trip there in late June. Lescot, in fact, had been taking a position against the Dominican dictator since at least 1943 when he suspected Trujillo was using Dominican spies to undermine his regime. Whatever the reasons, Lescot's regime now raised the ire of the Trujillo government across the border.

In a series of letters between the two men, Trujillo revealed his disgust for what he perceived as Lescot's ingratitude to him based on several speeches Lescot made against the Dominican Republic in the spring of 1944. Trujillo exposed his financial support for Lescot's election, and revealed the details of a shocking plot conjured up by Lescot in 1940 for Trujillo to precipitate a "serious agitation on the frontier" akin to the massacre of 1937 in an effort to weaken Vincent's position in Haiti and create for himself "the easiest way to the presidency." In June the following year at the San Francisco conference, the translated letters were published and presented to each delegate. Later, part of the correspondence was circulated in Port-au-Prince.[138] The tensions between the two men and the controversy that resulted from the publicity of the letters reached new heights later in the year. When Trujillo planned a peace meeting at the border in 1945, Lescot refused to participate, claiming that he was fearful for his life. He then made public certain death threats he received from Trujillo as early as 1941.

Growing increasingly suspicious of Trujillo, Lescot made a vain effort to drag the United States into the quarrel by suggesting that Trujillo had spies in Haiti whose purpose was to destroy the SHADA project and that Trujillo was working in concert with the Axis powers. He further stated that given Trujillo's past actions, there was "the possibility of the repetition of the sad situation of 1937."[139] Such efforts, however, did little to win support as Washington had by then recognized that Axis strength was weakening. The powers that once sustained Lescot could now be counted among his opponents.

Conclusion

The Lescot era was critical for the development of radicalism in Haiti for three main reasons. First, the strengthening of U.S.-Haitian economic relations and the failure of SHADA during the war years produced mixed results. Instead of improving the local economy, these new relations contributed to the harsh conditions faced by the peasantry and the urban workers, and added to popular dissatisfaction with the regime. Second, the traditional power elite—the Catholic church, the urban bourgeoisie—in an effort to cope with the social changes of the period exercised a greater degree of prejudice toward the very elements of Haiti's past that radicals were promoting. The anti-superstition campaign was the most prominent example of this. The response of the government to perceived threats against the state was to strengthen control in the hands of the *milat* elite, a move that made the social divisions more apparent to an increasingly politicized urban population. According to Trouillot, "By 1945, for the first time in Haitian history, the distribution of power had become explicitly colorist."[140]

Finally, the politicians of the Lescot administration, in spite of attempts at cooptation, failed to appreciate the potential of the various radical movements that grew during the war years. The combined effect of these movements was an intensification of black consciousness in the country at a time when the financial burdens and misappropriation of funds were most severe. The end of the war and the enthusiasm with which it was received globally, coupled with growing radicalism locally, was too much for the Lescot government to bear. U.S. chargé d'affaires to Haiti Robert S. Folsom, who began his tour of duty in 1941, noted that initially the Lescot government had the "advantage of unity inspired by war." How different the mood was by late 1945 when, according to Folsom, the Lescot regime was "collapsing from the weight of its own mistakes."[141] By the time the collapse arrived, it was obvious that Haitian politics would never be the same again.

CHAPTER 3

The Haitian Revolution
of 1946

†

We are the men who prepared the Revolution
of January 1946. Men of the bourgeoisie you lost
1930. But the Revolution of 1946 will not lose.
—JACQUES STEPHEN ALEXIS, *La Ruche*, 1946

For us Marxists, the color question, despite current
appearances to the contrary, does not lie at the heart of
the Haitian problem. —MAX MENARD, *La Ruche*, 1946

In today's Haiti, we consider false any communist
movement that is not directed by the black majority.
—*Chantiers*, 1946

When after the revolution you hear the people
and its leaders express certain aspects of their
desire . . . it is so that an authentic representative of
its majority can govern the country. You cannot tell us
that we are spreading division. The country has not been
united for even a brief moment over the past few years.
—ROGER DORSINVILLE, *Lettre aux hommes claires*, 1946

In 1946 the political history of Haiti changed course. The overthrow
of the Lescot regime that year during what is commonly referred to as
"the five glorious days," intensified unresolved tensions and fomented a
decade-long political conflict. The radical movement born in the occupation and nurtured during the Vincent-Lescot years, matured with incredible force following the fall of the government with the revolution of 1946.
More broadly, the revolution was the first popular response against a U.S.-
supported government in postwar Latin America and the Caribbean. The

triumph of the movement did not lead to the creation of long-term economic recovery from the abuses of the deposed government, nor eradicate political corruption, and only minimally improved the material benefits of the country's impoverished majority. It did, however, signal a breakdown in the legitimacy of elite political supremacy; forcefully asserted radical ideology as a political weapon; gave the black middle class unprecedented political leverage; announced the crucial role of the labor movement as a force in national politics; and strengthened the role of the military. Most symbolic of the major changes in the political culture was the coming to power of the black peasant-born Dumarsais Estimé in August. From that moment onward, a member of the light-skinned elite has not been elected to the highest seat of power in the country.

This chapter traces the emergence of these forces on the political scene and analyzes the elaboration of the conflict within the Haitian left that marked the long and tumultuous course of events leading to the election of Estimé and the consolidation of his regime. To understand these developments and their importance to national politics it is necessary to begin with a discussion of the instigators of the revolutionary movement, the Marxist youth, and their pivotal role in the revolt.

"We Are the Reds": The Young Marxists and the January Revolt

The movement to topple Lescot emerged not from the socialist writers of *La Nation* nor the disparate *noiriste* factions, but from the young Marxists in Port-au-Prince. As noted in the previous chapter, the split in the communist movement in the early forties weakened its ability to organize but did little to contain the spread of Marxist thought among a new generation of young intellectuals. This interest was not entirely linked to the PCH or the writers of *La Nation*. The victories of the Allied forces in the war invigorated young Haitians with a new sense of self-confidence, optimism, and the possibility to effect lasting change in their society. This new cohort did not experience the occupation nor the Damien strike but they had first-hand encounters with the repression of the current government. For the minority who attended the University of Haiti the desire for change was urgent.

Since the existing faculties of tertiary education in Haiti—medicine, applied science, engineering, ethnology, law, and agriculture—were not unified into a state university system, general control of each fell within the jurisdiction of various ministries. Of all the faculties, the medical was the most vociferous in the demand for reorganization. The National Medical School, founded in 1863 and including the medicine, surgery, pharmacy, and later dentistry schools, was under the directorship of the minister of public instruction, Maurice Dartigue. By a decree of October 1938, the school was elevated to the status of faculty with an increase in the period of study from four to six years and with the admission of female students. In the mid-forties total attendance in the medical school was fewer than one hundred with most students coming from the ranks of the middle class.[1] A small number of private doctors were responsible for instruction, and the directorship of the school remained under a dean appointed by the president. Lescot suggested a reorganization of the university system in December 1944, but the heavy influence of government bureaus on the faculty and its resultant lack of academic freedom created opposition among the student body.[2]

The formation of the Association des Étudiants en Médecine, Pharmacie, et Art Dentaire (ADEM) in 1945 was an attempt to create a fraternity of students concerned with the state of the profession. ADEM also became an important forum where political ideas were discussed. The president of the association was a brilliant, energetic, twenty-three-year-old black student from Gonaïves named Jacques Stephen Alexis. Alexis's father, Stephen, was a respected militant journalist of the twenties and later ambassador to Paris. Alexis's interests extended far beyond the medical profession. In 1945 he was president of the country's most prestigious intellectual organization, Club Intrepid, a high honor considering his young age. A staunch communist who had been exposed to radical thought through discussion with his father's colleagues, Alexis used ADEM's journal *Le Caducée* as an opportunity to express his views on world politics.[3]

On a wider level, global intellectual currents further enhanced the impact of revolutionary thought on the young intellectuals. A figure of great influence among the students was French cultural attaché Dr. Pierre Mabille, who settled in Haiti during the occupation of France in 1941.[4] During his Haitian tenure, Mabille was instrumental in strengthening cultural links with France through the formation of the Institut Français, and the founding of an important cultural and literary journal in January 1946, *Conjonction*. He was also supportive of the Medical Faculty where he occasionally lectured. His presence among the Haitian literati and on the campus of the faculty strengthened his impact on the medical students. Mabille maintained in the French embassy library an extensive collection of Marxist literature and of the works of poets and writers of the French resistance, which he openly shared with the students close to him. For many of the revolutionary youth these books were their first encounter with concepts of historical materialism and heavily shaped their political conscience.[5]

Of the several radical students in the medical school, Gérald Bloncourt, the son of a French woman and an elite Haitian, was one of the more prominent. In spite of his youth, the twenty-year-old distinguished himself in several areas. He was an athlete of some repute and respected artist and director at the Centre d'Art before enrolling in the medical school in 1945. On the posthumous release of Roumain's *Gouverneurs de la Rosée* that year, Bloncourt, a strong admirer of Roumain, had a fortuitous meeting with senior medical student and fellow Roumain follower Jacques Stephen Alexis.[6] The two young students fast became close friends and often met after classes and on weekends to discuss current trends in art, literature, and the international communist movement.[7] Alexis and his colleagues Théodore Baker and Gérald Chenet, like many other young radicals, heard of the bravery of Bloncourt's brother Tony, a member of the French Resistance who was tortured and killed in a Paris prison in 1943, and thus had great respect for the rebellious younger brother.

In April 1945 René Depestre, a nineteen-year-old high school student from Jacmel who had relocated to the capital four years earlier, published a book of poems entitled *Étincelles*, which was received with great enthusiasm among the young militants. The works of the French resistance poets, Éluard, Aragon, and Emmanuel, influenced Depestre's work.[8] Like the other students, he was a fervent communist who idolized Jacques Roumain. "Camarade Roumain," wrote Depestre in his ode *Le baiser au leader*, "you are our ideal. You are our flame. You are our God. [You] cried a voice and the present choir will respond."[9] For the young radicals, Depestre's work was a reflection of their own political sympathies, and a confirmation that a new generation of intellectual youth was becoming politically conscious. In late spring, Bloncourt arranged the small reading group he cofounded "Les amis de Jacques Roumain," to meet the young poet at a gathering of left intellectuals at communist Edris St. Armand's house. At that meeting a bond quickly formed.

The international expansion of Marxism in the postwar world, the Spanish Civil War, and the flurry of radical ideas among the intellectual youth in Port-au-Prince excited them. These young men, many of whom were poets, writers, and artists as well as students, agreed that their revolutionary ideas deserved an outlet for expression, and thus decided to start an activist journal. In order to avoid financial and licensing problems, the journal was named after a short-lived two-page weekly that Baker started in 1942 while still a student at the Lycée Pétion, *La Ruche*.[10]

On 7 December 1945 the first issue of the revamped *La Ruche* appeared in Port-au-Prince. The editorial board was a group of fifteen students, the most important being Alexis, Depestre, Gérald Chenet, Baker, Bloncourt, Gérald Montasse, George Beaufils, Raymond Pressoir, and Max Menard. The writers often went into the popular areas of Port-au-Prince and read the articles in Kreyòl for their largely illiterate audience.[11] The *La Ruche* writings were often bold, defiant, and idealistic, driven by a revolutionary zeal and naïve optimism in Marxism. Unlike the *noiristes*, their resistance to Lescot did not derive from color politics but from the repressive nature of the state, which they equated with fascist Italy. As Gérald Montasse remarked, "Our movement is not directed against the person of Élie Lescot. It is against colonialism and bourgeois greed . . . that is the greatest sorrow of the proletarians and Haitian people. We have given ourselves to a new politics. This new politics is national, anti-bourgeois, democratic, and socialist."[12]

The potent discourse of the *La Ruche* collective was fashioned not only from Marxism but also from French cultural theory. None proved more influential than surrealism. In early December André Breton, the doyen of the surrealist movement, visited Haiti for a series of lectures on surrealism and modern art. In exile from France since 1944, Breton came to Haiti on the invitation of Mabille and with the aid of Lévi Strauss, then French cultural attaché in New York.[13] Although the surrealist movement was then losing influence in its native France, it was the latest in a series of European intellectual movements enthusiastically received by the Port-au-Prince intelligentsia. Until the mid-forties, Haitian intellectuals, with the notable exception of Magloire St. Aude, paid little attention to surrealist claims.[14] The succeeding generation of poets and writers deeply motivated by négritude, which in turn drew on surrealism's emphasis on liberating the creative mind to form a new aesthetic, found the movement novel and alluring. According to Paul Laraque, the young Marxist-influenced soldier and poet who was close to the members of *La Ruche*, many poets of his generation had no idea of surrealism before Césaire visited the island in 1944.[15]

The majority of this group, as Laraque, Depestre, Bloncourt, and Pressoir later admitted, had a narrow and blind view of surrealism and were unfamiliar with the critical writings of Breton's contemporaries or the limitations of the movement. Notwithstanding, the presence of the revered Breton, whose visit coincided with that of Cuban artist Wilfredo Lam in Port-au-Prince over Christmas 1945, stirred considerable excitement among the members of *La Ruche* and their peers, who religiously attended his discussions at the Savoy club and his lectures at the Rex Theater.[16]

They were most fired by Breton's nonconformism and staunch denigration of dictatorship of all kinds, given powerful emphasis by his refusal to greet Lescot after his third lecture on 20 December.[17] Emboldened by Breton's presence, the writers of the paper decided that the special edition they were planning in honor of Haitian independence on the first of January would instead be a tribute to Breton. The paper bristled with harsh critiques against dictatorship. The opening of Depestre's front-page article crystallized the exuberance of the youth: "The year 1946 will be a year of profound experiences. . . . January will no longer be called January but Justice, February, liberty, April will be called deliverance, May, union etc. A new future for man will begin." It was, however, the scathing page-length pronouncement they ran on the second page that proved most incendiary:

> 1946 will be the year of Freedom, when the voice of real democracy will Triumph over all forms of fascist oppression.
> Down with all the Francos!
> Long Live Democracy in Action!
> Long live the Youth!
> Long Live Social Justice!
> Long Live The World Proletariat!
> Long Live 1804![18]

The appearance of that page, which was widely circulated in the city, was the drop that caused the cup to overflow. Two days after the paper appeared, police acting on Lescot's orders stormed the Ruelle Roy headquarters of the newspaper and forced its immediate suspension. Depestre and two other members of the group were arrested and released the following morning. On the afternoon of 4 January, Franck Magloire, the editor of *Le Matin*, whose printing press was used by *La Ruche*, was temporarily detained by the Garde and questioned about his involvement with the students.[19]

That night at Alexis's house, Raymond Pressoir, Alexis, Depestre, Baker, Chenet, and Bloncourt met to strategize. They agreed that drastic action had to be taken against the government's banning of the paper. The young men reasoned that the best way to demonstrate their anger would be to organize a student strike similar to the Damien revolt.[20] Damien's success owed much to the marines' reluctance to open fire on the students in the streets. A student strike, they averred, would precipitate a social revolution and the overthrow of the regime. For the remainder of the weekend group members busied themselves contacting fellow students in the law and medical faculties of the university and in the high schools, informing them of the plan to strike on Monday morning. The strike organizers devised various coded messages to relay information to the high school students. According to Emerante de Pradines Morse, then a student participant, the students were given a simple question to ask each other in order to determine which of their classmates supported the strike effort: "Are you going to the funeral today?"[21]

Alexis, who informed the socialists of the students' intentions, contacted Max Sam of La Nation. Since December, the socialists were secretly working with members of the Garde to stage a protest against the government to take place sometime around the congressional elections in May.[22] The students hoped to galvanize support from the older Marxists in Port-au-Prince, many of whom were expected to appear at Breton's fourth lecture on Sunday night at the Rex Theater. On Sunday afternoon, Gérald Bloncourt visited Breton at Mabille's house in Pétionville on behalf of the "Jeunesse Révolutionnaire d'Haïti" and pressured him to dedicate his fourth lecture that evening to freedom, as the next day the country would be in revolution. As Bloncourt later recalled, "This was the first revolution that had a date and time already set!"[23] A shaken Breton agreed, and under heavy security delivered a stirring lecture on surrealism and freedom. Capitalizing on the fervor of the moment, Depestre and Baker led a small demonstration in front of Champs de Mars immediately following Breton's lecture. Both were arrested and released later that night, while the other members of the group went into hiding and plotted to continue the strike as planned.[24]

Shortly before ten o'clock on Monday morning, 7 January, the students alerted the press and the U.S. embassy to the impending strike, which would culminate with a demonstration in the embassy's courtyard. The task of contacting the embassy was given to Depestre, who, fearing repeated arrest by Gontran Rouzier, seized the opportunity to plead for U.S. asylum but was refused and immediately went into hiding.[25] That morning the strike began in earnest.

The members of La Ruche along with their supporters from the law and agricultural faculties filed out of their classes and congregated outside the Medical School, shouting "Vive La Revolution!" No sooner had they gathered than police arrived and beat the students with batons. Alexis, who was badly beaten, urged Bloncourt to rally students from the nearby all-girls Lycée des Jeunes Filles, where Bloncourt's mother taught. After convincing the female students that soldiers were abusing university students, they entered the courtyard of the Medical school and formed a wall around the students, forcing the soldiers to desist. They marched toward the Champs de Mars, attracting a large crowd of secondary school students and workers along the way.[26]

With clenched fists raised high above head, the students passed through the leading secondary schools, Lycée Pétion, St. Martial, St. Louis de Gonzague, and St. Rose de Lima, singing the Haitian national anthem, "La Dessalinienne." The numbers of protestors grew remarkably as workers and street people joined the khaki-clad students as they marched through the central streets of downtown Port-au-Prince. Using word of mouth, leaders of the strike rallied support by spreading false news that the purpose of the protest was the assault of two students by the soldiers. As the crowds moved through the heavily populated slum areas of Bel-Air, La Saline, and Croix des Bossales, nearby businesses closed down. The newspapers quickly issued appeals for order demanding the intervention of the parents of the rebellious students. Once the protestors arrived at the U.S. embassy, members of the Garde were already on hand and temporarily detained several activists, most notably Max Menard, Bloncourt, Max Pennet, and the poet Jean Brierre. Several other students were severely beaten during the melee. Military intervention did little to dampen the resolve of the protestors, some of whom spent the night hiding in the popular neighborhoods, preparing Molotov cocktails.[27]

Lescot, who clearly underestimated the determination of the students, was shocked at the demonstration. Previously he ordered the head of the secret police, Lucien Marchand, not to keep the students under surveillance and to desist from harassing them, claiming that "the youth were not dangerous. They are only dialecticians."[28] Though he expected the strike to have subsided by Monday evening, he took no chances.

As soldiers packed themselves into jeeps and patrolled the deserted streets of the city Tuesday morning, the students put into effect their new plan of attack. A manifesto by Le Comité de la Grève was sent to the leading press, calling for the recognition of constitutional freedoms and international democratic guarantees. Around midday in front of the Henri Deschamps bookstore on Grande Rue, Bloncourt, who had made his way downtown in disguise, attacked an unarmed soldier. Panicked storeowners closed their stores as bystanders began hitting pots on the telephone poles, sending signals of protest throughout the streets. Employees from the Departments of Labor, Agriculture, and Education joined the students. Strong support also

Crowds gather in front of the National Palace during the January revolt, 1946. Courtesy of U.S. National Archives, Record Group 59.

came from the Morne-a-Tuf region near the medical faculty, where a student from the community had died from beatings sustained during the protest the previous evening.[29]

By five thirty later that day, the four thousand strong protest that had marched through the main arteries of the downtown streets climaxed on the Grand Rue. The movement then broke into two flanks, one led by Alexis and the other by Bloncourt. By the time the latter reached Place Geffrard, awaiting soldiers arrested him. Bloncourt escaped, jumping out of a pickup truck en route to the Dessalines barracks. After making contact with Mabille, he found refuge in the library of the French Embassy, where he stayed until leaving to rendezvous with Alexis's column on Rue Pavée the following morning.[30] Lescot and his family escaped from the palace by hiding in the back of cars belonging to the U.S. embassy and passed through the protestors led by Alexis before arriving at Lescot's manor in Bourdon. From his home that evening, Lescot issued his first statement since the revolt began. Broadcasting on the radio, he urged the student leaders to end the protests and warned them that if they continued the Garde would "take the most drastic measures to reestablish public order."[31]

On Thursday the revolt intensified. In the morning, the Comité Démocratique Féminin, a women's movement headed by Jacques Roumain's wife,

Nicole, led a march to the Cathedral to appeal for peace, freedom of the press, and the liberation of political prisoners.[32] When a few supporters shouted "A bas Lescot," nearby officers fired into the crowd, killing two young men and wounding two women. In retaliation, large mobs began to spread throughout the city, storming the police headquarters and hurling rocks at Garde officers before dispersing in the streets. The houses and property of leading ministers and their henchmen were ransacked and destroyed and stores looted. In the hillside areas that surround the capital, the sound of vodou drums and *vaksins* (hollow wooden instruments made from bamboo) reverberated throughout the city as the factories of Gérald Lescot, Gontran Rouzier, and a host of other government officials burned to the ground.[33]

By that afternoon it was clear that the government was unable to deal with the crisis. Over two dozen people were reported killed and many more injured during the week of *dechoukaj* (uprooting). A wide range of workers, including bus drivers, agricultural workers, bakers, and butchers, went on strike for the first time in the city's history, and the U.S.-run companies of SHADA, Standard Fruit, and the Atlantic Refining Company were forced to close their operations. Led by Dr. Georges Rigaud, a coalition of professionals, businesspeople, journalists, and opposition leaders formed the Front Démocratique Unifié (FDU) in Port-au-Prince, which openly supported the students and called for the right to form political parties. Similar groups formed among students and businesspeople in the southern department of the Grand'Anse.[34] The movement spread to the other departments by the end of the week. In Jacmel, where large numbers of students at the Lycée Jacmel had received and read *La Ruche*, student strikes on the seventh were augmented by the participation of workers and peasants over the following two days, by which time, according to one participant, "the Revolution had conquered Jacmel."[35]

In an effort to avoid overthrow, Lescot agreed to have the cabinet dissolved and met with George Rigaud and other political leaders, intimating that he would resign on 15 May, the anniversary of his installation. In a private audience with Colonel Lavaud, the head of the Garde, a desperate Lescot ordered Lavaud to use all necessary force to break up the mobs. Lavaud refused and Lescot ordered his immediate arrest. The second ranking officer of the Garde, Colonel Antoine Levelt, instead counseled with Lavaud and U.S. Ambassador Wilson to decide the best course of action. In conjunction with the embassy they formed that evening a Conseil Exécutif Militaire (CEM), which demanded and successfully obtained Lescot's resignation once

Members of La Ruche *celebrate Lescot's overthrow, 11 January 1946. Left to right: Jacques Stéphen Alexis, George Beaufils, Gérald Bloncourt, Théodore Baker, and Gérard Chenet. Courtesy of Collection Gérald Bloncourt.*

they convinced him his life was in danger if he remained in Haiti a day longer. Petrified, the rest of the cabinet submitted their resignations that afternoon and fled the country. The three-man junta that headed the CEM, which included Paul Magloire, Levelt, and Lavaud, put Lescot under house arrest. At three o'clock on the morning of 11 January, Élie Lescot and his family huddled in the back of a police car drove to Bowen Field, then boarded a waiting plane to Miami, becoming the republic's first exiled president since the occupation.[36]

To allay protests the CEM informed the public that Lescot was to make a radio address at one o'clock that afternoon. By four o'clock, Lavaud, on behalf of the CEM, announced on radio HH3W that Lescot had left the country. Lescot's departure was received with immediate jubilation across Haiti. Crowds continued to loot and raid the homes of public officials, forcing Jean Brierre and several student leaders of the riots to drive around the city and broadcast speeches on the radio appealing for calm and order.[37] By Monday, order was slowly restored, with commercial activities resumed and fifty-one political prisoners released.

The CEM's first act was to dissolve Lescot's congress and declare new congressional elections in May. They inducted a six-man military congress to handle state affairs. They also appointed civilian Sylvio Cator, a renowned Olympian, as mayor of Port-au-Prince to demonstrate they did not intend to create a military state. There was still much anxiety when Washington failed to grant immediate recognition of the CEM, despite repeated pleas from U.S. officials in Port-au-Prince, who feared that U.S. neutrality could strengthen the influence of the local Marxists.[38] Tensions were heightened when a U.S. destroyer was spotted off the coast of Port-au-Prince and a squadron of navy planes hovered over the city Saturday evening. Many feared that reoccupation was imminent.

Concerned with the threat that these developments posed in the face of a highly radicalized and still protesting populace, the CEM scheduled parliamentary elections for 12 May. When foreign recognition was still not forthcoming, the CEM sent elder diplomat Dantès Bellegarde to Washington to plead their case and win support among black activists there. This quelled increasing rumors that the revolution was a military coup. Bellegarde's diplomacy, which argued that delayed recognition could lead to a Trujillo overthrow or, worse, a communist state, was crucial in obtaining U.S. support of the junta on 8 April.[39]

The revolt was closely followed elsewhere in the region.[40] The revolutionary fervor of the strike held particular interest for blacks in the United States. In the *Pittsburgh Courier* Raymond Pace Alexander, who visited Haiti under Vincent, wrote a five-part column on the events. Similarly, Mercer Cook, a Howard University professor who also spent nearly two years in Haiti teaching English at the university, published a series of articles on the incident in the *Washington Afro-American*, imploring blacks in the United States to lend moral support to Haiti: "Our task as the racial brothers of these descendants of Toussaint L'Ouverture, Dessalines, Christophe and Pétion, is to offer them friendship and understanding. But let's hope that the gains today will not be lost, as in 1930, to the old-school politicians."[41] His colleague Rayford Logan writing in the *Pittsburgh Courier* was careful to point out that the strike was a result of U.S. involvement in Haitian affairs during the war. It was not a sign of the incapacity of black people to govern.[42]

André Breton, who distanced himself from the hysteria in the capital since *La Ruche*'s tribute to him, returned to present his fifth lecture on the eighteenth. Neither he nor Mabille said much about the revolt, doubtless aware of their tenuous status in the country.[43] By March the CEM under pressure by the United States decided that Mabille was far too dangerous a presence to remain in Haiti.[44] On the advice of his superiors at the Quai D'Orsay, Mabille returned to Paris that year, where he remained until his death in 1952. Both Haitian and U.S. officials were equally fearful of the influential Gérald Bloncourt, whom U.S. civil attaché Jack West called "the principal leader of the strike that overthrew Lescot" and an individual "who possesses extremely radical tendencies."[45] Bloncourt, after inciting small protests against the CEM, was forced to flee the city and seek refuge in the hills of Kenscoff.[46]

An Unstable Front: The Rise of Parties and Polemics

The immediate success of the radical movement in deposing Lescot was but the beginning of a wider movement for social change. Within days of Lescot's exit, the Haitian press was liberated, with an unprecedented explosion in the number of political and social papers—over a hundred in Port-au-Prince alone.[47] On the radio, popular personalities such as Languichatte Debordus, the alter-ego of Théodore Beaubrun, delighted in being able to ridicule Lescot on the national airwaves without fear of reproach: "Lescot, why is it that whatever you heard Hitler do, you wanted to do it too?"[48]

This freedom and the collective sense of hope that accompanied it was manifest in the widespread formation of political parties for the first time in the country's recent history. Nearly one hundred political parties formed across the country. On the day of Lescot's overthrow, *milat* conservatives resurrected the old Liberal Party, renamed Parti Libéral Socialiste under the leadership of François Dalencour. Other conservative groups included Edouard Tardieu's Parti Populaire Social Chrétien (PPSC) and F. Burr Reynaud's Union Démocratique Haïtien.[49] It was readily apparent, however, that popular currents would not sustain these traditional groups. Radical groups figured more prominently on the political scene and none were more influential than those that derived from *noiriste* and communist ideologies.

The *noiristes* associated with Emile St. Lôt's L'Amicale club formed the Parti Populaire Nationale (PPN) in January, with Daniel Fignolé as the vice-president and including Denis, Duvalier, Léger, and Désinor. The party's organ *Flambeau* became the central paper for *noiriste* propaganda in 1946. For the PPN, 1946 was, after 1804 and 1930, the third national revolution in the country's history and the most important because it promised the total liberation of the black majority.[50] As Duvalier and Denis ominously concluded one week after Lescot's exit, "Finally the Haitian bourgeoisie is no longer the master of power."[51]

During the first days of February, a cadre of former Roumain supporters and other Marxist sympathizers led by Edris St. Armand revived the PCH and launched its daily newspaper, *Combat*, which chose a red star and a scythe and hammer as its logo.[52]

Il est évident que l'arme de la critique ne saurait remplacer la critique des armes ; la force matérielle ne peut être abattue que par la force matérielle ; mais la théorie se change, elle aussi, en force matérielle dès qu'elle pénètre les Masses.

DIRECTEUR :   Félix Dorléans Juste
Rédacteur en Chef :   Edris St Amand
Administration   Gérald Bloncourt
                        Gérard Chenet
                        Fréda Seide
           Rue Pavée No. 60
Abonnement : 1 gde P-au-P.
           1 gde. 50 Province

Organe Officiel du Parti Communiste d'Haiti

1ère Année, No. 1   -   Hebdomadaire Politique et Social   -   Mercredi 6 Février 1946

Masthead of the first issue of Combat, *organ of the Haitian Communist Party, 6 February 1946. Courtesy of U.S. National Archives, Record Group 59.*

The Communist Party was swept up by the enthusiasm of the moment, likening the events of January to the Russian Revolution of 1917.[53] In an editorial in the second issue of *Combat*, St. Armand remarked that communism was the "only possible solution for the country to get out of the social stagnation and poverty."[54] The party's initial program, which argued for the creation of a "Socialist Soviet Republic of Haiti," advocated *inter alia*, the socialization of all industries and land, Soviet-style organization of all political institutions, and the democratization of the Haitian Garde, which was to be renamed "the people's army."[55] Following severe criticism of the plan by Cuban communists who closely followed the events in their neighboring island, the party later outlined a far more tempered twenty-point minimum program for Haitian development. The most radical provisions were the revision of all contracts signed by Lescot and Vincent; the participation of women in public office; a democratic and socialist constitution; labor union organization; reduction of working hours; and a repeal of all anticommunist legislation.[56] Despite these revisions, as Michel Hector has pointed out, the 1946 proposals of the PCH were out of step with the direction that international communism was taking after World War II.[57]

Although subscribing to Roumain's ideals and philosophy, the new PCH did not include his closest compatriots among its members. The leader of the party was Felix Dorléans Juste Constant, an Episcopalian pastor from Arcahaie, who was a Marxist since the early thirties and remained close to Roumain following the split with the socialists. Once he declared his presidency of the party, he temporarily gave up his parish and became part of the non-parochial clergy.[58] Juste Constant, St. Armand, Max Menard, and Roger Mercier composed the political bureau of the party. All contributed to *Combat*, and Gérald Bloncourt was appointed the paper's administrator. It is difficult to determine the party's reach in this period but some estimates suggest that in the early months of 1946, *Combat* had a subscription of approximately 1,000 readers throughout the country, and there was an alleged 1,307 registered party members.[59] Though this figure may likely be inflated, it is clear that the party was not confined to Port-au-Prince, having established cells in Gonaïves, St. Marc, Cap Haïtien, and the Grande'Anse.

The young radicals of *La Ruche* were immediately drawn to the PCH. The party they formed in the wake of the strike, the Parti Démocratique Populaire de la Jeunesse Haïtienne (PDPJH), became the communist youth arm. *La Ruche* reemerged in late January and, following a split with Baker and Gérard Martelly, became *La Nouvelle Ruche*, the PDPJH organ, which was circulated mainly among university and secondary school students.

Despite its efforts to gain international recognition, the PCH had no apparent links with Russia or direct connections with regional communists. The Cuban PSP dismissed them outright as "infantile leftists" with an unrealistic program, and severely criticized the authenticity of a Communist Party with an Episcopalian preacher as its leader.[60] The PCH also had no apparent links with the CPUSA, though the U.S. embassy was concerned that they had received funds from U.S. leftists.[61]

The PCH supported the Front Révolutionnaire Haïtien (FRH), a coalition of eleven radical groups including the PPN, the PDPJH, and the Ligue d'Action Social et Démocratique, which formed on 8 February. The formation of the FRH indicated a certain unity among the radical groups during the first months of 1946. St. Lôt led the FRH, and Juste Constant and Daniel Fignolé were vice-presidents. On the afternoon of the eighth, shortly after the formal meeting of the FRH, a parade was held in downtown Port-au-Prince in which large groups of urban workers participated, many carrying red flags alongside the Haitian blue and red flag, wearing red bands with revolutionary slogans, and singing the Communist Internationale and "La Dessalinienne."[62] The parade was a first for Haiti and evidence of the initial strength Marxists in the FRH exercised over the urban workers. Such open displays of sympathy toward communism worsened the pervasive fears of the CEM and the United States over the strength of the Marxists. The CEM thus decided to send a message to the young communists, and on 16 February Gérald Bloncourt, the most radical of the student communists, was caught by the Garde and exiled to Paris two days later.[63]

Given its heterogeneous composition of Marxists and *noiristes*, contention within the Front was inevitable. Fignolé began to compete with the communists for control of the Port-au-Prince laborers. He used his remarkable influence over the slum dwellers and workers to create a popular force of mass protestors that he referred to as the *woulo konmpresè* (steamroller), still a pervasive feature in Haitian popular protest. The *woulo* was a large amalgam of disenfranchised and impoverished blacks that Fignolé could at the shortest notice arouse with a simple call to march: *woulo deyò* (steamroller outside). More important, they were his urban troops, a constant reminder that of all the political entities in the city, he more than any other had the loyalty of the popular forces.

The forceful image of the *woulo* in 1946 was noted in an editorial in *Demain*, which commented on the "extraordinary" and "fanatical" "attachment of the entire population from Bel-Air, Croix des Bouquets, La Saline, and Morne-à-Tuf," to "the Moses of Port-au-Prince."[64] This devotion to Fignolé inspired an outpouring of essays, editorials, and panegyrics in the press. A poem entitled "Leader" by a Fignolé supporter captured the popular mood: "Young teacher of the proletariat . . . black friend of the blacks . . . sincere comrade loved by the crowd on whose orders they swell into an immense sea . . . [we] love, adore, and adulate Daniel Fignolé."[65]

The defining factor of the predominantly black Front, then, was the ideological and numerical strength of the *noiristes*, most of whom had little tolerance for Marxism. On 23 March, the PCH formally withdrew, claiming that "the historical role of the Front has ended," and the Communist Party resumed its independent activities.[66] Shortly thereafter, the PDPJH also withdrew from the Front, dissolving itself as a separate party. As the other Marxist groups operated outside of the FRH, it remained a coalition of various *noiriste* parties.

Perhaps the most important radical group to reform in these early months was the socialists. In late January, the Parti Socialiste Populaire (PSP) was officially formed, comprising, in the main, contributors to *La Nation*, which had reappeared around the same time.[67] The redoubtable Max Hudicourt, who returned from exile two days after Lescot left the country, became the leader of the PSP. The party's other principal members were Anthony Lespès, Étienne Charlier, Jules Blanchet, and Max Sam. The Marxist convictions among the members of the party differed somewhat, as Hudicourt, though referring to himself as a socialist, retained the liberal nationalist outlook he cultivated during the thirties, whereas Sam, Charlier, and Lespès were more fervently Marxist.[68] The party structure and ideology closely resembled both that of the Socialist Party in the Dominican Republic and the Cuban PSP (Partido Socialista Popular) with which it was aligned. The PSP was also the only radical party formed in 1946 that had some experience in political organization, as its leaders held revolutionary credentials dating back to the 1930 strike. This organizational experience and the connections with socialists in Cuba worried U.S officials. When Lespès traveled to Havana in February to purchase a printing plate from the defunct communist daily *Gaceta del Caribe*, the FBI interpreted the purpose of his visit to obtain "money and firearms from Cuban communists" and thus closely watched the PSP.[69]

The philosophy of the PSP represented the most stark contrast to the *noirisme* of the other radical groups. The mostly elite intellectuals in the PSP privileged class struggle over color divisions as the most important threat to Haitian society. Like the PCH in the thirties, they argued that a reorientation of the polity based on color would not bridge the country's fundamental economic cleavage. *Noirisme*, for them, was a political weapon used by the black middle class to attain control of the country but that promised little for the welfare of the poor.

This position created an interesting polemic between both leading Marxist parties. The predominantly black and middle class PCH was markedly different in 1946 from its first incarnation twelve years earlier. It positioned itself against the *milat*-led PSP by claiming to be the "Front Révolutionaire des Partis Gauches Authentiques."[70] In a departure from the orthodox Marxism-Leninism they held as their guiding doctrine, the communists emphatically declared the color question as an "essential aspect of the present class struggle in Haiti" that, if ignored, would lead to the reinstallation of a bourgeois dictatorship.[71] The PSP, they argued, evaded the color question because the party was largely *milat* and consequently feared the threat a black government might pose to their status.

The PCH's strong emphasis on color did not mean, however, that they agreed with the ideas of the *noiriste* politicians in the PPN. On the contrary, their exit from the FRH was in large part due to the disagreements they found with the *noiristes*. Alexis, one of the most profound social critics in the party, argued that the *noiristes* were solely driven by a fight against the light-skinned elite but they never attacked those he considered the real exploiters in the country, the Arabs, Italians, and U.S. whites.[72] *Noiristes*, moreover, never advanced any meaningful political doctrine that sought to rebuild the country's damaged economy.

Although they remained outside of the conflict between the PSP and PCH, there were at least two other small communist parties that formed in Port-au-Prince during this early period. Authors Robert and Nancy Heinl mention a small Parti Communiste Manchousite, a Maoist organization of which little is known.[73] The second was the Parti Socialiste Haïtien (PSH), which was led by the founder of Cenacles des Études and grandson of President Lysius Salomon, René Salomon. Though having limited appeal, the PSH adopted a fascinating position that melded traditional socialist theory with the ideas of the *noiristes*. The party's manifesto, published in its organ *Classe Moyen et Masse*, summarized its program: "The rights of the authentic black cannot be satisfied [only] by the formation of a ministry of blacks, but from the extension of the revolution and formation of a new nation."[74] This "new nation," Salomon claimed, must be socialist. He argued that 1946 was the first opportunity since the 1806 assassination of Dessalines at Point-Rouge that black Haitians had to assert their claim to national politics. Recalling his grandfather's political program, he maintained that a "homogenous bloc" would facilitate stronger black rule and allow the dictum of the nineteenth-century Nationalist Party to be rewritten for the benefit of all, "authentic Haitians: The greatest benefit for the greatest number and power for the authentic representatives of the majority."[75]

Both the PCH and PSP extended their influence among the laboring classes through the formation of several unions. The CEM issued a major decree on 28 January legalizing labor unions. The Marxist syndicates organized several strikes, the first notable one being leather workers in early February led by Alexis, one of the country's first organized strikes.[76] For the most part, however, the worker strikes that continued into the first two months following the fall of Lescot were spontaneous occurrences, with wageworkers striking for greater pay and recognition.

Despite the efforts of these groups, ultimately Daniel Fignolé had the strongest support among the majority of urban workers in Port-au-Prince. His dominance in the Front grew as he began to lead several labor unions that organized during the first months after Lescot's ouster. In mid-February he was easily elected president of the HASCO union. Fignolé led a strike of HASCO workers later that month that succeeded in improving working conditions and wages. The power base of the PPN was beginning to unravel as Fignolé, aware of his immense popularity, began to spend more time on labor activism than party affairs. On 26 March, he officially resigned from the PPN and the Front, choosing to devote his time to campaigning for a seat as deputy of Port-au-Prince in the legislative elections and to leading sot.[77] He wasted no time following his withdrawal from the PPN to rally his supporters in the Port-au-Prince shanties.

The 1946 Elections

The CEM upheld the provision of the 1932 constitution that the successor of a deposed president had to be elected by a majority in the National Assembly. It also decided that the constitutional committee would meet after the congressional elections in order to prevent violent challenges from the left-wing parties. The congressional elections on 12 May were therefore crucial. Early in the presidential race U.S. officials speculated that the leading candidates were conservatives Edgar Néré Numa and Bignon Pierre-Louis.[78] This initial prediction would change dramatically during the long summer.

Over two hundred mainly black candidates presented themselves for election to the twenty-one senatorial seats and thirty-seven deputy seats.[79] After two successive dictatorships, the political field was wide open and the promise of a democratic Haiti finally seemed to be realized. For the first time in the country's history, leftist candidates had a large representation in the election campaign. Juste Constant from the PCH was running for president, mayor, and senator; PSP executives Max Hudicourt, Max Sam, Georges Rigaud, Étienne Charlier, and René Salomon all ran for seats in the Chamber of Deputies. Labor leaders Fignolé and the popular Henri Laraque in the north also sought positions as deputies for Port-au-Prince and Cap Haïtien, respectively. Both candidates and the electorate grew restless. On 1 May, the PCH staged a massive demonstration downtown highlighted by powerful speeches by Depestre, Alexis, and St. Armand.[80] Fignolé also put the *woulo* in full effect to support his candidacy in the first week of May.

As the congressional elections drew close, tensions increased in the streets of the capital. Rumors circulated across the country that peasants and urban workers were conspiring to slaughter all light-skinned Haitians if their leaders were not elected. Recent events added drama to such fears. In April, a group of unemployed workers squatting in the hills around the city approached a large downtown business and demanded immediate employment. When they were refused, they began to damage the building and allegedly threatened to kill the owner.[81] The international press picked up these events as they continued to closely monitor developments in the country, especially the growing strength of the Marxists.[82] The anxieties in the city proved unbearable. Two days before the election the CEM declared a curfew and banned the sale of alcohol.

On the 12 May most of the registered voters turned out to vote. Once the votes were publicized two days later, it was clear which group was the deciding force in the presidential race. Conservatives and *noiristes* associated with the PPN won most of the seats. Daniel Fignolé was unelected and Max Hudicourt, who won a seat in the Senate, was the only member of a Marxist party in the Assembly.

The results of the election were staggering, and the defeat of the majority of the left's candidates sent shockwaves through radical circles. Salomon and the PSH blamed the defeat on the disunity of the Marxist left, which should have buried ideological conflicts and fought the "common peril" in the election campaign.[83] Radicals were most aggravated by the reelection of several cabinet members closely associated with the Vincent and Lescot regimes, namely Charles Fombrun, H. Bourjolly, and Dumarsais Estimé. Most leftists charged that the Ministry of Interior, headed by Colonel Paul Magloire, had tampered with the election results.

Their claims were not without foundation. The U.S. embassy also suspected Magloire's complicity in the elections when it was discovered that hundreds of electoral cards were sold the week before.[84] In addition, Lavaud and Levelt were worried about their partner's political aspirations.[85] Of the three, Magloire was most popular among the lower ranks in the Garde and had spent considerable energy in the months following the protests in January, forming alliances with key members of the economic and political elite. Being the darkest-skinned member of the triumvirate and having climbed to the highest ranks of the Haitian military, Magloire, by virtue of his favored position during the color-charged climate was assured a great deal of respectability among the populace.[86] Still, he was keenly aware that whatever power he exercised over the political situation was a result of his military position and refused to jeopardize this by giving up his post and running as a civilian candidate. Haiti was not yet prepared for a military leader.

Nonetheless, the results of the legislative elections infuriated Port-au-Prince leftists, who feared that the CEM killed the achievements of the January revolt. Defeat prompted them to form a temporary alliance and create a Comité de Défense Nationale (CDN) that included Depestre, Alexis, Juste Constant, and the majority of the PSP and PCH. They issued a manifesto calling for the dissolution of the CEM, the annulment of the elections, and the creation of a civilian provisional government.[87] They warned that failure to meet these demands would force them to incite a national strike to overthrow the CEM. The young communists clearly felt they retained the command over the Port-au-Prince workers that they had in January. Though the prospect of a provisional government headed by renowned leftists was unlikely, it was sufficient to raise serious concern among the military government and U.S. officials.[88]

But much had changed in the four months following the Lescot overthrow. The CEM had effectively used the military apparatus to maintain social control and, more important, the urban workers responded more readily to the *noiriste* rhetoric of Fignolé and his associates than to the Marxism of the student leaders of the January revolt.

Thus, the expected fierce riots followed Fignolé's defeat at the polls. When the dust settled, several Fignolists were seriously injured by the Garde. This event propelled the CEM to take drastic measures. Before the results were made official, Fignolists barged into the headquarters of his opponent, Georges Voltes.[89] In Cap Haïtien, Laraque also incited riots that resulted in six people killed and twenty-five wounded.[90] The CEM took the threats seriously and immediately declared martial law, issued a curfew, dissolved the CDN, banned all political demonstrations for presidential candidates, and arrested almost fifty, mainly light-skinned signatories of the manifesto, a move that was well received by U.S. officials.[91]

With their hopes of achieving success in the upcoming elections impeded, the leftists took to the press to object to the harsh new impositions. In *La Nation*, Max Sam wrote that five months after the fall of Lescot the CEM had created a tragic situation and reintroduced totalitarianism, the "grave menace for the future of democracy in Haiti."[92] The PCH chose not to back any candidate in the presidential race, since, according to St. Armand, "the next government cannot bring any improvement whatsoever in the situation of the masses."[93]

Not surprisingly, the loss of the seats in the National Assembly intensified the battle between the *noiristes* and Marxists in the radical press. When Dumarsais Estimé, in an effort to gain support for his presidential campaign, sent out congratulatory cards to the new senators and deputies, Max Hudicourt refused to accept the gesture. In *La Nation*, he issued a bitter assault against Estimé. Calling himself "a militant socialist," Hudicourt castigated the "reactionary fascist" Estimé, whose political career had been rife with contradictions and vacillations. Hudicourt drew particular reference to an article Estimé wrote in *Le Glaneur* in the 1920s while a professor at the Lycée Pétion, in which he called for a wall to be erected at Champs-de-Mars to keep the elite from contaminating the authentic Haitians that lived below the palace. He contrasted the deputy's early position with his marriage to a light-skinned member of the bourgeoisie, Lucienne Hertelou, and his close personal relationship with Vincent.[94]

The *noiristes* in the PPN who now emphatically backed Estimé responded in unison. Yves Jeannot wrote in *Demain* that Hudicourt's actions were "dictated against the entire majority class" of the country and fueled by "his hate of all blacks."[95] In Estimé's defense, Jeannot claimed that his early ideas as writer in *Le Glaneur* and his reforms in school curricula at Lycée Pétion were not contradictions but "precursors to the ideas of the Revolution."[96]

Hudicourt spawned another clash when he suggested in June that the National Assembly should be moved to the province of Jérémie since the constant pressure of the Fignolists made it difficult to complete the constitutional debates.[97] The *noiriste* assault on the PSP was harsh and personal. Marxism, led by the "Pseudo Socialiste Populaire," was a western ideology used to justify *milat* control.[98] The black Max Sam was a "servant of the *milat*," and Rigaud and Hudicourt were "strange socialists" who "are already suffocating at the thought of a black man like Estimé becoming president."[99]

Notwithstanding this hostility, the PSP made a judicious evaluation of the political situation and acknowledged that their candidate Georges Rigaud had little hope of success. They decided, therefore, to back Edgar Néré Numa, the conservative black deputy from Les Cayes. The decision to back Numa, according to Sam, then general secretary of the party, was not taken because Numa was black but because he appeared most sympathetic to the goals of the Socialist Party even though he himself was not a socialist.[100] Still, the fact that a light-skinned candidate would never win in the heated political climate of 1946 was not lost on the socialists. They were well aware, as Sam conceded, that Haiti was not prepared for socialism and that a strong nationalistic president with no direct ties to *noiriste* factions would be the most realistic option. *Noiristes* like Roger Dorsinville, who thus far supported Numa, withdrew their support, claiming that they refused to "back an understudy" and put their efforts behind "the peasant" Estimé.[101]

During the dispute between Hudicourt and the *noiristes*, the PCH chose to temporarily side with its socialist rival. The party leadership grew disillusioned with the political process after the March elections. At a party meeting in mid-June, Juste Constant argued that the party no longer supported the "dangerous" color question created by French and U.S. forces to divide the nation and now used by the Fignolists and *noiristes* to gain power: "The history of Haiti reveals that the color question has never been anything but a weapon in the hands of the foreigner to divide and weaken the country for civil war. Proletarians have no color line and the same hunger pinches all. The problem is international."[102] He also reorganized the political bureau of the party, withdrew his candidacy for presidency, and urged party members who supported *noiriste* ideas to resign.[103]

Thereafter anti-imperialism became the party's strongest ideological concern. Communists took the position that U.S. economic control of Haiti was the main source of its dire poverty. Alexis championed the party's position on imperialism. In an address at a PCH meeting in late July, he argued that the inter-American economic climate was far more decisive to the future of Haiti than the political wrangling among candidates. The Soviet opposition to the imperialistic design of Britain and the United States, he argued, was the only real source of hope for Third World countries. Haiti faced a "slow death" if the next president did not try to break the stranglehold of U.S. hegemony. The SHADA experiment, in Alexis's view, was a conscious effort by the United States to damage Haitian agriculture and to force the country into greater dependence on its northern neighbor.[104] Prior to the elections, Théodore Baker also emphasized that whichever candidate won, he should strive to fight against U.S. imperialism and not color politics: "We are anti-imperialist. We fight against all forms of imperialism. For more than thirty years we have been controlled by America and have not seen the benefits. . . . When we vote in a few months it should be against all those who since 1915 have worked toward our ruin."[105] Anti-U.S. sentiments were also apparently strong outside of the capital, where one regional journal took issue with the "Anglo-Saxon caudillos" in the U.S. embassy, whose interference with the elections denied Haiti the democratic promise of January.[106]

For the irrepressible Daniel Fignolé, defeat at the polls was not an end to his nascent political career but a beginning. With his former ally St. Lôt in the Senate, Fignolé was quick to realize the new emphasis on party politics to electoral success. It was thus necessary for him to be part of a political organization that he could lead, one that would incorporate all the various unions he directed and rely on his political personality.

In 1945 several former working-class students of Fignolé's at Collège Odéide had formed a small discussion group that they named MOP, a direct reference to the English word with the implicit suggestion of sweeping out of the old order in Haitian politics.[107] In late February, the students approached their former professor, expressed their intention of extending their group to a worker's party, and offered him the presidency. Fignolé readily agreed and officially formed MOP as a party on 13 May, transforming its name into an acronym for the Mouvement Ouvrier Paysan, with *Chantiers* as their official organ. Under his leadership, MOP became the most organized labor party in Haitian history and the largest mass organization in the pre-Duvalier era. Apart from the HASCO union, which Fignolé led, MOP incorporated unions from the largest companies in Port-au-Prince and its environs, including workers at the BATA shoe factory, dockworkers, hydraulic workers, gas station workers, confectioneries, and barbers.[108] Fignolé's charisma and popular appeal guaranteed MOP a following far wider than the unions. As he stated in *Chantiers* shortly after the party's formation, "We have formed MOP which will assure the majority class effective direction of the country. . . . Our party is strong and put to the service of our class."[109]

Once formed, MOP did not take long to get its foot in the presidential race. Fignolé expressed a strong desire to run for office.[110] But at thirty-three he was too young to be considered a candidate, the minimum age for which had been fixed at thirty-five in the 1932 constitution. His impassioned speeches, while important in gaining popular support, could prove a liability in the presidential elections. The directors of the party thus decided that a more prominent member of the black middle class would provide the political advantage the party needed in the ensuing presidential contest.[111] Fignolé would guide this leader from behind and then accede to presidential power once the moment was opportune.

For the mopistes, the most suitable candidate for the position was forty-year-old François Duvalier. The older members of the party were familiar with Duvalier's presence at the heated discussions in Louis Diaquoi's drawing room in the early thirties.[112] The younger members of the party followed with interest his writings in *Les Griots* and were impressed by his political ideas, expressed with greater regularity in his contributions in *Chantiers*. His *noiriste* politics appeared starkly conservative when compared to the forceful rhetoric of the communists and, they believed, would win MOP the support of the U.S. State Department. Perhaps most alluring was his social stature, which grew as a result of his position as a medical examiner in the American Health mission, which he held following his return from Michigan. Duvalier worked on controlling the spread of malaria and started work on an anti-yaws campaign, a project that would eventually win him notable acclaim. His work, particularly in the provinces, strengthened the young doctor's popularity among the peasants, an important factor for the young mopistes, considering Fignolé's difficulty to build a constituency beyond the capital.

But Duvalier was politically inexperienced. He had no prior position of leadership and displayed little ambition to hold public office. Nor did he want to become Fignolé's puppet, a position he and Lorimer Denis agreed could destroy any chances of building a meaningful political career later on. Both men were, however, sympathetic to the party's policies and therefore agreed to join MOP in another capacity. Duvalier became general secretary and Denis an important member of the party's braintrust.[113]

One of their primary tasks was to find an alternative candidate for the presidential election. They suggested Démosthènes Pétrus Calixte, the former head of the Garde who had recently returned to Port-au-Prince. They argued that Calixte had gained significant influence in the north and the south over the course of the past year. Popular support from the Fignolists in Port-au-Prince would provide him with the greatest chance to win the election.

Fignolé was disappointed at the choice of Calixte, whom he felt had been out of the Haitian political scene far too long. He much preferred Duvalier's taciturn and unassuming demeanor to Calixte's strong personality, which often clashed with his own. The former colonel was equally unimpressed with Fignolé, whose fantastic promises that a Calixte presidency would guarantee slum-dwellers with automobiles and houses in the suburbs of Pétionville and Delmas were constant sources of embarrassment.[114] Nonetheless, both men appreciated the exigency of their union. Calixte knew that an alliance with the professor would provide him with the surest chance to enter Haitian politics. Fignolé appreciated Calixte's commitment to being his frontman. Furthermore, if MOP had any intention of achieving success in the upcoming elections, an extensive campaign had to be launched immediately. Personal dissatisfactions became secondary to the objective of gaining political power. By the middle of May Fignolé began to invest all his energy in campaigning for Calixte. He was successful in gaining the endorsement of noiriste papers including La Voix des Jeunes, L'Action Nationale, and La Presse.

The decision to back Calixte as the popular leader provoked considerable opposition among other radical groups. The radical students from the PDPJH who thus far had respected Fignolé were disappointed with MOP's decision.[115] In the pages of La Nation, Georges Petit, who took sides with the socialists on several issues, launched a harsh critique against Calixte, pointing to his training under the U.S. marines, his close association with Vincent prior to the 1938 plot, his role in the assassination of several officers, and his decision as former chief of the Garde to seek haven in the Dominican Republic less than a year after the 1937 massacre.[116] Petit also took Fignolé to task, pointing to his contradictory endorsement of a military candidate following the harsh treatment he received by the CEM during the congressional elections. "Why," he asked, "should we take Démosthènes over Paul [Magloire] when Paul is already in place and also black!"[117]

Calixte's political background was indeed suspect. Rayford Logan, who met Calixte at the border town of Fort Liberté on his trip to the Dominican Republic in 1942, remarked on his startlingly close relationship with Trujillo while in exile there and the respect that the staunchly anti-Haitian Dominican border patrol had for him.[118] In his 1940 correspondence with Trujillo, Lescot indicated Calixte's willingness to become Trujillo's dupe to challenge Vincent in exchange for a position in a Lescot government.[119] Notwithstanding the opposition from the intelligentsia, Calixte was the labor party's candidate, which alone made him a force to be reckoned with during the months that preceded the election.

On 26 June, a conspiracy among lower-ranking members of the Garde to bring about a mutiny of the enlisted personnel against their officers and to overthrow the CEM was discovered. Rumors circulated that Calixte and Fignolé engineered the plot to ensure Calixte's election. The mastermind of the plot, Audain, was arrested and over thirty accomplices were transferred to the provinces or relieved of their duties. Such events only served to reinforce the CEM's commitment to martial law.

Meanwhile the debates over the constitution that were postponed until after the March elections resumed. Crowds packed the legislature every day to hear the passionate debates over the constitution led by St. Lôt, Hudicourt, Louis Déjoie, and Jean David. Since the CEM provided no limitations on the time of debate, both chambers spent the entire summer deliberating the suggested provisions. Many of the new members of Congress relished the opportunity to wax unceasingly on the political situation.[120]

As the deliberations over the constitution wore on during early August, the popular forces in the city grew impatient. Fignolé, ignoring the laws against political demonstrations, used the machinery of the *woulo konmpresè* during the first week to get protestors to pressure the Assembly to vote for Calixte. These frenzied protests were fueled by Fignolé's powerful speeches on the radio. He was immediately banned by the CEM from the only medium legally granted to him for broadcast.[121]

The anxiety in the streets reflected the contentions in the Senate. In such a polarized atmosphere, it was clear that the prolonged and theatrical legislative discussions would not bring about a swift decision. Three recently elected senators fearful of the chaos that was threatening to erupt and desirous of bringing the campaign to an end conspired with other delegates and hatched a coup on the night of Sunday, 11 August. In a private session these three men, Philippe Charlier, Thomas Desulmé, and Jean David persuaded thirty-five of their colleagues to agree to a suspension of the review of the new constitution and the temporary enforcement of an amended version of the 1932 constitution Vincent had thrown out.[122] To ensure little opposition, they cleverly convinced the more antagonistic members of the Senate, Emile St. Lôt, Castel Demesmin, and Max Hudicourt, that there was a private meeting in Kenscoff.[123] The following morning Charlier put the resolution to the National Assembly. Strong protests came from St. Lôt and Hudicourt, who called the resolution a "trick to deny the country of a democratic constitution."[124] St. Lôt vigorously challenged the proposal and influenced several other deputies to side with him. After hours of debate, the majority of the legislators accepted Charlier's provisions. It was then decided that both houses would reconvene four days later to complete the vote. No sooner was the announcement made public that scores of Fignolists besieged the legislature, protesting for five hours before the police dispersed the crowds with tear gas and guns.[125]

On the morning of the sixteenth, as tanks and reinforced troops surrounded the cordoned off streets and the Palace Garde armed with submachine guns stood at strategic points around the Legislative Palace, the senators, dressed in white suits and some carrying sidearms, took their seats and cast their votes for the republic's new president.[126] Only two of the customarily four ballots were necessary. Estimé won the first with twenty-five votes. Six votes were counted for Calixte, seven for Numa, and eight for Pierre-Louis. Following much discussion, the results of the second ballot were pulled from the urn and proved more decisive. Estimé again won the plurality with thirty-two votes. Elected to serve a six-year term, the deputy from Verettes became the first black president of postoccupation Haiti. A few minutes later the new president surrounded by the Garde delivered his inaugural address to the Assembly in which he promised to form a broad coalition, including people from both sides of the political divide, encourage unionization, and promote financial liberation of the country.[127]

Estimé's election was received with surprise and disbelief throughout the city. As he made his victory tour through the streets of Port-au-Prince, people shouted threats and slurs at him, while many women were, according to one observer, "on their knees wailing miserably."[128] Small groups of mopistes marched spontaneously throughout the city crying, "Vive Calixte! Vive Fignolé." Their leaders, however, were nowhere to be found. Fignolé and his advisers went into hiding immediately following the election. Duvalier was enraged at the outcome of the elections and, according to Roger Dorsinville, threatened a violent retribution.[129] Fignolé would later claim that Duvalier, Denis, and himself found it prudent to strategize before launching an attack on the government. No sooner had all three men congregated than they received word from one of Estimé's officials that they were being considered for positions in the new government. For Fignolé, the self-acclaimed *chef des masses*, this was obviously a victory, as he felt that no progressive government could hope to last without his participation. Two days later, the trio had a secret meeting with the president in which they all accepted his offer and agreed, according to Fignolé, "to begin the constructive phase of the Revolution."[130]

Calixte, terrified of imprisonment, consulted Ambassador Wilson about seeking asylum.[131] He issued a statement the following day thanking his supporters and declaring that since the Assembly chose "[his] personal friend Dumarsais Estimé," he supported the decision and asked all fellow mopistes to do the same. A week later Estimé made Calixte the inspector general of diplomatic posts in Europe, and the former commander left the country to take up permanent residence in Paris.

Fignolists in the poorer districts expressed their immediate frustration later that night; unorganized mobs smashed streetlights and defaced public buildings.[132] Estimé capitalized on the absence of the popular leaders and the next day paid huge sums of money to shopkeepers and bar owners ordering them to supply free food and alcohol for the entire weekend. With his close supporters he drove through the slum areas he had dared not enter a month before, throwing money, soap, and spare change through the window. In the midst of the three-day, government-sponsored carnivalesque celebrations, the popular song *Papa Gede* became *Papa Estimé* and the new president paid a visit to the General Hospital, where, ironically, many pro-Calixte demonstrators lay recovering from police-inflicted wounds.[133] The man the popular classes christened *Titime* had successfully used political tactics to gain the popular support he lacked throughout his campaign.

The Collapse of the Radical Coalition

But if Estimé was able to win the approval of the Haitian majority through largesse, the discordant political factions would require greater skill to assuage. The strongest objection came from the daunted PSP. They were gravely disappointed in Numa for agreeing to the Charlier-Desulmé coup, and Étienne Charlier refused Estimé's early offer of a cabinet post.[134] Estimé attempted to remedy this situation by creating a coalition cabinet that included communists, labor leaders, and *noiristes*. The day after the election Estimé invited Fignolé to accept the post of minister of education and public health in the new cabinet, which the radical labor leader readily accepted. For Estimé this was a masterstroke, as he was well aware that such a high-profile position would satisfy the ambitious Fignolé and his followers. He also appointed Price-Mars minister of foreign relations and religion. The other radical extreme in the cabinet was socialist Georges Rigaud, who became minister of commerce and agriculture. Rigaud accepted the position after a long deliberation with the PSP executive. The members agreed that Haiti was obviously not ready for a socialist state, but having key members in the cabinet was the party's best hope.[135]

As minister, Rigaud's priority was to eradicate the flourishing black market in soap, oils, textiles, and other goods by creating price ceilings, and to control the profits of wholesalers and retailers. In designing his plan, he drew on the expertise of his socialist comrades. Jules Blanchet became a technical adviser and Lespès held the same position in the Department of Agriculture. Max Sam took a post as director of the information service of the Department of Commerce.[136]

In early September a proposal that passed in the Assembly to remove all anticommunist legislation from the Haitian penal code received strong support in both chambers. With the euphoria of political victory, *noiriste* politicians such as Emile St. Lôt no longer viewed the communists as a serious threat to their political control and felt some concession was in order.[137] Estimé, however, shrewdly avoided passing final judgment on the resolution, claiming that since the communists had been allowed to practice freely since January it was not necessary. The retention of the law was a weapon he would later use against his opponents in an effort to gain U.S. support.

Rigaud's socialist projects aroused much resentment in the cabinet, especially from the new minister of education, Fignolé, whose fierce public addresses increased with his newly won position of authority.[138] Although Fignolé was responsible for several key education programs, he was accused by the socialists of advocating a system of discrimination against all light-skinned officials in government posts, highlighted by the discharge of *milat* administrators from the schools.[139] Fignolé was equally angered by Rigaud's inclusion of other members of the PSP into key positions in the new government. With the confidence afforded by his new position, Fignolé took to the radio and admonished his opponents: "If anyone thinks they can stop what I am doing for my people, I will be forced to use my *woulo* to destroy them!"[140]

Despite the harsh tone of his radio addresses, Fignolé never used the *woulo* for anything other than a demonstration of his popular strength. Nonetheless, his speeches were linked to sporadic outbreaks in the streets of the capital. *Le Matin* ran an article on street terror pinpointing Fignolé's speeches as being largely responsible, and a few reports of U.S. citizens being harassed came into the embassy.[141]

Fignolé's radio addresses against Rigaud were most offensive to the socialists. The PSP responded by attacking Fignolé's "demagogic" radio campaign of "violence and anarchy" in *La Nation*. The party also criticized the government for allowing Fignolé to say what he wished on the airwaves, and jokingly ridiculed the new president, "Estimop," for his feeble response.[142] The clash between Fignolé and Rigaud erupted on 21 October. At eight o'clock that night, during MOP's weekly fifteen-minute broadcast on Radio HH2S, Fignolé delivered an incendiary radio address. He charged Rigaud and Hudicourt as conspiring with Senator Louis Déjoie to overthrow Estimé. He claimed that their aim was to get rid of all blacks who rightly belonged in power, and ultimately institute a communist system in Haiti in which blacks would be subservient to the light-skinned elite. Immediately following Fignolé's address, Roger Dorsinville appeared on the air at the same station and, on behalf of the president, appealed to all Haitians not to foment a color war in the country.[143] Later, Max Sam delivered a cautionary speech to "the black people of Haiti" on behalf of the PSP.[144]

A week before, Fignolé's address, Estimé received reports from Haitian officials in the United States that his government was generally considered as being a radical left-wing administration and thus deserved scrutiny.[145] Concerned over the impact such perceptions could have on diplomatic relations, Estimé capitalized on the Fignolé-Rigaud controversy by remaining silent on Fignolé's actions in an effort to ease Rigaud out of the cabinet. Two days after the radio address, an embarrassed Rigaud handed in his resignation, taking the other socialists with him. In solidarity, the other cabinet members also resigned, but the president, who was holding out on a collective resignation, refused them.[146] Fignolé incited another clash in an emergency session of the National Assembly. When a resolution proposed by Hudicourt was passed, Fignolé was forced to demonstrate whether a plot had actually existed. He avoided the issue, declaring that he was the leader of two million men and was too busy to attend to trivial affairs.[147] At the same session, the still functioning 1932 constitution was further amended to allow members of the legislature to hold a dual seat in the cabinet.

During that week, Estimé sent agents into the troubled areas of La Saline and Bel-Air in an effort to drum up support for his office and split some of Fignolé's base.[148] Dorsinville, Love Léger, and other functionaries visited the same districts a day later, urging the people not to follow the advice of leaders who threatened to destroy the national unity that had been created since the election. The Department of the Interior issued a statement later retracting Fignolé's statements. The PSP, supported by the PCH, did not accept the statement since it did not come directly from Fignolé. Under pressure, Fignolé resigned. On 24 October, Estimé accepted the resignation of the entire first cabinet and began to form a new one of legislators supportive of his policies.[149] Both Fignolé and the PSP would lead the offensive against the administration.

Conclusion

The events from January to October 1946 marked a watershed for Haitian politics. Through the combined force of *noirisme*, Marxism, and populism, Haitian radicals successfully overturned the Lescot administration and introduced radical programs on the national agenda. More important, the revolutionary movement and the subsequent elections animated the popular classes and gave them a stake in political participation. With the slogan "les noirs au pouvoir," black political elites could claim victory over the traditional *milat* elite and present black rule as a necessity rather than a privilege. But state power brought with it the potential for greater division among competing black groups in the postelection climate. In the face of competition from leftists with popular appeal, Estimé and his supporters carefully presented themselves as the only real hope for social reform in late 1946.

The departure of the socialists and the militant Daniel Fignolé from the cabinet completed the first phase of this Estimist transformation. The new president masterfully coopted his political opponents and used their internecine rivalry to consolidate his regime and weaken their influence. The new black politicians rejoiced in these early achievements. For them, it was proof that Estimé shared their *noiriste* vision, and they readily placed the aspirations of the black middle class squarely on his shoulders. What he did with this mandate is the subject of the next chapter.

CHAPTER 4

Now Both Sides of the Hand Have a Chance

Noirisme *and Opposition under Estimé, 1946–1950*

†

My friend what is happening?
The country has changed
Shoulder to shoulder
Together we bend
Together we rise
For the earth is ours
I now see a beautiful country
It is the time
It is the hour
I am rebuilding my country with the help of my brothers.
—FELIX MORISSEAU LE ROY, "Natif Natal," 1948

By late 1946, as Haiti's *noiriste* government gained momentum, the new president experienced extraordinary popularity among the peasantry, black middle class, and urban workers. For these social groups, previously disenfranchised and often treated as second-class citizens, Estimé's victory was a triumphant symbol of a new day. Robert Bazile, the young army officer, was by then a staunch Estimist, promoted above his light-skinned colleagues to First Lieutenant of the Garde in 1946. He later recalled the optimism of those first exuberant months: "At the beginning . . . [there] was a song for Estimé. '*Machin Estimé woule-m de bo.*' Estimé's caravan turns on both sides. . . . You see with Estimé we now had two chances. Two sides. *De bo!* Before it was only one side of the hand [which was light-skinned] and now the other [darker] side had a chance. It was a very very good start."[1]

These sentiments echoed across the region. In a *Pittsburgh Courier* editorial Estimé was described as a "black moderate," whose regime is expected to give fair treatment to "both the so-called 'blacks' and 'mulattoes.'"[2] As these comments and the previous chapter suggest, the Estimé era represented a period of great importance in the advance of Haitian politics, as it was the country's first real attempt to create a stable democracy. Indeed, nearly another half century would pass before a democratic regime would reemerge.

But if the presidency started out on a positive footing, it fast became a victim of the cold war environment that remained hostile to a regime perceived as radical, and presented the new leader with unparalleled challenges and frustrations. Estimists proved equally susceptible to internal tensions produced by the explosion of radicalism the decade before. Progressive Haitians expected a social revolution with Estimé; what they got was a period of unsustainable hope rife with color resentment, ideological polarization, and a bitter, occasionally violent struggle for political power among forces inside and outside the government. All this occurred against a backdrop of heightened color awareness during the late forties, when the ideological and cultural dimensions of post-1946 black consciousness reached their apogee.

The Nationalization of Black Power

The Estimé years witnessed a reorientation in the character of Haitian radical thought. The divisions among *noiriste* groups that emerged during the presidential elections carried over to the national scene once competing black groups gained access to state power. The rhetoric of black power that resounded loudly throughout the campaign gave rise to a systematic attempt to create policies and programs aimed at its inclusion in national life. In the pages of *Flambeau*, *La République*, and several other pro-black journals, *noiriste* ideas of governance and social progress were discussed on a daily basis. Among the more prominent advocates of this new politics were the ideologues of the thirties, who saw in the black government the culmination of their earlier aspirations.

François Duvalier and Lorimer Denis, who thus far closely associated themselves with Fignolé and MOP, left the party and permanently severed ties with the professor in late 1947 for reasons elaborated below. With André Séjour, Lelio Dalencourt, Kléber Georges Jacob, and Lamartinière Honorat, a young writer and secretary of L'Institut d'Éthnologie, they revived *Les Griots*, defunct for nearly a decade, as a daily newspaper in 1948.[3]

In contrast to its previous incarnation, the new version of the paper was a political and social organ that dealt explicitly with the practice and application of Haitian black power and only peripherally with scientific or psychological concerns. Its most dominant feature, however, was the strong support of its contributors for what they frequently referred to as the "Estimist revolution." Duvalier and Denis explained this obvious irony by arguing that even during their support of Calixte and Fignolé in 1946, they always believed less in partisanship than in the fundamental problem of "class." Estimé was a "preeminent member of the majority class" who "after thirty years of errors and regression" had "put the country back on the road to its destiny and instituted a political system of national prestige."[4]

In 1948 they updated and published in book form the study that first appeared in 1946 in Chantiers, Le problème des classes à travers l'histoire d'Haïti. Brandishing Dessalines's imperial flag of black and red on its cover, this work represented the most radical elaboration of noirisme and signaled a definite shift in its philosophy. In the survey of Haitian history that opens the work, the authors argue that since the days of earlier presidents Salomon and Antoine Simon (1908–11), blacks had no access to political power until the ascension of Estimé, the real, "authentic son of the peasant masses."[5] They celebrated the expansion of the black power movement they began among the intellectual groups in the thirties and continued through the policies of the new government.

The book's most distinctive feature, however, was its analysis of the social and color divisions in the country. The superiority of black rule, once a social scientific argument, was now axiomatic. The fundamental reasons for the domination of the black majority by the light-skinned minority was, they argued, a result of elite attempts to maintain "exclusivity" by dividing blacks along class lines. As long as blacks remained complacent with minimal political and economic power, the problem in social relations was destined to persist. The only solution for this predicament was the creation of a powerful and unified black "class." "If we are to rise as a strong class and be respected for achieving Equilibrium in our Nation, we must meditate on these serious faults which have haunted us since the birth of our natural life."[6]

For Duvalier and Denis, as David Nicholls has pointed out, "equilibrium," the opposite of milat "exclusivity," meant black power in all areas of political and social life.[7] In this "era of the masses," after nearly a century and a half of independence, Haiti had finally found equilibrium.[8] This equilibrium, Duvalier outlined in an insightful address to the law school in early 1950, was the final and perfect stage in the cycle of modern Haitian politics, preceded by an intellectual mission and preparation, revolution, and a period of reaction.[9] With a black head of state emerging in the wake of a revolution, the fundamental realignment of Haitian politics was, he argued, finally realized.

As racial consciousness deepened in the writings of black intellectuals, so did its expression among the popular classes. Once more music and the arts were frequently used to assert identity and a maturing social consciousness. Groups such as Jazz des Jeunes were closely linked to the movement of 1946, proudly celebrating the ideas of the black government in song. Other acts such as Jazz Saïeh, master drummer Ti-Roro, and the haunting singer from Gonaïves Lumane Casimir became frontrunners in the post-1946 renaissance in *vodou-djazz* performing regularly at nightclubs and theaters around the country. These performers drew heavily on the multilayered folk wisdom of Haitian proverbs to express sentiments of pride in their new social recognition. Much of the music of the era moved beyond the mid-forties celebration of Haiti's African heritage to include incisive critiques of the rearrangement of the political order. These conditions breathed new meaning into traditional songs. A notable example is the late forties rendition of the *rara* song "Kote moun-yo" by Jazz des Jeunes, which features the lines, "Where are the people? I can't see the people? I can't see the people who are saying these bad things about us."[10] In the sociopolitical context of the Estimé era, the lyrics of the song were taken as a commentary on the withdrawal of the light-skinned elite from national prominence.[11]

At other times, performers were more explicit in declaring admiration for the cultural achievements of the new government and the beloved president *Titime*. A 1946 song by Luc Jeanty contained the following refrain: "Our hearts are truly happy, we've been asking for President Estimé for a long time. The country is coming out of its darkness. I can tell you now with a guarantee, we are going to have a new Haiti."[12] Similarly, in the song "Isit nan Ayiti" (Here in Haiti), Lumane Casimir delivers an ode to a "marvelous new Haiti" founded on "peace" and "union."[13]

The transformation in popular attitudes to *noirisme*, manifest in the expression of black consciousness in the arts, owed much to the government's enthusiastic support of the movement. *Indigénisme*, the foundation on which *noirisme* stood, explicitly stressed national development of local culture. A 1949 tourist bureau brochure suggested that the "half gay, half sad" *vodou-djazz* "may well become as popular as the rhumba in the United States."[14] The Bureau d'Ethnologie, under the directorship of Lorimer Denis in the late forties, heavily promoted vodou aesthetics, especially the rhythms and music as part of the government's nationalist program. According to Denis, "as with literature and art, songs are an important part of our national unity."[15] That the state encouraged these developments was, for U.S. writer Edith Efron, who visited Haiti in 1949, nothing less than a "vital cultural revolution": "The scientific interest in popular customs and folklore moved suddenly from the library to the public stage when the black government of 1946, sharing the new sympathy for native expressions, and interested in stimulating the tourist trade, encouraged for the first time in Haiti's history the formation of native song, dance and drum troupes, and brought out of hiding these native art forms, which had so long been educated Haiti's shame."[16]

The greatest symbol of the government's commitment to the promotion of black consciousness on a social level, and one of Estimé's lasting legacies, was the lavish Bicentennial Exposition that ran from December 1949 to April 1950. Organized to celebrate the two hundredth anniversary of the founding of Port-au-Prince, the Exposition was a world-class showcase. Along the palisades that extended across the Port-au-Prince bay, the structure of a modern city was erected at considerable cost to the government. To facilitate this, the capital received a new urban look. Street cleaning and sanitation projects were initiated and scores of beggars and vagrants were rounded up and sent to the remote La Gonâve.[17] The government also created a Department of Tourism in September 1947, which over the course of the next two years was successful in initiating a broad public relations campaign in the United States and across Latin America. Over a dozen hotels were built to accommodate the large numbers of foreigners the government expected to flock to the island.[18] Official figures suggest that tourism rose steadily in 1947–1949, reaching a total of 5,663 visitors the year the Exposition began.[19] Apart from the massive restructuring of Port-au-Prince, the Exposition exposed Haiti's indigenous culture to the world. The showcase of the Exposition was the folkloric performances that took place in the newly erected Théâtre du Verdure and the rich display of ethnological artifacts.[20]

This state sponsorship of indigenous culture in Haiti must, however, be understood in its regional context. In the postwar period, U.S. cultural interest in the Caribbean grew substantially as economic expansion facilitated greater travel. After the war Pan-American Airlines expanded its service to regions North Americans seldom visited. Port-au-Prince became a leading Caribbean destination along with Havana, San Juan, and Port-of-

Spain, attracting North Americans with their attendant vices. In all these sites North American interest in "exotic" African-based cultural forms were widely appreciated and thus exploited by local governments.[21]

The political context in Haiti, however, distinguishes its experience from that of its neighbors. The promotion of a commercialized form of vodou music was clearly geared toward exploiting the tourist trade. Some commentators such as Georges Ramponeau, an artist and director of the Centre d'Art, were cynical about such endeavors. Ramponeau argued that the significance of the ceremonies was lost on a young generation that only viewed vodou rhythms, music, and dance as fashionable and paid little attention to the significance of the ceremonies. Even worse, this new interest in vodou culture encouraged commercial exploitation of vodou priests and "primitive" artists.[22]

Nonetheless, as Anne Greene has pointed out, the Estimé government gave a larger public profile to the symbols and culture of the religion than its predecessors.[23] These efforts at cultural nationalism strengthened the bonds between Haitians and regional black organizations. In the United States, Walter White of the NAACP became a tireless advocate of Haitian promotion, and in 1947 he began a public relations campaign aimed at correcting negative stereotypes of the country.[24] While sharing similarities with movements elsewhere, the cultural awakening in Haiti thus had deeper social meaning. By supporting the popular culture and articulating its aspirations, the regime was able to secure moral and cultural legitimacy. All this came at a heavy price. The next section reviews the political achievements and failures of the new government and critically analyzes the reaction of the traditional power structure to its rule.

The "Reign" of the Authentiques

The defining characteristic of the new regime was the transformation in the composition of the ruling political elite. In a marked reversal of previous administrations, members of the black intelligentsia ran all major areas of governance and state affairs. This pattern was extended to the coveted foreign posts including, for the first time, the appointment of a black ambassador to Washington in 1946. The cabinet, once the hub of elite political control, was in 1947 almost entirely devoid of *milat* membership.[25] In the spirit of the times, the men who assumed the prominent positions in the government proudly referred to themselves as *authentiques*, the real inheritors of the legacy of Dessalines furthest removed from Europhile culture and appearance.[26] Their fiery black nationalism drew on the ideology of the Griot writers with whom they were closely associated. They were the public face of the *noiriste* cause and included the writers who, in the wake of Lescot's departure, vigorously championed the color argument: Jean Rémy, Joseph Déjean, Love Léger, Marc Séïde, Roger Dorsinville, and Emile St. Lôt. Blessed with the social and educational privileges denied most blacks in the country, the *authentiques* represented the intellectual pinnacle of the black middle class. Black power was for them a national mission. Dorsinville, the most committed of the group and head of Estimé's cabinet (1946–1949), defined the vanguard of the new government as having a "strange idealism" in which "'class' was defined to include all blacks," and black power meant "a black leader and group leading the masses like a shepherd."[27] The "exploiters of class," Dorsinville explained in reference to the *milat* elite, "could be converted to this philosophy" or risk being "destroyed by black power."[28] There was a great deal of naïveté in this organic vision of national unity. Dorsinville recognized as much in a later autocritique of the *authentiques*, who, despite their rhetoric of "a black nation" with "peasants, prostitutes, and intellectuals coming together," had no intention to depart from "social norms."[29]

The *authentiques*, then, were essentially *noiristes* with political power, bonded by their collective desire to build an inclusive political system under the leadership of a black directorate. They were the bright young Turks assiduously courted by Estimé in the months following the collapse of the first cabinet to become the nucleus of his braintrust. They, in turn, found in Estimé a black leader who, in spite of his previous political associations, was sympathetic to the ideas they espoused and willing to realize a truly nationalist policy.

But if the *authentiques* were all Estimists, not all Estimists were *authentiques*. Among the members of this new "classe politique" were many devotees whose loyalty to the president was not rooted in the same ideological foundations as their radical counterparts but rather in an admiration for the symbol of democracy and social justice that Estimé represented for the majority of black professionals. Indicative of this tendency is the experience of Minister of Finance Noé Fourcand (1948–1950). A dark-skinned lawyer from Jérémie, Fourcand celebrated the color equality that Estimé strived for rather than the loud call for black supremacy of his peers: "Estimé opened everything. With Estimé, the blacks and mulattoes got closer. . . . As a black man I could go into the Rex Theater and sit down. Before [the government of 1946 came to power] I couldn't do that. . . . He gave all advantages to blacks. . . . He said we, black Haitians, are good and he gave us opportunities and showed us we were as brilliant as the mulattoes."[30] That these divergent views, one more radical than the other, could coexist within the government was to a large degree attributable to the person of Dumarsais Estimé, one of the most misunderstood heads of state in Haitian history.

In the literature on modern Haiti there are two distinct schools of thought regarding Estimé. Haitian historians, in keeping with a strong tradition of nationalist writing, tend to mythologize him as in the platitudes of Joseph Baguidy, "a sincere patriot not afraid to put his genius and intelligence to the service of his country."[31] In contrast, foreign writers typically offer a less heroic portrayal. Robert and Nancy Heinl define him as a "peasant popu-lis[t]" guided by a "fierce black racism," whereas Robert Rotberg offers an even less sanguine evaluation of a "mere opportunist with no real love for or support from the masses."[32] Katherine Dunham, who maintained a long association with Estimé, described him as "disliking white people" and a tragic figure whose personality and vision of a unified black nation were "strikingly similar" to those of Toussaint.[33]

Yet Estimé was neither racist nor revolutionary. His biography suggests as much.[34] He was born on 21 April 1900. After a poor upbringing in the small town of Verettes in the Artibonite plain, he was spared a life of poverty by the generosity of an uncle in the capital who financed his studies at the Law School in Port-au-Prince. Upon graduating in the mid-twenties, he practiced law briefly before accepting a post as instructor at the Lycée Pétion. After being discharged by the Borno government for sedition, he became a vigorous opponent of the occupation and aligned himself with the nationalist movement in 1930. During the early phase of his public career, Estimé developed a reputation as one of the more faithful politicians working in the much criticized Vincent government.[35]

But if Estimé was incorruptible, he was not beyond using corruption to achieve political ends. Once one of the few black members of the lower chamber, he was a seasoned and skillful politician closely wedded to the machinery of Haitian politics. He worked hard to form the right associations, married into the elite, and consistently lent his support to the more powerful light-skinned members of the Senate in return for political advance. Such devotion paid off as he quickly rose through the ranks in the Vincent government. It is no surprise that he was excluded from the several legislative dissolutions of the mid-thirties. He eventually became minister of education and the president of the Chamber of Deputies, a position that gave him the confidence to make an unsuccessful bid for the presidency in

President Dumarsais Estimé (center) faces the nation at a ceremony marking his assumption of executive powers from the Comité Exécutif Militaire, election day, 16 August 1946. Members of the CEM triumvirate, Paul E. Magloire (at Estimé's right), Franck Lavaud, and Antoine Levelt (at Estimé's left) salute the new president. Courtesy of Collection Georges Corvington.

1941. Although he experienced the Lescot years with much frustration, he never rose in opposition to Lescot's misdeeds. He was, however, alert to the changing political tide in the country in the years leading up to the collapse of the old regime.

As a black member of the Assembly he was in a position to see the growing importance of color in the political maelstrom and positioned himself accordingly. The youngest Haitian head of state at the time, his willingness to promote black politicians won him the support of new aspirants such as St. Lôt, Dorsinville, and, most important, Paul Magloire. Once in power Estimé viewed himself as a man of destiny with the responsibility to lead his country on its path to progress. Although his political record suggested otherwise, he believed in the rhetoric of his black power supporters who argued that his regime had a historical mission. His inaugural speech, a brilliantly crafted discourse written by Dorsinville, outlined a program of national renovation. "You have chosen among those who have sought your votes a man who is not widely known nor has a famous name, nor illustrious birth. It is one of the masses you have chosen and I am committed to devoting myself to their cause."[36]

Estimé committed himself to the reformism that his administration promised, and it was from his attempts to realize this that his unprecedented popularity among the black middle and popular classes derived. He embarked on several regional tours that drew enthusiastic responses, particularly from people in the northern and central provinces who supported his reformism. Most beneficial were the large-scale innovations in education reform. The new government finally realized the *noiriste* vision of a new technical and intellectual elite class drawn from the black middle class.[37] Government scholarships were given out in great regularity and dozens of young non-elite Haitians traveled to Europe and the United States to pursue post-secondary studies. Estimé, who created several schools in the provinces, instituted the L'École Normale Supérieure for the training of secondary school teachers, used state funds to develop the National Archives, and continued the new school project initiated by Fignolé during his brief tenure as minister of education.[38] The government's school rehabilitation led to an enrollment increase of 45 percent in the primary schools. The expansion of social services was complemented by several public works projects including road building, literacy campaigns, a national census in 1949, as well as an extensive UNESCO-sponsored rural development campaign in 1949–50.[39] The importance of these pioneering reforms was superseded by the state's new attitude toward labor.

In his inaugural address, Estimé pledged that the government would protect "all the hardworking against the abuses of employers."[40] A serious attempt was made to adhere to this promise by including for the first time freedom of labor organization in several articles of the new constitution and initiating a broad legislative program for the protection of workers.[41] The ministry of labor, which up to then had a nominal role in the government, became one of the most important ministries under the leadership of Emile St. Lôt and Clément Jumelle. A labor bureau was created under the rubric of the ministry and the government organized a national labor conference, the first of its kind, in May 1949 around the theme "three years of experience in labor problems," which produced an exhaustive volume on the state of labor in the country.[42]

As positive as these new measures were, they were not without problems. Since Haiti had virtually no prior experience with labor laws, legislation was often faulty and confusing, at times revealing a misunderstanding of the Haitian labor situation. There were also several problems spawned from the rapid development of labor institutions, such as the unexpected influx of temporary workers into Port-au-Prince in the late forties, many of whom wrongly believed that the new bureau would create jobs for the country's unemployed. Not only did this affect labor in the countryside, it also added to the material problem of overpopulation in the capital.[43] More problematic was the intermediary role of state institutions in labor disputes. As we shall see, this created serious tensions with independent unions that claimed that state interference in trade unionism revealed tacit support of U.S. imperialism. Large U.S. firms such as SHADA and HASCO also made much of this new role on the part of the Haitian government, labeling labor officials "communists" and occasionally threatening diplomatic intervention.[44] These faults notwithstanding, the government did succeed in improving the status of urban workers by increasing the daily minimum wage from 1.50 to 3.50 gourdes per day; establishing the framework for a social security system; organizing social cooperatives; creating landmark child and female labor laws; and creating provincial labor inspectors to ensure application of these laws in the rural areas.[45]

The regime's economic record, though boasting notable achievements, was ultimately less stellar. The electoral promise of financial liberation became a *cause célèbre* of the new government. *Authentiques*, staunchly nationalist by nature, bitterly resented Lescot's 1941 agreement with the United States, which facilitated U.S. interference in the national budget and imposition of stringent tax controls. Although agricultural exports increased after the war, briefly providing Haiti with relative prosperity, the economy remained fragile. The new regime, moreover, inherited the economic problems of the Lescot years and needed to reduce its outstanding debt, especially those accrued during the occupation and due for repayment in 1947. A delegation including Price-Mars, Gaston Margron, Hudicourt, and Rigaud traveled to Washington in the early months of 1947 to negotiate a moratorium on the loans, forgiveness of a 1938 loan, and a new $20 million loan to help with the repayment of the occupation debts and the development of agri-business. The EX-IM bank denied the request on the vague grounds that the proposal contained a "lack of detailed information on individual projects" that the loan was intended to service.[46]

Gravely disappointed, the delegates suggested that Estimé's decision to reduce U.S. control over the internal economy accounted for the harsh reaction. At a press conference in Washington, Price-Mars argued that EX-IM's reason for refusal was unfair and that "world conditions do not justify foreign interference or control of Haitian finances."[47] The U.S. black press was equally outraged, arguing that it was blatant racism toward a black president who "refuse[d] to deliver his nation to Wall Street in a neatly wrapped parcel."[48] The United States, they argued, preferred to support rebuilding efforts in war-ravaged Europe and leave Haiti in turmoil and confusion. An upset Rayford Logan writing in the *Pittsburgh Courier* stated, "Even Germany will receive more favorable consideration from the American people, Government, and financiers than the Negro Republic of Haiti."[49]

In Haiti, the new government was left with few alternatives but to raise the money to pay the debt by its own means. In one of the most patriotic demonstrations in the career of any Haitian politician, a determined Estimé made a stirring radio address imploring the nation to assist him in raising an internal loan for the repayment of the debt. Calling the refusal "a happy disappointment" and claiming that "with them or without them we will liberate the country," he appealed to the country's nationalistic sentiment, arguing that it was everyone's responsibility to ensure full repayment.[50] It was a speech of remarkable potency and effectiveness. Senators agreed to take a drop in their salaries and state revenues and private donations were put toward repayment. On 28 March university and secondary schools students staged a large protest favoring financial liberation. The slogan *Payons cinq millions* became a popular cry of schoolchildren and workers.[51] The effort was a tremendous success for the financial status of the country and elevated Estimé's prestige higher than any other president before him. The government raised an internal loan of $7.6 million in July, of which five million was used to pay off the outstanding debt, an extraordinarily rare occurrence in Haitian economic history.[52] Estimé also strengthened Haitian control of the National Bank by reducing its board of directors from six to five and appointing only Haitians to the board instead of the previously required three U.S. representatives and two Haitians. Equally significant, the *noiristes* managed to rally the country, if only temporarily, around a national cause. Reflecting on the moment, Fourcand surmised: "The white Americans had done nothing to help the country. They controlled the banks and still they did not help. I was Minister of Finance and decided we had to deal with the problem [of the debt] internally. . . . The bourgeoisie did not like Estimé, especially because the three-month program of financial liberation proved so successful. It was something very important in our history. Dessalines liberated the country politically and now Estimé liberated the country economically."[53]

With the triumph of financial liberation, Haiti made another bid in September for U.S. assistance and was once again rebuffed. Fortunately, the government had the support of new U.S. ambassador Harold Tittmann and former minister to Haiti Norman Armour, who by mid-1947 was head of the Latin American Affairs section of the State Department. Armour in particular was most interested in campaigning for U.S. economic assistance to Haiti, arguing that Haiti had always occupied a "somewhat different category from the other American Republics," and the United States therefore had a "moral responsibility" toward the country.[54] It was not a historical obligation, however, that most concerned both men but the volatile political climate in Haiti of which they both were well aware. Haitian anti-imperialism became most pronounced once the government began to enforce nationalist policies. Armour and Tittmann were "disturbed by the state of opinion towards the United States in Haiti," caused by the loan refusal and "the use to which it might be put by communist influences," and thus urged State Department officials to adopt greater sensitivity to foreign relations with the island.[55] They made a convincing case and succeeded in gaining a favorable loan of $4 million and technical support for the development of the Artibonite valley, the tourist industry, and a readjustment of the SHADA debts, which, because of "the anti–United States feeling [it] engendered," was deemed the most "important thing to placate."[56]

While the retiring of the occupation loan eased somewhat Haiti's dependence on the United States, it was only a temporary relief. The projects the new government proposed demanded more money than it was able to raise. U.S. officials still chafed at the administration's policies. The debate over the 1946 Constitution reflected much of this concern. The initial constitutional draft sought to reverse the most stringent provisions of the 1932 constitution and included limitations on foreign ownership of land, the banning of expatriate clergy, and the limiting of foreign intervention in retail. In the end, the protest of several foreign legations persuaded the government to remove the objectionable clauses.[57]

The most important example of the new government's attempt to exert greater control over local finances was the nationalization of the banana industry in 1947. Standard Fruit, which was in operation in Haiti since the thirties, experienced a period of relative prosperity during the postwar years. Bananas became the country's second largest income earner with a total of $6 million in 1946. The banana industry thrived throughout the first quarter of the forties as United Fruit made favorable offers to peasants in the rich and fertile Artibonite valley to increase production and built wharves and roads at all the major ports. The prosperity of the banana trade was an economic revolution for provincial trade by providing greater income for peasant farmers, opening regional ports, and diversifying the export of smaller crops, a welcome reprieve following the problems endured during SHADA.[58]

In April 1947, eager to gain control over these revenues and to finance several proposed projects, Estimé, well aware of the profitability of the Artibonite crop, passed legislation providing for a state monopoly over the parceling and distribution of bananas.

A few months later the government denied the renewal of the Standard Fruit contract and relations with the company deteriorated. Estimé disbursed concessions to six companies owned and operated by political allies, including Magloire, a program that would be repeated a year later with the issuing of state monopolies over tobacco. In launching this venture, the government proved to be extremely shortsighted. The newly contracted ships lacked refrigeration and were overall inferior to Standard Fruit's vessels. Haitian bananas, moreover, never commanded a large demand on the international market and, as one of the directors of United Fruit averred, suffered greatly without the company's important trade connections.[59] In the event, Standard Fruit ceased entirely its operations in the north of Haiti. The new concessions were all mismanaged and made little attempt to offer peasant farmers incentives such as insecticides and fertilizers. The peasants, paid reduced rates by the concessionaires, ended up devoting more time to other crops, though a devastating drought in 1948 severely impaired their ability to do so successfully. Estimé renegotiated with Standard Fruit in 1949, but by that time the industry suffered from high debt. Early shipments to Miami were seized to pay the debt.[60] By the beginning of the fifties bananas accounted for virtually none of the national income.[61] Benefiting only the local companies that exploited the unchecked system of state patronage, the project was an unmitigated disaster from which the regime would never recover.

What is most apparent from the preceding discussion is the contradictory nature of black power. On one hand, black power meant a rearrangement of the political order and an opportunity to advance desperately needed reforms seldom achieved under *milat* rule. On the other, it was an extension of the black middle class into the economic sphere and was quite often used to justify nepotism, corruption, and political opportunism. The change in the political fortunes of black politicians encouraged several of them to exploit their new positions in order to feather their own nests. Rumors of ministerial abuse, such as reports of a prominent government official who diverted barrels of cement for a public works project to the construction of a personal villa in the suburbs, were all too common.[62] As the Estimé years wore on, such abuses of power became more apparent. For all its rhetoric of social equality, *noirisme* could not eradicate the fundamental problem of rampant graft and corruption intrinsic to the administrative structure of the state.

The new prestige of middle-class blacks, along with the controversial state reforms, provoked resentment from the traditional power elite. The Catholic clergy, angered by the government's call for an indigenous clergy to replace the Breton priests, was most vociferous in its condemnation. The French clergy was noted for its unfavorable treatment of Haitian priests, often giving them assignments in distant provincial towns and keeping them out of the preferred Port-au-Prince posts.[63]

Church officials employed various means to undermine the regime. On a visit to Washington in 1948, the director of the schools operated by Les Frères de L'Instruction Chrétienne, distraught over new government policies that several subjects had to be taught by Haitians instead of foreign priests, called on former U.S. ambassador Norman Armour. In a lengthy diatribe, he claimed that the Estimé government was supported by international communism, and the attempt to reduce the influence of the foreign clergy was the first stage in a program to break completely with U.S. and European interests and establish the first communist state in the Caribbean.[64] The more influential Père Foisset, one of the fervent opponents of vodou and *noirisme*, launched a campaign in the local press in which he reproached the government for giving vodou national prominence. He advanced the fantastic argument that Estimé sought the intervention of vodou priests to ensure his victory in 1946 and was now repaying them by building new vodou temples. The ethnologists who he claimed influenced the government's policy toward vodou sought to elevate the religion because most of them were devotees themselves.[65] Duvalier and Denis, in response, accused the Catholic church of being responsible for the ignorance of the peasants.[66] By 1948 Foisset was declared persona non grata in Haiti and forced to leave the country on the grounds that he sought to disrupt government affairs.

The propaganda battle between the *noiristes* and the Catholic church paled in comparison to the distressing and intense atmosphere of animosity between the black political class and the *milat* bourgeoisie during these years. While his social policies were intended to grant middle-class blacks greater parity, Estimé's political experience made him sensitive to the centrality of the bourgeoisie to the local economy. He knew the importance of economic power to the status of the elite and recognized their crucial role in the social balance of the nation. His electoral success, after all, owed much to the financial support of *milat* businessmen who, despite their skepticism of his *noiriste* agenda, saw in him the only connection to the ancien régime. Yet maintaining a privileged position in the economic sphere was insufficient for an elite that was increasingly marginalized from government positions. They most feared the hostility of the *authentiques* who formed the president's inner circle and were determined at all costs to protect the new status quo. During the first two years of the administration, light-skinned members of Haitian society were routinely denied important posts in virtually all social institutions. More important, the *authentiques* were not above sanctioning violence to remain in power. The immediate victims of this retribution were Lescot's former ministers and functionaries. In December 1946, for example, Gontran Rouzier, former undersecretary of state of the interior, returned to Haiti and was immediately arrested and imprisoned as part of the inquiry into the Lescot regime where, according to U.S. embassy reports, he was so horribly mistreated that he became mentally unstable.[67]

Estimé therefore found himself in a precarious position, caught between a traditional bourgeoisie from whose goodwill he benefited and a new political elite on whose devotion he depended. The clamor for radical change among his black supporters in the legislature and in the streets forced him to reluctantly take measures against the elite that he would otherwise have avoided.

On occasion he was compelled to overstep the carefully demarcated boundaries between economic and political control to demonstrate his commitment to social reform. His treatment of the pervasive problem of the black market provides a useful example. The increase in demand for imported goods after the war proved to be a mixed blessing for elite businessmen. They gained substantial returns from the brief postwar boom, and the black market in cooking oil, basic food items, soap, and fabrics, which the more powerful participated in, thrived. Responding to pressures by his cabinet, Estimé introduced severe restrictions on the market. Much to the chagrin of the elite, he also introduced the first income tax in 1948. As a show of force, Jamaican-born tycoon O. J. Brandt, who not only benefited from the brief rise in coffee exports, but also saw his fortunes grow in the black market, was imprisoned for three days, though he was made an honorary citizen of Port-au-Prince shortly after his release.[68] Yet such obvious efforts at appeasement did little to alleviate the *noiriste* attitude of the new politicians or create an environment of reconciliation between the social axes.

For the light-skinned elite the sudden loss of political prestige was a great shock. The government propaganda on the radio and in the newspapers, stripping the bourgeois politicians of their national identity by denouncing them as *non-authentiques*, only added insult to injury. The conflict between these two social groups often played out in the National Assembly, where the minority of *milat* senators frequently challenged their black colleagues on a variety of issues. Alphonse Henriquez, one of the few black members of the legislature who supported the *milat* senators, frequently attacked Estimé in his paper *Le Justicier* for raising color prejudice far greater than Lescot ever did.[69]

Political sparring in the legislature underscored the raging tensions building in the city. A striking incident that occurred in July 1948 provides a clear illustration of the level of tension between the two groups during these years. In late June, Gérard Viau, a young light-skinned law student and son of Alfred Viau, a judge from a prominent middle-class family, was named frontrunner for a government scholarship to study in Paris. A few weeks later, however, Viau was not listed among the three recipients of the scholarship. On Sunday, 2 July, in an editorial in *Le Nouvelliste*, an outraged Alfred Viau accused the minister of education of replacing the younger Viau's name with that of his own son Ernest on grounds of color discrimination.[70] The *noiriste* paper, *La République*, responded strongly to the accusation by stating that Laraque "like others quite naturally thought of his son" for the scholarship. "The real indecency," the paper argued in an oblique reference to the bourgeoisie whom Viau represented, was "on the part of those who after having used and abused their privileges believed they were now able to correct others."[71]

Three days later, the younger Viau appeared at the Imprimerie de L'État and confronted Estimé's personal secretary and director of *La République* Jean Rémy as he arrived for work. The altercation between the two men ended after a few minutes when Viau drew a pistol and shot Rémy three times in the chest.[72] The victim was taken to the hospital where he was pronounced dead shortly after receiving a visit from the president. The reasons Viau brought the dispute to a violent conclusion remain obscure. On the surface it appears that he was swept up with the emotion of the debate between his father and the *noiristes* and decided to exact retribution. Lyonel Paquin has suggested that Viau's actions were part of a larger plot concocted by powerful members of the bourgeoisie. Disgusted by the "mortal peril" their class faced under the black regime, they planned to topple it.[73] If this was indeed the intention of Viau and his supporters in the upper classes, it was ill conceived, for shortly after the incident Viau was arrested. During his interrogation, a mob of angry Estimists drove to the station, barged through the police guards, dragged Viau out, and proceeded to mercilessly beat and stab him to death. The group allegedly included a few government ministers who, according to several reports, instigated the beating on the orders of the president.[74]

Whether or not Estimé had anything to do with the murder, his government was implicated in the incident. A public inquiry into the event was launched the following day but was not sustained. Members of the Senate as well as the opposition were stunned by the violent outcome and the government's failure to launch a full investigation. For several days the city was paralyzed and the threat of a color war was imminent. Members of the Haitian bourgeoisie were most terrified. After a failed attempt to secure U.S. asylum, Alfred Viau and his family abandoned their home and lived for two weeks in the Cuban Legation before successfully gaining permission to relocate to the Dominican Republic. At least one *milat* opposition member in the Senate, Franck Lanoix, resigned his position and temporarily relocated to the United States, claiming that "Haitian mulattoes [were] in physical danger."[75] U.S. officials remarked on the "unsettling feeling" caused by the serious and ever-present "possibility of violence."[76] The aftermath of the incident proved less conflictual. Estimé diverted attention from the affair by issuing a speech the following week in which he called for national unity and shortly after headed a lavish ceremony laying the first cornerstone of the Cité de L'Exposition. In an interview he would later publicly condemn the "new style racism" in the country and modified his approach by giving two light-skinned politicians portfolios in his cabinet.[77]

Still, color bitterness continued to surface in smaller episodes throughout the summer of 1948, most notably at the Miss Haiti beauty pageant in late July. The winner, Paulette Guichard, was the only black contestant among a host of light-skinned rivals, most of whom hailed from the bourgeoisie. After the announcement of her victory, she was accosted backstage by several disappointed contestants and a fight ensued, leaving her in such a disheveled state that she was unable to return to the stage to accept the award.[78] The government responded strongly by launching a press campaign proclaiming Guichard as a "typical Haitian beauty," and Estimé hosted a large dinner in her honor at the National Palace.[79]

Both these episodes emphasize the degenerative relationship between the *milat* elite and the new government, which bore the near-constant threat of open conflict. Although Estimé avoided confrontation with the light-skinned elite, his controversial role in such bitter disputes as the Rémy-Viau murders was sufficient to unify the bourgeoisie in opposition. The state's handling of these incidents also left no doubt as to the strong position of the black government in these heady years and its willingness to resort to authoritarian methods to secure its rule. If the *milat* elite were to have any success in toppling the regime, the events of the summer of 1948 made it abundantly clear that they would need the support of other powerful factions opposed to Estimé. The plurality of radical ideas unleashed by the movement of 1946 and exemplified by a disunified yet vibrant left made such allies easy to find.

Centers of Resistance: Militant Labor and the Marxist Left

Haitian black radicalism ceased being a unified movement with the revolution of 1946. Under Estimé this problem grew more obvious as popular pro-black factions, blocked from government posts by rivals in the government, maintained a strong opposition. Foremost among them was MOP and its indomitable leader Daniel Fignolé. Fignolé fast grew disillusioned with Estimé's politics following his exit from the cabinet. This attitude doubtless stemmed from a resentment of the way in which the president maneuvered his resignation. Yet his antagonism to Estimé drew on differences far deeper than mere power struggle. In the division between the two we find writ large the crucial disjuncture in *noiriste* politics of the late forties. The most ardent champion of black supremacy, Fignolé found the politics of the new government far too conciliatory to the *milat* elite. He was equally abhorrent of the intellectual elitism of the *authentiques*, which he argued ran counter to the demands of a poor black nation. For him, they constituted a new black bourgeoisie, replete with all the attributes of social superiority and condescension of past administrations. He reviled the greed of the inexperienced new black politicians, who were content with waving the flag of black power while using state funds for personal wealth. Black conquest of political power was insufficient for Fignolé; the economic strength of the *milat* elite had to be destroyed and the status of the urban workers and peasantry elevated. Fignolé derided the Estimé regime as "asthenic" rather than "authentic."[80] It was not a truly revolutionary black government, as it offered only marginal benefits to the popular classes while the country remained "the property of sixty privileged families."[81] Moreover, the rampant corruption and opportunism that accompanied the regime created wider cleavages within the black population: "To our mind, the Revolution has not completely triumphed if . . . the black intellectuals who pretend to hold political power are not attentive to the tactics of the mulattoes whose existence is based on the division of the blacks."[82]

Both U.S. observers and Fignolé's enemies in the government interpreted his analysis of Haitian polity as Marxist and were wont to characterize the professor as a communist.[83] Indeed, in the context of postwar politics his extreme color-class analysis was sufficient to worry liberal interests in the country. Nonetheless, Fignolé remained staunchly opposed to communism and, despite his open admiration for Léon Blum and Mao Zedong, he consistently criticized Marxists in his public statements. Furthermore, unlike the anti-imperialist PSP and PCH, Fignolé's critique of *Estimisme* and *milat* economic control in fact seldom extended to an attack on U.S. capital and presence in Haiti. On the contrary, he was careful to avoid the enmity of U.S. officials in the country, aware of their decisive role in domestic politics.

Concerned with negative perceptions of his party, in late 1946 Fignolé, accompanied by MOP's reticent general secretary, Duvalier, held a private meeting with U.S. Chargé d'Affaires Horatio Mooers, in which he made clear MOP's anticommunist stance, arguing that the party's only purpose was "to bring help to the black masses."[84] Fignolé was so fearful of negative remarks about his party's ideology, which he claimed his enemies were "whispering to the embassy," that he urged the U.S. official "not to take his public declarations too seriously," especially statements that may be construed as anti-U.S. He further remarked that he welcomed U.S. interest in Haiti, but resented the fact that officials since the occupation displayed mistrust in the capacity of the black majority by consistently allying themselves with the elite.

As alluring as his rhetoric was, Fignolé was most feared by the administration for his unmatched popularity and the remarkable organization of his party. Described by Jack West, chief of U.S. central intelligence in Haiti, as a "racist organization, which condemns mulattoes for all of Haiti's economic and political woes [comprised of] an inarticulate mass of disinherited Haitian blacks, illiterate, loyal only to their [mystical] chief," MOP remained the foremost opponent of the new regime from late 1946.[85]

During his brief period in the government, Fignolé used his cabinet position to build MOP into a well-tuned and formidable force. His creation of several schools in the more poverty-stricken areas of the capital won him new fame among the poorer classes and greater devotion from the laborers affiliated with MOP. Party dues were deposited regularly in a Social Welfare Fund, which the leaders put to effective use to ensure member loyalty.[86] Fignolé's organizational success owed much to his own self-discipline. Rodrigue Casimir, editor of *Chantiers* and a leading member of MOP's inner circle, who knew Fignolé since they were young students, notes that Fignolé afforded himself very little time for recreation, devoting his days almost completely to party matters.[87] He seldom participated in the socializing Haitians generally relish and expected like asceticism from his younger charges, occasionally calling emergency meetings during national festivities. Though demagogic in his political persona, Fignolé keenly understood the importance of intraparty collaboration and rarely took a major decision without first consulting his political bureau. As party president he earned a reputation for probity that won him the confidence of the several unions he headed.

Fignolé stressed the importance of education and family as central to "the concept of revolution."[88] To this end, MOP began a literacy program for workers with the creation of a night school at its Rue Du Peuple headquarters. This was complemented with a day school for members' children of primary school age. These activities extended to the rural areas, where MOP organized schools in a few local unions; in 1948 it planned to create its own lycée for the award of secondary school certificates. In a subsidiary paper, *La Famille*, which was under the directorship of Fignolé's wife, Carmen, the party stressed the importance of parental guidance, gender relations, and child rearing to the future life of the country.[89] Under its "bureau of propaganda," the party also created an Institut Mopique, a small building adjacent to the party headquarters where senior members gave public addresses in Kreyòl on history, geography, and politics and held bi-weekly screenings of documentary films on world affairs. Along with the institute, the party formed a social club called Club Mopiste, which featured sporting events and wedding receptions and organized among the youth through a Bureau de L'Action des Jeunes and the paper *Notre Jeunesse*.

By early 1947 MOP gained both in membership and syndicates. Numerical strength and the freedom to organize allowed the party to become more radical in its outlook. As if to emphasize this new hard-line image the party held a large ceremony in mid-October where it unveiled the MOP flag. The flag boasted a green background representing the "hope of the Haitian masses in the struggle for Justice" with a large red circle in the center representing the "blood of all the popular leaders who have died in the service of the cause of the masses."[90] The most dramatic feature of the flag, however, was the design in the left-hand corner; a replica of the Dessalines imperial flag with two bands, black and red, placed vertically beside each other with the black nearest the mast.[91] What was most significant about this was the new meaning mopistes attached to its colors. The black symbolized the "shadow of Africa," pushing the "true leaders of the race and the protectors of the country." The red, unlike the imperial flag of 1805, however, did not represent light-skinned Haitians, but "the rust of the chains of slavery, a reminder of the exploitation of the race and the blood offered as sacrifice at Bois Caïman."[92] The symbolism of the flag points to the fundamental aspect of MOP's self-assessment in 1947 that it represented more than the *authentiques*, the most radical form of *noirisme*, and that it was by virtue of its popularity among the popular classes, the real descendant of the revolutionary tradition.

Notwithstanding the party's commitment to *noirisme*, its radicalism in the late forties cannot be explained solely on the basis of ideology. As mentioned above, the state consolidated its paternalistic hold over the working class by developing a program of total domination of the labor scene through state sponsorship of unionism. The success of this measure in producing progressive labor laws during the late forties has also been noted. The preceding years, however, were marked by an intense competition for influence over organized labor that pitted the government against the left-wing unions. The state's legal role as intercessor in disputes between independent unions and patrons aggravated such tensions. In this struggle, the MOP leadership positioned itself against the government by emphasizing the class tensions in social relations. As is now apparent, Fignolé's appeal to the urban workers and the underemployed derived from his fundamental critique of the Haitian class structure.

For most of 1947, labor disputes often found the government at loggerheads with leaders of unions that fell under the SOT banner. The way many politicians used these labor issues to further their own ends cannot be discounted. It is significant that urban labor in Haiti, unlike elsewhere in Latin America, was in its infancy and the support of a working-class constituency was, at least early on, considered essential for political aspirants mindful of labor's role in the revolution. Furthermore, the rapidity of unionization in a country riven with poverty meant that unions were inevitably absorbed into ongoing political battles. The dissolution and reformation of unions was a common phenomenon. Statistical data on independent union membership are woefully unreliable since many syndicates inflated these numbers to elevate their importance. MOP was most guilty of this practice,

Daniel Fignolé addresses a crowd of supporters at Institut Mopique. The MOP flag hangs in the background. From Chantiers, *1947. Courtesy of Bibliothèque Nationale d'Haïti.*

claiming repeatedly that it had upward of 40,000 members at any given time.[93] It is safe to assume, however, that at its peak in 1947 total membership of all the independent unions never exceeded 10,000.[94]

In view of the difficulties of mass illiteracy, low demands for labor, and general political apathy, it is clear that labor unions stood little chance of surviving without the leadership of prominent political figures. Thus labor bargaining, while seeking to improve the standard of living of urban workers, was more often a stage for political competition among labor leaders. This was certainly a significant factor in the battle between SOT and the government. Frequently strikes were encouraged for the primary purpose of frustrating the government. The government, to be sure, did accede to the repeated demands of SOT leaders, who implored their workers to strike for better conditions, as in the recognition of the eight-hour workday.[95] But these were rare occurrences and unions were in the main an antagonizing force in the political war between labor militants and state officials.

The aggressive presence of Fignolé and the Marxists as directors of important unions frustrated the state's labor programs. In July 1947, the government reacted firmly to this rivalry by promulgating a new law that regulated labor disputes. The most salient elements of the law were sections 33 and 34, which severely restricted strikes of a certain category.[96] These restrictions were extended in October when an obfuscating addition to the law was passed. Although the right to organize strikes was retained, the law included several legal limitations; in its broad application, strikes by all labor groups except the unorganized workers in the handicraft industry were deemed illegal and subject to strict sanctions.[97] The purpose of the law was twofold. First, it was clearly an attempt to secure government control of labor by rendering impotent the power of the independent unions. Second, it was a concession to the U.S.-owned companies and the landholding bourgeoisie engaged in sisal, coffee, and sugar production that complained bitterly about the interference of antigovernment personalities in labor issues.[98]

In late October Fignolé and other members of the SOT hierarchy, after precipitating small strikes among wharf workers and bottling employees, planned to launch a general strike against the new law and the retention of St. Lôt as minister of labor. Communiqués were circulated to the press and Fignolé made announcements on the radio two days before the scheduled strike. On the morning of the strike only a small number of workers affiliated with SOT unions and Fignolists turned up. Fignolé greatly underestimated the strength of the government and the popularity of the president. The secretary of the interior issued a public declaration denouncing the strike. At the same time, several unions publicly acknowledged their disapproval.[99] Within Fignolé's own ranks there was some satisfaction with Estimé's performance on labor issues, and thus less than half of the twenty-nine unions grouped under the SOT agreed to support the strike. Blinded by his fervent anticommunism, Fignolé fatally limited the impact of the strike by failing to make overtures to the Marxist-led FTH, which, in any event, was locked in talks with the government about improvements for the railway workers the FTH represented.[100]

The failure of the strike was a serious blow to Fignolé's political image. The harsh backlash it caused alienated him from some of the union members who began to defect to the FTH. These supporters read Fignolé's efforts as rooted solely in political self-interest with little regard for workers' concerns. In the face of public ridicule, Fignolé resigned from SOT.[101] The government capitalized on the incident and attempted to break Fignolé's strength once and for all by officially dismantling SOT and issuing harsher regulations against union organizations that in effect led to official repression of MOP activists.[102] At the Lycée Pétion, for example, teachers who were party members were terminated under new measures taken by the Department of Education. In Port-au-Prince most of the MOP-affiliated unions were forced to dissolve. Union organizers were attacked most viciously outside of the capital, where the representatives of the army were more openly aggressive. The socialists, who held an emergency meeting a week later to discuss the implications of the failed strike, called the new measures a "major defeat" that unfortunately left the workers as the inevitable victims.[103]

Ultimately, the most damaging outcome of the aborted strike for Fignolé and MOP was the internal division it created within the party hierarchy. MOP's General Secretary Duvalier, who thus far had silently supported Fignolé's actions, rejected the premature strike from its inception and disapproved of the labor leader's vehemence. A bitter dispute erupted between the two men and a few months later Duvalier left MOP permanently, eventually accepting a post as undersecretary of state in the Ministry of Labor, his first government position.[104]

These events limited MOP's strength on the political scene. The party's rural offices were targeted by the police and forced to operate underground. *Chantiers* also began to appear less regularly. Fignolé, however, did not stop his active opposition to the government. On the radio and in public he continued to attack government officials, actions for which he was periodically arrested and imprisoned.[105] A February 1948 law against public assembly led to the decline in the political strength of the party but did not entirely hinder MOP activities. Education programs continued and the party regularly arranged "picnics" at Club Mopiste, which provided an occasion for members to meet informally and discuss current events. At these gatherings, party leaders creatively used popular songs with new lyrics to transmit political messages.[106] For the most part, however, by the middle of 1948 MOP's force was lessened.

Amid the color conflicts and restiveness in the labor movement, the state had to contend with challenges posed by the communist movement. We have seen how the events of 1946 precipitated a shift in the ideology of the PCH from orthodox Marxism-Leninism toward a peculiar form of Marxism in which the color issue became infused in the party ideology. Still, it was an organized left-wing party with some of the strongest personalities of 1946 in its membership. Estimé dealt with this potential threat early by granting the younger, more fervent party members such as Alexis, Depestre, and Roger Gaillard scholarships to study in France in the fall of 1946. Thereafter, the remaining leaders of the party adopted a defensive strategy, supporting the "anti-bourgeois" government's "civic courage" and "policies favorable to the masses," while attacking U.S. imperialism.[107] They also openly rejected the color argument, holding that the "communist party is the party of reconciliation of blacks and mulattoes."[108]

The presence of an organized Communist Party in Haiti troubled several nations with interests in the region. Great Britain, for example, concerned with the clamor for self-government in neighboring Jamaica, closely observed communist activities in Haiti. In March 1947, the British foreign minister received a lengthy and astonishingly inaccurate report entitled "Communism in Haiti," which claimed that 90 percent of the Haitian youth were members of the Communist Party, and that it was a dangerous threat to the stability of the government. The Soviet Union, through communist parties in Mexico and Cuba, supposedly financed the PCH, which deliberately set out to sabotage other political parties and institutions, particularly the Catholic church, with the hope of launching a color war and the Sovietization of Haiti. The report, which was severely criticized by the United States embassy, was indicative of the exaggerated international opinion on the strength of communism in Haiti.[109]

Contrary to these concerns, the PCH in 1947 was handicapped by serious internal difficulties. The removal of its most articulate young members, Depestre, Alexis, Bloncourt, and Baker, lessened its appeal among the young intelligentsia.[110] In the medical school, only a year before the fulcrum of youth activism, there was a general admiration for Estimé, who was careful to display respect for the students.[111] Most debilitating were the crucial changes in the leadership of the party. On 10 March, Juste Constant resigned his post as secretary-general when an unauthorized tract, bearing his name and urging the lower classes to "have confidence in the government of President Estimé which is the best we have ever had," circulated around the city.[112] Edris St. Armand then became the de facto head of the party and sought to rebuild the political bureau, but his efforts suffered as a result of limited popular appeal. On 22 April 1947, yielding to pressure from its opponents, the party issued an autodissolution. Considering the state of communist parties in the rest of Latin America, particularly the persecution of the Cuban PSP, Haitian communists decided that their party was also threatened.[113]

> All over the world communists are hunted and persecuted the same way Hitler hunted the Jews. The national bourgeoisie has called their imperialist allies and claimed that the entire country is communist even though there is no communist in an important post in the administra-

tion. . . . The Bourgeoisie is playing the card of [economic] strangulation with their imperialist allies . . . and thrown on the PCH all the burdens that derive from their exploitation in an effort to return the Haitian people to their defenseless state. . . . The PCH will not be used as a ploy by our aggressive neighbor who takes the pretext of our existence to create irreparable misfortunes for the Haitian people. After analyzing this situation, the Parti Communiste d'Haïti, in all lucidity, has decided to issue its dissolution until there is strong resistance in the Americas to the opposition of the proletariat and history necessitates its participation in the GLOBAL STRUGGLE FOR THE ABOLITION OF ALL CLASSES.[114]

The decision to abolish the party, according to Michel Hector, was essentially an outgrowth of their "imbibed *noirisme*" and conscious support of the "anti-bourgeois government."[115] This, however, is only a partial explanation. The party hierarchy suffered several problems in the wake of Juste Constant's resignation and was in financial turmoil by 1947. The increasing anticommunist state repression also weakened its organizational abilities. Hector's explanation, moreover, suggests unanimity in communist support for Estimé and a large degree of tolerance in the regime's attitude to the party. The situation was quite the opposite, as communist leaders Edris St. Armand, Roger Mercier, and Gérard Montasse, continued to struggle individually against the government throughout 1947 and well into the next year. In January 1948 they regrouped and attempted to renew the PCH by forming another Communist Party, the Parti Ouvrier Progressiste Haïtien (POPH). They were marginally successful in gaining labor support, but the party suffered greatly when a month later the Senate, in violation of Articles 24 through 26 of the constitution legalizing party organization, passed a modified version of the 1936 anticommunist law.[116]

The government's decision to outlaw communist activities did not pass unchallenged. In the highly charged debate that led to the approval of the law, the Assembly remained divided on the issue as government opponents in both houses voiced strongly their disapproval. The debate in the Chamber of Deputies found Rossini Pierre-Louis of the PSP, the sole Marxist in the lower chamber, admonishing the deputies that the law would lead to further regulations against all parties, both communist and liberal.[117] Leading the opposition in the Senate was the elderly black senator from Port-de-Paix, Alphonse Henriquez, himself not a communist, who argued that the new bill was a tyrannical law designed only to win favor with the United States, then still deliberating on the proposal for a second EX-IM loan. To suppress the communists on these grounds, he argued, was a dangerous violation of the country's fragile democracy as it would lead to persecution and eventually greater opposition. "All this furor . . . just to obtain a loan and a few vague scholarships?"[118] He chastised his fellow senators as being mere sycophants motivated only by personal interests and the promise of political gain. The debate was so heated that the large audience had to be ejected because of occasional outbursts in protest of the bill.[119] In the end, Henriquez's lone voice was unable to sway the Senate. Estimé later admitted to a U.S. official that the law was directed against "small groups of leftwing intellectuals who have absorbed too much Marxism" and were "able to infiltrate the government positions."[120]

Increased concern over the state of communism in the country and the fear of destabilization was essentially a response to the internal and external pressures visited upon the regime. The rapid and dramatic change in global politics after the war, marked by the onset of cold war tensions, intensified U.S. foreign policy concerns over the spread of communism in the western hemisphere. Where the Good Neighbor Policy meant nonintervention, cold war diplomacy found the United States exerting indirect pressure on Latin American states that had prominent communist parties. From this perspective, the history of postwar communism in Haiti accords with the pattern of brief legalization, followed by harsh repression found elsewhere in Latin America.[121] However, the strength of the ideological color conflict, notably absent from communist repression elsewhere, distinguishes the Haitian case. Estimé was gravely concerned with rumors that the 1947 loan request was denied because the United States viewed his regime as communist.[122] U.S. officials in Washington and the mainstream U.S. press often confused the radical nationalism of the *authentiques* with communism, although officials in Haiti were aware that the Communist Party was no real threat to internal stability.[123] From the moment *noirisme* was consolidated at the state level, through the government's nationalist policies, the black government was frequently portrayed as being communist.[124] It is significant to recall that the policy of the PCH had in several ways accepted the basic policies of the *noiristes*, and after the dissolution of the party remained less forceful and thus less threatening.

Thus the government's push to abolish communism in 1948 was part of a broader attempt to remove the taint of radicalism from its international image, strengthen economic ties, and repair the fractured political relationship with the United States. In defense of his regime Estimé told a *New York Times* reporter in 1947, "Haiti is in no danger of becoming

A Socialist Party meeting at party headquarters. Seated at the head of the table are Étienne Charlier and Max D. Sam. From La Nation, *1947. Courtesy of Bibliothèque Nationale d'Haïti.*

communistic. The conditions in Haiti are not suitable to communist penetration. [The peasants] are too individualistic to be led off by foreign ideology."[125] Yet even after the passage of the law and the repression of the communists, Estimé played the communist card by telling U.S. officials of the constant threat they posed and the state's attempts to silence them.[126] Spontaneous manifestations against his regime were unfailingly explained as communist-inspired attempts at destabilization.[127]

The PCH, however, comprised one half of the Marxist campaign against the state. The post-1946 Socialist Party had an altogether different experience under Estimé. Following the dissolution of the PCH and the repression of MOP, the PSP remained the only true party in the country, with the daily *La Nation,* and its affiliated paper *L'Action,* run by Georges Petit, the principal opposition papers. St. Armand and his communist associates found their way to their former rivals in the PSP once the POPH floundered, though not without some resistance.[128] The Socialist Party thus became an umbrella organization for dissident leftists, socialists, communists, and Marxist sympathizers in the late forties.

The PSP's increased social presence was augmented by a marked improvement in its involvement with organized labor. In 1947, the small Marxist-led unions joined with the Fédération des Travailleurs Haïtiens (FTH), the first central labor organization in the country, founded in November of the previous year with four unions of electricians, sailors, mechanics, and chauffeurs. Four of the eight directors of the FTH were socialists, the principal ones being Fernand Sterlin and St. Armand, the latter of whom, after ending the PCH, brought five communist-led unions—wharf workers, soft drink bottlers, manufacturers of foodstuffs, customhouse workers—to the Fédération.[129] In contrast to MOP, the FTH had significant reach in the provinces, with regional federations in Port-de-Paix, the Northwest, the South, and the Artibonite. Through its union activities the Socialist Party established local sections throughout the country with dues-paying members.[130] During this period, the FTH crested with over fifty-one unions, though several of these unions dissolved almost as fast as they emerged. The presence of the dominant St. Armand in the FTH extended membership in the Fédération and illustrated the early importance of the Marxists in the organization. The extent to which union members supported Marxist ideas during this period is not known, though it appears that at the peak of this influence, in the period following the dissolution of SOT, there was much sympathy for the organization and the democratic principles that PSP spokesmen in the FTH advocated. *La Nation* also published regular columns in Kreyòl aimed at the FTH's union members.[131] The party's success among labor unions was complemented by the formation of a youth arm in early 1948. The Jeunesse Progressiste de Port-au-Prince (JPP) included radical *milat* youth such as Albert Joseph, Andrée Roumer, and a fiery young agronomy student at the dawn of what would be a long and turbulent engagement with radical politics, Jean Dominique.[132]

The infiltration of socialist ideas in the labor movement expectedly raised the concern of the pro-government forces intent on extirpating left-wing influences from working-class activism. The dual image of the Haitian labor movement, at once ideological and color-based, was made manifest in the composition of the FTH. That the most active leftist personalities in the FTH were from the defunct Communist Party only intensified division. This rivalry was played out, for example, in the contrasting attitudes of left and centrist leaders to party affiliations. The principal figure and secretary-general of the FTH, René Victor, was anti-imperialist but more fervently anticommunist and advocated a collaboration with the American Federation of Labor, then seeking to make inroads in Haitian labor, to counterbalance the growing influence of the Marxists.[133] His Marxist counterparts, on the other hand, pushed the FTH to establish ties with the left-wing of the Confederación de Trabajadores Cubanos. The anticommunist position was strengthened by its crucial political links with the National Labor Bureau, where Victor eventually accepted a post as director. Although his successor, the French-born and anti-U.S. Victor Vabre, was affiliated with the PSP, the promise of greater benefits with the National Labor Bureau proved more alluring to union leaders.[134]

The alliance between the FTH and the government effectively meant a reduction in the Marxist orientation of the FTH. In March, the titular head of the FTH, Milien Josué, a seaman whose anticommunism deepened after a brief residence in Cuba, decidedly split the union along ideological lines, resulting in a sharp decline in the role of St. Armand, Sterlin, and the other Marxists.[135] By the middle of 1948 Josué and the other anticommunist leaders left and formed the Fédération Haïtienne des Travailleurs (FHT), taking with them the largest unions. By 1950 the FHT, remaining under the suzerainty of the state, was the largest federation in the country, with nearly thirty-six unions, two of which, the tobacco union and coffee washers union, were composed almost entirely of women. The FTH worked more closely with Estimé following the repression of militant labor in 1948, and deepened its connections with workers through the establishment of night schools, programs on trade-unionism, and the issuing of FTH jackets to union members.[136] The removal of the stronger unions from the FTH and the repercussions of the legislation against antigovernment unions reduced the FTH to nothing more than a board of directors by the end of the decade.[137] Despite the strong influence of Marxists in 1947, they became increasingly marginalized in the labor movement once the FTH began to cooperate more closely with the government, and like MOP ultimately fell victim to state efforts to destroy militant labor. The socialists claimed that government sanctions against independent unions was indication of Estimé's subservience to "yankee imperialism."[138]

Although the PSP had mixed results with the labor movement in these years, owing to the strength of its leadership it maintained its importance as a central party of opposition. By virtue of its intellectual provenance the PSP was the most articulate leftist voice after 1947. Its radical approach owed much to unexpected and tragic circumstances that occurred in the middle of the year. On the evening of 4 May, in a bizarre turn of events, the party's enigmatic leader, Max Hudicourt, was found slumped over his desk in his home office with a gunshot wound to the chest and a revolver clutched in his right hand, an apparent suicide. The reasons that drove Hudicourt to take his life have never been clearly ascertained. The night before, he had attended a party meeting at George Rigaud's house at Rue Camille-Léon, offering little hint of his intentions.[139]

Radicals were stunned by his death and several explanations were proffered. Georges Petit hinted that his death was an assassination, retribution by the *authentiques* who despised his constant agitation and wanted to send a loud message to the government's opponents.[140] Such claims carried much weight in Port-au-Prince when it was learned that Hudicourt had planned to reveal in *La Nation* the names of the civil and military authorities most responsible for graft (ironically, a draft of the article lay on his desk when his body was found).[141] Others rumored that a U.S. agent had been responsible for the deed, an explanation that persists to this day.[142] Those closest to him, however, claim that in reality the suicide was wholly unrelated to political intrigue. Rather, it was a tragic end to a month-long depression.[143] Whatever the reasons, the death of the articulate and influential Max Hudicourt signaled the important loss of one of the few remaining members of the first generation of Marxist-influenced Haitian leftists.

It nonetheless did little to defuse the convictions of the more committed Marxists in the party. Under the leadership of Rigaud, Lespès, the doctrinaire Étienne Charlier, and Hudicourt's wealthy brother-in-law from Les Cayes, deputy Rossini Pierre-Louis, the party began to hew more closely to a more orthodox Marxism-Leninism. Hudicourt's death forced Charlier to assert a stronger leadership role as secretary-general of the party. As the party's leading voice, he wrote several thought-provoking editorials in *La Nation* that outlined the evolution of Haitian politics and the necessity for a radical agenda.[144] At the party's general meeting in 1948, Charlier in his annual report presented a clear and insightful self-assessment of the party and critique of the *noiriste* regime. He admitted that the color question was at the base of the country's social structure and would not disappear by itself. In moments of economic crisis, it emerges as the dominant political alternative. "If the PSP did not have the support of the masses in 1946," he argued, "it was because as a Marxist party [it was] forced to look at the situation in terms of class where the collective psychology was embroiled in a struggle of color."[145] The banana scandal, the economic bane of the Estimists, had exposed the administration for what it was, a "black petit bourgeois" minority, different from the previous regime in color only. Such disasters could only intensify class-consciousness. With confidence, Charlier, paraphrasing Roumain, could claim that in these conflict-ridden years "the color question is passing and more and more the masses are realizing that color is nothing, class is everything."[146]

The darker-skinned members of the PSP strongly supported Charlier's critique of Estimist *noirisme*. In a 1949 interview with Robert Alexander, Roger Leonard, editor of *La Nation*, insisted that the revolution of 1946 was "an anti-imperialist revolution" made by Haitians of different classes and colors, and that was now falsely depicted by *noiristes* as a "revolt of blacks against mulattoes." It is for this reason, Leonard argued, that Fignolé lacked the "moral right" to oppose the government, as ultimately there was "no basic difference" between MOP and the government.[147] Max Sam, the most prominent black member of the PSP, argued that Estimé's color politics was a distraction from the more pressing issues of social and economic exploitation. What the country desperately needed was a program for the development of its most deprived and illiterate majority. "Estimé only appealed to the emotions of the poor by rousing them to the belief of 'blacks in power.' But there was no real ideology. In the black government, there was no unity. . . . No ideology to save Haiti."[148]

Despite its provocative critique of *noirisme*, it would be unfair to suggest that the PSP blindly opposed all the policies of the Estimé administration. The party disapproved of the reactionary politics of the Catholic church and commended the government for its nationalist position in its battle with the French clergy, arguing that Haiti was an "island of blacks in the middle of a continent of whites," which perpetuated the "semi-colonial state" of the country through its agents in the church.[149] The government's stance on financial liberation also won much favor among party members. Lespès and Rigaud created an economic plan for the redistribution of income and development of food crops that sought to improve desperately needed agricultural revenues.[150] Jules Blanchet, the Columbia University–trained agronomist, resigned from the party and became undersecretary of national economy and director of the government's tobacco monopoly office. Likewise, in October 1947 Sam and Michel Roumain accepted two-year ambassadorial posts to Rome and Brussels, respectively, a decision that Sam maintains was taken to demonstrate the party's support of democracy in the country and gain greater exposure to European socialism.[151] The party's affirmation of a nonracial ideology and repudiation of *noirisme* fueled attacks against it as a bourgeois organization of "young aristocrats."[152] That socialists denounced most of the light-skinned leaders for their ideas mattered little to the staunchly *noiriste* groups.

Even so, U.S. officials were extremely disturbed by the more radical approach of the party, which, despite its "relative insignificance in light of the predominant position held by President Estimé," deserved to be watched "very carefully."[153] As was the case with the communists, they also kept a watchful eye on Estimé's policies toward the PSP. In several instances officials complained that he was not as vigilant in repressing the PSP as he was with Fignolé and MOP, insinuating an interest in socialism at the state level.[154] An exhaustive report on the Haitian left, completed in April 1948 by U.S. embassy representative Jack West, arrived at the following conclusion about the PSP: "The PSP is the only organized political group in Haiti and as such inspires certain respect as well as fear. The danger that this party will take over the reins of Government in Haiti is not imminent, but it exists and will tend to increase unless checked by Governmental repression."[155]

From the above portrait of the Haitian left in the late forties, two conclusions may be drawn. First, the level of organization and success in the labor movement, albeit short-lived, demonstrates that the left was at its most powerful after 1946. Yet the divisions within the movement along class and color lines proved as prohibitive to its development and expansion as state repression. Second, the *noiristes* in power assumed an autocratic role in dealing with their enemies outside the government. On one level, this continued a well-developed tradition in Haitian politics. It was also a reaction to the growing importance of radicals among the popular classes facilitated by the post-1946 political context. The conflict between the *noiristes*, themselves an integral part of the protest movements of previous years, and the militant left must be seen as part of a broader contest among radical forces. The continuing divisions among radicals left open the possibility that the *milat* elite would capitalize on this weakness and foment a serious challenge to black political dominance. This issue of division among radical forces and within the structure of the government itself would play a significant role in weakening the foundation of the state and inciting its sudden and dramatic collapse. To appreciate this, we need to closely examine the political narrative of the last phase of the "Estimé revolution."

Internal Struggles and Estimists in Retreat

The forces with the greatest potential to fell the presidency proved to be the very ones that brought the *noiristes* to power. As the beginning of this chapter revealed, the popularity and support Estimé claimed among the poorer classes was in large measure due to the reformism of his administration. Yet the true guarantors of power on the national political scene were not state officials, the weakened bourgeoisie, the *authentiques*, or the popular classes, but the commanding officers in the military whose support had assured Estimé's political victory. Estimé demonstrated his gratitude to the armed forces by promoting several high-ranking black officers to privileged positions in the upper echelons of the military bureaucracy. For many officers like Robert Bazile, who was given a two-year scholarship to study statistics in Washington and who headed the census bureau in 1949–1950 upon his return, these were grants denied them under the previous regime and a further incentive to support the *noiriste* cause.[156] Estimé also elevated the Garde to the status of Armée d'Haïti in 1947. As empowering as these measures were, they did not redress the fragile alliance between the state and the army, nor did they remove the ever-present threat of opposition from powerful army officers, particularly the one most closely associated with the president, Paul Magloire.

By the summer of 1947, Estimé, on the advice of his most radical partisans in the National Assembly, decided that the expulsion of potential opponents in the cabinet was necessary to reduce the threat of opposition growing within the administration. Chief among them was Minister of Commerce Phillipe Charlier, who made declamatory speeches on wage conditions to strikers. Recognizing the growing power of the armed forces, Estimé sought to profit from the large-scale cabinet shakeup by getting high-ranking officers out of the country through subterfuge. A post as ambassador to Chile was hurriedly created for Magloire. The colonel, however, was notified by a palace spy of Estimé's intention and left the capital for two weeks, forcing the president to give the appointment to another functionary.[157] On Magloire's advice, Levelt and Lavaud both turned down similar offers. The incident drove a wedge between Magloire and the president that led to the gradual deterioration of their relationship. In late 1947, Estimé, hoping to gain support from other officers, replaced Magloire's appointee as chief of police, Stephen Woolley, with one of his staunchest military supporters, Marcaisse Prosper, a young black major in the army whose influence was increasing among the lower-ranking officers. Magloire recognized the president's attempt to undermine his position on the political scene, and in private conversation he confessed a desire to overthrow the government and run as president.[158]

Although they maintained a public friendship and worked closely together in the fight against the left opposition, by the fall of 1949 the relationship between the two men had soured and rumors of overt attempts to usurp the president's power were rife.[159] The political climate, however, was unsupportive of opposition to the popular president. Magloire, too, was involved in the corrupt banana concessions he managed. Still, the ambitious colonel was far too strong a force to be underestimated. He continued to have overwhelming popularity among light-skinned and black members of the officer corps and grew closer to powerful members of the traditional elite and U.S. representatives in Haiti. He won much favor among these groups by privately opposing the government's labor policies, xenophobia, and the black supremacy of the cabinet. The Haitian army thus remained divided in its allegiance to Estimé and Magloire.

If Paul Magloire was the regime's most dangerous ally, he was by no means its only military threat. Prior to Magloire's support of his presidential campaign, Estimé owed a considerable debt to another officer who ensured his election in the Chamber of Deputies in May 1946, Colonel Astrel Roland. During the heated months following Lescot's ouster, the appeal of *dechoukaj* reached fever pitch and virtually all politicians who served under Lescot or Vincent stood little chance of reelection. Aware of this, Estimé sought the aid of Colonel Roland, a *milat* of significant influence, who had been the Garde's chief officer in the Artibonite region for nearly twenty-five years and who was the directing officer for the Verettes elections.[160] Roland's intervention on Estimé's behalf proved crucial in securing his reelection to the Chamber of Deputies and in bolstering Magloire's support for him in Port-au-Prince.

Desirous of a swift victory in the turbulent campaign and faced with challenges from all sides, Estimé unwittingly promised the antagonistic Roland a high position in the government and may even have suggested that he would be his first choice as successor on the expiration of his term of office.[161] When the president, overwhelmed by demands from his anti-*milat* supporters in the cabinet, failed to make good on his promise, Roland became restless. His first demand was to be transferred from the distant Artibonite post and stationed in the privileged Palace Guard in Port-au-Prince. Since Magloire, who was wise to Roland's political aspirations, already occupied this position, Magloire devised a plot with the president's consent to remove Roland as a threat. In 1947 Estimé gave Roland a position as head of the Haitian delegation attending an international conference in Ecuador. In Quito, Roland received orders not to return to Haiti but to leave directly for Washington, where he was to serve as military attaché. Realizing the complicity between Magloire and Estimé, an enraged Roland left Ecuador for the Dominican Republic. There he took refuge with his close ally Anselmo Paulino, head of Trujillo's secret police and former Dominican minister in Port-au-Prince. Both Estimé and Magloire seriously underestimated Roland's determination, as once in Santo Domingo Roland formed alliances with other exiled *milat* dissidents, including Alfred Viau.

With considerable support from Trujillo they launched a formidable opposition against Estimé from Ciudad Trujillo. Following a much publicized clash in 1946 resulting from Estimé's decision not to have Trujillo appointees serve as ministers in Port-au-Prince, the Dominican dictator, who falsely accused Estimé of plotting a 1948 invasion of the Dominican Republic, quietly waited for an opportunity to launch a full assault on the Haitian government. Roland and Viau provided the impetus. Their most powerful weapon was the radio and on the station *La Voz Dominicana*, widely received in Haiti, Roland broadcast inflammatory and vulgar anti-Estimé attacks beginning in early 1949. Dominican planes flying over Port-au-Prince dropped pamphlets and called for a popular overthrow of the regime. In order to gain U.S. support, a lengthy letter was sent to the State Department in Washington signed by the three men outlining the failures of the Estimé regime. They accused the government of encouraging blacks to enact "violent action against the unarmed colored class," which was under constant threat from an army "composed exclusively of blacks of the lowest social level." They further argued that Estimé was officially prescribing the replacement of Christianity with the "barbarous and primitive voodoo cult, the ritual of which is bloody sacrifice," and, with the help of the army, ordered the assassinations of Hudicourt, Viau, and several other light-skinned opponents.[162]

Trujillo's support of Roland renewed the serious tensions between the two countries. In Haiti, a national state of siege was declared. Although several public statements were made in support of a court martial of Roland supporters, little effort was made to enforce it. The government, on the other hand, preferred to use harsh measures to deter local opponents from siding with Roland.[163] During the state of siege, a ban was placed on all public meetings, thus limiting the influence of opposition parties. These actions drew immediate protest from conservatives such as Paul Cassagnol, president of the PPSC, who saw them as justification of government repression.[164]

Estimé rightly recognized that even with support in Haiti, once Roland had as powerful a protector as Trujillo, he would not be easily silenced. After seeking intervention from the Inter-American Peace Commission, Haiti and the Dominican Republic signed a joint declaration advocating intolerance to groups or individuals who attempted to disturb the national security of either party.[165] Despite this, throughout the year Haitian officers on the border betrayed several conspiracies and plots of invasion as the intrigue between Estimé and Roland continued. Roland's strong attacks aroused a patriotic response on the part of the poorer classes in favor of the government and widespread support of Estimé in Haiti. The local press and radio revived the painful memory of the 1937 massacre and disregarded Roland as a traitor against the progressive government. Even the antigovernment PSP in *La Nation* criticized Roland for dishonoring the presidency.[166] Such rare universal support for Estimé changed dramatically later in the year once the president made obvious his intentions to succeed himself.

One can only speculate on the reasons that motivated Estimé to press for a second mandate. There is obvious historical precedent for his actions, as most of his predecessors, including his political mentor, Vincent, had used the same method to secure political power. Given the power struggle in Haiti of the late forties, there seem to have been other precipitating factors. Most certainly the *authentiques*, desperate to retain their privileged position in Haitian society, pressured the president to consider a second term. Some feared that a weakening of his position could allow for a return to the old order. There was also a fundamental element in *noirisme*, which from its modern inception advocated authoritarianism as a necessary evil in the competitive Haitian political arena. To this must be added Estimé's political personality and high sense of self-importance. Indeed, the grandiosity of the Exposition and the recognition he received for it, and Estimé's handling of the Roland affair, definitely created illusions of grandeur. To varying degrees these factors figured in Estimé's attempt to revise the constitution of 1946 to include a provision for reelection.

Government officials hinted at the president's desire to succeed himself in the next election from as early as January 1949 during speeches celebrating the third anniversary of the 1946 revolution.[167] That Estimé made calculated moves toward reelection is found in his banning of the PCH and restrictions on labor activism the year before. It was, however, the legislative electoral campaign, which began in October 1949, that presented the government with the first opportunity to prepare the stage for reelection. Estimé's term of office was set to terminate on 16 August 1952, the same year senators would be elected to the Senate. Although Estimé had limited support in the Senate, sitting senators seeking reelection depended on his good favor and consequently revealed little indication they would challenge a constitutional revision tabled in the lower chamber. It was therefore critical for the government that a chamber of deputies loyal to the president be elected in the January 1950 elections. The government spared no measure in realizing this. The state of siege was lifted for the duration of the electoral campaign and opposition groups were allowed to meet freely. In early September, a new electoral law was passed in Congress bestowing on the three-member communal councils the responsibility for voter registration, the conduct of the elections, and the final counting of the ballots. To guarantee support, nearly all of the communal councils elected for four-year terms in 1946 were removed from their posts for various reasons after 1947 and replaced through executive appointment by known Estimists.[168]

The government's actions precipitated extreme opposition from leftists in MOP and PSP and from disparate, generally uncooperative sectors of the opposition now united against the government. To weaken the growing challenge from the dissident groups, the government passed another anticommunist decree in November prohibiting all activities and meetings deemed by the government to be of a communist nature. As expected, the government interpreted the law broadly and labeled all opposition groups communist. The president's opponents in the Senate, Henriquez and Franck Lacroix, formed a new political group called L'Union des Indépendants, and Fignolé, having been relatively inactive for nearly a year, revived MOP, holding large general meetings of thousands at the party headquarters. The joining of these forces presented a popular resistance to the electoral campaign in Port-au-Prince. Opposition to the government was not limited to the capital. Reports suggested that government candidates in several southern provinces were forced to leave their homes for fear of mob action against them.[169]

In Port-au-Prince the situation worsened. In early November MOP joined forces with the PPSC, which included several influential *milat* businessmen and Catholic organizations, and the Henriquez and Lacroix movement to form the Front Démocratique. Fignolé defended his alliance with the conservatives, as an effort to fight the widespread communist influence of the government. In an effort to deflect accusations against his party, Fignolé argued that the government's anticommunist policies were "merely a cloak" to "impress" democratic countries. In reality, "communists" from the PSP such as Max Sam were influencing the government's direction toward "terror" and "totalitarian methods against all opposition."[170] Relying on the strength of the Fignolists, the Front planned and organized a general strike against the government. The Front issued a ten-point manifesto that called for the reinstatement of the communal councils, whose members were replaced by the executive, and the removal of all anti-labor legislation. The protest was intended to precipitate a general commercial strike and merge with other anti-Estimé demonstrations nationwide.[171]

Concerned over the upcoming Exposition and international attention, Estimé was reluctant to take violent action against his opponents, but he also realized the severity of this threat and the Front's wide support. On the advice of Magloire and Lavaud, he immediately reimposed the state of siege and ordered the arrest of all the leaders. The Haitian police were ruthless in adhering to these orders, violently beating student leaders and jailing six members of various opposition groups, including Marcel Fombrun, son of prominent senator Charles Fombrun, and Lespès of the PSP. Fearful of the opposition alliance escalating into popular unrest, Magloire issued a series of repressive policies that recalled the harshest days of the Vincent presidency. Eight newspapers were immediately shut down, the presses of *Chantiers* and *La Nation* among them being smashed, and three political parties, the PPSC, L'Union des Indépendants, and the PSP, were dissolved. All radical leaders were forced into hiding. Étienne Charlier fled the capital incognito and Fignolé narrowly escaped arrest by hiding in the Argentine embassy. Senator Jean David, the president's close advisor, who was accused of trying to overthrow the government by Magloire factions, was also forced to leave the country.[172]

With the opposition effectively silenced, the plans for the legislative elections continued. In the face of threats from rabid pro-Estimé groups, all independent candidates including Rossini Pierre-Louis and Edgar Néré Numa boycotted the elections and withdrew their candidacy. Estimé, with very thin evidence, publicly blamed the strike on communist complicity with Roland and used the occasion to clamp down on the Socialist Party.

Although Roland had nothing to do with the activities of the opposition movement in Haiti, he was far from out of the picture. In the Dominican Republic the campaign against Estimé continued to gain momentum. Viau published a pamphlet that was printed in full in the Dominican paper *El Caribe* and circulated widely across the region. Entitled "Impressions of the Hospitable and Democratic Dominican Republic during the era of Trujillo," it was presented as a conversation between Viau and Trujillo, with the dictator assuming the role of comforter. Aside from lionizing Trujillo, the pamphlet was a scathing attack on the black government. Calling Estimé a "cannibal, thief and bandit," Viau argued that the Haitian government was "the most dangerous Bolshevik cell in the Antilles, [ruled by] bloody anarchy."[173] The wide circulation of this pamphlet was but the first stage in a new assault against the Haitian government.

In December, through sheer good fortune, Estimé received word of a large-scale plot orchestrated by Trujillo and Roland. In the border town of Jimaní, Haitian police officers discovered a large cache of weapons in the home of a Roland associate, Jean Dupuy, who was subsequently killed by the

Haitian police. In the ensuing investigation conducted by the Organization of American States, it was discovered that a cadre of expelled *milat* officers and Dominican associates were given ammunition and money by Trujillo and planned to launch a raid that would culminate in Port-au-Prince with the assassination of Estimé, Magloire, Lavaud, and Prosper.[174] The details of the adventurous plot included the burning of the Dominican Legation in Port-au-Prince by Trujillo agents, giving them reason for a Dominican invasion and overthrow of the regime. Fearing for his life, the Dominican minister in Port-au-Prince, Sebastián Rodríguez Lora, betrayed the conspiracy to Haitian foreign minister Vilfort Beauvoir shortly after fleeing to the United States. Over forty officers, including a U.S. national, were arrested, and fighting continued between Dominican forces and the Haitian army for several days along the border. Estimé received diplomatic support from Venezuela and Cuba. International solidarity forced Trujillo to back down. An extensive OAS investigation into the events was launched and its report presented in March 1950 confirmed the undeniable and extensive involvement of Trujillo in the plot.[175] Trujillo withdrew his support of Roland and his associates and ordered that they immediately leave the Dominican Republic. International attention succeeded in quelling a potentially dangerous advance by the Dominican Republic and temporarily strengthened Estimé's hand.

Still, it had little effect on political and economic tensions in Haiti. Estimé threw himself obsessively into the Exposition, reveling in the attention it brought Port-au-Prince. The glowing reviews it received in foreign publications such as *Life*, which called it the Caribbean's "bravest adventure," was for Estimé validation of the importance of his regime to Haitian history.[176] But good international press could not camouflage the economic damage the Exposition wrought, which only added to popular dissatisfaction. Although there was a consistent increase in sisal production, the country's major export, coffee, experienced considerable increases in costs of production, forcing many commercial interests in the city to support anti-administration causes.[177]

The impact of the banana scandal was accentuated by a series of economic failures related to the tourist industry. In an effort to boost the country's tourism, Estimé, acting on poor advice, contracted with two unscrupulous U.S. businessmen to develop casinos. During the two-year preparation for the Exposition, they expropriated funds from the government coffers for shady ventures, including several hotels and a boxing arena where fixed fights were staged, and convinced the president to contract with their associates for architectural developments.[178] Not surprisingly, none of this money yielded positive returns for the country and one of the casino owners could boast to a U.S. observer that the funding for the government's ambitious adult literacy program depended entirely on the success of the casino.[179] The casino, and the newly erected amusement fair, attracted only the tourists that came to the country. To this was added the $2 million the government used in developing the frontier town of Belladère into a modern city. The general extravagance of the Exposition, moreover, worsened the economic problems. Over $4 million of a national budget of $13.4 million was appropriated for the Exposition.[180] Public opinion was harsh and unforgiving in its condemnation of the state's misguided and wanton expense, arguing that Haiti had neither the material nor moral means to withstand a venture as grand as that proposed by Estimé.[181] To his own detriment, the president threw himself into the Exposition with little thought of the consequences, like Henri Christophe and the Citadel over a century before.[182]

The January elections succeeded in creating a lower house in the National Assembly wholly subservient to the president. With this support, on 3 April Estimists pushed through a revision of provision 81 of the constitution that barred reelection. The provision was unanimously approved in the Chamber of Deputies and, given the color divisions in the Senate, was expected to have a similar hearing there as well. To the surprise of the *authentiques*, and no doubt Estimé himself, the Senate, after a week of intense debates, voted against the passage of the bill on 18 April. Leading the opposing senators was Emile St. Lôt, recently returned from a diplomatic post in France with possible presidential aspirations. The enigmatic St. Lôt, thus far an Estimist, shocked the president by switching sides and using his considerable influence over several other senators to support him in opposing the revision.[183] It was widely held by U.S. and Haitian sources that a desperate Estimé promised the opportunist St. Lôt a large sum if he supported the amendment but reneged on it when he thought St. Lôt's demands became more extravagant. As a result, one of Estimé's staunchest *noiriste* supporters in the Senate became his most dangerous political enemy. U.S. officials had already questioned St. Lôt's allegiance to Estimé in 1948.[184] It was also believed that Magloire promised St. Lôt the presidency if he swayed the Senate against Estimé. The defection of several black leaders strengthened the opposition bloc in the Senate, which previously had been led by Henriquez and a small group of light-skinned senators, most notably Louis Déjoie. After the debate only three senators leaned on the side of revision.[185]

The unanticipated rejection of the proposal in the Senate and the backlash in the chamber created a fierce three-week crisis that shattered the hold of the *noiristes* on the state. On Déjoie's prompting the dissident majority in the Senate called for a full inquest into the financial manipulations of government officials since 1947. Both ministers of finance were accused of extra-constitutionally spending nearly twenty million gourdes for various projects without the approval of the Senate. Several government officials, including Duvalier and Fourcand, refused to attend the sessions, which became so hostile they had to be monitored by police officers.[186] The debates took on a clear class bias. The pro-Estimé *noiriste* paper, *La République*, reacted strongly by issuing harsh criticisms of Déjoie in particular. Déjoie was accused of accepting funds from Trujillo and supporting Roland in an effort to embarrass the government and justify *milat* intervention.[187]

Fearful of the long-term potential of the crisis, Estimé's enemies outside of the legislature, black and *milat*, reinvigorated their challenge to the regime. The most powerful opponent of reelection was Magloire. The tensions between the two men increased over the course of the two months preceding the constitutional debate. By this time, bourgeois factions also began to court the army chief.

On 21 April, showing signs of increasing weakness, Estimé requested that the United States ambassador approve a proposal he drafted for a U.S. army mission to reorganize the Armée d'Haïti.[188] He clearly felt that following his support for the OAS investigation and his pro-U.S. policies over the past two years, the Truman administration would forgive his earlier nationalist policies and support him in the case of a coup d'état.[189] Equally cognizant of this fact, Magloire scrupulously refrained from taking action against the *authentiques*, aware that the continued exposure of government scandals in the Senate would force the government to resort to drastic unpopular action. As the crisis reached boiling point, Estimé continued to block the publication of the senatorial decree. Such efforts did little to mollify the intransigence of the Senate. Déjoie and Henriquez drafted a resolution calling for the lifting of the state of siege, hopeful that if the resolution passed, in Déjoie's words, "Estimé won't last three weeks."[190] The president realized that the survival of his regime lay in his ability to weaken the army high command. He offered Major Prosper money and a political position if he incited a sergeants' revolt against Magloire. Recognizing Estimé's desperation and the futility of fighting the dominant Magloire, Prosper refused.[191]

With little support from the legislature or the military, a desperate Estimé placed his fate in the hands of his most extreme enforcers. Chief among them Léon "Ti-Roi" Bordes, a businessman utterly devoted to the president. When it became known that Fignolé, now backing Magloire in the fight against

Estimé, agreed to use his influence to launch a large-scale workers' strike against the regime on 6 May, Bordes arranged for a counter-demonstration of rioters and politicized gunmen who completely overwhelmed the anti-government strikers.

Had the efforts of the Estimists stopped there, it would have weakened the capacity of his opponents and possibly provided him with more time to negotiate with the senators. Estimé, however, had little control over the violent mob assembled by Bordes. Brandishing machetes and shouting "Vive Estimé! A bas le Sénat," the mob marched to the Senate, then in session, barged in, torched the archives, and completely ransacked the chamber, destroying everything within its reach before eventually pulling the tiles from the floor. Demonstrators moved throughout the streets and popular neighborhoods to the gates of the National Palace, beating drums and carrying pieces of furniture and Senate documents as trophies of the destruction. The dissident senators narrowly escaped the onslaught. At St. Lôt's house, a large mob stormed the gates and a shootout ensued before the police arrived. There was great fear that the demonstration would escalate into a civil war and possibly a color conflict. Indeed, the ferocity of the actions of the Estimists supported this notion. Estimists captured *milat* businessman Lucien Chauvet and accused him of attempting to lead a *milat* strike against the government. According to his testimony, he was viciously beaten before the police intervened.[192]

Apparently believing the force of his opposition weakened, the support of the United States guaranteed, and the popular classes behind him, the president unconstitutionally dissolved the cabinet and the Senate and the next day announced his new cabinet. It included Joseph L. Déjean as head, Duvalier as minister of health and labor, Castel Demesmin as minister of interior and national security, and Love Léger as minister of education, all of whom were Magloire's most vocal enemies.[193] That same evening, moved by the public demonstration in his name, Estimé made an emotive radio address from the steps of the National Palace in which he commended the crowds who stormed the Senate for being the true defenders of democracy, "demonstrating a political maturity" and displaying "an eloquent attitude without precedent in the history of the nation."[194] This open support of one of the country's most violent public demonstrations since the slaughter of President Vilbrun Guillaume-Sam in 1915 was the death knell of the Estimé regime.

The dissolution of the Senate on 8 May created immediate tensions within the army high command. Lavaud and Levelt argued that they were forced by their position to support the president in his decision. Several black officers sided with them. Magloire, on the other hand, claimed he would resign his post in order to protect the senators. Lavaud on the president's orders prepared to arrest Magloire that evening.[195] The influential police chief Prosper supported Magloire and threatened a violent retaliation against his pro-Estimé colleagues if the orders were carried out. Summoned to a private meeting at the Cassernes Dessalines, Lavaud and Levelt capitulated. A military committee, formed for the protection of the senators, guarded the National Assembly and reportedly uncovered lists of senators who were to be assassinated. Lavaud personally went to the government printing office that night and stopped the printing of the decree dissolving the senate.

Estimé was desperate. An eleventh-hour pledge to withdraw the proposal for reelection found no support.[196] On the morning of the tenth, he summoned U.S. Ambassador DeCourcy to his office and confessed that Magloire, Levelt, and Lavaud had presented him with a coup d'état.[197] He attributed the astonishingly rapid breakdown of his political power to the betrayal of Magloire and St. Lôt, whose avarice led them to make unrealistic demands of him. Shaken and erratic, Estimé pleaded with the ambassador for U.S. intervention to "save Haiti," stave off potential anarchy, and restore his administration.[198] When it was refused, he unsuccessfully sought the intervention of the Mexican embassy. An hour later, with little hope of salvaging his regime, a vanquished Dumarsais Estimé signed the resignation letter Lavaud had prepared for him and in one stroke brought to an end the most *noiriste* regime the republic ever experienced.

Conclusion

By 1950 the progressive forces that four years earlier envisaged a radical transformation of Haitian politics were all but defeated. The military junta that oversaw Lescot's ouster once again took its position as the transition government. Why did Haiti's black nationalist regime so quickly reach an inglorious end? There are several explanations. The failure of the Estimé government to hold on to state power was in large measure a result of a misreading of political attitudes. The opening of black middle-class access to state power after 1946 promised to fulfill the goals of the January revolt. The government did make a genuine effort to improve social conditions. Yet there was little attempt to bridge the gap between the state and civil society. Black consciousness, while an important aspect of the regime's appeal, was insufficient to address the economic and social problems of the country. Estimists also made little effort to eradicate the spoils system entrenched under Lescot. Black power was often used as justification for black participation in the corruption of the state bureaucracy. These factors served to underline the disconnect between the government and the populace. By overestimating his strength and appeal, Estimé was unable to come to terms with the growing alienation of his regime. In the face of mounting popular protest from the Marxist left and independent labor, the state responded with repression.

Finally, the *noiriste* government was unable to control the growing strength of the Haitian army that helped to install it. Once the shaky alliance between the state and the armed forces was broken, there was little chance of survival.

CHAPTER 5

Blacks without Color

*Military Rule and Radicalism
in Transition, 1950–1957*

†

Shaking the head will not break the neck.

—HAITIAN PROVERB

In 1950 I fought my enemies, and today I will put
back on my iron pants and fight them once more.

—PAUL MAGLOIRE, 1954

Forward on Electors! We can find happiness. In April 1957,
Fignolé says they want him to be president of the republic.

—CAMPAIGN SONG, 1957

We are going to vote so we can make the country evolve.

—CAMPAIGN SONG, 1957

Let us not forget that 1956 will complete 1946.

—FRANÇOIS DUVALIER, *Souvenirs d'un campagne*, 1957

Few observers who witnessed the fall of Estimé, the reassertion of
military rule, and the general political changes in 1950 could have
predicted that Haiti was on a chaotic path. In the wake of Estimé's
fall, his former ally Paul Magloire became president, ruling with a firmer
hand than his predecessors. Under his administration a disoriented left
fought to pick up the pieces of its late forties destruction. A sharp turn to the
right in Haiti and the region as a whole impaired their chances of success.
The drift from Estimé-era black consciousness and an increasingly desperate
economic situation created an urban environment markedly different from
that of the forties.

The preceding chapter emphasized the divisions within the radical opposition and the forceful response of the government to its challenges. This chapter argues that during the fifties, a decade frequently misunderstood as an era of stability and prosperity, this relationship became more volatile. In an effort to maintain dominance, the military government adopted a series of measures aimed at destroying its opposition. Persecution, a more vigilant U.S. foreign policy, and a debilitating political and economic system contributed to the resurgence of a new and more confused form of radicalism, and ultimately to the near anarchic battle for power in the presidential campaign of 1956–1957. This campaign, which marked an end to the postoccupation promise of political renewal, forms the centerpiece of the present discussion. To begin, however, we must first explain the institutionalization and consequences of military governance.

The Consolidation of Military Rule

The removal of Estimé by a military junta created both a political vacuum and dilemma. Participants in the coup from the left and center expected political rewards for their part in deposing the popular leader. The most opportunistic of them ambitiously hoped for the presidency. The junta, however, aware of its importance as the arbiter of power following its experience in 1946, did not intend to relinquish state control to civilian authorities. The promotion of army personnel the previous four years, all part of Estimé reformism, placed high-ranking officers in a stronger position than ever before to determine political direction. Moreover, the political context of 1950 was considerably different from that of 1946, as Estimé's fall was not precipitated by a popular uprising, but by an internal political clash between two dominant groups within the power elite. The ideological furor that contributed to the erosion of the Lescot presidency also began to recede in 1950. The junta thus emerged at a time when elements of opposition had not only become more divided but were also more easily contained. Still, the immediate crisis required that the democratic rhetoric of the past four years be preserved and some respect for electoral procedures be pursued. This was even more necessary considering the state of international opinion regarding Estimé's sudden and unexpected downfall. Walter White, for example, in a letter to Magloire, commented that he regretted the loss of a president who "within the past two years [transformed] the reputation of Haiti from being a poor country inhabited by uneducated people to its true status as one of the most charming places in the world."[1]

It was thus necessary for elections to be held. Local garrisons easily controlled small protests against the junta in the provinces, and the triumvirate was able to regain international recognition and public confidence by appointing a civilian cabinet of Estimé's staunchest parliamentary opponents, Henriquez, Lanoix, and Rosinni Pierre-Louis, and a Consultative Council led by Dantès Bellegarde, which was also civilian-dominated. Foreign posts were also reshuffled and all Estimé associates removed from office. Most important was the support the military received from the business community, which did not want to see the return to power of another *noiriste*. The junta also introduced universal male suffrage in the summer of 1950, legally allowing all males over the age of twenty-one to vote.

Paul Magloire, now the undisputed leader of the Haitian army, did not immediately present himself as a presidential candidate, although he long harbored such aspirations. Instead, it was his close associate Luc Fouché whom many assumed would be the colonel's handpicked choice for president. The established bourgeoisie was not willing to accept anyone other than Paul Magloire, and Magloire, despite his repeated statements to the contrary, had every intention to become Estimé's successor.[2] In the summer of 1950 Magloire began to make goodwill visits across the island, offering reassuring promises of material improvements, employment, the development of agri-business, and maintaining the ideals of democracy. His most appealing promises were to decentralize power from the capital, thereby allowing the provinces, especially his native city of Cap Haïtien, to reassert their prominence. His supporters referred to the ebullient Magloire, who had already charmed the French clergy and *milat* elite as the "apostle of national unity." Newspaper reports of the tour record similar receptions at each stop: lavish balls and street dances, ceremonial award ceremonies in which sundry titles were presented to local magistrates, visits to families and friends, honorific Catholic masses, and large outdoor meetings highlighted by long-winded speeches and promises.[3] On his return to Port-au-Prince in July, Magloire toured the poorer districts, distributing money and food, showing free movies in neighborhood cinemas, and participating in local dances organized by the CEM in conjunction with the local business community. The fanfare that accompanied Magloire across the country made clear long before his election who would be the next head of state.

Throughout his brief campaign, Magloire continued to exploit the theme of national union, declaring himself a "citizen-soldier" willing to correct the inherent mistakes of *Estimisme* and bridge the social divide. To give credence to these claims and to gain even greater popularity, Magloire openly brought into his camp several political opponents, most notably Fignolé, whom he supported as Deputy for Port-au-Prince. The Magloire campaign, not surprisingly, proved triumphant. Running against a little-known Estimist, Fénélon Alphonse, he received 99 percent of the popular vote, becoming the first military president since 1915.[4]

Magloire's election signified a victory for the bourgeoisie, now able to regain the political prestige they considered stolen by Estimé. They took every occasion to fête the president and shower him with parades, and in 1952, a radio station, Radio Commerce, was put entirely at his disposal.[5] The Catholic church, too, celebrated the change in government, referring to the new president in Christian terms as the "savior of the country."[6] Magloire cultivated a reputation of a bon vivant who fraternized freely with members of all social classes. As far as the country's diplomatic relations were concerned, Magloire won the approval of officials in Washington who long regarded him as a bulwark in their design for the preservation of U.S. interests in the country. Magloire also sealed a rapprochement with the country's longtime adversary Trujillo in 1951, when both men signed an anticommunist pact.

In national politics, the Magloire presidency was a return to conservatism, a reprieve from the socially charged forties. With Magloire, a new cultural context emerged in which black consciousness enjoyed limited support and the celebration of Haiti's African heritage was seen as having little more than commercial value. The Catholic church, although losing much of its earlier power, resumed its public attacks on vodou without state resistance.[7] The shift in attitudes to vodou and black consciousness was even reflected in the music of the decade, as the vodou-djazz revolution of the forties began to give way to Nemours Jean-Baptiste's fast-paced *kompa-dirèk*, a carefree form of dance music that drew its influences from meringue and contemporary Cuban music. Clubs in Cap Haïtien and Port-au-Prince throbbed nightly to the sounds of *kompa* groups such as Jazz Septentrional and Symphony Jazz. This new lifestyle received government support, and the president himself was a frequent visitor to the nightclubs.[8]

Magloire and his conservative black cabinet projected the image of black middle-class progress, which Magloire termed "social equilibrium." Magloire claimed that his policy was to have "a majority of blacks" but to always include "some mulattos in [the] cabinet."[9] The rhetoric of national unity wore thin quickly, however. The black middle class, which essentially was still directing the country, was powerless against the dominant military and commercial interests that made up the Magloire camp.

Magloire's relations with the elite, in fact, had been an important part of his political background. Born on 19 July 1907, Magloire rose to prominence as a member of a respected black elite family in Cap Haïtien. The young Magloire was schooled to accept the supremacy of the military by his father, a general who served under Nord Alexis (1902–1908). From the moment he entered the L'Ecole Militaire in 1930 to his promotion as chief of the Palace Guard by Lescot in 1944, he benefited greatly from the support of powerful members of the elite. His mentor, Colonel Gustave Laraque, a *milat* from the north, ensured that the young Magloire would be among the few black beneficiaries of Lescot's exclusionary policies.[10] His limited tolerance for ideological concerns endeared him to the bourgeoisie, who placed their faith in him as they patiently awaited Estimé's fall. But Magloire was by no means a puppet president willing to do the bidding of the old elite. Having engineered the resignation of two presidents, one of whom he had helped to impose, he had long prepared for the day he would become president. His support of strongman rule was predicated on a deep mistrust for the process of Haitian politics and civilian authority. Thus the political climate he constructed in the fifties, while serving elite interests, was one of his own design; one that his *authentique* rivals referred to as the rule of "noirs sans couleur."[11]

On the surface, the change in Haitian politics as expressed by the new administration appeared to be one of reconciliation and modernity. Yet underneath the pomp and ceremony, which Magloire reveled in, lay a sinister concomitant of military rule: state-sanctioned violence. The constant threat of force against opponents was nothing new in Haitian politics. We have seen how Vincent abused his power and intimidated his opposition with imprisonment. The army, often the instrument of this intimidation under previous governments, was now in control of the state. No group suffered more from this than the already devastated left.

Kansonfèrisme *and the Left in Abeyance*

By 1950, the Haitian left had confronted a series of political and ideological challenges in the form of negotiating entry to national politics, internecine rivalry, and state repression. The Magloire dictatorship, which took antiradicalism as its leitmotif, brought no relief to this predicament. Since 1946 Paul Magloire had been the driving force in government suppression of left-wing activity, and now as president he was determined to eliminate all forms of radicalism. Where Estimé's position and the nature of his coming to power forced him to make promises to various political groups, Magloire

President Paul E. Magloire leads the military parade at the Haitian Flag Day celebration at Champs de Mars, Port-au-Prince, 18 May 1954. Courtesy of Collection du Cidihca.

wielded control of the army to forcefully break up all groups perceived as a threat to the regime. He reinstalled the secret police abolished by Estimé, and targeted all dissidents regardless of political persuasion. The independent press virtually ceased to exist by the beginning of the decade and the leading dailies, *Le Matin* and *Le Nouvelliste*, were muzzled. At a public address in 1954 Magloire coined a Kreyòl term that became a popular description of his method of governance: *kansonfèrisme* (iron pants).[12]

The success of *kansonfèrisme* owed much to changes in inter-American diplomacy. The expansion of global anticommunism in the fifties afforded Latin American and Caribbean leaders extraordinary latitude in dealing with anti-state opponents. The twin effects of McCarthyism and the Korean War fueled a more pronounced U.S. paranoia over the growth of communism in the hemisphere. The Eisenhower administration's Latin American policy therefore led the United States to supporting dictatorial regimes and discouraging economic nationalism as a necessary measure in preserving regional security against communist infiltration.[13] Although Haiti in the 1950s was classified as having "secondary priority" among Latin American nations with strong communist influences, U.S. intelligence found it nonetheless important to support state efforts to combat radical activity.[14] This was considered all the more urgent following the overthrow of Jacobo Arbenz in

Guatemala in 1954, when White House officials noted a rise in communist "societies" in several Latin American countries, including Haiti.[15]

Much like his contemporaries Trujillo and Fulgencio Batista in Cuba, Magloire portrayed himself as a beacon of anticommunism in Haiti and set about proving this with ruthless abandon. A *Port-au-Prince Times* editorial opined, "This government is in the vanguard of the anticommunist nations. [It] has shown itself to be zealous in its guarding of the nation against all communist encroachment."[16] As was the case with Vincent in the early thirties, global anticommunism played to the advantage of the Haitian government. The intensification of cold war politics and the commitment to fight against Soviet expansionism provided Magloire with the opportunity to use state terror to settle old scores by applying the communist label indiscriminately to all political dissidents.

The passage of official decrees to prevent the growth of leftism supplemented the use of state repression. The PSP, which since 1947 remained the only openly Marxist party in the country, was hardest hit by this policy. The government passed a law on 30 December 1950 abolishing the PSP and Fignolé's MOP. It cited the "dangerous maneuvers" of both parties, whose political programs would "only result in Haiti's collusion with Moscow and the execution of a series of plans against American democracy."[17] Their journals *Chantiers*, *La Nation*, *Notre Jeunesse*, and *La Famille* were also closed and all future newspapers related to either party were prohibited. Party members who resisted the law found themselves either imprisoned for brief periods or forced into exile. The remaining members of the PSP, Max Sam, Étienne Charlier, and Anthony Lespès, tired of constant harassment by the police, ended their political activities, and resumed nonpolitical occupations.[18] According to Sam, "since the fall of Estimé the leftist movement decreased rapidly. Under Magloire, we could not be politically active. We could no longer be militant. . . . We were followed everywhere we went and with the anticommunist law we had no choice but to remain out of politics or get thrown in prison."[19] Not all of the socialists gave up fighting against dictatorship. Rossini Pierre-Louis remained one of Magloire's foremost critics. The PSP's unstable influence over the labor unions ended also with the 1951 death of Francis Vulcain, one of the party's foremost labor leaders.[20] The Socialist Party, however, remained a frequent scapegoat used to raise the concern of the U.S. embassy and justify the dictatorship. For example, in 1951 the government suspected former PSP members of continuing recruitment and indoctrination in the provinces and attempting to foment a peasant uprising.[21]

As the demoralized PSP retreated from activism, their younger followers in the JPP fought to maintain a political presence, circulating radical literature among urban workers. The government responded by occasionally arresting its leaders.[22] In 1951 when police raided the party headquarters and found communist literature, the party was officially dissolved.[23] Former members of the JPP continued radical activity in reduced form during the decade and in November 1956 formed the Parti Populaire de Libération Nationale (PPLN), a party strongly influenced by Marxism. Two other prominent leaders of the student movement of 1946 who returned to Haiti in 1955 from studies in France and who gave impetus to the younger radicals were Jacques Stephen Alexis and Roger Gaillard. The groups met secretly with other Marxist sympathizers from the forties.[24] The PPLN, though having cells in Gonaïves, Pétionville, Jacmel, and Port-au-Prince, was a relatively weak organization; it would have a larger impact in the early Duvalier years.[25]

A lack of reliable documentary evidence on this period makes it difficult to determine the extent to which it influenced other groups. Nonetheless, it is safe to assume that the party as a whole was politically underdeveloped. The underground nature of its activities also meant it was unable to build a popular base. Clandestine activity, as the party bureau later admitted, required "organization, cadres, a popular basis and an experience of revolutionary struggle which the Haitian socialist movement generally lacked."[26]

René Depestre, who had been working closely with communist groups in France and Cuba and was then living in Havana, desired to return to Haiti to rebuild the Communist Party in 1952. His plans were thwarted when the Batista government arrested him for communist activities. Batista attempted to have him deported to Haiti. Magloire, however, refused to have his passport validated, declaring, "Depestre is a communist not a Haitian." Depestre was sent to France and did not return to Haiti until after the election of 1957.[27]

To combat communist influence, which they claimed emanated from contact between Haitian students and French radicals, the Magloire administration significantly reduced the number of government scholarships awarded to Haitian students to study in France. Another measure taken was the banning of all literature perceived to be communist. In Cap Haïtien the army raided a bookstore operated by an Italian national, and several Marxist books were seized. The owner along with his colleagues and family were deported.[28]

The success of military repression of Marxists in these years accounts for the extremely limited influence of these groups in the political battle of the late fifties. Notwithstanding organizational difficulties, the formation of groups such as the PPLN indicated a shift among urban youth toward new strategies of political resistance. A consideration of the activism of university students, who were unaffiliated with the Marxist left, supports this conclusion.

In the forties, the students at the graduate faculties of the university, the center of student activism, supported the *noiriste* state and its promotion of Haitian over French directors at the university. In the medical faculty, students therefore became upset when the new government reversed the moderate reforms in curricula under Estimé, and the Ministry of Public Health decided to send graduates to practice in provincial hospitals indefinitely, restricting their ability to practice medicine in Port-au-Prince. The more politically minded students associated with ADEM became most resistant.[29] Their protest against the government policies came to a head in January 1952. What began as a minor clash between a professor of pediatrics, Pierre Salgado, and a third-year student escalated into a serious political affair. When Salgado, an unpopular professor, accused a student of stealing a flashlight from one of the labs, ADEM intervened on the student's behalf, claiming that Salgado's charges offended the integrity of the entire student body.[30] The students refused to attend classes for two days, demanding a public apology from Salgado. The protest assumed political overtones when students from other faculties as well as interns in the General Hospital joined in sympathy. Minister of Labor and Health Clément Jumelle and the dean of the Medical School issued an ultimatum that the students return to classes or risk expulsion, a demand that went unheeded.

Once the protest attracted national attention, Daniel Fignolé mobilized the disparate supporters of MOP to rally to the students' cause. The attempt of the medical students to launch a general strike was, for the government, a frightening reminder of the events of 1946. Punishment was harsh. The entire third-year class was arrested and forced to sign a declaration calling off the strike. The most prominent leaders were sent to distant provincial prisons. Fignolé suffered most for his participation in the strike, as his house was stoned and set on fire by government-assembled thugs.[31] Though largely ineffectual, the strike demonstrated that political consciousness remained a crucial if latent issue during the period of "social equilibrium."

The government's attitude to Fignolé during the student strike provides further illustration of its blurring of divisions among radicals. Daniel Fignolé's support of the Magloire campaign in 1950 had a dual effect on his political career. To a certain extent, it was his fervent belief in his supremacy and role as the popular leader in the election campaign of 1946 that fired Fignolé's antagonism toward Estimé. His decision to support Magloire in 1950, therefore, was not political opportunism but a genuine view that with Magloire, who built a popular campaign on the basis of national union, he could finally assume the prominence he felt was denied him under Estimé. Still, Magloire's conservatism and aversion to radicalism made his pairing with Fignolé in 1950 awkward. It also further divided MOP leadership. In April 1953, Fignolé's trusted vice-president, Michel Romain, resigned from the party, taking with him a handful of the brightest members. Romain's reason was that "Professor Fignolé wandered from the principles and political line which MOP had followed since 1946 and [rejoined] with the common enemy."[32]

The strength of antiradicalism, the change in government in 1950, and the dissolution of MOP on grounds of "communist subversion" had indeed forced Fignolé to reconsider some of his earlier political views. From 1952 he refined his radical *noiriste* attacks against the bourgeoisie, presenting himself as a "National-Democrat" who firmly believed that "Haiti must be anticommunist . . . [and] truly democratic. Moscow-styled communism is certainly dangerous for the normal evolution of this little country."[33] He upheld this position in forming the Grande Parti National Démocratique, which was explicitly anticommunist and pro-labor. Changes in political orientation, however, could do little to relieve the worries of U.S. officials, who remained concerned over his popular strength.[34]

Nor could it stop his activism. In the legislature he repeatedly attacked fellow deputies who failed to support his proposals.[35] Moreover, once the illusory nature of the military government's democracy became more apparent, he resumed his attacks on the state. An editorial in his new paper *Construction* commented, "If the present government is as they claim all for the people, we are not beneficiaries of their plan. It is not with Mr. Magloire that we find this union as he has come to power with the former collaborators of Lescot and Estimé."[36]

In December 1953 he cofounded the Ligue de Défense des Libertés Publiques, a group of twenty-one oppositionist politicians, including Alphonse Henriquez and former PSP director Rossini Pierre-Louis. The main aim was to combat tyranny and antidemocratic tendencies in Haitian politics. Following the government's closure of *Chantiers*, Fignolé used a new journal, *Haïti Démocratique*, which operated out of his home, to publicize the ideas and activities of the group against the antidemocratic tendencies of the regime. The party's critique of Magloire was indirect. Nonetheless, after only two weeks of existence the government banned the league and on 6 January arrested eighteen of its members.[37] That night police barged into Fignolé's house, destroying the press of *Haïti Démocratique*, and arrested the professor and his associates. A decree permitting members of the National Assembly to be jailed was hurriedly passed and Senator Marcel Hérard, Pierre-Louis, and Fignolé were arrested and put in solitary confinement for three months.[38] Around Port-au-Prince Fignolé supporters were followed and in some instances violently beaten. Police Chief Prosper announced that the government had incontrovertible proof that the league was sponsored by international communists, that Fignolé and Pierre-Louis had planned to start an islandwide revolution, and that arms and bombs were discovered in the houses of its chief members, though this evidence was never made public.[39]

The retreat of the Fignolists was also indicative of a rapid decline in labor activity. Although labor laws under Estimé were upheld in the 1950 constitution, unionism was severely crippled. All major unions were closed down and even the half dozen that remained lapsed into inactivity. Labor leaders attempting to revive the activities of independent unions or incite strikes were imprisoned or murdered. In 1954 the strongest of the remaining unions, the chauffeurs (public transport operators), launched a strike in response to the high taxes imposed on professional drivers' licenses and the imprisonment of recalcitrant drivers. The chauffeurs were not only the best organized group of urban workers but also held the greatest leverage in the fifties, owing to increasing demands on public transport created by the growth in urban population. Thus the three-day strike, which found most bus drivers in Port-au-Prince hindering urban transportation through their refusal to drive, affected all sectors. In responding to the strike, the government arrested Ulrick Joly, the general secretary of the union, and tortured several of the striking chauffeurs as an example.[40] In the end, the union was forced to split and organized labor continued its slow death.

At the other end of the *noiriste* spectrum were the *authentiques*, once the directors of national affairs and now considered marginal enemies of the state. During the first half of the dictatorship, the most persistent fear for Magloire and his allies was the return to power of Estimé. To prevent this, Magloire launched a far-reaching smear campaign in which Estimé was painted as a communist whose regime accepted funds from the Communist Party. From Kingston, where he spent part of his exile, Magloire agents tried to convince the Jamaican government that Estimé was a "dangerous communist" and was to be kept under constant surveillance by local police.[41] State Department officials knew better but did play on lasting fears Washington had toward Estimé and worked to undermine his base of support.

In actuality, Estimé, embittered by forced exile and weakened by a lack of financial and popular support abroad, was in no position to effectively challenge Magloire, although he did consider the idea. Writing to a colleague from Jamaica during his first year of exile, he commented on the "isolation" he suffered outside Haiti and that despite Magloire's victory the support of black nationalism was strong enough among the population to ensure his return.[42] Whatever plans Estimé may have had to go back to Haiti were unrealistic: Magloire's spies kept close watch over the ex-president's movements in Jamaica, and the U.S. government, content with the order the new president brought to Haiti, were unwilling to support Estimé's efforts.[43]

Upon leaving Kingston and taking up residence in New York, Estimé continued to petition State Department intervention on his behalf to prevent the dictatorship, which, he maintained, was a contradiction to Haiti's democratic ideals. In his private communication with U.S. officials, Estimé sought to repair the image of his regime as black supremacist, highlighting the supportive role he gave to U.S. policy initiatives in his last year in office. He argued that it was in the interest of the democratic ideals of the United States to oust Magloire and reimpose his presidency. U.S. officials steadfastly refused all forms of assistance to the ex-president and showed little sympathy for his complaints that he had neither assets nor adequate housing, was ineligible for employment, and constantly victimized by racism.[44] The Estimists' dream that their leader would return to Haiti despite obstacles from the new government ended when Estimé died on 10 July 1953 of ulceric poisoning. Magloire organized a large state funeral for Estimé and arranged for an open casket to be held at Bicentenaire, the site of the Exposition. It was a clear sign to all that the *noiriste* leader was gone for good and with him, Magloire assumed, the ideas of 1946.

But in death Estimé's stature grew in ways the new government did not anticipate, and with it a blind determination among his adherents to avenge him. The Estimists who remained in Haiti, including several lower-ranking officers in the army, were under threat. Several who resisted Magloire's directives were forced into exile or, according to some reports, killed.[45] A few of the *authentiques*, including Séïde, Dorsinville, Vieux, and Bordes, were arrested and temporarily jailed for alleged communist activities.[46] Under threat and fearful of further reprisals, several former members of the Estimé administration reconciled with their military adversary and found their way into the administration. For Magloire, their presence completed the veil of national unity and political cohesion his regime claimed to espouse.

Not all were willing to side with the government. One Estimist who had some experience with labor and was willing to use the disunited unions to broaden his urban base was François Duvalier. Following Estimé's ouster, Duvalier like most, was relieved from his post in the Ministry of Labor. His medical expertise, however, allowed him to gain employment on a team of local doctors who worked with the U.S. Health Commission, the Service Coopératif Inter-Américain de la Santé Publique (SCISP), which launched a program to fight against a debilitating yaws epidemic then claiming the lives of hundreds of Haitians. During this time when anti-vodou opinion re-emerged, *Les Griots*, like the other *noiriste* papers, closed down permanently and Duvalier and Denis stopped entirely their ethnological writings.

Duvalier maneuvered his way into becoming a key figure in the post-Estimé *noiriste* movement. In 1950–51 he organized secret meetings from the safety of his office in the SCISP compound with other Estimists, members of the judiciary, and some lower-ranking officers, where they plotted the return of the ex-president. It was during this time that Duvalier began to lay the groundwork for his presidential campaign.[47]

Estimé's death also created divisions among his partisans. Jean David, Estimé's trusted lieutenant who held firm to his hostility to the Magloire presidency and who had the strongest support among the *noiristes*, presented himself as the heir apparent.[48] David's followers depicted Duvalier as untrustworthy, emphasizing his initial support of Fignolé and sudden switch to the Estimé side as a sign of his opportunism. David was clearly the stronger of the two, having shared a close relationship with Estimé. The shrewd Duvalier capitalized on the few political assets he had in order to win support. His work with SCISP has put him in contact with the peasants, a crucial base of support he would later draw on. Others were impressed with his asceticism and reputation for honesty. But it was the blessing of Estimé's wife, Lucienne Hertelou, that turned the tide for Duvalier, when she declared that shortly before his death Estimé had named Duvalier his political successor. Whether or not this was true or simply a political tactic, it opened the door for the doctor to become more politically involved.[49]

In the final analysis, the Magloire presidency represented more of a transition toward an uncompromising form of dictatorial rule than a return to the pre-1946 political order. The somewhat simplified view of his *caudillo*-style leadership, common in scholarly assessments of this period, belies his political background. Since the occupation, the Haitian armed forces remained the only autonomous political institution in the country, a fact Magloire appreciated and did not hesitate to use to his advantage. It is indeed ironic, then, that the first president technically voted into power by direct popular vote also closed the avenues of political participation.

Scholars have not always agreed on how to evaluate the Magloire era in Haitian history. Michel-Rolph Trouillot offers an interesting interpretation of the period, arguing that during Magloire's presidency one finds the beginnings of a totalitarian order that assumed full form under Duvalier.[50] David Nicholls challenges this view, arguing that Trouillot grossly misapplies the totalitarian label, as "it would be hard to think of any Latin American ruler who conformed less to the totalitarian model than the playboy Magloire."[51] It is true, as Nicholls has pointed out at length, that totalitarianism, in its most widely accepted sense, has no parallel in Haiti before or after Magloire. Trouillot does overstretch his argument by applying the totalitarian label to include army officials under Magloire, whose main purpose for implementing state terror was not allegiance to a particular ideology, but the preservation of personal power. In the fifties there was a more obvious shift away from ideology to a more blatant form of power struggle, one in which ideas occupied increasingly limited space. Nonetheless, Trouillot makes an important observation: that the nature of Haitian dictatorship began to change during the Magloire years and, by institutionalizing state violence, or at least the threat of it, Magloire presented a violent political alternative.

This repressive context is important to consider in explaining the state of the left during these years. First, it significantly undermined leftist morale. Radicals found themselves operating more clandestinely than during the thirties and early forties. With the collapse of the PSP early in the decade and with fewer radicals of the Lescot era still politically active, Marxist ideology became less powerful and the movement itself suffered a loss of political direction. In the long view, the epoch of *kansonfèrisme*, therefore, represented the end of an era for the left. Resistance became ambiguous, less ideological, and more diffuse. Even among the *noiristes* it is clear that in the struggle for supremacy between David and Duvalier, there was a shift to a greater personalization of the movement and less of a focus on cultural and ideological concerns. More than anything, Duvalier's ascendancy to the leadership of the *noiriste* camp represented a victory only for him. The fundamental difference between the political situation under Magloire and the one that prevailed under Lescot was that the suppression of the left (the brief formation of the Ligue de Défense notwithstanding) did not facilitate a forging of alliances.

On the other hand, by stretching the limits of the repressive machine of the state, Magloire ensured that future challenges against the state would be more virulent. The absence of opposition journals for most of the fifties essentially closed a vital forum for radical expression and contributed to greater tensions. Equally important was the creation of a revolutionary mystique surrounding 1946. Young radicals began to look to the movement of 1946 in ways quite different from their predecessors. As the decade wore on, fewer radicals were able to recall the corruption and factionalism of the Estimé years. Instead, a picture of the era as one of popular participation, democracy, and social justice was promoted. This allure, as we will see, would be exploited fully in the 1957 presidential campaign.

But political frustration only partly explains the background to the catastrophic state that defined the last half of military rule. Inherent in the resistance of the fifties was a growing sense of desperation on the part of the middle and popular classes. To properly explain why this arose with such force during a period of relative stability, we need to depart from the political narrative and discuss more fully the state of the Haitian economy in the 1950s, which thus far has only been briefly touched upon.

Beneath the Glitter: The 1950s Economic Decline

The Haiti that Magloire inherited was already experiencing economic difficulties. These problems, as noted in the previous chapter, took effect in the late Estimé years and were partially attributed to the financial backlash to the Exposition and the collapse of the banana trade, which created deep ruptures in the economy. Where Estimé directed his energies to social reforms, Magloire formulated a pragmatic plan of modernization encouraging the development of new industries, tourism, and the improvement of the financial sectors.

It is this feature of Magloire's administration that has inspired the common perception of the fifties as a golden era, one in which progress and development emerged for the first and only time in the country's history.[52] Magloire's most recent biographer, Raymond Bernardin, has emphasized that "his government was distinguished by the important realizations" which "gave a better life to all Haitians."[53] When measured against the economic disaster of the Duvalier years it is easy to see why this view is often repeated. Yet the perception is deficient because it ignores the critical decline that existed beneath what Brenda Plummer calls "Haiti's reputation as a carefree tourist fantasia" in the fifties.[54]

There were, to be sure, visual signs of improvement that flowed from the tourist industry. Tourism provided a qualitative improvement in the national image and international recognition. Plummer has convincingly argued that a changing attitude from anxiety to sympathy within the United States fostered a positive view of Haiti and served to promote tourism and a fashionable interest in Haitian culture. There were multiple manifestations of this. For example, *Lydia Bailey*, a major Hollywood film set during the Haitian Revolution, had its premiere in Port-au-Prince in 1954.[55] All of this was nonetheless cosmetic and reveals far too little. Statistical data suggest that during the early fifties there was an unprecedented increase in tourist traffic. By 1952 the numbers of tourists visiting the island more than doubled 1949 figures. Yet the same data show a decline by 1956, when the economic pressures were becoming more unbearable.[56] When compared with the numbers of tourist visitors to its closest island neighbors, Jamaica and Cuba, the tourist boom in 1950s Haiti was hardly striking. Between 1949 and 1956 the numbers of tourist visitors to Haiti averaged between 10,000 and 52,000. In Jamaica, for the same period it was 55,000–155,000, and for Cuba, 150,000–275,000.[57] Moreover, the revenue accrued from tourism, insufficient to begin with, was seldom regenerated into long-term development programs.

A more telling indicator of the country's economic status by mid-century was its experience in agriculture, on which the national income remained heavily dependent. Magloire's aim was to diversify the agricultural sector through the expansion of foreign investment. A political environment of stability, real or apparent, encouraged private investment. The government's open and favorable attitude to U.S. interests also resulted in a great outpouring of aid and technical assistance to the country. The United Nations, the World Health Organization, a U.S. Point IV program, and various missionaries began work in Haiti during the fifties toward promoting a higher standard of living for the peasantry. The impact was varied.[58] Most of the funds and assistance were incorporated in an ambitious Five Year Plan (1951–56) that Magloire hoped would lead to greater agricultural expenditures.[59] Magloire's pragmatic approach to development involved the promotion of coffee exports, which experienced yet another brief increase on the international market the year he took office.

To a degree, the government's development plan produced notable achievements. A desperately needed dam was built in the Artibonite (a project that originated in the Estimé era) for the irrigation of the neighboring provincial zones and eventually for hydroelectricity. There was also some development in transportation as several major roads were rebuilt connecting Port-au-Prince to distant provincial towns in the interior and north.[60] As with the changes created by tourism, these were surface improvements that only disguised deep-seated problems. They were also unsustained as the new dam failed to provide adequate irrigation and the road improvement project never extended beyond the major urban areas.

Similar to the ISI (Import Substitution Industrialization) programs of the time, attempts were made to expand industry from sisal and sugar to include cement, textiles, iron, soap, wax, hats, iron, and flour.[61] The government reactivated trade with France, dormant since the beginning of the war, and a French cement factory began operations in 1954.[62] Efforts were also pursued to exploit the country's small bauxite deposits through a concession to the U.S.-owned Reynolds Mining Corporation. Any benefits derived from these ventures proved nominal, as agricultural revenues in 1954 still accounted for an overwhelming 86 percent of the GNP.[63] The greater problem was that most traditional exports, including cotton, cacao, and castor oil, were in a state of rapid decline, regressing, as some writers have suggested, to low nineteenth-century levels. The situation was worsened by ecological degradation, deforestation, and soil erosion.[64]

The problems of the Haitian economy negatively affected the conditions of the majority population. Low productivity raised the cost of living of the peasantry, which since the forties was experiencing a demographic increase. The government claimed that the new projects promised more jobs but the small-scale industries that relied on basic technology and artisan labor could not employ sufficient numbers of peasant laborers.

The grim reality was that the country was very close to its economic nadir during Magloire's administration. Even at its height, coffee production in 1951–52 made very little improvement over its nineteenth-century figures.[65] Haiti, like Cuba, Colombia, Brazil, and Costa Rica, which faced similar problems due to a slump in coffee prices, received little U.S. assistance in price stabilization.[66] When coffee prices fell sharply by 1954, the government was unable to recover. The national debt rose sharply in the mid-fifties, nearing its highest figure ever for the fiscal year 1956–57.[67]

The weak reliance on one crop left the national economy open to unexpected crises in the export-oriented sector. The worst of them came in October 1954, when Hurricane Hazel roared across the island. An especially terrible disaster, Hazel increased dramatically the plight of the peasantry by leveling several southern towns, leaving approximately 5,000 peasants injured or dead, another 250,000 homeless and countless others suffering from various diseases.[68] The long-term damage to the economy was immense. Nearly half of the island's coffee and cacao crop was destroyed and with it the nation's leading source of revenue.[69] Although the United States offered over $7 million in emergency aid, it could not remedy the problems of mismanagement and regression that followed the dismal loss of the country's most vital exports. Food prices went up as the hurricane was quickly followed by an equally unanticipated drought.

In the urban sectors conditions were dire. The steady stream of peasants into Port-au-Prince, fleeing the plight of unemployment, malnutrition, and sickness in the interior, only added to the problems of overpopulation and underemployment. Estimates suggest that by the mid-fifties at least half of the population in Port-au-Prince was born in the provinces.[70] With a limited supply of jobs to meet the new labor demands, the numbers of unemployed swelled to alarming rates. Among the laboring classes, the problems grew more acute. Again, there was a false impression of progress. For example, Magloire increased the minimum wage rate from 3.50 gourdes to 5.00. But this figure is misleading as the cost of living rose steadily during the period 1952–56.[71] Although the government made much of its creation of new schools, primary school enrollment never rose above 20 percent for the duration of Magloire's term.[72] Furthermore, the living conditions in the city deteriorated as more than 60 percent of urban housing in Port-au-Prince was found in the squalid *bidonvilles* that ringed the wharf and less than 2 percent of the population had running water.[73] Public services were in shambles and telephone access became a luxury found only in government offices and the private homes of the elite. Murders in the cities and suicide rates in the provinces increased as a result. An editorial in a Port-au-Prince paper noted the deteriorating social conditions: "Haitian society has become a jungle where the knife is king. We kill to live or we kill [ourselves] to escape the suffering."[74]

The greatest obstacle to sustained economic development was the perennial problem of the corruption, nepotism, and graft in the government bureaucracy. This was an even more troubling concern in the fifties as Magloire's political clientele, in the words of one U.S. official, proved to be "far greedier than their predecessors."[75] The squandering of foreign loans inhibited the development of useful programs such as the Artibonite dam, which was poorly constructed at more than double its projected cost. Emergency relief funds for victims of Hurricane Hazel never found their way past the hands of government officials. The government exploited its limited resources to maintain an impression of development. Magloire officials who paraded in new gold-braided uniforms and lived in large villas in the hills above Port-au-Prince bore a striking contrast to the increasing numbers of urban poor. The chasm was difficult to disguise. In 1954 *Time* magazine ran a cover story on Magloire lauding his "black magic of dams, roads, and schools," but also questioned the fact that Prosper lived in a "lavishly furnished house the size of a U.S. small-city high school on $350 a month."[76] Magloire's version of Estimé's Bicentennial Exposition, the expensive Tricinquantenaire in January 1954 celebrating the 150th anniversary of independence, only added to the problems.

Economic and financial devastation not only created tremendous pressures on all sectors of the urban population, but also emphasized class divisions. Magloire's project of "social equilibrium" seemed to benefit only the contracting circle of bourgeoisie. However, even the more privileged sectors of the urban population felt the strains of the economic crisis. The low yields from coffee for the fiscal year 1954–55, the worst in the country's postoccupation history, weakened the economic power of the urban bourgeoisie and underlined the depth of the malaise.

The instability caused by the lack of outlets for political frustration made matters worse. In Washington U.S. officials commented on the nature of the Haitian economy and the potential problem it could have on political events.[77] The election of deputies in January 1955 provided a rare opportunity for popular resentment of the economic turmoil to be voiced. Running for reelection in the Chamber of Deputies, Daniel Fignolé threatened that the government would be faced with grave problems if it did not accept its responsibilities and gain desperately needed funds from the United States to lift the country out of its quagmire. The government responded in characteristically dictatorial fashion by rigging the elections and once again censoring Fignolé. Fignolé's miserable loss at the polls (93 votes to 12,823 for a virtually unknown candidate) was more than a personal defeat, but further proof of the government's unwillingness to open debate on the crisis.[78] When Fignolé protested, he was arrested, imprisoned, and reportedly beaten.[79] During election week, Duvalier, with help from his driver, Clément Barbot, organized a small strike of disparate members of the chauffeurs union. The strike, however, was betrayed before it could commence and the government came down hard on the plotters.[80] Duvalier was removed from his post in the SCISP and immediately went into hiding.

In sum, the economic and financial conditions in the republic reached crisis proportions by the middle of the decade. Although the economic program served to increase foreign attention and investment, underlying degradation exacerbated social and political inequalities and laid the basis for greater depression. We shall see how these circumstances produced different responses among the urban sectors. Still, even among certain sectors associated with state institutions, particularly the lower-ranking officers and lower government bureaucracy, there was growing disenchantment with Magloire's handling of economic affairs. This point is significant if we consider the gross disparity in wealth between the army high command and the underpaid rank and file. Even mid- to upper-level government bureaucrats were suffering in ways they never had before, as Magloire was forced to introduce austerity measures such as reducing payrolls and salaries and close some of the more favored diplomatic posts.[81] But these groups still occupied the lower rungs of the socioeconomic ladder. The economic downturn occurred at a moment when the political structure was beginning to alienate sectors of the power elite that had sustained it.

Thus, unlike the crises of 1946 and 1950, there was no single group beyond those directly linked with the state leadership willing to support the government.[82] The economic situation in 1956, for the first time since 1915, found all social and economic sectors opposed to the government. When this is considered with the repressive nature of the regime, it is easy to see how the economic understructure would reopen festering problems and erode the political base of the military state. The crisis of the fifties was more a result of intensifying socioeconomic frustration than it was a consequence of political discontent. The combined result was the eruption of a yearlong conflict beginning in the spring of 1956.

"A Question of Life or Death": The Presidential Campaign of 1956–1957

In many ways the 1956–57 political crisis accents the main issues treated throughout this book: a volatile contest for power sharpened by ideological resistance to the legacies of the occupation; intraparty rivalries; the reaction of a highly politicized army to changes in civil society; the decisive role of popular resistance in affecting national politics; the role of the United States in influencing local political events; and the transition from a black consciousness project of national unification to a struggle for partisan domination. Yet in other respects the events of 1956–57 were much more. A new political landscape created by the shift to universal suffrage increased the stakes. Far from being a repeat of old battles, the campaign's foremost character was not ideological but partisan warfare intensified by the personalization of politics. Direct elections, a recent innovation in Haitian politics, meant that candidates could no longer rely solely on surreptitious alliances with parliamentarians but had to contend with an enfranchised electorate. The result was political tribalism and violence. The use of violence to preserve political status had been introduced during the last phase of Estimé's presidency and extended through army rule under Magloire. In 1957 it was deemed a necessary strategy for victory. But what is most noteworthy is that the campaign of 1956–1957 was the last explicit political conflict along color and class lines. To follow the confused course of events our analysis must begin by carefully tracing the reanimation of popular resistance against military rule.

The movement to topple the Magloire government was sparked by political events at the beginning of 1956 and the urgent need for change, a consequence of the economic dislocation just described. According to a false reading of the constitution, 15 May 1956 was the official date of the end of Magloire's presidency. In February opponents and political hopefuls agitated public interest by circulating pamphlets and handbills calling for the government to honor this date and officially declare general elections. "The choice of the future president," according to one commentary hinting at the economic problems, "is for the laboring classes a question of life or death."[83]

The strongest of the emerging factions was the one associated with Louis Déjoie, the dissident *milat* senator who encouraged the fall of Estimé. Although the most powerful opposition bloc, the Déjoists were not the only ones prepared to openly challenge the regime over the question of the election. At least one of several underground radical groups, the Haitian Revolutionary Committee, surfaced and its anonymous leaders, many of whom were Duvalierists, began issuing bulletins calling for the overthrow of the regime.[84] When Magloire responded to his critics by announcing that his administration would last another year, students immediately rallied around various opposition leaders and began to protest. In Jacmel, Les Cayes, and Port-au-Prince student protestors organized strikes and burned tyres, which were immediately quelled by police with firearms and clubs.[85] Expectedly, the greatest display of violence occurred in the capital, where students at Lycée Toussaint tore down a picture of Magloire and burned it in the schoolyard before attacking the police.[86] Small groups of urban workers joined the students but proved no match for Prosper's forces. Magloire declared a state of siege and had thirty-five protestors arrested.

The events of May were a portent of greater problems. Radicals and various oppositionists had demonstrated that *kansonfèrisme* had not completely incapacitated their ability to provoke public disorder to their advantage. The violent reaction of the student protestors indicated a distinct change in the nature of popular protest. The peaceful "*bras croisé*" protest of 1946 had now become something more urgent.[87] By removing civil liberties and imposing a state of siege, the government only aggravated the problem while overlooking the main point of the demonstrations. Perceptive officials in the U.S. embassy noted that as a result of the demonstration, the "position of the government had been weakened and could become serious."[88] What prevented the strike from escalating into chaos was not merely police brutality but the lack of cross-class support among the opposition. Business interests, sensing that Duvalier and other Estimists were the principal instigators, refused to collaborate with their *noiriste* rivals. Similarly, Fignolists and the few remaining unions, which still felt pressured from the repressions of 1955, were unwilling to rally the labor groups to support the strike without real guarantees of success. Over the course of the next six months the opposition began to work together to build the coalition needed to topple the regime. Déjoie managed to convince the reluctant *milat* business interests that a brief alliance with Duvalier was necessary.[89]

In the meantime, the government fought in vain to restore its popularity and broaden its base of support. Magloire feigned an interest in democracy by encouraging the establishment of new political parties, though all leftist groups remained suppressed. The new parties that emerged were in reality a façade consisting of low-level government bureaucrats forced to declare allegiance to the president. What was most interesting about this new tactic was the government's willingness to couch Magloire's achievements in *noiriste* terms in an effort to weaken the growing support for the strongest of his opponents, Louis Déjoie. No longer the "apostle of national unity," Magloire was now the "black champion of the masses" who "struggled for ten years to render impossible any attempt to return to the regime of corruption." "To permit the return of the oligarchy to power is to betray the revolution of 1946," which gave "the sons of Dessalines the same rights as the sons of Pétion."[90] These transparent maneuvers to exploit *noirisme* had little effect on the majority of Haitians, who had not seen any of the purported benefits of Magloire's ten-year struggle. The excesses of the administration, the blatant disregard for political improvements or civil liberties and worsening social repression, could not be masked by rhetoric. Where Magloire could hide behind the achievements of Estimé in the late forties, his personal record lessened any popular support for him in 1956. Finally, during the six years of *kansonfèrisme*, the revolutionary mystique of 1946 began to take hold of the young urban poor, who collectively perceived Magloire as the very negation of the ideals of the movement. It bears mentioning that the main leaders of the May strikes, the high-school students, held no strong recollection of the struggle against Lescot.

Following the announcement of Magloire's intention to step down in 1957, the presidential race became more strident. While it contributed to the silencing of his opposition, it also opened the political field through the promise of free and fair elections. Various underrepresented groups began to increase their pressure on the government for inclusion. The Women's League and Women's Union, the two leading feminist organizations, also rose in protest against the government and began to push for suffrage rights denied them in the 1950 election.[91]

The government backed as Magloire's successor Clément Jumelle, a young technocrat who had held a post in the Department of Labor under Estimé. He served under Magloire as minister of finance and, like most of the prominent members of the cabinet, had strong presidential aspirations. He also had some support in the center and the south. Meanwhile, in the second week of September, the race intensified when François Duvalier officially declared his candidacy.[92]

With 1956 coming to a close, the political situation fast deteriorated. Factions among the elite openly criticized the regime and campaigned for Déjoie. The response on both sides was most often violent. For example, in November upon returning from a trip to the United States, Déjoie and several local businesspeople who had gathered to welcome him narrowly escaped being beaten by a small contingent of army soldiers acting on Magloire's orders.[93] The incident was only one of a series of horrifying episodes that erupted in the last two months of 1956. Duvalier supporters, working underground, launched a series of bombings around the city. The densely packed Marché de Fer became a popular site for such disruptions. Shots randomly fired by political thugs would frequently induce panic and result in the flight of vendors from the market and the closing of merchant stores and commercial offices.[94]

By early December Magloire's alternatives were dwindling. The efforts of the opposition to impede commercial activity proved successful. A "coup by word of mouth" followed and a weeklong general strike took effect. Peasants from the provinces, prompted by oppositionists, refused to bring food to Port-au-Prince, bus drivers parked their vehicles and intimidated private motorists to do the same, and shopkeepers and businesspeople refused to open their stores. The lower-ranking officers, many of whom were loyal to either Duvalier or Fignolé, did little to help the situation. To silence his opponents, Magloire resigned on 6 December and turned executive power over to the Supreme Court. As part of a prearranged plan with Levelt, he retained the post of commander-in-chief of the army. Under this ruse, Magloire immediately jailed over a hundred oppositionists, including Déjoie, and forced the Supreme Court to reject the executive power. With no executive, Levelt passed the power of the state to Magloire, who was to serve as a provisional president. Magloire attempted to force Washington into supporting his move. But the State Department, fearful that his presence would further larger strikes and perhaps a revolution that could be used by Soviet interests, was unsympathetic. Magloire unnecessarily angered U.S. officials when he suggested that the U.S. embassy was mostly responsible for the paralyzing strikes through their "interference with Haitian affairs."[95] When soldiers confiscated U.S. food supplies sent to lessen the economic plight, U.S. officials decided it was time for Magloire to "step aside."[96] A large general strike was again launched on 10 December. Two days later Magloire boarded a plane to Jamaica, and thus it was that the military dictatorship ended and Haiti plunged headlong into a political battle of proportions hitherto unknown.

The history of the long and chaotic second phase of the presidential campaign (12 December 1956–22 September 1957) is widely covered in the literature.[97] Conventional analyses tend to treat it as an isolated occurrence, disconnected from the march of postoccupation politics. As a result, the underlying importance of the battle and its significance in relation to the history of leftism and political opposition is underemphasized.

The more critical analyses of the campaign have pointed out that its defining characteristic was the strong emphasis on partisanship. Michel-Rolph Trouillot has lamented the absence of a sustained debate on the central issues facing the country during the late fifties, and the fact that candidates were merely content to build a popular base of support.[98] Patrick Bellegarde-Smith has gone further, arguing that the candidates represented "differing emphases, different social classes, or factions thereof, but no full-fledged ideological split as generally understood."[99] Indeed, the campaign as a whole marked a definitive break from the ideological battles that dominated political discourse in the forties. Nonetheless, there were signs of traditional antagonisms from that era. Some likened the euphoria of Magloire's ouster to Lescot's fall a decade before.[100] Significantly, all of the four principal candidates were linked to the revolutionary movement of the forties and drew heavily on this fact in combating each other. Analysis of pamphlets, editorials, and campaign speeches of the leading candidates highlight the ferocity of this contest.

Within days of Magloire's departure, a new provisional government was set up, headed by Joseph Nemours Pierre-Louis, head of the Supreme Court. The objective of the new government was to restore public order and set a date for elections that the new government and the U.S. State Department anxiously hoped would be 15 May. Nineteen candidates surfaced, all contending for the presidency. Among them were, for the first time since 1941, two light-skinned candidates, Déjoie and Alfred Viau, Trujillo's accomplice in the Roland affair, who had recently returned to Haiti. But the principal candidates were Duvalier, Fignolé, Jumelle, and Déjoie. That Daniel Fignolé decided to enter the presidential race came as a surprise to no one given his incredible popularity in the capital. Dockworkers chalked "Vote Fignolé" along the wharf, and posters of the young leader were pasted to locomotives and buses around Port-au-Prince.[101] Fignolé's entrance in the presidential race, however, worried his opponents early in the campaign.

Duvalier and Fignolé, both *noiristes* and former allies in MOP, were now sworn enemies unable to contain their aversion for each another. So divided were they that both men spent considerable energy in the early phase of their campaigns in a corrosive verbal war. Fignolé, who knew well the political views of his party's former general secretary, was especially wary of Duvalier, taking every occasion to warn that the doctor's political views could only lead to brutal dictatorship.[102] Fignolists contrasted their leader's constant agitation with Duvalier's perceived cowardice. Duvalier was referred to as the *"Captain' en bas Caban,"'* who had little record of physical bravery.[103] "Today," an editorial in Fignolé's *Mopisme Intégral* commented, "after ten years of preparation, initiation, and labor, . . . the religion of Fignolisme has taken over [the streets] of Port-au-Prince."[104] For their part, Duvalierists painted an image of Fignolé as a radical communist. A popular Duvalierist tract featured a "Fignolé of yesterday" with a photograph of a young Fignolé in a Maoist uniform and excerpts of his most radical statements from the 1946 campaign.[105]

Of the four, Jumelle was the least favored as far as U.S. interests were concerned. He was too closely associated with Magloire and held by many to be a main contributor to the country's dismal economic state. Color and class issues, as expected, were most venomous in the battle between Louis Déjoie and the black candidates. Déjoie was, in the language of the Fignolists and Duvalierists, a *"colon moderne"* and an *"aristocrat anti-peuple"* who "exploited without pity the Haitian masses."[106] Déjoie, the favored candidate of the U.S. embassy, did not shirk from upholding an anti-*noiriste* position in the face of resentment, calling the 1946–56 period "ten years of social regression."[107] He also drew attention to the contradictions in Duvalier's politics, warning that regardless of color, terror would be the result. "The candidate Duvalier has chosen his company . . . and it is the diabolic group of the reign of Magloire-Prosper-Estimé! Those men who used brutal force, call for the extermination of mulattoes and radical blacks and are not afraid to use bombs!!"[108]

The dominance of personal politics over party issues was also reflected in the minimal role played by labor and the Marxist left in the campaign. Independent unionism had by 1957 endured almost ten years of repression. During that period, unemployment increased significantly, further reducing the potential to organize. Workers thus invested their hopes in the success of political leaders who convinced them that they had the welfare of the laborers at heart. Duvalier achieved some level of success in securing the support of certain sectors with this tactic, and Fignolé remained the idol of the unorganized urban workers during the fifties. All this meant that the current of independent unionism experienced in the Estimé years had receded significantly and the demands of urban workers were framed in political terms rather than labor concerns. To be sure, unionism did reemerge. The chauffeurs, the most organized sector of the urban workers, held a national conference and attempted to start an independent union under Ernst Coulanges. There were also small-scale strikes early in the year, such as a HASCO strike for improved wages. Nonetheless, attempts at independent political organization among laborers were rare, as the majority of workers organizations were easily absorbed into the electoral combat.[109]

The Marxists shared a similar experience. The years of underground activity left Haitian Marxism in disarray. Tentative attempts to form organizations in the provinces, or to launch an independent Marxist journal, achieved little success, and thus once the crisis of 1956–57 broke out, the younger socialists were caught unprepared. Former members of the PSP who were unwilling to fight the tide of the debate could do little more than watch the events unfold.[110]

In fact, it was only Georges Rigaud's Alliance Démocratique that continued to maintain a liberal democratic platform amid the chaos and hinted at the independent organization of the previous decade. Its failure to make incursions in the camps dominated by supporters of the rival parties rendered it largely uninfluential. Other groups with Marxist tendencies, such as the PPLN, lent unequivocal support to Fignolé in the form of mobilization and financial support. Although this may seem somewhat contradictory given Fignolé's vehement anticommunism, it should be made clear that the relationship derived from reasons other than an acceptance of Fignolé's platform.

For many of the young radicals, Fignolé, being the only major veteran of 1946 at the forefront of the presidential campaign, held a revolutionary allure. His superior command over the majority of the workers in the capital won the admiration of a generation that increasingly privileged charismatic leadership over ideology. More pragmatic members of the PPLN argued that he was the candidate most closely linked to the laboring classes, and the party could have no hope of gaining a popular foothold without siding with him.[111] Jacques Stephen Alexis lent his talents to speech writing for Déjoie, whom he supported, a move that was heavily criticized by other Marxists. Justifying his decision in a letter to his estranged friend René Depestre, he argued, "In the desert of ideas and men that defines our nation after the overthrow of Magloire, Louis Déjoie appears to me to be the only one with a program which although incomplete, appears to be the best."[112] Lucien Daumec, former secretary-general of the PCH, became a speech writer and key figure in Duvalier's campaign. Thus the confused state of the Marxist left in 1957 precluded a collective allegiance among the disparate groups of leftists.

The tempo and tenor of the campaign also brought out the regional differences and tensions in the country. Fignolé continued to be the undisputed leader of Port-au-Prince and its suburbs. In the provinces, however, his influence was significantly weaker. There, the battle was strongest between Déjoie and Duvalier. In the south and southwest the majority stood behind Déjoie, whose platform and experience with agricultural development promised a more pragmatic solution than claims to black power.[113] Duvalier, however, dominated the north and Artibonite. The central base of popular support for all candidates was the large numbers of unemployed workers that migrated to the capital in droves from the interior willing to offer their services to the various candidates. All four men would make good on this as the campaign wore on.

In February, however, it was Déjoie who exercised considerable control over events in the city through his financial strength and merchant and commercial support. Thus when he called a strike in February against Pierre-Louis, who many suspected made a move in favor of Jumelle by supporting the resignation of the provisional cabinet, Déjoists succeeded in bringing business to a halt and forcing Pierre-Louis's resignation. The economy was paralyzed as returns from the coffee crop the previous year were much lower than anticipated and tourism had all but ceased since the outbreak of political violence. The immediate problem, however, was the interminable battle among the candidates. After much deliberation it was decided by vote in the National Assembly that Franck Sylvain, a black lawyer from Grand Goâve, would become the second provisional president charged with the task of calming the fractious partisans.

The Sylvain government was little prepared for the developments and daily political clashes. The army was also yielding to the divisions among civilians and saw its internal cleavages widen considerably. Among the lower-ranking officers there was a strong allegiance to Fignolé. The army superiors for the most part supported Duvalier, whom they saw as the most malleable of the four. A minority of *milat* officers backed Déjoie. Sylvain was pro-Duvalier and made it clear that Jumelle, Fignolé, and Déjoie would not have fair representation in the caretaker cabinet he set up.[114] For the next month, Sylvain and the army high command barely managed to keep up a profile of neutrality as they systematically worked to install the mechanism to ensure Duvalier's victory.

As tensions built in the city, Sylvain revealed his true colors. Acting on a questionable claim that Jumelle extorted nearly half a million dollars while serving as minister of finance under Magloire, Sylvain ordered the arrest of the candidate, who was in hiding.[115] He also dissolved the Senate and the Chamber of Deputies and attempted to arrest Fignolé, claiming that his popular radio broadcasts were illegal. His fatal move was to use voter registration in the provinces as a means of instituting the electoral machinery for a Duvalier victory. Not surprisingly, the Déjoie strongholds in the south launched riots and Fignolé's supporters in the capital followed suit. Along the wharf, a popular movement to overthrow Sylvain was threatening to erupt. On 1 April, a Fignolé-Déjoie led strike brought Port-au-Prince to a standstill. When a cache of homemade bombs and Molotov cocktails was uncovered the following day, Sylvian was among several Duvalier sympathizers implicated. The embarrassing affair left the chief of the army, Léon Cantave, with little choice but to force Sylvain's resignation on the grounds that he was an accessory to civil unrest.[116]

Two provisional presidents had failed to neutralize partisan tensions. A series of meetings of candidates and their supporters aimed at resolving the pressures caused by interim rule produced nothing of consequence. The army therefore determined the only solution was to form a civilian governing committee, a Conseil Exécutif Gouvernement (CEG) comprising thirteen representatives of the six principal candidates. It was entrusted with the task of restoring stability and setting a date for the election, which had been postponed because the fraudulent machinery installed by Sylvain had had to be dismantled.[117] Less than three weeks after its formation, the CEG collapsed when Duvalier withdrew his supporters, claiming that the other ten were plotting against his candidacy. In an impassioned speech that has since become legendary, Duvalier took to the radio imploring his supporters to remain strong, as the other candidates had "all gone mad."[118] Duvalier's speech was an adroit political maneuver to reignite public disorder in the main cities, weaken the influence of the civilian committee, and force a military junta that he hoped would ensure his victory.

The CEG, nonetheless, persevered and continued its task of voter registration and electoral preparation without Duvalier's supporters. This move also played to Duvalier's advantage as the CEG now appeared to be working on behalf of Fignolé and Déjoie. When the CEG, in an effort to stabilize the volatile environment for the proper conduct of electoral planning, banned all political meetings and prohibited radio broadcasts, the scene was set for disaster. Once a date for elections was declared for 16 June, Duvalier propagandists called it a coup to bring about the election of Fignolé. Duvalier's supporters in the Estimé strongholds of St. Marc, Cap Haïtien, and elsewhere in the north, refusing to accept the directives of the CEG, immediately set up their own committees and threatened to break away from Port-au-Prince. The scene was most dramatic in Cap Haïtien, where farmers in support of Duvalier erected a sixty-foot roadblock intended to prevent the transport of food to the capital.[119] All across the country, efforts at voter registration were marred by violence and rioting.

By the second week of May, it was clear that Haiti was perilously descending into full-fledged anarchy. U.S. representatives feared that the disorder would spread to other Caribbean and Central American states, and sent Gerald Drew, a veteran of the occupation, to replace the aged U.S. ambassador in Haiti, Roy Tasco Davis, whose ill-health was considered a liability at a time when the United States needed a strong presence in Haiti.[120] The national bank and the legislature closed down in protest at the CEG's handling of affairs. In Port-au-Prince, Fignolists engaged in regular conflicts with supporters of Duvalier. Hired thugs clubbed a group of women in the capital who had organized a peaceful protest in support of Déjoie.[121] Along the campaign trail candidates and their supporters were beaten, stoned, or harassed by rivals. A bloody battle on Flag Day, 18 May, which ended only when soldiers fired into a crowd carrying the blue and red flag in front of the

Cathedral, forced Cantave to oust the CEG and swiftly declare martial law.[122] Since Cantave was among the members of the army hierarchy with leanings toward the Duvalier camp, the move was read as a further attempt to block the democratic process and secure a Duvalier presidency. Supporters of the other candidates responded emphatically to their leaders' call for a general strike. Déjoie, using his significant influence, capitalized on the divisions among the soldiers and garnered support from various allies in the army to support the appointment of police chief Pierre Armand, who was also favored by the U.S. embassy as Cantave's replacement.[123] Cantave, however, was unwilling to give up power. With the dissolution of the CEG and the rivalry between Cantave and Armand, Haiti was literally without a government or a unified military.

On 25 May, the looming civil war came frighteningly close to materializing. A daylong battle took place outside the Casernes Dessalines, where Cantave and his supporters were in refuge fending off the onslaught of Armand's forces outside. Over a dozen civilians were killed and scores fatally wounded in the shooting. A contingent of Armand's soldiers from the Air Force attacked the Casernes and in one instance dropped a bomb (which miraculously did not detonate) in the heavily crowded street adjacent to the Casernes.[124] At the same time, Fignolé's *woulo*, under the impression that their leader had been arrested by Cantave, stormed throughout the city, stoning police and burning buildings, vehicles, radio stations, seeking to destroy everything in their path. Déjoie also capitalized on the moment, organizing his shock troops in the city with the intention of eliminating all of Duvalier's support. The homes of known Duvalierists, including Duvalier's own house on Ruelle Roy, were stoned and nearly torched. With neither side able to end the protests, the three black candidates held an emergency meeting under heavy gunfire in the Casernes that resulted in the official resignation of Cantave and Armand and the appointment of General Antonio Kébreau, then making secret deals with Duvalier, as the army's new leader.

The standoff between the army and civilian leadership reached its climax on 25 May. It was the first of two crucial victories for Duvalier. Déjoie's desperate attempt to turn the tide of the campaign in favor of the bourgeoisie was exposed by his participation in the bombing of the Casernes. That a member of the elite was willing to resort to such measures and exploit an already fragile situation discredited his campaign significantly. The alliance among the black candidates against Armand and Déjoie brought the class issue out into the open. The most decisive outcome of the conflict, however, was the decision of Jumelle and Duvalier, acting on the advice of Emile St. Lôt, that "in the interest of the country and the people," Daniel Fignolé was to be made provisional president.[125] The following day Daniel Fignolé, the man who for a decade was the centrifuge of urban protest, the most popular political figure in the country, and the only candidate with enough influence to stabilize the worsening situation, was sworn in as provincial president of the republic.

Fignolé in fact had become the frontrunner of the campaign a month before being named provisional president. He reformed MOP and, reflecting a less militant ideology, had its name changed to Mouvement Organisation du Pays (National Organization Movement) in 1956. Thus the day of his inauguration proved historically significant for his followers. Outside the palace and throughout the Champs de Mars his supporters were barely able to contain their excitement. From the headquarters of his new journal *Foi Sociale* in Carrefour Feuille, and from the buildings along the central roads of the cities, Fignolé's supporters poured out of the balconies, corridors, roofs, and into the streets.[126] Once Fignolé stepped down the steps of the Palace, he was barely visible in the sea of MOP flags, dwarfed by his legion of joyous followers.

Fignolé had a large mandate. In Port-au-Prince the efforts of the Duvalier-ists in the provinces to strangle the capital had moderate success, as many of the slumdwellers were starving and in desperate need of the restoration of food supplies. The closing of the national bank in the preceding months meant that there was limited money in circulation and the national treasury reserves were down to $6 million (U.S.).[127] The urban poor thus invested a lot of hope in the Fignolé government. Fignolé made promises to increase wages, made visits to the provinces where he examined agricultural condi-tions, and attempted to build a cabinet of technocrats to assist in restoring production, which had suddenly halted.[128] But a presidential campaign was still in effect, and despite a constitutional law barring a provisional president from running for election, Fignolé showed no intention of leaving the Na-tional Palace. His firmness in maintaining this and the way in which he set about instituting a series of reforms designed to strengthen support, such as raising the daily wage, both shocked and angered his opponents.

News of the leftist Fignolé's appointment was not only a serious problem for the Haitian elite, but also of grave concern in the United States, where the events in Haiti featured prominently in major newspapers and maga-zines.[129] That the Haitian crisis occurred only three years after the Guate-malan debacle only created greater fears among U.S. interests over the emergence of a potentially Communist government. At a meeting of the National Security Council (NSC) on 27 May, which included President Eisenhower and Vice-President Nixon, the Fignolé appointment was the first item on the agenda of developments affecting U.S. security. CIA director Allen Dulles warned that although Fignolé was "not exactly a communist," he had "a strong leftist orientation" and "was not especially friendly to the United States."[130] He was also worried that the "disturbing" situation in Haiti presented great difficulties to political stability in the region.[131] Eisenhower himself revealed his concern, in conversation with the Secretary of the French Embassy in Washington, that Fignolé "might eventually become another Arbenz."[132] The president's comment reflected the implacability of U.S. opposition to Fignolé. There was no formal U.S. recognition of the Fignolé government and officials began to publicly demonstrate their disapproval. Former U.S. ambassador Roy Tasco Davis, who had left the island in March, fanned the flames of distrust in Washington, claiming that he believed Fignolé to be the next Arbenz.[133] In dispatches to Washington, U.S. officials in Port-au-Prince commented that Fignolé's initial political program was "comparable with the Soviets."[134]

Fignolé found little help from U.S. blacks then engrossed in the civil rights movement. The U.S. black press that closely observed Haitian affairs a decade before now refrained from extended commentary on the campaign, partially betraying an inability to fully grasp the perplexing political situation.[135] Moreover, with the death of Walter White in 1955, Haiti lost its greatest supporter and lobbyist in the NAACP. Thus, all of Fignolé's strength following 25 May lay in his local supporters.

Popular support, though sufficient to worry traditional interest groups, was not enough to guarantee the survival of Fignolé's presidency. His left-wing reputation made it virtually impossible for him to garner necessary support from the established power structure. Fignolé's greatest failure in his campaign was to rely almost exclusively on the popular classes in Port-au-Prince without making inroads into the influential sections of the armed forces or business interests. Moreover, the fatal divisions among the black middle class, which had discredited him since his battle with Estimé, broke any strong support he could have gained from that constituency. Fignolé thus realized that any intention of using his provisional president status to remain in office would involve neutralizing the powerful leaders of the armed forces, the sector he most distrusted.

On 12 June, he attempted to weaken the military by ordering the dismissal of police and the addition of three hundred civilians, all of whom were his partisans. The palace guard troops were also disarmed and the lower rank and file officers who were devoted to him were promoted to key posts.[136] These orders created a serious problem between him and the new Chief of Staff of the Army, Kébreau. Fignolé's obvious plan was to reduce the threat of the army by undermining its leadership. What he did not know was that the army leaders, with U.S. knowledge, were already plotting to remove him from office.[137] Two days later the plan was executed. Kébreau gave the pro-Fignolé lower-ranking officers the night off, making sure they were disarmed before leaving the barracks.[138] At an emergency cabinet meeting, a small contingent of army officers broke into the president's chambers, kidnapped Fignolé, forced him at gunpoint to sign a resignation letter, and rushed him into a waiting car, sending him into what would become a thirty-year exile.

The army high command gave as the reason for the overthrow Fignolé's intention to take advantage of his position and weaken the army.[139] Not surprisingly, Fignolé did not accept the move and from New York, where he was exiled, he blamed Duvalier and petitioned Kébreau to have him reinstated, as he was still a presidential candidate.[140] But it was clear that no one would intervene on his behalf, least of all the U.S. government, which was relieved to see him go. In the following weeks, after failed attempts to win U.S. support for his presidency, Fignolé reconciled with Déjoie and decided to work with a base of exiled Haitians in New York to try and block Duvalier's election.[141]

The removal of Fignolé from the presidential seat changed the course of the campaign immeasurably. In retrospect, Fignolé's decision to accept the post of provisional president appears to have been a poorly conceived plan to obtain presidential power and use it to remain in office. But in the heated days of May, with army and bourgeois support split between Duvalier and Déjoie, it seemed the only solution to the crisis. Fignolé quite possibly thought that as president he would be able to curb the influence of the army high command. Yet there is evidence which suggests that his adversaries had been planning the move from before the fatal events of 25 May, and it was not, as is often assumed, a last-minute decision taken in the interest of public order.[142] Jumelle and his temporary ally Duvalier created a trap for Fignolé from the outset. Making the ardent Duvalierist Kébreau the chief of staff at the very moment Fignolé was given the appointment was a fait accompli assurance of Duvalier support.

But Daniel Fignolé was far more than a political leader; he was a phenomenon. The army had to contend with the reactionary force of his supporters in the streets of Port-au-Prince. Thus when word of the professor's forced exile was made public, the city broke out in protest. From La Saline to Bolosse and out of the cramped hovels that lined the waterfront, legions of Fignolists took to the streets, beating pots and calling for revolution. As hundreds of angry protesters marched through the streets of the capital destroying street lamps, Kébreau put the army into action. Truckloads of soldiers armed with submachine guns and flashlights drove around the darkened center of Port-au-Prince shooting as many protestors as they could find. When the protestors, wounded and frightened, retreated to the *bidonvilles*, the soldiers followed them and for another day continued the killing. The two-day massacre cast a frightening premonition of the mass terror imposed by the Duvalier regime. Contemporary journalists were astonished at the exactitude with which the order was carried out. Carleton Beals, a journalist for *The Nation* covering the campaign, offered a chilling description of the event:

> The new Caesar turned his soldiers loose on the slum districts—which comprise most of this city. . . . Unarmed people, demonstrating in favor of their fallen idol, Fignolé, were mowed down by machine guns. The hospitals are jammed and the latest estimate of dead reaches 476. The actual number cannot be known because all but the few bodies taken to the morgue were loaded into lorries and buried in the plain. . . . Many demonstrators and people dragged at random from their homes were dumped without food or shelter on La Gonâve. Every day trains of people are led down the streets by the soldiery, and every day soldiers have been terrorizing, by illegal search or arrest, the followers of Fignolé.[143]

Once Fignolé's supporters in Port-au-Prince were brutally silenced, the country lapsed into a state of controlled terror. A reunified army was again at the helm under a three-man junta, the Conseil Militaire de Gouvernement (CMG) headed by Kébreau. Washington offered little response to the brutality of the military and granted it full recognition within a week of the slaughter of Fignolists.[144] Kébreau capitalized on this international recognition and immediately censored the press. Editors of any paper, including MOP's own *Foi Sociale*, who published a photograph of Fignolé were subject to arrest. The judiciary was forced to comply with the army and strict bans were enforced against political meetings and debates.

The success of the army's efforts to eliminate Fignolé, the greatest obstacle to a Duvalier victory, strengthened the prestige and position of the doctor. All major leaders of the opposition were threatened and the two former PSP members, Rigaud and Pierre-Louis, were forcibly taken out of Port-au-Prince and exiled to remote peasant villages in the north, where they were kept under close watch.[145] After the press was silenced and a series of restrictive laws passed, in early August an election date was set for 22 September.[146] There is evidence to support the notion that Kébreau's support for Duvalier was not entirely assured, as Trujillo, fearful of an Estimist in power, made overtures to Kébreau to have him support Déjoie instead.[147] Although Kébreau wavered, there was little chance that any other civilian candidate was able to challenge Duvalier after mid-June. He had the support, no matter how uncertain, of the army.

In his analysis of the election, Patrick Bellegarde-Smith has argued that the real strength in Duvalier's campaign was the "decisive" support he received from the State Department, which believed he "represented progress and the emergence of the middle-class to political maturity."[148] While it is true that Duvalier received U.S. support, it came much later in the campaign than Bellegarde-Smith indicates. Duvalier's position as a member of the black middle class and staunch Estimist was precisely why the United States remained wary of him throughout the campaign. Concerns over radical reformism under a Duvalier presidency were indeed at the forefront of U.S. evaluations of the situation. We have seen how easily U.S. officials confused black nationalism in Haiti with communism. All the black candidates, at one time or another, were suspected of having communist affiliations or tendencies.[149] It was Déjoie, the candidate who seemed the strongest guarantor of the status quo, who received the strongest backing of the State Department until the month before the election.

After two frustrating meetings with the CMG, in which the U.S. ambassador pleaded with Kébreau to set a date for the election, Kébreau and Duvalier played their hand. Widespread rumors that the army would torch the U.S. embassy and "break relations" with Washington if it did not get support reached the ears of State Department officials.[150] In a letter to the State Department, Ambassador Drew noted his fear that if the U.S. resisted the army's handling of the election and push for Déjoie, there was "the danger Haiti might at least threaten to turn to the Soviets for help or that the Communists in [the] hemisphere or elsewhere might try to make propaganda."[151] By antagonizing Drew, and playing on fears of communist infiltration, the CMG won reluctant support. Thus, U.S. support for Duvalier came

François Duvalier and members of the army during the 1957 presidential campaign.
Photograph by Robert W. Kelley, Time & Life Pictures, courtesy of Getty Images.

late in the campaign and was not determined by a belief in his candidacy, but out of fear that, without support of the army, a Déjoie presidency would collapse and possibly open the country to communist influence.

With new confidence, Duvalier embarked on a countrywide campaign to galvanize support. Duvalier's campaign speeches made only veiled hints of the *noirisme* of the previous decade, cloaking his intentions and political beliefs behind a vague discourse he called *Estimisme*. This may have been a result of Duvalier's courting of members of the bourgeoisie during his campaign, which most observers suspected to be more crucial than Duvalier let on.[152] Throughout his campaign Duvalier never failed to exploit the revolutionary mystique of 1946 and to present himself as Estimé's political heir. A speech in Cap Haïtien was typical of the dozens he gave across the country on the last leg of the campaign: "The Revolution of 1946 broke the circle of iron. The progressive government of Dumarsais Estimé infused in the entire country a new blood. The peasant, the worker, the intellectual, the professional, were no longer molested, unknown or scorned. . . . I firmly believe in all these great ideas and sentiments, and that the people will be guided and will see past the materialism and vulgarity of the enemies of all spiritual authenticity and determine my victory on September 22."[153]

Conclusion

Support in the north and the commitment of important sectors of the army and black middle class were seen as insufficient guarantees of a Duvalier victory. In an election that relied on the popular vote, the CMG ensured that Duvalierists held all key positions in the communal councils, Supreme Court, and provincial electoral boards. Army officers loyal to the CMG were placed at the polls and, according to the U.S. embassy's report, ordered to intimidate Déjoie supporters and influence voters to vote for Duvalier.[154] In the south, pro-Duvalier sheriffs arrested Déjoie supporters on the eve of the election and placed them in jail until after all votes were cast. In certain provinces, fraud was so rampant that votes for Duvalier outnumbered by 50 percent the number of the local population. Two days before the election, the U.S. embassy learned of a plot hatched by Duvalier and Kébreau to arrest Déjoie and Jumelle immediately after the election results was announced.[155] Primarily out of fear, Jumelle withdrew from the election and urged his followers to abstain from voting.

Even such techniques proved unsatisfactory for Duvalier, whose supporters mobilized themselves into commandos known as *cagoulards* (masked thugs) and invaded the slum districts in Port-au-Prince, terrorizing all non-Duvalier supporters. On 22 September Duvalierists won the majority in all the *départements*, and their leader received 679,884 votes to Déjoie's 266,992 and Jumelle's 9,980.[156] Although Déjoie won the majority in Port-au-Prince and Les Cayes, his supporters were unable to gain any seats in the Senate. Extreme use of force, intimidation, and fraud, coupled with little interference from the United States, ushered François Duvalier into power and launched a dictatorship far more brutal than Jacques Roumain, for all his prescience, could have ever imagined.

CONCLUSION

†

The trees are cut down from time to time
but the voice of the forest never loses its power.
—JACQUES STEPHEN ALEXIS,
Les arbes musiciens, 1957

ess than a month after his November 1957 inauguration, during the debates over the new constitution, François Duvalier made a proposal to the National Assembly that startled many people in Port-au-Prince. Now that the *authentiques* were back in power, he insisted the Haitian flag be changed from its traditional blue and red bands to black and red, which, he argued, were the true colors of Haiti. Reporting on Duvalier's first month in office to his superiors at the State Department, Virgil Randolph III, the Secretary of the U.S. embassy, called the proposal a "new low" that did nothing but arouse "popular disgust." He also noted that given Duvalier's "impotence" he would be unable to carry through such a "trivial manifestation."[1]

It would be another seven years before a more powerful Duvalier would change the colors of the flag, and, by declaring himself president for life, announce to the world that he and the black and red flag were "one and indivisible." By then, Duvalier had systematically uprooted his opposition through forced exile, torture, and murder. Magloire, Fignolé, Kébreau, and Déjoie were in exile. Jumelle, who had remained in hiding since 1957, succumbed to hypertension two years later, not long after Duvalierists summarily executed several members of his family. The few leftists who braved this tyrannical rule suffered.[2] A form of militant communism briefly surfaced within the leadership of the Parti d'Entente Populaire in the wake of the 1959 Castro revolution, but it was effectively silenced with the brutal murder of Jacques Stephen Alexis in 1961. Across the country, terror-ridden Haitians shook under the tight grip of Duvalier's sinister militia, the Tonton Makout. In retrospect, then, Duvalier's 1957 proposal was further indication that an era that began with a vision of democracy and progressive social change had passed.

A nationalist movement that was unified in its aims defined the period of *désoccupation*. At the dawn of the thirties, the intellectual movement of the writers and poets of the twenties and the burgeoning political organizations among the elite youth worked in tandem to combat foreign occupation. By 1934 the struggle was shaped in terms that were primarily a reaction to the new social context that Haitian urbanites were forced to accept. By concentrating the balance of political power completely in favor of the bourgeoisie, the U.S. occupation served to intensify the conflict between the *milat* elite and the black middle class. The responses of radicals to this scenario were varied. On the one hand, elite radicals, led by Jacques Roumain and Max Hudicourt, clamored for a Marxist restructuring of Haitian society and greater attention to class differences. On the other hand, the small black middle class transformed an emphasis on cultural difference into a political discourse that advocated black power. Both groups drew on European theory in positing a political alternative for postoccupation Haiti. However, despite emerging from the nationalist movement, they shared little else in common.

In the thirties the divisions among the more prominent radical groups were clearly drawn along ideological lines. The dominance of the Vincentist state allowed little space for large-scale political mobilization. Moreover, the majority of the urban population, suffering from the effects of the Great Depression and underemployment, remained alienated from the radical groups despite the tentative efforts of the communists to build a working-class base. This began to change slowly as the decade wore on. The massacre of 1937 provided the first political challenge to the postoccupation political system. Popular protests against the government's weak response to the event, though having little short-term success, shattered the nationalist claims of the regime and contributed to a more fervent struggle for political participation.

During the Lescot years resistance continued. State suppression of organized political activity sought to limit the entry of radical activism in the political sphere. Lescot, however, proved incapable of containing the spread of radical ideas, and political dissidents from various social backgrounds worked together and employed different strategies to undermine the regime. Nonetheless, the ideological divisions remained, surfacing most dramatically in the first months of Lescot's demise. Ultimately, the tensions among radical groups after 1946 strengthened the armed forces and the established political institutions.

Ideological disagreements were but one factor that weakened radicalism. The fractious political history of Haiti during these years unfolded during a period of great change in the region. Radicals were constrained by an international environment that did not completely understand their objectives and was quick to apply the communist label to all forms of political activism. The attitude of the United States, which sought to maintain the political framework instituted under the occupation, had a dual effect on the revolutionary thrust of the movements. During the war years the expansion of U.S. capital and the attempt to "Americanize" Haiti intensified the resistance movement.

The combined efforts of the socialists, and a new group of *noiristes* led by Daniel Fignolé, sharpened the debate against the antidemocratic state. In many respects it was as much a critique of U.S. impositions as it was a challenge to *milat* hegemony. At the same time, however, pressure from the United States forced radicals to reevaluate their programs and platforms. Fignolé, for example, altered his *noiriste* rhetoric of the mid-forties the following decade, partially to avoid the antagonism of U.S. officials in Haiti. The result of all this was a great deal of ambiguity, as class analyses were, at times, confused with *noiriste* appeals to color.

The greatest outcome of the changing political environment was an intensification of the fratricidal battle among political groups. The concerted efforts of *noiriste* and Marxist factions in the struggle to topple Lescot dissipated with the clashes during the revolution of 1946. The elaboration of color conflicts and the opening of access to state power to the black middle class changed the face of political competition.

For all radical groups, the post-1946 period was a story of gradual decline. The pyrrhic victory of the revolution and its aftermath gave way to the ambiguities of the Estimé era. Urbanites profited from the Estimist emphasis on black consciousness that deepened the reappraisal of national identity started in the twenties. But the competition for state domination proved far more dangerous to the survival of progressive political parties and the opposition. Moreover, as the Estimé regime struggled to adjust to the new political arrangements, it was unable to overcome the inherent problems of a fragile state. Early attempts to improve social welfare receded as the *noiristes* fought to preserve their weak hold on the state. The new black politicians who formed part of the *noiriste* vanguard of the early forties succumbed to corruption and opportunism. For its duration, the Estimé government was threatened by the challenges of its *milat* and black opponents and leftist demands for greater inclusion. Faced with the constant agitation of independent labor and Marxist parties, Estimists adopted the same type of repression they fought against earlier.

By 1950 the socialists, communists, and labor militants were weak and marginal. With the emergence of the military dictatorship this situation grew worse. The failure of radical groups to remain a viable opposition was due to their inability to find a consensus in the face of a hostile state and cold war anticommunism. The opportunity for left solidarity occasionally arose, but leftists fell victim to the internal divisions and personalism that continued to plague Haitian politics. The PSP made no overtures to MOP even though the government often conveniently linked them to each other. The election campaign of 1957 presented an opportunity for a resurgence of the left. Yet the political context had changed considerably during the Magloire presidency, and conflicts among groups were reduced to personal battles for power.

The relevance of radicalism in the postoccupation era cannot be evaluated solely by these limited achievements. Divisiveness may have been the most enduring characteristic of postoccupation radicalism, but it did not mean that the movements failed to shape political events. Considered from several perspectives this contribution becomes clear.

The radical opposition's sustained critique of historical social divisions and dominant elite ideology, manifest in the rise of opposition newspapers and the formation of left-wing parties and unions, constituted an important element of protest. The politicization of the largely illiterate urban populace was in large measure a result of the efforts of these groups. By raising public consciousness, radical movements occasionally influenced state policy. MOP's call for greater benefits for urban workers provoked the Estimé government's passage of progressive labor laws. Although such achievements were few, they illustrate the influence of radical agitation.

At the individual level, the commitment of radicals to social justice served to inspire generations of militant youth. Radical journalists, intellectuals, students, and popular leaders took personal risks in their efforts to realize a vision of a democratic Haiti. Ostracized by their social class, elite radicals endured repeated hostility, arrest, exile, and even death. Non-elites suffered a great deal as well. Indeed, part of Daniel Fignolé's magnetism was due to his courage and stubborn refusal to accept the abuses of the state despite the harsh repression he received. The result of these efforts can be found in the high regard the revolutionary youth of 1946 held for Jacques Roumain, and the unceasing popularity of Fignolé and MOP throughout the period.

Through their influence over other groups, radicals of the forties and fifties provided an example for future protests against the state.

The activities of radicals also exposed the inherent weaknesses of the state. The most visible outcome of the occupation was the reaffirmation of the power of the traditional political elite that claimed legitimacy based on superiority. Under Vincent and especially Lescot, the Haitian bourgeoisie experienced its greatest period of domination since the turn-of-the-century. The radical vanguard from the elite and middle class sectors, through radical organs, strikes, and protests, was chiefly responsible for bringing the contradictions of elite rule to the surface. The bourgeois nationalism championed by Vincent faltered following the urban protests of 1937–38. Over the course of the next two decades, the postoccupation state had to adopt an increasingly repressive stance in order to combat the expansion of political dissidence. That all the governments from 1934 to 1957, in spite of their increasingly repressive styles, reached an end in the wake of political crises and popular unrest owes as much to the spirited influence of radicalism as to the provocations of presidential aspirants. In the end, it was only through state terror that these movements were silenced.

A further indication of the significance of radicalism during these years was its direct role in changing the political culture. This was a result of the expansion of radical ideas from the militant elite to incorporate the radical youth, professionals, and the popular classes in Port-au-Prince. These groups, once excluded from political discourse, became an important part of the movements of the forties. To be sure, much of this expansion derived from social and economic conditions in the country. Cyclical economic crises, typical of a poor and unstable export economy, worsened social conditions. The Haitian economy, while experiencing brief periods of relative success, made only marginal improvements. The negative results were high rates of unemployment, rapid urbanization, and a desperately low standard of living. Such factors aggravated tensions between civil society and the state. The failure of all the postoccupation administrations to address these problems contributed to the influence of the opposition.

The Lescot regime's policy of limiting black inclusion in the government and its emphasis on foreign capital penetration allowed the protests of the period to be framed in terms that went beyond politics. The ideological foundations of the radical movements—color and race consciousness, anti-elitism, Marxism, and revolutionary nationalism—became powerful weapons in the protest against the Lescot presidency. This appeal did not end with the rise of a black government. The *noiristes* of the late forties, while promising to build new political institutions, met the same fate as their predecessors.

The efforts of the radicals were also integral to the creation of a culture of resistance reflected in the expressions of black consciousness in music and the arts. This cultural protest against social contradictions in Haiti broadened the appeal of black radicalism. An emphasis on an authentic Haitian culture, which included recognition of Kreyòl and vodou, was an important part of the radical discourse of the *noiristes* and, to a much lesser extent, the Marxists. Much of this drew on a romanticized view of peasant culture. The attitudes of the *noiristes*, for example, were often self-serving claims to political legitimacy. Still, they were able to effectively challenge the dominant francophilia and political control of the ruling elite, and complemented the exposure of radical political ideas among the popular classes.

Similarly, the emergence of a small yet significant labor movement in 1946 allowed radicals a large degree of influence among the popular classes. The brief period in the mid-forties when political meetings and labor unions were legalized facilitated greater contact with the laboring classes. For some groups such as MOP, this proved key in allowing the party to exert its influence and to score small victories for workers.

Perhaps the greatest testimony of the impact of postoccupation radicalism is its influence on the post-Duvalier years. The popular movement that overthrew Jean-Claude Duvalier in February 1986 bore striking resemblance to similar events forty years earlier. The nationwide protests that toppled the once monolithic Duvalierist state grew among a militant opposition that galvanized support from elite radicals and the popular classes.

In the immediate aftermath, it was to the radicals of the postoccupation era that the popular classes looked for guidance. An ailing Daniel Fignolé returned to a hero's welcome in Haiti in March 1986 with scores of excited supporters awaiting his arrival at the airport. His death a few months later dashed many of their hopes of him returning to the seat of power. Other militants of the fifties also returned to Haiti and achieved some success in reviving the labor movement and developing opposition parties. One prominent voice of the post-Duvalier opposition was Jean Dominique, a former member of the youth arm of the PSP, who used radio to inform the popular classes of the machinations of the post-Duvalier regimes. The outpouring of international attention over his assassination in 2000 bears witness to the wider influence of postoccupation radicals.

This influence has extended to a new generation of politically conscious and militant movements. In contemporary Haitian popular culture we find some of the more obvious incarnations. The emergence of the *rasin* (roots) movement in Haitian music in the post-Duvalier years, with its conscious appropriation of vodou chants and motifs, harkens back to the black consciousness movements of the forties. Groups such as Boukman Eksperyans and RAM celebrate indigenous culture in ways that recall their vodou-djazz forebears.

In the rise of popular leaders such as Jean-Bertrand Aristide and the powerful *Lavalas* movement, we find shades of Fignolisme and the enduring symbolism of the *woulo*. Indeed, comparisons between Fignolé and Aristide are found in discussions of contemporary Haitian politics.[3] While there are obvious similarities in their popular appeal, both men have notable differences. Aristide's massive support outside the capital was something the urban leader Fignolé was unable to achieve. Nonetheless, the roots of Aristide's use of political symbolism, popular appeal, and mobilization can be traced to Fignolé.

In several ways, then, we may conclude that Haitian radicalism despite its many shortcomings played a leading role in influencing the politics of the postoccupation period and beyond. By focusing on its limitations and failures, historians have underappreciated its significance. This general view in the literature stems from an overemphasis on color divisions in Haitian politics and society. As this book has shown, the color question has always been central to political relations in Haiti. Yet color conflicts were but one of a multiplicity of concerns that guided radicals and informed political protest. Issues of class, a struggle for democracy, anti-imperialism, and competition for state control were quite often equally pronounced.

The concerns of Haitian radicals refracted on broader pressures for change within the African Diaspora. From Senegal to Selma, black activists saw themselves as part of a global battle against legacies of imperialism and colonialism. U.S. black activists looked to Haiti during their own struggles for civil rights and placed Haiti firmly within the orbit of African Diaspora politics. Penny Von Eschen has argued that in the period between 1937 and 1957, U.S. blacks developed an "internationalist politics" that "linked African-Americans with Africa and the Caribbean."[4] Organizations and personalities in the United States, such as the small group in New York that formed the "Committee for the release of Jacques Roumain" in the early thirties, Rayford Logan, Walter White, and the NAACP, found solidarity with Haitian political actors even if, at times, they were unable to make sense of Haiti's perplexing politics.

Similarly, the experience of radicalism in postoccupation Haiti can be seen as part of a pattern of resistance in the modern Caribbean. Although the conditions and scale were quite different, Cuban politics followed a similar trajectory to the Haitian experience in the period between the fall of the Machadato in the revolution of 1933 and the victory of Fidel Castro in 1959.[5] For the Anglophone Caribbean, the height of political radicalism arrived the following decade. During the thirties and forties, labor upheavals and an anticolonial fight against British imperialism swept across the British Caribbean. The real gains of these movements resulted in the granting of self-government in the sixties. In Trinidad and Jamaica, both of which gained independence in 1962, the period from the early sixties to the early seventies was characterized by a pronounced struggle for radical change in the face of a gradual shift in political power from the colonial authorities to a local elite. In these postcolonial states, issues of color, race, anti-imperialism, heritage, and class-consciousness figured prominently in the political clashes between charismatic black nationalists and Marxists. Although Anglophile radicals did not explicitly follow a Haitian model, the contest for power among them evolved in ways that closely resembled the Haitian experience.[6]

In this sense, the political experience of radicalism in Haiti from 1934 to 1957, with its expansion of historical struggles and tensions, foreshadowed developments elsewhere in the Caribbean and may therefore be regarded as an important chapter in the history of Caribbean resistance.

Conclusion

One of the first things the astute visitor notices upon entering Haiti's Musée Panthéon in Port-au-Prince is the absence of any displays on the twin regimes of François and Jean-Claude Duvalier. Amid the rich collection of pre-Columbian artifacts and relics of Haiti's impressive past, there is scarcely a hint of an era that lasted three decades. This absence is noted in the country at large. The Duvalier name, once emblazoned on schools, hospitals, the national airport, and the national currency, is today nowhere to be found. The blue and red colors have long returned to the national flag and the Duvalierist black and red is now an image most people do not care to remember. If in nothing else, *dechoukaj* in 1986 successfully erased the physical memory of the harsh years of Duvalierism.

But that process of forgetting involves a further separation from the pre-Duvalier past. As the years advance, this past dims in the collective memory of the nation. An earlier era of red and black, defined by a struggle between

Marxists and *noiristes*, *milat* and black, and state and civil society, remains distant for Haitians in the twenty-first century confronting interminable obstacles to political stability. Considered in the midst of the political chaos that followed the end of Duvalierism and the fall of Aristide in 2004, the postoccupation period becomes at best a missed opportunity, and at worst a complete failure.

Yet the positive legacies of the era continue to resound in many ways. The resistance to color and class prejudice, an emphasis on grassroots political organization, and the enduring fight for the realization of true democracy in Haiti are rooted in the indefatigable efforts of the men and women who refused to accept the legacies of foreign occupation. It is true that the power struggles of the period inflicted deep scars on the nation. But the clamor for radical change in the face of escalating repression, a legacy of the era, has served to invigorate post-Duvalier Haiti. In the end, the postoccupation period should be remembered for what it was: a defining moment in the long history of the Caribbean and Latin America's first independent nation.

Abbreviations

The following abbreviations are used throughout the notes.

ANH	Archives Nationales d'Haïti, Port-au-Prince
BHFIC	Bibliothèque Haïtienne des Frères de L'Instruction Chrétienne, Port-au-Prince
BHPSE	Bibliothèque Haïtienne des Pères du Saint-Esprit, Port-au-Prince
DDEL	Dwight D. Eisenhower Library and Museum, Abilene, Kansas
FDRL	Franklin D. Roosevelt Library and Museum, Hyde Park, New York
FRUS	United States Department of State, *Foreign Relations of the United States, 1941–1957* (Washington, D.C.: Government Printing Office, 1962–87).
HSTL	Harry S. Truman Library and Museum, Independence, Missouri
LC	Library of Congress, Manuscript Division, Washington, D.C.
MAE	Ministère des Affaires Étrangères, Archives Diplomatiques, Quai D'Orsay, Paris
MSRC	Moorland-Spingarn Research Center, Howard University, Washington, D.C.
NAACP Papers	National Association for the Advancement of Colored People Papers
NSC Papers	National Security Council Papers
OF	Official File
POF	President's Official File
PPF	President's Personal File
PSF	President's Secretary's File
RG	Record Group
RU	Special Collections and University Archives, Rutgers University, New Brunswick, N.J.
SCRBC	Schomburg Center for Research in Black Culture, New York Public Library, New York
UF	Special Collections, University of Florida, Gainesville
USNA	U.S. National Archives II, College Park, Maryland
WHCF	White House Central File

Introduction

1. *Le Nouvelliste*, 3 January 1934.

2. There are some notable exceptions. In particular, Michel Hector's pioneering study,

Syndicalisme et socialisme en Haïti, and the collection of period documents and interviews in *Trente ans* and *Pouvoir noir*.

3. See, for example, Rotberg, *Haiti: The Politics of Squalor*; Heinl and Heinl, *Written in Blood*; and Bellegarde-Smith, *Haiti: The Breached Citadel*. A glance at Laguerre, *The Complete Haitiana*, and Lawless, *Haiti: A Research Handbook*, reveals the dearth in studies of the postoccupation period.

4. Lewis, *Main Currents in Caribbean Thought*, 317.

5. On popular perceptions of Arab-Haitians see Plummer, "Race, Nationality, and Trade."

6. In this book I use the Kreyòl term *"milat"* as opposed to "mulatto" or *"mulâtre"* in reference to the predominantly light-skinned Haitian elite, in an attempt to provide a more inclusive definition of the various social groups that compose the elite. The common usage of "mulatto," or *"mulâtre,"* which refers to someone of mixed white and black ancestry, is often misapplied in the Haitian case where there exist several categories ascribed to light-skinned people (for example, *griffe, grimelle, grimault, brun, marabou, clair*). Moreover, there is a strong correlation between color, class, and culture in Haiti that impacts significantly on the way people of different phenotypes are perceived. Reference to a light-skinned person as "mulatto" in Haiti acknowledges phenotype but does not necessarily refer to social status. In Kreyòl, however, the term *milat* contains reference to class and not just color, as exemplified by the oft-cited Kreyòl quote credited to nineteenth-century army leader Jean-Jacques Acau, "Neg rich se *milat*, *milat* pòv se neg" (the rich black is a *milat*, the poor *milat* is a black). Considering these differences, *milat*, though imperfect, is a more encompassing definition of someone who is both light-skinned and of a certain social class. For similar reasons, *milat* is used by Daniels in "Review," 156, 159, and Largey, *Vodou Nation*. The term "mulatto" is used only when quoting directly from the sources.

7. The historical relationship between social status, color, and class in Haiti is well treated in Labelle, *Idéologie de couleur*, and Michel-Rolph Trouillot's provocative discussion on these issues, "Culture, Color, and Politics in Haiti." Though brief, Manigat's *Ethnicité, nationalisme, et politique* contains some insightful comments on the uses of color in Haitian political history since the nineteenth century. On the racial ideologies of the nineteenth-century Liberal Party, see Lewis, *Main Currents in Caribbean Thought*, 261–64.

8. For more on the ideologies of the nineteenth-century thinkers see Dash, "Blazing Mirrors," and Bellegarde-Smith, "Haitian Social Thought." For an examination of non-elite political activity during the nineteenth century, see Sheller, *Democracy After Slavery*.

9. Leyburn, *The Haitian People*. Leyburn's thesis drew heavily on John Lobb, "Caste and Class in Haiti." It also sparked a major debate among Haitian scholars of the forties. See the critique by Jean Price-Mars, "Classe ou caste?"

10. Leyburn, *The Haitian People*, 4.

11. Ibid., 101.

12. Nicholls, *From Dessalines to Duvalier*, xliii.

13. For further critique of Nicholls's thesis, see Lundahl, "Economies of Colour," and Smith, *"From Dessalines to Duvalier* Revisited."

14. Trouillot, "Culture, Color, and Politics in Haiti," 154–55.

15. Trouillot, *Haiti: State against Nation*, 110.

16. Haitian scholars have done the best work on peasant resistance during the occupation. See, for example, Roger Gaillard's seminal multivolume study *Les Blancs débarquent* and Georges Michel's monograph *Charlemagne Péralte*.

17. Corvington, *Port-au-Prince au cours des ans*, 5:235.

18. On the background of the more prominent of these writers see Trouillot, "Jeux de mots, jeux de class."

19. Price-Mars in *So Spoke the Uncle*, 7.

20. Ibid., 218.

21. Fowler, *A Knot in the Thread*, 59.

22. See the account of one of the commissioners, Fletcher, "Quo Vadis Haiti?," 541.

23. These events are covered in detail in Plummer, "Black and White in the Caribbean," 663–73. On the strike at Damien see Savaille, *La grève de 29*. The details on the Forbes Commission are analyzed in Shannon, "U.S. Commission." See also Logan, "International Status of the Negro," 36–38, and Péan, "Unité et conjoncture," 29–31.

24. Nicholls, *From Dessalines to Duvalier*, 166.

25. For example, in 1936 the journal *La Relève* devoted an entire issue to Vincent, the "Second Liberator" of Haiti. See *La Relève*, March–May 1936.

Chapter 1

1. Gunther, "Hispaniola," 776.

2. On the confusion between radical black nationalism and Bolshevism in the United States during the twenties, a situation that closely resembles the discussion here, see Kornweibel, *"Seeing Red,"* and James, *Holding Aloft the Banner of Ethiopia*, chap. 5, 284–86.

3. Commandant of the Garde d'Haïti to the American High Commissioner, 18 February 1930, Port-au-Prince, USNA, RG 59, 838.00/1830, M-1246, roll 1.

4. Fowler, *A Knot in the Thread*, 303. See also Péan, "Unité et conjoncture," 32–33.

5. Fowler, *A Knot in the Thread*, 1.

6. Based on information in Fowler, *A Knot in the Thread*, 6–12.

7. Jacques Roumain to Tristan Rémy, n.d. [ca. 1932], reprinted in *Haïti Journal*, 4 January 1933. The purpose of this letter, as Roumain later explained, was to provide Rémy with biographical information for a proposed French edition of his novel *La Montagne ensorcelée*. Haitian authorities, however, later used it against him. See the article "Une Lettre de Jacques Roumain," *Haïti Journal*, 6 January 1933. The substance of the letter is discussed in Fowler, *A Knot in the Thread*, 140–41.

8. Rey-Charlier, "Note d'introduction," 279–81. Information on Christian Beaulieu's background is sparse. Apart from being an instrumental member of the communist movement, Beaulieu was also a pioneer in the teaching of Kreyòl in Haiti, developing a program against illiteracy that involved instruction in the native language, an initiation that would take decades to be realized. Some indication of his political life from the twenties and contribution to public education is given in Hector, *Syndicalisme et socialisme en Haïti*, 31.

9. Fowler, *A Knot in the Thread*, 142.

10. Ibid., 143.

11. "Memorandum of Conversation with Sténio Vincent Re-Communists in Haiti," enclosure to Norman Armour to Secretary of State, 13 January 1932, Port-au-Prince, USNA, RG 59, 838.00B/12, M-1246, roll 6.

12. Norman Armour to Secretary of State, "Communist Activities in Haiti," 6 January 1933, Port-au-Prince, USNA, RG 59, 838.00B/11, M-1246, roll 2.

13. Auguste, Manigat, and Dominique, *Haití*, 82.

14. Norman Armour to Secretary of State, "Communist Activities in Haiti," 6 January 1933, Port-au-Prince, USNA, RG 59, 838.00B/11, M-1246, roll 6; Fowler, *A Knot in the Thread*, 144; Hector, *Syndicalisme et socialisme*, 182.

15. Norman Armour to Secretary of State, "Communist Activities in Haiti," 6 January 1933, Port-au-Prince, USNA, RG 59, 838.00B/11, M-1246, roll 6.

16. See for example, *L'Action National*, 5 January 1933; *Le Nouvelliste*, 2 January 1933; *Haïti-Journal*, 6 January 1933; "Press Statement of International Labor Defense," enclosure to Norman Armour to Secretary of State, 3 January 1933, New York, USNA, RG 59, 838.00B/12, M-1246, roll 6.

17. See "Une Lettre de Max Hudicourt au Directeur du 'Temps,'" in *Le Nouvelliste*, 15 June 1933.

18. *Haïti Journal*, 6 January 1933.

19. *Le Nouvelliste*, 12 February 1933; Fowler, *A Knot in the Thread*, 147.

20. Rey-Charlier, "Note d'introduction," 280; *Combat*, 6 February 1946.

21. The PCH was the most important progressive movement formed in the summer of 1934 but not the only one. The womens' movement also organized in 1934, forming the Ligue Feminin d'Action Sociale, led mainly by women from the elite. The Ligue had its own journal, *Voix des Femmes*, and protested for female suffrage, the repeal of child labor laws, and education reform. On the early activities of the Ligue, see the articles in *L'Assaut*, 12, 15, 19, 20 April and 29 March 1935. See also Chancy, *Framing Silence*, 38, and Seza, "Koudèy sou istwa."

22. *Manifeste de la Réaction Démocratique*; Fowler, *A Knot in the Thread*, 150.

23. Comité Central du Parti Communiste, "L'Analyse schématique 32–34," 1934, typescript, BHFIC.

24. Ibid., 33–34.

25. Ibid., 35.

26. Ibid.

27. Ibid., 35.

28. Ibid., 36.

29. Ibid.

30. Fowler, *A Knot in the Thread*, 155.

31. Roumain in his defense argued that *L'Analyse schématique* was not a secret brochure and had in fact been made available to the Department of Interior as stipulated by law. For details on the trial see *Haïti Journal*, 16 October 1934; *Le Nouvelliste*, 16, 20, and 23 October 1934; Roumain, "Haiti," 14; Auguste Manigat, and Dominique, *Haití*, 89–91; Trouillot, *Dimensions et limites de Jacques Roumain*, 102; Fowler, *A Knot in the Thread*, 153–56.

32. [Illegible] to Secretary of State of the Interior and his Bureau, 6 December 1934, Port-au-Prince, Corréspondence Ministère de la Justice, folder 1272, ANH.

33. Robert Cummings to Secretary of State, 24 March 1933, Mexico City, USNA, RG 59, 838.00/3124, M-1246, roll 3.

34. Stanley Woodward to Secretary of State, 12 October 1934, Port-au-Prince, USNA, RG 59, 838.00B/17, M-1246 roll 6; Fowler, *A Knot in the Thread*, 156.

35. *Haïti Journal*, 16 October 1934.

36. [Illegible] to Secretary of the State of the Interior, 11 January 1935, Port-au-Prince, Corréspondence Ministère de la Justice, folder 1272, ANH.

37. See, for example, *Opportunity* 12 (October 1934): 3–4.

38. F. N. Shepherd to Eden, 23 June 1936, Port-au-Prince, *British Documents on Foreign Affairs, 1936*, 340. In 1936 Vincent, in an effort to appear democratic, declared that he would serve a second term only if there was popular support. The government thus installed a popular referendum. The U.S. minister described the "travesty" of Haiti's first experience with voting since the occupation this way: "The whole day is a holiday. . . . Voters are rounded up and brought to the polling booths in camions wholesale by the unofficial electoral managers. In most cases no attempt is made to explain to them what they are voting for or why, but they are handed free drinks of clarine [Haitian white rum] . . . in recompense for their electoral patriotism. . . . Ballots printed 'yes' and 'no' on different colored slips are used in the voting. . . . At most of the booths there were no 'no' ballots to be had. When the peasant comes up to the booth he is merely handed his ballot which he then stuffs in the box, and then receives his clarin. The camions full of electors frequently stop at more than one polling booth and cast double votes." See Gordon to Department of State, 16 May 1936, Port-au-Prince, USNA, RG 59, 838.00/-M-1246, roll 5.

39. The death of the popular Jolibois *fils* was glossed over in the Haitian press that also gave virtually no reportage of his funeral. There was, however, great speculation that he was murdered in prison on orders of the president. U.S. representatives reasoned that the conditions of forced labor and poor sanitation in the national prison may have contributed to his instability and hastened his early death. Gordon to Secretary of State, 17 June 1936, USNA, RG 59, 838.00/3346, M-1246, roll 5. On his political activities and influence on the small urban working class, see Hector, "Solidarité et luttes politiques en Haïti."

40. Roumain, "Haiti," 14–15.

41. *Combat*, 6 February 1946.

42. Doubout and Joly, *Notes sur le développement du mouvement syndicale en Haïti*, 11.

43. See, for example, the description of a bus drivers strike in *Le Nouvelliste*, 22 September 1936, and for an earlier association, *L'Assaut*, 25 March 1935.

44. *Le Nouvelliste*, 26 November and 2 December 1936; *Le Moniteur*, 23 November 1936.

45. "L'Anticommunisme Haïtien," in *La Rèleve* 6 (December 1936): 32. See also *Le Matin*, 27 November 1936; George Gordon to Secretary of State, "Government's efforts to suppress communism in Haiti," 3 December 1936, Port-au-Prince, USNA, RG 59, 838.00/3361, M-1246, roll 5; George Gordon to Secretary of State, "Dictatorship advocated to combat communism in Haiti," 15 December 1936, Port-au-Prince, USNA, RG 59, 838.00/33621/2LH, M-1246, roll 5.

46. Nicholls, *From Dessalines to Duvalier*, 165.

47. Ibid., 165–66.

48. Nicholls, *From Dessalines to Duvalier*, 168.

49. Oriol, "In Memoriam: Lorimer Denis," 9.

50. Nicholls, *From Dessalines to Duvalier*, 168. Diaqoui died in his early twenties. On his profound influence on his colleagues, see Duvalier's tribute to him in *Le Nouvelliste*, 18 June 1932.

51. Carl Brouard, "Les Griots," in *L'Action Nationale*, 9 June 1932, reprinted in Gaillard, *Le destinée de Carl Brouard*, 59.

52. The differences between "anciens" and "nouveaux" perspectives among Haitian intellectuals was noted by the British representative in Haiti. See Shepherd to Eden, 24 June 1936, Port-au-Prince, *British Documents on Foreign Affairs, 1936*, 341.

53. Trouillot, "Jeux de mots, jeux de class," 46.

54. *Les Griots* (July–September 1938): 1. See also Carl Brouard, "Doctrine de la Nouvelle Ecole," in the same issue.

55. Duvalier's interpretation of Gobineau's theories is best expressed in his series of articles, "En quoi L'État d'âme du noir se différencie-t-il de celui du blanc?" in *Le Nouvelliste*, 30 December 1935 to 3 January 1936. For a fine analysis of the influence of Gobineau on the Griots biological approach to Haitian history, see Nicholls, "Biology and Politics in Haiti."

56. *Les Griots* (October–December 1938): 153.

57. *Les Griots* (July–September 1938): 4.

58. *Les Griots* (July–September 1939): 3.

59. Nicholls, *From Dessalines to Duvalier*, 116–17; 171.

60. *Les Griots* (July–September 1939): 3. Emphasis included.

61. Nicholls, "Biology and Politics," 209.

62. Ibid.; *Les Griots* (July–September 1938): 4.

63. *Les Griots* (July–September 1939): 3.

64. Carl Brouard, "Hommage au President Vincent," in *L'Assaut*, 27 February 1935, also quoted in Nicholls, *From Dessalines to Duvalier*, 166. See also René Piqouin's interview in *L'Assaut*, 11 March 1935. This is probably due to the enthusiasm many black nationalists shared for Vincent's policies of inclusion during his first term, and the enthusiasm that accompanied the end of the occupation.

65. Nicholls, *From Dessalines to Duvalier*, 170.

66. Nicholls, "Biology and Politics," 210.

67. This point is noted in Nicholls, *From Dessalines to Duvalier*, 172. See also the series of articles on the Italian invasion in *L'Assaut*, 11, 12, and 13 March 1935.

68. *L'Action Nationale*, 28 July 1936.

69. Nicholls, "Ideology and Protest in Haiti," 16–17. Duvalier's early writings scarcely address the issue of communism in Haiti, though he would frequently argue that materialist theories were of little relevance to analyses of the Haitian situation. For some of his comments on communism in the thirties see, for example, *Le Nouvelliste*, 15 December 1942. He would, of course, have much to say against communism during the sixties when he brought the debate between the *noiristes* and the communists to a violent conclusion.

70. Trouillot, *Haiti: State against Nation*, 132.

71. Dantès Bellegarde, interview by Robert J. Alexander, 30 August 1949, Port-au-Prince, Alexander Papers, RU.

72. Dantès Bellegarde quoted in Dash, *Literature and Ideology*, 125.

73. For more on Bellegarde's views on race, color, and politics in Haiti, see Bellegarde, *Dessalines a parlé*, 90–97, *Haïti et ses problèmes*, 11–18, 101–10, and Bellegarde-Smith, *In the Shadow of Powers*.

74. On Brouard's life during this period, see Gaillard, *La destinée de Carl Brouard*, 42–50.

75. For a discussion of the political motivations behind the Good Neighbor Policy see Wood, *Making of the Good Neighbor Policy*, and Green, *Containment of Latin America*.

76. See Gruening, "Withdrawal from Haiti," 677–79, and Verna, "Haiti's 'Second Independence.'"

77. Scholarly interest in the massacre has increased substantially over the past two decades. The general narrative is best covered in Fiehrer, "Political Violence in the Periphery: The Haitian Massacre of 1937"; Derby and Turits, "Historias de terror y los terrores de la historia"; Malek, "Dominican Republic's General Rafael Trujillo"; de Matteis, *Le Massacre de 1937*; and Aquino, *Holocaust in the Caribbean*. Roorda, *Dictator Next Door*, chap. 5, and "Genocide Next Door," address the impact and long-term effect of the massacre on inter-American relations; Vega, *Trujillo y Haití*, vol. 1, chaps. 8–10, offers a detailed analysis of the event from a Dominican perspective. The different racial and cultural features of Haitian-Dominican relations in the disputed frontier zones are exceptionally well treated in Derby, "Haitians, Magic, and Money." Richard Turits offers a richly detailed and provocative discussion of the complicated reasons and consequences of the massacre for the border towns as well as the Trujillato in Turits, *Foundations of Despotism*, chap. 5, and "A World Destroyed." The episode is also featured in several popular novels such as Jacques Stephen Alexis's classic *Compère général soleil* and Edwidge Danticat's *Farming of Bones*.

78. On anti-Haitianism in the Dominican Republic see Sagás, *Race and Politics in the Dominican Republic*; Derby, "Haitians, Magic, and Money," especially 510–12; and Turits, *Foundations of Despotism*, 146–61.

79. Roorda, *Dictator Next Door*, 131.

80. *Le Nouvelliste*, 17 March 1937; Turits, *Foundations of Despotism*, 160.

81. Derby and Turits, "Historias," 73; Roorda, *Dictator Next Door*, 130.

82. R. Henry Norweb to Secretary of State, Ciudad Trujillo, 13 October 1937, USNA, RG 59, 738.39/36, *Records of the U.S. Department of State relating to Political Relations between the United States and Latin America and the Caribbean States, 1930–1944*, roll 87.

83. Ibid.; Fiehrer, "Political Violence in the Periphery," 11. Lauren Derby makes the important point that anti-Haitianism in the border towns was not primarily driven by racism as most scholars assume. Dominican attempts to safeguard the border in the thirties derived from the gradual breakdown in legislation on Haitian immigration dating back to the mid-nineteenth century. These concerns were cultural, nationalistic, and economic. Before and after the U.S. occupations, border police lamented the acceptance of Haitian religious practices by the Dominican peasantry, the spread of Kreyòl as a second language in the frontier zones, and the circulation of Haitian currency in Santiago and Barahona. Heavy commercial traffic between the two countries confounded the

difficulty of containing the spread of Haitian currency and culture. Haitian-Dominican contraband also presented a problem for Dominican officials (many of whom benefited from the trade) who resented the higher tariffs placed on Dominican goods entering towns on the Haitian side of the border while Haitian contraband penetrated the Dominican side unchecked. The 1937 policies were thus an attempt to link state racism with the popular anxieties of Dominican border residents who were gravely concerned with preserving nationality and the local economy. See Derby, "Haitians, Magic, and Money," 500–505, 526.

84. R. Henry Norweb to Secretary of State, 13 October 1937, Ciudad Trujillo, USNA, RG 59, 738.39/36, *Records of the U.S. Department of State relating to Political Relations between the United States and Latin America and the Caribbean States, 1930–1944*, roll 87.

85. Evremont Carrié to Georges Léger, 3 June 1937, 10 July 1937, 5 May 1937, Ciudad Trujillo, Haitian Collection, SCRBC.

86. Harold Finley to Secretary of State, "Report of Telephone Call from Melville Monk, at nine o'clock," 7 October 1937, USNA, RG 59, 738.39/26, *Records of the U.S. Department of State relating to Political Relations between the United States and Latin America and the Caribbean States, 1930–1944*, roll 87.

87. R. Henry Norweb to Secretary of State, 11 October 1937, Ciudad Trujillo, USNA, 738.39/34, *Records of the U.S. Department of State relating to Political Relations between the United States and Latin America and the Caribbean States, 1930–1944*, roll 87.

88. Fiehrer, "Political Violence in the Periphery," 12.

89. R. Henry Norweb to Secretary of State, 25 October 1937, Ciudad Trujillo, USNA, RG 59, 738.39/57, *Records of the U.S. Department of State relating to Political Relations between the United States and Latin America and the Caribbean States, 1930–1944*, roll 87.

90. It is difficult to state with accuracy the numbers of Haitians and Dominicans born of Haitian parents murdered. Early estimates ranged from 2,000 to 8,000. Richard Turits in his sophisticated analysis of the massacre suggests a figure closer to 15,000. Turits also makes mention of a brief subsequent slaughter the following year in the southern part of the border. See Turits, *Foundations of Despotism*, chap. 5.

91. *Listín Diario*, 16 October 1937.

92. R. Henry Norweb to Secretary of State, 13 October 1937, Ciudad Trujillo, USNA, RG 59, 738.39/36, *Records of the U.S. Department of State relating to Political Relations between the United States and Latin America and the Caribbean States, 1930–1944*, roll 87.

93. Harold Finley to Secretary of State, 11 October 1937, USNA, RG 59, 738.39/32, *Records of the U.S. Department of State relating to Political Relations between the United States and Latin America and the Caribbean States, 1930–1944*, roll 87.

94. Secretary of State of the Exterior, to Secretary of State of the Interior, 12 October 1937, Correspondance générale Expédiée, folder 88, ANH.

95. See, for example, Roorda, *Dictator Next Door*, 133; Malek, "Dominican Republic's General Rafael Trujillo," 142.

96. Fiehrer, "Political Violence in the Periphery," 14.

97. "Quartier Général du District du Palais National Garde d'Haïti, Interrogation of Capt. Pierre L. Mont Rosier," enclosure to F. Mayer to Secretary of State, 15 March 1938, Port-au-Prince, USNA, RG 59, 838.00B/20, "Internal Affairs—Haiti, 1930–39," M-1246, roll 6. See also Turits, "A World Destroyed," 622–23.

98. Sténio Vincent to Franklin D. Roosevelt, 12 November 1937, Port-au-Prince, Box 178, Folder, "Haiti," Welles Papers, FDRL.

99. Franklin Roosevelt to Sténio Vincent, 14 November 1937, Washington D.C., Box 178, Folder "Haiti," Welles Papers, FDRL; *New York Times*, 9 November 1937.

100. See the tract "Vive la Révolution!" attached to Harold Finley to Secretary of State, "Activities of a Revolutionary Party in Haiti," 21 October 1937, Port-au-Prince, USNA, RG 84, 800/-. See also the comments on an anti-Trujillo article in *L'Assaut*, in Secretary of State to Secretary of Justice, 31 December 1937, Port-au-Prince, Correspondence générale expédiée, folder 32, ANH.

101. See the report, Harold Finley to Secretary of State, "Haitian Psychology following recent border disputes," 25 October 1937, Port-au-Prince, USNA, RG 59, 738.39/58, *Records of the U.S. Department of State relating to Political Relations between the United States and Latin America and the Caribbean States, 1930–1944*, roll 87.

102. Harold Finley to Secretary of State, 23 October 1937, Port-au-Prince, USNA, RG 84, 800/-.

103. See the tracts "Bref Historique d' L'Incident," "Camarades," and "Une Déclaration de la Jeunesse Universitaire," all in Mangonès Collection, BHPSE.

104. Tract entitled "Une Declaration de la Jeunesse Universitaire," November 1937, Mangonès Collection, BHPSE.

105. Sténio Vincent to Franklin D. Roosevelt, 12 November 1937, Box 178, Folder— "Haiti," Welles Papers, FDRL.

106. Harold Finley to Secretary of State, "Haitian Psychology following recent border disputes."

107. The antigovernment protests in 1937–38 occurred during a time of intense popular upheaval across the Caribbean caused by widespread economic distress. Following small-scale protests in the Lesser Antilles in the mid-thirties, a wave of labor riots erupted in Trinidad, Barbados, and Jamaica by 1938. Although the events in Haiti fit with the pattern of popular resistance during this period, there was apparently little direct connection with the British Caribbean labor riots. Haitians may have been well aware of developments in neighboring islands, but the existing sources reveal no inspiration from them. The protests in Haiti were attributed almost entirely to the popular despondency, particularly in Port-au-Prince, over the government's handling of the massacre. In fact, up until the end of World War II, Haitian radicals had little direct contact with contemporaries in the British islands. This disconnect may be explained by differences in political systems and histories as well as the surface problems of language and culture. The strong history of democracy in the British colonies was a notable distinction from Haiti's unstable political history. By contrast, postoccupation Haiti bore many similarities with Cuba, which also experienced dictatorship, a tumultuous postindependence political transition, and an enduring and controversial U.S. presence. Given this, it is not surprising that Haitian radicals such as Roumain and Hudicourt found greater affinity with Cubans than with Jamaican radicals. On the riots in the British Caribbean see Ken Post's major studies, *Arise Ye Starvelings* and *Strike the Iron*, Bolland's *On the March*, as well as Hart's *Towards Decolonisation*. On developments in Cuba during these years, see De La Fuente, *A Nation for All*, and Pérez, *Cuba Between Reform and Revolution*.

108. Secretary of State to the Secretary of Justice, 3 December 1937, Port-au-Prince,

Correspondence générale, folder 32, ANH; Meyer to Secretary of State, 31 October 1938, Port-au-Prince, USNA, RG 59, 838.00/3431, M-1246, roll 6.

109. See, for example, the tract "Vincent Must be Overthrown," enclosure to F. Mayer to Secretary of State, 24 September 1938, Port-au-Prince, USNA, RG 59, 838.00/3427, M-1246, roll 6. General critiques of Vincent are mentioned in Rigaud, *Sténio Vincent*. See also the correspondence between Lescot and Vincent cited in Verna, "Haiti's 'Second Independence,'" 26.

110. See the report of the court martial proceedings attached to F. Mayer to Secretary of State, 15 March 1938, Port-au-Prince, USNA, RG 59, 838.00/3411, M-1246, roll 6. The Communist Party would later claim that members played an organizing role in the unrest. See *Combat*, 6 February 1946.

111. Fowler, *A Knot in the Thread*, 182–85.

112. Quartier Général du District du Palais National Garde d'Haïti, "Interrogation of Capt. Pierre L. Mont Rosier," enclosure to F. Mayer to Secretary of State, 15 March 1938, Port-au-Prince, USNA, RG 59, 838.00B/20, M-1246, roll 6.

113. See "Memorandum of Conversation, de la Rue, Briggs, and Chapin," 13 December 1937, Washington, D.C., USNA, RG 59, 838.00/3386, M-1246, roll 5.

114. Calixte's appointment as the first black head of the Garde was part of Vincent's policy of giving key positions to blacks in order to appear more nationalistic. On the formation and structure of the Garde, see McCrocklin, *Garde d'Haïti, 1915–1934*.

115. For details of the conspiracy and its aftermath, see Calixte's own account of the affair, *Calvary of a Soldier*, especially chaps. 2 and 3. On Calixte's part in the plot see F. Mayer to Secretary of State, 19 May 1938, Washington, D.C., USNA, RG 59, 838.00/3326, M-1246, roll 5, and "Memorandum of Conversation with Colonel Calixte," attachment to F. Mayer to Secretary of State, 1 December 1937, Port-au-Prince, USNA, RG 84, 800/-. For further mention of the plot and general urban unrest in early 1938, see Faustin Wirkus to Frank Crumbie, 18 January 1938, Crumbie Papers, Box 1, UF.

116. Borno's conversation with the Ambassador is the substance of "Memorandum of Conversation with de la Rue, Briggs, Chapin," 13 December 1937, Washington, D.C., USNA, RG 59, 838.00/3386, M-1246, roll 5.

117. Samuel I. Rosenman, "A Memorandum giving the circumstances surrounding a dispute between Haiti and the Dominican Republic, 1937–1938," Box 36, Rosenman Papers, FDRL; Roorda, *Dictator Next Door*, 142; Fiehrer, "Political Violence in the Periphery," 15; Maleck, "Dominican Republic's General Rafael Trujillo," 148–49; Logan, *Haiti and the Dominican Republic*, 46. The Dominican government later filed a counterclaim on the debt for alleged damages caused by Haitian bandits on the border. The Haitian government quietly agreed to a lump sum of less than half of the original figure, eventually reduced to $25,000, most of which was grafted by officials leaving, according to Thomas Fiehrer, "around two cents per victim." With little formal international resistance Trujillo was able to restore his public image as international attention to the event gradually abated. Roosevelt, who celebrated the "peaceful solution" to the crisis, was criticized in the U.S. press for not insisting on a thorough investigation. For coverage of the massacre in the United States, see, for example, the report of Haitian specialist Harold Courlander, "Not in the Cables."

118. F. Mayer to Secretary of State, 19 March 1938, Port-au-Prince, USNA, RG 59,

838.00/3409, and F. Mayer to Secretary of State, 11 February 1938, Port-au-Prince, USNA, RG 59, 838.00/3403, M-1246, roll 6.

119. Delince, *Armée et politique en Haïti*, 86.

120. *Haïti Journal*, 20 December 1938; F. Mayer to Secretary of State, 22 December 1938, Port-au-Prince, USNA, RG 59, 838.00/-, M-1246, roll 6. See also Heinl and Heinl, *Written in Blood*, 503.

121. *Le Nouvelliste*, 1 November 1938; F. Mayer to Secretary of State, 1 November 1938, Port-au-Prince, USNA, RG 59, 838.00/3430, M-1246, roll 6.

122. F. Mayer to Secretary of State, 3 November 1938, Port-au-Prince, USNA, RG 59, 838.00/3433, M-1246, roll 6.

123. J. P. Audain to L. Duggan, 19 April 1939, Port-au-Prince, USNA, RG 59, 838.00/3479; J. P. Audain to L. Duggan, 4 December 1939, Port-au-Prince, USNA, RG 59, 838.00/3506, M-1246, roll 6.

124. Walter White to Cordell Hull, 22 December 1937, New York, Box 178, Folder— "Haiti," Welles Papers, FDRL.

125. See the letters attached to C. Weiss to Cordell Hull, 6 January 1939, New York, USNA, RG 59, 838.00/3442, M-1246, roll 6.

126. F. Mayer to Secretary of State, 1 November 1938, Port-au-Prince, USNA, RG 59, 838.00/3430, M-1246, roll 6; See also Hull's reply, C. Hull to F. Mayer, 1 November 1938, Washington, D.C., USNA, RG 59, 838.00/3430, M-1246, roll 6.

127. F. Mayer to Secretary of State, 1 November 1938, Port-au-Prince, USNA, RG 59, 838.00/3430, M-1246, roll 6.

Chapter 2

1. This biographical sketch on Lescot is based on information from the president's son, Roger Lescot, interview by author, 16 June 2003, Laboule, Haiti; *Le Matin*, 10 April 1941; Heinl and Heinl, *Written in Blood*, 507; Rotberg, *Haiti: The Politics of Squalor*, 168; Alfred Nemours's panegyric *Les présidents Lescot et Trujillo*, 19–25; Lescot, *Avant l'oubli*, 1–2 and overleaf; Paquin, *Haitians*, 81–84.

2. Sumner Welles, "Memorandum of Conversation with Élie Lescot," 19 October 1940, Washington, D.C., USNA, RG 59, 838.00/3540.

3. The advocacy of a black president was also a factor that raised concern in the U.S. State Department, which privileged support of a candidate more favorable to their wartime program. For a discussion of this, see "Naval Intelligence Report," 6 April 1941, Havana, USNA, RG 165, Box 1578. Vincent himself apparently favored Duval early in the campaign referring to him as "the most likely candidate" for the presidency. Edward J. Sparks to Secretary of State, 13 January 1941, Port-au-Prince, USNA, RG 59, 738.00/3526.

4. J. C. White to Secretary of State, 12 April 1941, Port-au-Prince, USNA, RG 59, 838.00/3594.

5. Quotations taken from *Le Matin*, 9 April 1941.

6. J. C. White to Secretary of State, 12 April 1941, Port-au-Prince, USNA, RG 59, 838.00/3594; J. C. White to Secretary of State, 8 April 1941, Port-au-Prince, USNA, RG 59, 838.00/3587. White advised the secretary of state that since other candidates were "presumably tainted with Axis affiliations the non-election of Lescot might produce an

unfortunate impression in Washington." On Vincent's moves to remain in power, see *L'Action Radicale*, 26 February, 25 March, and 8 April 1941; Edward J. Sparks to Secretary of State, 31 January 1941, Port-au-Prince, USNA, RG 59, 838.00/3561; Heinl and Heinl, *Written in Blood*, 506; *Le Matin*, 13 April 1941; J. C. White to Secretary of State, 10 April 1941, Port-au-Prince, USNA, RG 59, 838.00/3590.

7. J. C. White to Secretary of State, 29 March 1941, Port-au-Prince, USNA, RG 59, 838.00/3581.

8. Edward J. Sparks to State Department, 31 January 1941, Port-au-Prince, USNA, RG 59, 838.00/3561; Harold Finley to R. Bonsal, 19 February 1941, Washington, D.C., USNA, RG 59, 838.00/3569; Plummer, *Haiti and the United States*, 143.

9. See the description of the election in Hudicourt, *Haiti Faces Tomorrow's Peace*, 11. In one instance, an elector wrote a short poem of endorsement for Lescot. See J. C. White to Secretary of State, 16 April 1941, Port-au-Prince, USNA, RG 59, 838.00/3618, and *Le Matin*, 16 April 1941.

10. See the article "White is Right in Haiti: Inside Story of White Cabinet Rule," *Chicago Defender*, 19 January 1946.

11. *Le Matin*, 24 May 1943; U.S. Naval Attaché, Confidential Report, RG 59, 838.415/20.

12. *Le Nouvelliste*, 25 May 1944.

13. Trouillot, "Culture, Color, and Politics," 161.

14. Élie Lescot to American Chargé d'Affaires ad interim, 13 December 1941, Port-au-Prince, and Sumner Welles to Franklin Roosevelt, 3 January 1942, PPF, Box 162, FDRL.

15. Élie Lescot to Vinton Chapin, 30 March 1944, Port-au-Prince, War Refugee Board Files, Box 33, FDRL. On the Dominican experience see Roorda, *Dictator Next Door*, 144–46, and Turits, *Foundations of Despotism*, 196–97.

16. *Chicago Defender*, 19 January 1946.

17. J. R. Taylor to G. Rouzier, 15 March 1943, Jérémie, Box 1577, USNA, RG 165.

18. Plummer, *Haiti and the United States*, 145; Fennell, "Haiti Makes Rubber History"; Jones, *Harley Harris Bartlett Diaries*, 156–65; Willard F. Barber, "Memorandum of Conversation with Dennis, Duggan, Bonsal, Finley, Collado, Bressman, and Lescot," 26 April 1941, Washington, D.C., *FRUS, 1941*, 6:334.

19. Sumner Welles to T. A. Fennell, 7 and 15 November 1939, 28 March 1942. I am grateful to Thomas Dudley Fennell for supplying me with copies of this correspondence and other documentation that informs my analysis in this section.

20. T. A. Fennell to Atherton Lee, 10 February 1943, attachment, "SHADA Cryptostegia program—Condensed record as of 31 January 1943," War Production Board Records, Box 33, FDRL.

21. Élie Lescot to Franklin D. Roosevelt, 19 September 1942, PPF, Box 67, FDRL.

22. Élie Lescot, "Lettre au Délégué du Cap Haïtien," n.d., Dartigue Papers, SCRBC; See also the attachment to T. A. Fennell to Henry Wallace, 27 August 1942, Port-au-Prince, POF, FDRL.

23. He expressed as much in a conversation with U.S. black academic Rayford Logan during Logan's April 1942 trip to Haiti. He argued that France was the "greatest enemy of Haiti and the Negro" and "the United States is the most generous country . . . the greatest friend of Haiti." Lescot also outlined a broad plan of economic and social expansion that

included the teaching of English in all Haitian schools. See 6 April 1942, Logan Travel Diaries, Box 9, LC.

24. *Le Continental*, 2 February 1942.

25. See the collection of *A Propos de SHADA* in Dartigue Papers, SCRBC.

26. Dupuy, *Haiti in the World Economy*, 145; Rotberg, *Haiti: The Politics of Squalor*, 169; Heinl and Heinl, *Written in Blood*, 511.

27. Maurice Dartigue to T. A. Fennell, 17 April 1943, Port-au-Prince, Dartigue Papers, SCRBC.

28. Maurice Dartigue to T. A. Fennell, 16 February 1943, Port-au-Prince, Dartigue Papers, SCRBC.

29. Dartigue's proposal was attached to the previously cited letter of 16 February 1943. One proposal that was pursued was the cultivation of subsistence crops such as plantains, particularly in the Artibonite valley where the local food economy decreased markedly since the introduction of the SHADA project and anti-U.S. sentiment was highest. See "SHADA planting Food" in *A Propos de SHADA*, 1 June 1943, Dartigue Papers, SCRBC.

30. Lt. Eddie K. G. Borjesson to Military Intelligence Division, "Inspection of SHADA Activities in the Department of the North," 12 June 1943, Cap Haïtien, USNA, RG 59, 838.00/3646; Thomas Dudley Fennell correspondence with author, 6 July 2006.

31. Leo T. Crowley, "Memorandum to the President," 10 May 1944, POF, Box 510, FDRL; Plummer, *Haiti and the United States*, 145.

32. J. W. McQueen, interview by Robert J. Alexander, 24 August 1949, Port-au-Prince, Alexander Papers, RU.

33. A. Chapin to Secretary of State, 14 April 1944, Port-au-Prince, telegram, *FRUS*, 1944, 7:1172–73.

34. Orme Wilson to Secretary of State, 28 June 1945, Port-au-Prince, *FRUS*, 1945, 9:1091; Orme Wilson to Secretary of State, 14 July 1945, Port-au-Prince, ibid., 1093, and 20 August 1945, 838.51/8-2045, ibid., 1098–1099; Charles C. Hauch, "Memorandum of Conversation with André Liautaud, Nelson A. Rockefeller, Corliss, Cochran, and Hauch," 6 August 1945, ibid., 1095–96.

35. By the end of 1945 agriculture accounted for only 5 percent of government expenditures, a mere 1 percent increase from its 1937 figures. Lundahl, *Peasants and Poverty*, 305.

36. Paquin, *Haitians*, 85.

37. *Cahiers d'Haïti* 4 (April 1945): 18. On a trip to Miami in late 1945 Brandt outlined his plan for economic expansion in Haiti in an interview with the *Miami Herald*. See *Miami Herald*, 10 January 1946.

38. Métreux, *Voodoo in Haiti*, 338. Métreux also refers to a short-lived series of skirmishes between Church representatives and vodouists that took place in 1913, which amounted to nothing of consequence.

39. Ibid., 339–40.

40. See "Haitian Field Trip-Notes," 23 June 1934, Herskovits Diaries, Box 13, folder 66, Herskovits Papers, SCRBC. See also Hurbon, "American Fantasy and Haitian Vodou," 189.

41. Ramsey, "Without One Ritual Note," 10–14.

42. According to Métreux, Catholic clergymen referred to *houngans* (vodou priests) as the "principal slaves of Satan," and their peasant supporters as being possessed by the devil. Métreux, *Voodoo in Haiti*, 339.

43. See Comhaire, "The Haitian 'Chef de Section,'" 622. This partially explains why in the Marbial region the crusades were particularly violent. For a detailed discussion on the effects of the campaign on the communities in Marbial see Métreux, *Voodoo in Haiti*, 344–51. See also the report in the regional paper, *Sud-Ouest*, 9 February 1942.

44. Peters, *Lumiére sur le humfort*, 55. The exact quote was "Moin promett' pour m'élever toutt pititt moin yo sans exception, n'en la religion Catholique Romaine, seule religion jesus-christ" (I promise to raise all my children without exception, in the Roman Catholic religion, the only religion of Jesus Christ). Métreux mentions another hymn that contained the verse, "Protestant[ism] is the religion of Satan—It doesn't lead to Heaven"; Métreux, *Voodoo in Haiti*, 351. Ironically, the Protestants, far from supporting vodou, held strong views against fetishism and superstition.

45. Georges Ramponeau, interview by Robert J. Alexander, 22 August 1949, Port-au-Prince, Alexander Papers, RU.

46. *Le Matin*, 30 January 1942 and 2 February 1942.

47. *La Phalange*, 24 February 1942; *L'Élan*, 23 February 1942; Métreux, *Voodoo in Haiti*, 343. For a discussion of other rumors that circulated around the time including possible ties with the French Archbishop and the Axis powers and the clergy's role in property theft in the countryside during the campaign, see J. C. White to Secretary of State, "Questionable Attitude of Certain of the French Clergy in Haiti," 25 February 1942, Port-au-Prince, USNA, RG 59, 838.00/40458.

48. *Le Soir*, 7 March 1942.

49. Élie Lescot to Pope Pius XII, 27 February 1942, Private Collection; Kerr [Military Attaché] to Military Intelligence Division, War Department, 6 March 1942, Ciudad Trujillo, USNA, RG 59, 838.404/93.

50. See, for example, Nicholls, *From Dessalines to Duvalier*, 182; Dash, *Jacques Stephen Alexis*, 10, and *Haiti and the United States*, 87; Fowler, *A Knot in the Thread*, 217; Trouillot, *Haiti: State against Nation*, 133; Rémy Bastien argued without evidence that the campaign was endorsed by Lescot in an effort to forcibly evict peasants from land needed for rubber planting. See Rémy Bastien and Harold Courlander, *Religion and Politics in Haiti*, 45. See also Anne Greene, *Catholic Church in Haiti*, 107, for a brief discussion on the event.

51. This letter is included in the preface to Peters, *Lumière sur le humfort*, 4. David Nicholls cites part of the letter as proof of Lescot's "explicit support of the campaign," in his discussion of the campaign in "Ideology and Protest," 12. Yet Nicholls, whose interpretation appears to have influenced the conclusions of others, only cites the first half of the letter. In the latter part Lescot clearly states he advocates only the conduct of masses in Kreyòl.

52. Élie Lescot, "Confidences intimes," typescript, 10 June 1962, Private Collection.

53. Nicholls, *From Dessalines to Duvalier*, 182.

54. Lescot to Trujillo, 11 April 1940, quoted in Trujillo to Lescot, 1 November 1943, in PSF, Box 39, FDRL; Roger Lescot, interview by author, 16 June 2003, Laboule, Haiti.

55. J. C. White to Secretary of State, 2, 19 February 1942, Port-au-Prince, USNA, RG 59, 838.404/48. See also Lescot's *Avant l'oubli*, 139–41, for his view that the church, for

no other reason but to embarrass his regime just after his election, orchestrated the campaign.

56. Jones, *Harley Harris Bartlett Diaries*, 164.

57. J. C. White to Secretary of State, 25 February 1942, Port-au-Prince, USNA, RG 59, 838.404/58; J. C. White to Secretary of State, "The Haitian Kulturkampf," 11 March 1942, Port-au-Prince, USNA, RG 59, 838.404/65.

58. See his articles in *Le Nouvelliste*, 9, 10, 12 March 1942. Some of this writing and the response of the Catholic church to Roumain's position are discussed in Fowler, *A Knot in the Thread*, 217–22.

59. Fowler, *A Knot in the Thread*, 211; Cobb, *Harlem, Haiti, and Havana*, 7.

60. For detail on his activities in Cuba during this period see Guillén, *Prosa de Prisa*, 324–25.

61. "FBI Secret File on the Republic of Haiti—March 1946," Chapter 3, USNA, RG 84.

62. J. Edgar Hoover to Adolphe Berle Jr., 20 September 1944, Washington, D.C., USNA, RG 59, 838.918/9-2044.

63. Secretary of the Interior to the Police General, 22 June 1941, Port-au-Prince, Haitian Collection, MSRC.

64. Secretary of the Interior to the Police General, 9 June 1941, Port-au-Prince, Haitian Collection, MSRC.

65. Secretary of the Interior to the Police General, 13 June 1941, Port-au-Prince, Haitian Collection, MSRC.

66. "FBI Secret File on the Republic of Haiti—March 1946," Chapter 3, USNA, RG 84.

67. Secretary of the Interior to the Police General, 9 July 1941, Port-au-Prince, Haitian Collection, MSRC.

68. See, for example, *Bureau d'Ethnologie Bulletin* 25 (October 1941), Mangonès Collection, BHPSE.

69. One notable work that he wrote during this period was *Le Sacrifice du tambour-assoto*, for which he spent several months visiting vodou ceremonies, documenting with great detail the manufacture of the main vodou drum. His aforementioned articles in *Le Nouvelliste* against the anti-superstition campaign were published in pamphlet form later that year, and he also wrote a preface to Edris St. Armand's *Essai d'explication de "Dialogues de mes lampes,"* an essay on Griot Magloire St. Aude's poetry. For a discussion of these writings, see Fowler, *A Knot in the Thread*, 220–22.

70. Roumain appears to have left for Mexico in late October. See Jacques Antoine to Carlos M. Paz y Diaz de Léon, 22 October 1942, Correspondence Générale, folder 117, ANH.

71. Dash, *Literature and Ideology in Haiti*, 141.

72. Secretary of the Interior to the Police General, 13 June 1941, Port-au-Prince, Haitian Collection, MSRC.

73. Hudicourt was refused documentation for admission to the Dominican Republic by the Dominican legation in Port-au-Prince but was admitted at the border. Hoover to Berle, 31 August 1944, Washington, D.C., USNA, RG 84, 838.918/9-2044; Legation Ciudad Trujillo to State Department, Santo Domingo, 20 September 1941, USNA, RG 59, 838.00/3544.

74. J. C. White to Secretary of State, "Communist Activities in the Republic of Haiti," n.d., USNA, RG 84, 838.000B/-.

75. *Le Matin*, 25 March 1941.

76. Max D. Sam, interview by author, 7 May 2001, Pétionville, Haiti.

77. *La Nation*, 5 April 1943.

78. Max D. Sam, interview by author, 7 May 2001, Pétionville, Haiti. The circulation of the paper was an issue of concern for the State Department and FBI, which monitored the directors closely. See J. Edgar Hoover to Adolphe Berle Jr., "Re: '*La Nation*,'" 31 August 1944, Washington, D.C., USNA, RG 84, 838.918/9-2044.

79. *La Nation*, 19 July 1943. The episode was also mentioned at length in J. Edgar Hoover to Adolphe Berle Jr., "Re: '*La Nation*,'" 31 August 1944, Washington, D.C., USNA, RG 84, 838.918/9-2044.

80. Max Hudicourt to Cordell Hull, n.d. [c. 1943], Port-au-Prince, USNA, RG 59, 838.00/3649. In another letter written while in exile in New York he was far more accusatory, claiming that it was the State Department that had "considerable and determining influence" over events in the "poor little country." Max L. Hudicourt to Cordell Hull, 29 May 1944, New York City, USNA, RG 59, 838.00/3651.

81. *Le Nouvelliste*, 15 April 1944; Hudicourt, *Haiti Faces Tomorrow's Peace*, 14; Heinl and Heinl, *Written in Blood*, 512.

82. *Le Nouvelliste*, 12 and 16 May 1944; Hudicourt, *Haiti Faces Tomorrow's Peace*, 15; J. Edgar Hoover to Adolphe Berle Jr., "Re: '*La Nation*,'" 31 August 1944, Washington, D.C., USNA, RG 84, 838.918/9-2044.

83. *Le Nouvelliste*, 20 May 1944; J. Edgar Hoover to Adolphe Berle Jr., "Re: '*La Nation*,'" 31 August 1944, Washington, D.C., USNA, RG 84, 838.918/9-2044.

84. Arthur Garfield Hays to Cordell Hull, 13 June 1944, New York City, USNA, RG 59, 838.90/3654.

85. Hudicourt, *Haiti Faces Tomorrow's Peace*.

86. *Le Nouvelliste*, 26 June 1944. It was during this period that the administration assumed its most repressive character. Other papers forced to close down included *L'Opinion*, *L'Action Nationale*, and *La Patrie*. Most of the directors of these papers were imprisoned, where two allegedly died from maltreatment.

87. Trouillot, *Dimensions et limites de Jacques Roumain*, 121.

88. Fowler, *A Knot in the Thread*, 225.

89. Beaulieu's death was rumored to be the result of political intrigue. Max Sam, who was very close to Beaulieu, claims, however, that the actual cause of death was due to wartime shortages on penicillin, which the sickly Beaulieu was unable to obtain. Max D. Sam, interview by author, 7 May 2001, Pétionville, Haiti.

90. *Cahiers d'Haïti* 11 (November 1944).

91. J. Edgar Hoover to A. Berle, 6 September 1944, Washington, D.C., USNA, RG 84, 838/00B/9-2444.

92. Not all shared this sentiment. Roussan Camille wrote a glowing report of the meeting in *Haïti Journal*, 22, 23 August 1944. See also Hoover to Berle, 31 August 1944, Washington, D.C., USNA, RG 84, 838.00B/9-1644.

93. Although they classified the communist movement as "weak" and "unorganized" in 1944, the FBI filed intermittent reports on the Haitian Marxists. See, for example, Hoover to Berle Jr., 6 September 1944, Washington, D.C., USNA, RG 84, 838.00B/6-944; Hoover to Berle Jr., 31 August 1944, Washington, D.C., USNA, RG 84, 838.00B/31-844;

Hoover to Berle Jr., 1 November 1944, USNA, RG 84, 838.00B/6-944; Hoover to Berle Jr., 10 November 1944, USNA, RG 84, 838.00B/12-1044.

94. Trouillot, "Culture, Color, and Politics in Haiti," 165–66.

95. See Césaire, *Cahier d'un retour au pays*; Dash, *Literature and Ideology in Haiti, 1915–1961*, 121.

96. A strong literature on the links between Haiti and U.S. blacks during the twentieth century has been developing in recent years. See, for example, Plummer, *Rising Wind*. Peggy Von Eschen draws frequent reference to the Haitian case in *Race against Empire*, 38–39, 105–7, 163–65; and Mary Renda offers a new interpretation of the way in which U.S. blacks appropriated Haitian themes in literature and the arts in *Taking Haiti*. The theme is also closely studied in Polyné, "Modernizing the Race," and Pamphile, *Haitians and African Americans*.

97. Rayford Logan diary entry, 4 April 1942, in Logan Diaries, LC. Logan was an important historian, Pan-Africanist, and civil rights activist. He studied at Harvard where he completed a dissertation on nineteenth-century U.S.-Haitian foreign relations, later published as *The Diplomatic Relations of the United States with Haiti*. Logan was an outspoken critic of the United States occupation and U.S. hostility toward Haiti. Although his political views were generally conservative, his support of Haitian causes won him the admiration of intellectuals and radicals in the island. On Logan's background, see Kenneth Robert Janken's biography, *Rayford W. Logan*.

98. Labelle, "La force opérante," in *Pouvoir Noir*, 143–45, and Dorsinville, "1946 ou le délire opportuniste," 46. Attendance at these clubs was by no means contingent on color. Many young elite students did not necessarily share the political ideas of *noirisme* but were excited by its cultural implications and regularly attended the meetings; Corvington, *Port-au-Prince au cours des ans*, 6:195, 198.

99. *Le Matin*, 15 September 1942.

100. On early efforts to develop tourism see "Haiti is today a Tourist Center," in *Haiti of 1936*, 66–7.

101. DeWitt Peters to Maurice Dartigue, 26 August 1943, Dartigue Papers, SCRBC. There is an extensive literature on the Haitian art movement. See, for example, Selden Rodman, *Miracle of Haitian Art*.

102. A compilation of reviews from U.S. papers was published in *Le Matin*, 25 February 1942. For more on this period, see also Largey, *Vodou Nation*, and Ramsey, "Without One Ritual Note."

103. Emerante De Pradines Morse, interview by author, 23 July 1999, Pélerin, Haiti. See also Averill, *Day for the Hunter*, 58.

104. Corvington, *Port-au-Prince au cours des ans*, 6:285. Elite interest in the folklore movement derived from both its entertainment value as well as its commercial potential. In Port-au-Prince of the forties, cultural elements of vodou became fashionable. Once it was clear that foreign interest in Haitian folklore could be exploited to the benefit of Haitian tourism, it was actively supported. As previously noted, Haitian elites and government officials were both enraged and embarrassed by the public image of Haiti abroad and saw folklore as serving the dual function of repairing negative stereotypes and promoting tourism, a point addressed in greater depth in chapter 5. This factor also explains why this appreciation never had cross-class support before the forties despite

Price-Mars's protestations. The awakening of the elites to vodou in the early forties was significant enough to warrant U.S. Minister White to report on the subject in 1942: J. C. White to Secretary of State, "Change in Attitude towards Voodoo on the Part of the Intellectual Classes in Haiti as Evidenced by Development of Expressions of Interest in Folklore," 24 September 1942, Port-au-Prince, USNA, RG 59, 838.404/85. It should also be apparent from the preceding discussion on the anti-superstition campaign that urbanites distinguished clearly between folklore as a national appropriation of ethnic art, and vodou, which they considered the mystical religion of the peasantry. Elite support and participation in the cultural movements of the era, in this regard, is not contradictory. Of course, outright denigration of vodou in certain quarters remained constant.

105. Largey, "Haiti and the French Caribbean," 133. For contemporary accounts of the impact of this new music on youth culture in the forties see, for example, *Le Courrier*, 26 April 1942, and *L'Action Radicale*, 17 March 1942.

106. Béhague, *Music and Black Ethnicity*, v.

107. For a detailed account of this incident and earlier musical protest in Haiti see Largey, *Vodou Nation*, chap. 2. Other examples of anti-occupation protest music are given in Harold Courlander, *Haiti Singing*.

108. Issa El Saïeh, interview by author, 13 July 1999, Port-au-Prince.

109. Taken from Averill, *Day for the Hunter*, 59.

110. Averill, "Haitian Dance Bands," 219.

111. Averill, *Day for the Hunter*, 63. See also Coulange, "Indigénisme et Musique en Haïti," 59–65.

112. Corvington, *Port-au-Prince au cours des ans*, 6:265.

113. Ibid., 150, and Herby Widmaïer, interview by author, 8 May 2001, Port-au-Prince.

114. Hartt, "Broadcasting in Haiti."

115. André Cameau, Victor Vabre, and Edouard Benodin, interview by Robert J. Alexander, 24 June 1948, Port-au-Prince, Alexander Papers, RU.

116. "Recensement de la ville de Port-au-Prince, 24 January 1949," Mangonès Collection, BHPSE. See also Lundahl, *Peasants and Poverty*, 93, and "Rise and Fall of the Haitian Labour Movement."

117. "Recensement de la ville de Port-au-Prince, 24 January 1949," Mangonès Collection, BHPSE.

118. Biographical information on Fignolé is drawn from Désinor, *Daniel Fignolé*, 18–19; Auguste, *La voix du M.O.P.*; Diederich, *Haiti's Bon Papa*, chap. 7; interviews with Fignolé, *Life*, 10 June 1957, and *Haïti Sun*, 27 January 1957; Fignolé and Romain, interview by Robert J. Alexander, 25 June 1948, Port-au-Prince, Alexander Papers, RU; Fignolé, interview by Robert J. Alexander, 5 May 1959, New York City, Alexander Papers, RU; Paul Laraque, interview by author, 5 July 2000, New York City; and Rodrigue Casimir, interview by author, 14 June 2003, Port-au-Prince.

119. Depestre, "La révolution de 1946," in *Pouvoir noir en Haïti*, 72–73.

120. *Chantiers*, August 1942.

121. Ibid.

122. Ibid.

123. *Le Réveil*, 23 October 1942, *L'Élan*, 17 October 1942, and *Chantiers*, 24 January 1946.

124. *Le Réveil*, 22 October 1943, quoted in *Chantiers*, 22 January 1946.

125. Fignolé's remarkable hold over the majority of urbanites and clever use of political symbolism remains unmatched in modern Haitian political history. His popular allure may be regarded as part of a tradition of charismatic and populist leadership in modern Caribbean and Latin American political culture. Such leaders emerge at times of political crisis and, through their appeals to the popular classes, galvanize a faithful following of supporters. Personalities such as Alexander Bustamante and Michael Manley in Jamaica, Uriah "Buzz" Butler and Eric Williams in Trinidad, Eric Gairy in Grenada, and Fidel Castro in Cuba fit firmly within this tradition. All these leaders masterfully manipulated political symbolism to build mass support and claim legitimacy. Fignolé, in his writings in *Chantiers*, occasionally likened himself to Juan Perón. The classic study of charismatic leadership in Caribbean politics is Singham, *The Hero and the Crowd*. For recent scholarship on this theme, see the essays in Allahar, *Caribbean Charisma*. For a comparison of Fignolé and contemporary Haitian political leaders, see Hector, "Charisme."

126. Depestre, "La révolution de 1946," 73, claims that on occasion in the mid-forties Fignolé wore a Maoist uniform to his classes and at public meetings, though this seems to have been mainly for theatrical effect.

127. *Le Réveil*, 22 October 1943, quoted in *Chantiers*, 25 January 1946.

128. *Chantiers*, 15 June 1946.

129. According to the report, the majority of the soldiers were untrained peasants. See "Combat Estimate of Haiti," 24 August 1942, Box 86, USNA, RG 218. See also Laguerre, *Military and Society in Haiti*, 87, and Delince, *Armée et politique en Haïti*, 45.

130. Tèt kole ti peyizan ayisyen, *Dosye Chef Section*, 6.

131. Robert Bazile, interview by author, 22 June 2000, Washington, D.C.

132. Paul Laraque, interview by author, 5 July 2000, New York City; *Le Matin*, 5 July 1941.

133. Similar strikes over grievances with pay emerged shortly before among members of the Aviation Corps and the artillerymen stationed at the Port-au-Prince harbor. Orme Wilson to Secretary of State, 28 June 1944, Port-au-Prince, USNA, RG 59, 838.00/6-2844.

134. Orme Wilson to Secretary of State, 3 July 1944, Port-au-Prince, USNA, RG 59, 838.00/7-344. The motives for the revolt were never fully ascertained. The State Department was, however, quick to assume that the revolt was the brainchild of leftists and had been motivated by Hudicourt. See Orme Wilson to Secretary of State, 15 July 1944, Port-au-Prince, USNA, RG 59, 838.00/7-1544.

135. *Le Matin*, 27 June 1944; Orme Wilson to Secretary of State, "Re: Closure of *La Nation*: Discontent in the Garde d'Haïti," 28 June 1944, Port-au-Prince, USNA, RG 59, 838.00/6-2844; Max D. Sam, interview by author, 17 May 2001, Pétionville.

136. Orme Wilson to Secretary of State, 10 October 1944, Port-au-Prince, USNA, RG 59, 838.00/10-1044.

137. Orme Wilson to Secretary of State, 14 October 1944, Port-au-Prince, USNA, RG 59, 838.00/10-1444; Lescot to Roosevelt, 27 October 1944, POF, FDRL. See the comments on the interview between Gérard Lescot, Haitian Secretary of State for Foreign Affairs, and the Dominican chargé d'affaires, Tomas Hernandez Franco, detailed in Gérard Lescot to Élie Lescot, "Notes pour son Excellence le Président de la République," 23 October 1943, Haitian Collection, UF. Others argued that even if Trujillo initiated the

plot, his agents exposed it out of fear that the rise in political consciousness could produce a new president even less tolerant of Trujillo than Lescot. For a discussion of these views, see Hicks, *Blood in the Streets*, 184–86, and Heinl and Heinl, *Written in Blood*, 512.

138. Lescot to Trujillo, 11 April 1940, quoted in Trujillo to Lescot, 1 November 1943, in PSF, Box 39, FDRL; Heinl and Heinl, *Written in Blood*, 512, 514.

139. Élie Lescot to Franklin D. Roosevelt, 17 February 1944, PSF, Box 39, FDRL. See also Roosevelt's reply to Lescot, 4 March 1944.

140. Trouillot, "Culture, Color, and Politics in Haiti," 167.

141. Robert S. Folsom to Secretary of State, 5 September 1952, Port-au-Prince, USNA, RG 59, 738.00/9-1952.

Chapter 3

1. Bordes, *Haïti*, 246. The low enrollment was attributed to the attraction many high school graduates had to military service following the reorganization of the military school in the late thirties.

2. Phifer, "Public Education in Haiti since 1934," 137; *Cahiers d'Haïti* 3, 4 (November 1945): 23.

3. See, for example, Alexis, "Les grand problèmes d'humanité générale."

4. Gaillard, "Je vous salue Mabille," 35. See also the special edition, "Surrealisme et révolte en Haïti," *Conjonction* 193 (April–June 1992), and Dash, "Le Je de l'autre," 90–94.

5. Gérald Bloncourt, interview by author, 18 June 2001, Paris.

6. Alexis was a follower of Roumain since he met him in 1942 at a poetry recital he arranged for Nicolás Guillén. Coates, introduction to Alexis, *General Sun, My Brother*, x.

7. Gérald Bloncourt, interview by author, 18 June 2001, Paris. The details on the early activities of the students and the launch of *La Ruche* are taken from this interview.

8. Dash, *Literature and Ideology in Haiti*, 45. See also Coates's introduction to *Festival of the Greasy Pole*, xx.

9. Depestre, *Étincelles*, 20.

10. Jean-Baptiste, "Étude thématique et bibliographique," 168; Gérald Bloncourt, interview by author, 18 June 2001, Paris.

11. Depestre, *Bonjour et adieu à la negritude*, 213.

12. *La Ruche*, 19 January 1946.

13. Polizzotti, *Revolution of the Mind*, 530.

14. Dash, *Literature and Ideology in Haiti*, 159.

15. Paul Laraque, interview by author, 5 July 2000, New York City.

16. Paul Laraque, interview by author, 5 July 2000, New York City; Raymond Pressoir, interview by author, 17 June 2000, Bethesda, Md.; Depestre, *Bonjour et adieu à la négritude*, 229. Gaillard, "In Memoriam: André Breton et Nous," 67. See also Laraque, "André Breton en Haïti," and Dash, "Le Je de l'autre."

17. Polizzotti, *Revolution of the Mind*, 605.

18. *La Ruche*, 1 January 1946.

19. Orme Wilson to Secretary of State, 4 January 1946, Port-au-Prince, USNA, RG 84, 800/10-446.

20. Raymond Pressoir, interview by author, 20 May 2000, Bethesda, Md.

21. Emerante De Pradines Morse, interview by author, 23 July 1999, Pélerin.

22. Max D. Sam, interview by author, 17 May 2001, Pétionville; E. Séjour Laurent to Max L. Hudicourt, 22 February 1946, printed in *La Nation*, 19 February 1946; A.J.H. to Department of State, 15 January 1946, Port-au-Prince, USNA, RG 59, 838.00/1-1546.

23. Gérald Bloncourt, interview by author, 18 June 2001, Paris.

24. Gérald Bloncourt, interview by author, 18 June 2001, Paris; Depestre, *Bonjour et adieu à la négritude*, 212; *Les Débats*, 25 June 1946.

25. John C. Howley, "Memorandum to the ambassador," 7 January 1946, Port-au-Prince, USNA, RG 84, 838.01/1-1946; Gérald Bloncourt, interview by author, 18 June 2001, Paris.

26. Details on the protest taken from Depestre, "La Révolution de 1946," and Gérald Bloncourt, interview by author, 18 June 2001, Paris; See also Bloncourt and Löwy, *Messagers de la Tempête*, and Collectif du Cinquantenaire, *Haïti*.

27. *Le Matin*, 8 January 1946; Emerante De Pradines Morse, interview by author, 23 July 1999, Pélerin; *Le Nouvelliste*, 7 January 1946; Depestre, *Bonjour et adieu à la négritude*, 213.

28. Élie Lescot quoted in E. Séjour Laurent to Max L. Hudicourt, 19 February 1946, reprinted in *La Nation*, 22 February 1946.

29. Gérald Bloncourt, interview by author, 18 June 2001, Paris; *Le Matin*, 9 January 1946.

30. Gérald Bloncourt, interview by author, 18 June 2001, Paris.

31. Élie Lescot, "Proclamation de son Excellence le Président de la République, le 9 Janvier 1946," Haitian Collection, MSRC.

32. Their manifesto appeared in *Le Matin*, 8 January 1946.

33. W. Abbott to Secretary of State, 11 January 1946, Port-au-Prince, USNA, RG 84, 838.000/1-1146; *Le Matin* 10, 12 January 1946; *New York Times*, 13 January 1946.

34. *Le Matin*, 11 January 1946.

35. Posy, "Jacmel 1946," 60.

36. On Lescot's personal reaction to the events, see Élie Lescot to Maurice Dartigue, 26 April 1946, Dartigue Papers, SCRBC.

37. *Le Matin*, 12 January 1946.

38. See the discussion on this issue in Abbott to Secretary of State, "Press Criticism of the United States," 19 February 1946, Port-au-Prince, USNA, RG 59, 838.00/2-1946. On opinions against the United States during these early stages, see *Le Nouvelliste*, 11 February 1946.

39. See the articles by Mercer Cook, "Bellegarde Back, to Speak for Haiti," *Washington Afro-American*, 30 March 1946, and "Situation in Haiti told Journalists by Ambassador," *Washington Afro-American*, 20 April 1946. See also Enoch P. Walters, "No Admittance: Haitians at State Dept. Door," *Chicago Defender*, 13 April 1946. Early in the military regime, Bellegarde expressed willingness to become a provisional president but was denied when the CEM felt that a civilian president would be easier for the communist militants to topple. See Orme Wilson to Secretary of State, 7 February 1946, USNA, RG 59, 838.002/2-746, and Orme Wilson to Secretary of State, 1 February 1946, USNA, RG 59, 838.002/2-146.

40. See, for example, the report in the Jamaican *Daily Gleaner*, 14 January 1946.

41. *Washington Afro-American*, 2 February 1946.

42. *Pittsburgh Courier*, 19 January 1946.

43. Polizzotti, *Revolution of the Mind*, 504; Depestre, "Pierre Mabille," 12–13; *Combat*, 12 March 1946.

44. Jack West, "Memorandum to the Ambassador," 26 March 1946, Port-au-Prince, USNA, RG 84, 838.00B/3-2646.

45. Ibid.

46. Gérald Bloncourt, interview by author, 18 June 2001, Paris.

47. Jean-Baptiste, "Étude thématique et bibliographique," 125.

48. Transcript of a broadcast printed in *Rasoir*, 13 January 1946.

49. Édouard A. Tardieu and Jacques A. Désinor, interview by Robert J. Alexander, 25 June 1948, Port-au-Prince, Alexander Papers, RU.

50. *Flambeau*, 19 January 1946.

51. *Flambeau*, 22 January 1946.

52. In 1940 an earlier anti-Vincent paper named *Combat* briefly surfaced as the "organ of the defense of Haitian Democracy."

53. *Combat*, 6 February 1946.

54. *Combat*, 8 February 1946.

55. *Combat*, 6 February 1946.

56. *Combat*, 12 March 1946.

57. Hector, *Syndicalisme et socialisme en Haïti*, 50–60.

58. *Combat*, 19 February 1946.

59. Jack West, "Report on Information regarding the Communist Party of Haiti," attachment to Orme Wilson to Secretary of State, "Memorandum on the size of the Communist Party of Haiti," 21 July 1946, Port-au-Prince, USNA, RG 84, 838.00B/7-2176.

60. The Cuban PSP's assessment of the PCH appeared in their organ *Hoy*, and was reprinted in the Haitian PSP's *La Nation*, 14 March 1946. Other Latin American communist parties that followed the developments in Haiti with great interest shared the Cuban PSP's decision not to recognize the PCH. For the PCH's riposte, see *Combat*, 19 March 1946. For further comparison between the Cuban communists and the PCH see Alexander, *Communism in Latin America*, 297.

61. Hoover to Frederick B. Lyon, 25 March 1946, Washington, D.C., USNA, RG 59, 838.00B/3-2546. There is no evidence that the CPUSA supported the PCH. Radicals in the United States did, however, comment on the developments in Haiti. The 18 January edition of the *People's Voice* reported on "the revolution of the Haitian masses" as "part of the worldwide determination of exploited peoples to throw off the shackles by which they have been bound by powerful industrial interests as an aftermath of the world conflict just ended." "clipping file—Haiti," Taussig Papers, Box 120, FDRL.

62. Orme Wilson to Secretary of State, 12 February 1946, Port-au-Prince, USNA, RG 59, 838.00B/2-1246; See also Dorsinville, "1946 ou le délire opportuniste," 48–49.

63. Gérald Bloncourt, interview by author, 18 June 2001, Paris.

64. *Demain*, 22 May 1946.

65. *Rasoir*, 7 July 1946.

66. Orme Wilson to Secretary of State, 26 March 1946, Port-au-Prince, USNA, RG 59, 838.00B/3-2646.

67. *Le Nouvelliste*, 23 January 1946.

68. Max D. Sam, interview by author, 17 May 2000, Pétionville.

69. J. Edgar Hoover to Frederick B. Lyon, 26 March 1946, Washington, D.C., USNA, RG 84, 838.00B/3-2646. The FBI's position was influenced by rumors circulated in Port-au-Prince by the PCH in an effort to attract Garde attention to its rival PSP. For commentary on these rumors see *La Nation*, 19 February 1946.

70. *Combat*, 28 February 1946.

71. *Combat*, 23 March 1946.

72. *Combat*, 16 April 1946.

73. Heinl and Heinl, *Written in Blood*, 516.

74. *Class Moyenne et Masse*, 19 February 1946.

75. *Class Moyenne et Masse*, 1 May 1946.

76. Doubout and Joly, *Notes sur le développement*, 21; Lundahl, "Rise and Fall of the Haitian Labour Movement," 198.

77. Daniel Fignolé, *Soixante-cinq jours*, 6 fn 8.

78. Jack West to Secretary of State, n.d., Port-au-Prince, USNA, RG 84, 800/CONFIDENTIAL.

79. "Album de candidats à la Députation et candidats au Sénat," BHFIC.

80. For details on the demonstration, see *Combat*, 7 May 1946.

81. *Le Matin*, 12 April 1946.

82. See, for example, the articles "Haitian Election May 12; Mulattoes Fear Massacre," *Washington Afro-American*, 16 February 1946; "Haiti's Communists Reported Leading Presidency Race," *Trinidad Guardian*, 6 March 1946; "Leftist Candidate Threatens Violence if Defeated," *New York Times*, 14 May 1946, all in "clipping file-Haiti," Taussig Papers, Box 120, FDRL.

83. *Classe Moyenne et Masse*, 26 May 1946.

84. Horatio Mooers to Secretary of State, 22 May 1946, USNA, RG 59 838.00/5-2246. There was also suspicion that Magloire had manipulated the results so that a Senate favorable to his preferred candidate, Estimé, could be installed. See Orme Wilson to Secretary of State, 19 August 1946, USNA, RG 59, 838.00/8-1946. René Depestre, in a published interview, made mention of a private meeting he had with Estimé and Bloncourt's father a week before the election in which Estimé promised the young radical reward in return for support from the revolutionary youth, an offer Depestre flatly refused. See Depestre, "La révolution de 1946," 88–89. The extent to which Estimé participated in a plan to secure reelection to the Chamber of Deputies is not known, though in July Ambassador Wilson noted his suspicions that Estimé had been buying votes from legislators. Orme Wilson to Secretary of State, 24 July 1946, USNA, RG 59, 838.00/7-2446. See also Dumas-Pierre, "La Garde d'Haïti."

85. Orme Wilson to Secretary of State, "Memorandum of Conversation with Major Levelt on Haitian Political Situation," 18 May 1946, Port-au-Prince, USNA, RG 59, 838.00/5-1846.

86. Dumas-Pierre, "La Garde d'Haïti."

87. *Le Matin*, 17 May 1946.

88. In a private meeting with U.S. Ambassador Orme Wilson, Major Levelt expressed the CEM's deep fear that the leader of the Comité, Dr. Georges Rigaud, would use a provisional government to support his bid for presidency and clear the way for a Marxist victory. For this reason, he argued, it was necessary for the Garde to prevent at any costs the success of the new Communist alliance. Orme Wilson to Secretary of State, "Memorandum of Conversation with Major Levelt," 27 May 1946, Port-au-Prince, USNA, RG 84, 800B/05-2746.

89. *New York Times*, 15 May 1946; *Le Réveil*, 16 May 1946.

90. *Le Matin*, 14 May 1946.

91. *Le Matin*, 24 May 1946; See the article "Jail Haiti Mulattoes," *New Amsterdam News*, 15 June 1946; J. Edgar Hoover to Frederick B. Lyon, 29 May 1946, Washington, D.C., USNA, RG 84, 838.005/5-2946.

92. *La Nation*, 26 March 1946.

93. St. Armand's comments were recorded at a Communist Party meeting on 12 July 1946. See the enclosure to Orme Wilson to Secretary of State, 16 July, USNA, RG 84, 838.00B/7-1646.

94. *La Nation*, 3 April 1946. U.S. State Department investigations on the elections later confirmed that some of the financial backing for Estimé's campaign came from the Vincent family. Orme Wilson to Secretary of State, 19 August 1946, Port-au-Prince, USNA, RG 59, 838.00/8-1946. Some mention of the contradictions in the *noiriste* program of 1946 is made in Watkins, "Social Role of Color in Haiti."

95. *Demain*, 30 May 1946.

96. *Demain*, 21 June 1946.

97. *Le Matin*, 12 June 1946. See also Nicholls, *From Dessalines to Duvalier*, 186–88.

98. *La République*, 9 June 1946.

99. *Flambeau*, 11 June 1946; Max D. Sam, interview by author, 17 May 2001, Pétionville.

100. Max D. Sam, interview by author, 17 May 2001, Pétionville.

101. *Demain*, 12 June 1946.

102. The meeting was reported in *La Nation*, 18 June 1946. The translation is taken from Orme Wilson to Secretary of State, 25 June 1946, Port-au-Prince, USNA, RG 84, 838.00B/6-2546.

103. Ibid.; *La Nouvelle Ruche*, 3 July 1946.

104. On Alexis's views see *Combat*, 12 July 1946. For his address to the party regarding the upcoming elections, see Orme Wilson to Secretary of State, "Memorandum Describing Meeting of Communist Party of Haiti on July 26," 29 July 1946, Port-au-Prince, USNA, RG 59, 838.00B/7-2946. At one point the PCH adopted the slogan "Haiti aux Haïtiens" and formed L'Union Haïtienne anti-Imperialiste, though there is no indication of how this union functioned. See *Combat*, 5 August 1946.

105. *La Ruche*, 2 March 1946.

106. See *Artibonite Journal*, 16 March 1946.

107. Désinor, *Daniel Fignolé*, 68.

108. Doubout and Joly, *Notes sur le développement*, 15; Hector, *Syndicalisme et socialisme en Haïti*, 45.

109. *Chantiers*, 15 June 1946.

110. Désinor, *Daniel Fignolé*, 40.

111. Ibid., 48.

112. Ibid., 45.

113. Ibid.

114. Ibid., 50.

115. See Depestre, "La Révolution de 46," 88.

116. *La Nation*, 30 July 1946.

117. Ibid.

118. Diary entry, 7 April 1942, Logan diaries, LC. Logan also recalled his initial observations on Calixte in a piece he wrote on the presidential campaign for the *Pittsburgh Courier*. See Logan, "Trujillo Meddles in Haitian Affairs," in *Pittsburgh Courier*, 13 July 1946.

119. Élie Lescot to Rafael Trujillo, 11 April 1940, quoted in Trujillo to Lescot, 1 November 1943, PSF, Box 39, FDRL.

120. See the reports on the debates in *Le Matin*, 2, 6, 8 August 1946.

121. CEM to Daniel Fignolé, 5 August 1946, Correspondence Général Expédiée, folder 883, ANH; Désinor, *Daniel Fignolé*, 78.

122. *Le Matin*, 13 August 1946.

123. Paquin, *Haitians*, 145.

124. *Le Matin*, 13 August 1946.

125. It was largely held that the strike was allowed to take place by Magloire, despite the CEM's strict laws against political demonstrations, in an effort to coerce the legislature to vote for Estimé. Jack West to Ambassador, 12 November 1946, "Political Situation in Haiti (A Review)," enclosure to Harold Tittmann to Secretary of State, 13 November 1946, Port-au-Prince, USNA, RG 59, 838.00/11-1346.

126. Jack West to Ambassador, 12 November 1946, "Political Situation in Haiti (A Review)," enclosure to Harold Tittmann to Secretary of State, 13 November 1946, Port-au-Prince, USNA, RG 59, 838.00/11-1346.

127. *Le Nouvelliste*, 17 August 1946.

128. Robert Bazile, interview by author, 22 June 2000, Washington, D.C.; Jack West to Ambassador, 12 November 1946, "Political Situation in Haiti (A Review)," enclosure to Harold Tittmann to Secretary of State, 13 November 1946, Port-au-Prince, USNA, RG 59, 838.00/11-1346.

129. Dorsinville, *Marche arrière*, 54.

130. See *Chantiers*, 10 July 1947.

131. Orme Wilson to Secretary of State, "Memorandum of meeting with Col. Calixte," 17 August 1946, Port-au-Prince, USNA, RG 59 800/8-1746. Calixte also revealed that influential *milat* businesspeople and former Lescot rival Frederick Duvigneaud, who, according to Calixte, raised $75,000 for Estimé's campaign, had backed Estimé. He also admitted that his decision to resign from politics was done in order to weaken Fignolé's popular strength since he "would never continue street agitations alone" and hence look more favorable to the new regime.

132. Jack West to Ambassador, 12 November 1946, "Political Situation in Haiti (A

Review)," enclosure to Harold Tittmann to Secretary of State, 13 November 1946, Port-au-Prince, USNA, RG 59, 838.00/11-1346.

133. Ibid.; *Le Matin*, 19 August 1946.

134. Jack West, "Memorandum to the Ambassador," 21 August 1946, Port-au-Prince, USNA, RG 84, 838.00B/8-2646.

135. Max D. Sam, interview by author, 17 May 2000, Pétionville. Sam also recalls that in a telephone conversation with Estimé informing him of his acceptance of the post, Rigaud, on the advice of the PSP executive, warned the president that if he wanted the new government to work it was not the leftists he had to fear but the ambitious Magloire. Rigaud suggested that Estimé create a diplomatic post for Magloire in a foreign country. Estimé responded that Magloire had been far too beneficial to the government and should remain in Haiti, a critical decision that Estimé would live to regret.

136. Max D. Sam, interview by author, 17 May 2000, Pétionville.

137. Jack West to Ambassador, 12 November 1946, "Political Situation in Haiti (A Review)," enclosure to Harold Tittmann to Secretary of State, 13 November 1946, Port-au-Prince, USNA, RG 59, 838.00/11-1346.

138. On Fignolé's activities and policies during this period see Fignolé, *Soixante-cinq jours*. See also his correspondence with Estimé reprinted in *Foi Sociale*, various issues, June–July 1956.

139. *La Nation*, 28 August 1946.

140. Taken from the transcript of a radio broadcast in *Rasoir*, 1 September 1946.

141. See *Le Matin*, 15 October 1946. One report that came into the embassy was of a U.S. customs agent who, driving through the district of Carrefour at night, drove off the road and fell in a ditch. When he asked for assistance fifty locals came and shook his car, threatening to kill him; they claimed that Haiti was now a black country with a black president and all white foreigners should respect that. His life was spared, he alleged, only after giving the mob all the money he had. Harold Tittmann to Secretary of State, "Memorandum on J. I. Grant," 13 October 1946, Port-au-Prince, USNA, RG 84, 800/840.1. For regional responses to these events see, for example, "Call Port-au-Prince City of Fears," in the Jamaican *Daily Gleaner*, 1 October 1946.

142. *La Nation*, 25, 29 August 1946.

143. Jack West to Ambassador, 12 November 1946, "Political Situation in Haiti (A Review)," enclosure to Harold Tittmann to Secretary of State, 13 November 1946, Port-au-Prince, USNA, RG 59, 838.00/11-1346.

144. *La Nation*, 28 October 1946.

145. Jack West to Ambassador, 12 November 1946, "Political Situation in Haiti (A Review)," enclosure to Harold Tittmann to Secretary of State, 13 November 1946, Port-au-Prince, USNA, RG 59, 838.00/11-1346.

146. Ibid.

147. *Le Matin*, 23 October 1946; Désinor, *Daniel Fignolé*, 84.

148. Jack West to Ambassador, 12 November 1946, "Political Situation in Haiti (A Review)," enclosure to Harold Tittmann to Secretary of State, 13 November 1946, Port-au-Prince, USNA, RG 59, 838.00/11-1346.

149. C. Stevenson to Walker, Barber, et al., "The Haitian Cabinet Crisis," 28 October 1946, Port-au-Prince, USNA, RG 54, 838.002/10-2846.

Chapter 4

1. Robert Bazile, interview by author, 22 June 2000, Washington, D.C.

2. *Pittsburgh Courier*, 24 August 1946. See also the follow-up article, "New Deal for Haiti Seen Under President Estimé," *Pittsburgh Courier*, 31 August 1946.

3. Lamartinière Honorat, interview by author, 8 May 2001, Port-au-Prince.

4. *Les Griots*, 16 August 1948.

5. Duvalier and Denis, *Le problème des classes*, reprinted in Duvalier, *Œuvres essentielles*, 357. Emphasis added. Also quoted in Nicholls, *From Dessalines to Duvalier*, 195.

6. Ibid., 360.

7. Nicholls, *Dessalines to Duvalier*, 200.

8. Duvalier, *Œuvres essentielles*, 421.

9. Ibid., 405–21.

10. "Kote Moun Yo?," Jazz des Jeunes, *Super Jazz des Jeunes*, Ibo Records ILP 113, n.d.

11. As with most other forms of protest music, lyrics in Haitian *vodou-djazz* often take on multiple meanings depending on the context. This particular song, with its battery of vodou drums and *rara vaksins*, is usually interpreted in Haitian national discourse as a defiant expression of indigenous pride and a pointed denunciation of the *moun sa-a yo* (those people), specifically, the light-skinned elite who slander the culture of Haiti's black majority. Still, the song assumed other meanings in the late forties. The latent battle between Jazz des Jeunes and Jazz Saïeh for dominance on the music scene during the latter part of the Lescot years exploded after 1946 into a feud along color lines, as bandleader Issa El Saïeh has pointed out (Issa El Saïeh, interview by author, 13 July 1999, Port-au-Prince). Since Jazz Saïeh was led by a Haitian of Arab and U.S. descent, and composed of more proficient musicians, it was dismissed by Jazz des Jeunes as *non-authentique*, despite the band's frequent incorporation of vodou chants and rara instruments in its repertoire. By contrast, the untutored orchestration of Jazz des Jeunes was heralded by their *noiriste* supporters who praised them in the pages of *Les Griots* as being closer to the true culture of the country. Here we find yet another instance of class-color antagonism operating on a terrain beyond that of national politics. For further discussion on the tension between the two bands and on music during these years see Averill, *Day for the Hunter*, 60–62, and Largey, *Vodou Nation*, chap. 5.

12. Lyrics taken from *Rasoir*, 24 November 1946.

13. The performance of this song is taken from a 1948 promotional recording issued by the government to launch vodou-*djazz* in the international market and encourage Haitian tourism. I am grateful to M. Herby Widmaïer of Radio Metropole (formerly HH3W) for supplying me with a personal copy of this recording. Casimir's legendary renditions of traditional songs such as *Papa Gede, Panama-m tombe* and the Kongo song, *Caroline Acao* won her international attention.

14. "News of Haiti—Department of Tourist Promotion of the Republic of Haiti," Elmer Lancaster Files, Box 1, Office Folder, USNA, RG 40. On similar promotion of Haitian art in the late forties, see Rodman, *Haiti*, 94–97.

15. Director's Report, *Bulletin du Bureau d'Ethnologie* (December 1947).

16. Efron, "The 'New' Movement in Haiti," 18.

17. Harold Tittmann to Secretary of State, 16 January 1948, Port-au-Prince, USNA, RG 59, 838.504/1-1648.

18. *Livre bleu d'Haïti*, 514; "Haiti Information Bureau Press Release—Exposition 1949," Box A295, Folder 2, NAACP Papers, LC, and *Le Moniteur*, 24 November 1949. Detailed contemporary sources on the Exposition, including government decrees, are compiled in Mathurin, *Bicentenaire de la fondation de Port-au-Prince*.

19. *Livre bleu d'Haïti*, 518.

20. The ethnological contribution to the Exposition is discussed in *Les Griots*, 4, 22 October 1948; *Le Nouvelliste*, 5 December 1949; and *Bulletin du Bureau D'Ethnologie-Rapport 1949*. For a rich description of the Exposition in general see Corvington, *Port-au-Prince au cours des ans*, 6:150–52, 298–99, 117–20, passim; For a critique of the Exposition from a foreign participant see Wilson, *Red, Black, Blond, and Olive*, 90–92.

21. The theme of Caribbean cultural links with North America in the postwar period is the subject of several thought-provoking works. See, among others, Hill, *Calypso Callaloo*, chap. 9; Neptune, *Caliban and the Yankees*; and Pérez's penetrating study *On Becoming Cuban*, which includes fascinating insight on the role of U.S. culture in the shaping of Cuban national identity.

22. Georges Ramponeau, interview by Robert J. Alexander, 22 August 1949, Port-au-Prince, Alexander Papers, RU.

23. Greene, *Catholic Church in Haiti*, 108.

24. Walter White to Joseph V. Charles, "Re: Present U.S. Opinion of Haiti," 20 September 1947, Washington, D.C., Box A297, Folder 2, NAACP Papers, LC; Walter White to Dumarsais Estimé, 21 June 1949, Box A295, Folder 6, NAACP Papers, LC. See also Polyné, "Modernizing the Race," chap. 2, for a critical discussion of the campaign.

25. The only two exceptions were the non-elite Jean David, who although light-skinned shared political views more closely identified with the *noiristes*, and Emmanuel Thezan, who temporarily held a position as minister of finance in 1947.

26. The term *authentiques*, used in reference to the radical wing of the *noiriste* politicians who served under Estimé, originated in late 1946 shortly after the election. The coining of the term is usually associated with Roger Dorsinville, the most prominent of the *authentiques*. Dorsinville, however, remembers the term having pejorative origins among the socialist writers of *La Nation* in their verbal assault against the *noiristes* in the early days of the administration. See Dorsinville, *Marche arrière*, 135. It should also be noted that the *authentiques*, though sharing the same name, appear to have had little to do with the *auténtico* party then in power in Cuba.

27. Dorsinville, "1946 ou le délire opportuniste," 139. For an example of Dorsinville's views at the time see his essay, *Lettre aux hommes claires*.

28. Dorsinville, "1946 ou le délire opportuniste," 139.

29. Dorsinville, "Les 'Authentiques,'" 165–66.

30. Noé Fourcand, interview by author, 14 July 1999, Pétionville.

31. Baguidy, *Dynamique d'une revolution*, 36–37. The nationalist myth regarding Estimé expanded greatly in the sixties and the seventies because of Duvalierist propaganda. François Duvalier was largely responsible for encouraging this eulogizing when in 1964 he held a state funeral for Estimé and erected a bust in his honor at Bicentenaire. The myth itself, however, predates Duvalier's rise to power as exemplified in Jean Magloire's

celebratory *Dumarsais Estimé*. The most recent example of this is the account of the Estimé years by Estimé's wife. See Estimé, *Dumarsais Estimé*, especially the tributes on 163–68 and 179–86.

32. Heinl and Heinl, *Written in Blood*, 519; Rotberg, *Haiti: Politics of Squalor*, 175.

33. Dunham, *Island Possessed*, 47–48.

34. The biographical information here is drawn from *Psyche*, 14 July 1939, Magloire, *Dumarsais Estimé*; Rotberg, *Haiti: The Politics of Squalor*, 171; Estimé, *Dumarsais Estimé*, 41–50, passim; *Au service d'une cause-souvenirs d'une campagne*; Lamartinière Honorat, interview by author, 9 May 2001, Port-au-Prince; and Noé Fourcand, interview by author, 14 July 1999, Pétionville.

35. See, for example, the character descriptions of him in Shepherd to Eden, "Records of Leading Personalities in Hayti," 12 November 1937, *British Documents October 1937– 1938*, 325, and *Intelligence Review*, no. 28, 22 August 1946, in War Department Intelligence Review File, Box 18, HSTL.

36. *Le Matin*, 16 August 1946.

37. On earlier *noiriste* views on education see Duvalier's piece, "Contribution au problème de L'enseignement en Haïti," in *Les Griots* (October–December 1939).

38. Dumarsais Estimé, interview by Robert J. Alexander, 25 June 1948, Port-au-Prince, Alexander Papers, RU.

39. Robert Bazile, interview by author, 22 June 2000, Washington, D.C.; Georges Ramponeau, interview by Robert J. Alexander, 22 August 1949, Port-au-Prince, Alexander Papers, RU. On the UNESCO project, see Wilson, *Red, Black, Brown, and Olive*, 91, 95–103; Heinl and Heinl, *Written in Blood*, 518; Lundahl, *Peasants and Poverty*, 472.

40. *Le Matin*, 16 August 1946.

41. *Livre bleu d'Haïti*, 350; see articles 19–21 and 26 of the 1946 Constitution in "Un siècle de constitutions haïtiennes," 70–71; Hauch to Barber, Briggs, Braden, Wright, Smith, "Annual Report on Labor—Haiti, 1946," 31 January 1947, Port-au-Prince, USNA, RG 59, 838.504/1-3147.

42. "Premier Congrès National du Travail, Avril 1949," typescript, BHFIC.

43. *Livre bleu d'Haïti*, 330. Robert H. McBride to Secretary of State, "Haitian Labor Legislation," 24 April 1948, Port-au-Prince, USNA, RG 59, 838.504/4-2448.

44. René Victor, interview by Robert J. Alexander, 24 June 1948, Port-au-Prince, Alexander Papers, RU.

45. Hauch to Barber, Briggs, Braden, Wright, Smith, "Annual Report on Labor—Haiti, 1946," 31 January 1947, Port-au-Prince, USNA, RG 59, 838.504/1-3147; Robert H. McBride to Secretary of State, "Haitian Labor Legislation," 24 April 1948, Port-au-Prince, USNA, RG 59, 838.504/4-2448; *Livre bleu d'Haïti*, 330, 349, 354, 367–68; Lundahl, "Rise and Fall of the Haitian Labour Movement," 98–99; Latortue, *Le droit du travail*, 315–37; St. Jean, unpublished manuscript on history of labor in Haiti, Private collection.

46. Spruille Braden to the Members of the Haitian Special Mission, 17 March 1947, Washington, D.C., *FRUS*, *1947*, 8:722.

47. See "U.S. refuses loan to Haiti," *Pittsburgh Courier*, 29 March 1947.

48. "Haiti Seeks to Ease Economic Ties to U.S.," *Chicago Defender*, 28 September 1946.

49. "Haiti's Plea for U.S. Finance Overlooked," *Pittsburgh Courier*, 14 March 1947. See also Von Eschen, *Race against Empire*, 106–7, and "Haiti seeks to End U.S. 'Overlord-

ship,'" *New York Times*, 20 May 1947. U.S. black protest intensified a few months later when it was learned that Haitian diplomats on an official visit to the United States were mistreated and harassed by U.S. authorities. See Walter White to Harry S. Truman, 22 October 1947, Box A297, File 5, NAACP Papers, LC.

50. *Le Nouvelliste*, 26 May 1947; Robert Bazile, interview by author, 22 June 2000, Washington, D.C.; Noé Fourcand, interview by author, 14 July 1999, Pétionville; See also Chayet report, MAE, and Pierre Charles, *Haití*, 29.

51. Robert Bazile, interview by author, 22 June 2000, Washington, D.C.; *Combat*, 29 March 1947.

52. For details on the repayment of the loan and the fervor of patriotism that it engendered, see, for example, F. Morisseau-Leroy, "Freed Finances and After?," *Le Matin*, 16 August 1947.

53. Noé Fourcand, interview by author, 14 July 1999, Pétionville.

54. Norman Armour to Secretary of State, "Memorandum of Telephone Conversation with William Martin [Chairman of EX-IM bank]," 3 June 1948, Washington, D.C., *FRUS, 1948*, 9:596; Norman Armour to Thorpe, Woodward, Daniels, Stenger, Cady, "Memorandum of Conversation with William Martin," 28 June 1948, Washington, D.C., Assistant Secretary of State for Economic Affairs Files, Box 15, HSTL.

55. Charles C. Hauch to Secretary of State, "Memorandum of Conversation with Assistant Secretary Armour and Ambassador Tittman—Haiti," 10 October 1947, Washington, D.C., *FRUS, 1947*, 8:733.

56. Ibid. On the Artibonite project, see W. Alan Laflin's report, "The Artibonite Valley Project in Haiti," 9 July 1949 attachment to Melvin D. Hildreth to John R. Steelman, 18 August 1949, New York, OF, Box 162, HSTL.

57. Plummer, *Haiti and the United States*, 164; Jack West to Ambassador, 12 November 1946, "Political Situation in Haiti (A Review)," enclosure to Harold Tittmann to Secretary of State, 13 November 1946, Port-au-Prince, USNA, RG 59, 838.00/11-1346.

58. Moral, *Le paysan haïtien*, 312; Giles, "War and the Trade Orientation of Haiti," 281.

59. Charles C. Hauch to Secretary of State, "Memorandum of Conversation with Kerwin, Braden et al," 10 April 1947, Port-au-Prince, USNA, RG 59, 838.5034/4-1047.

60. Raynol St. Cyr, interview by Robert J. Alexander, 1 September 1949, Port-au-Prince, Alexander Papers, RU, and Louis Decatrel, interview by Robert J. Alexander, 31 August 1949, Port-au-Prince, Alexander Papers, RU.

61. Lundahl, *Peasants and Poverty*, 44.

62. Wilson, *Red, Black, Blond, and Olive*, 91.

63. The tension between the foreign and indigenous clergy is discussed in Greene, *Catholic Church in Haiti*, 108–10. On contemporary views of the indigenous clergy see Gayot, *Clergé indigène*.

64. Norman Armour to Charles C. Hauch, "Memorandum of Conversation with Frère Gabriel Edouard, Norman Armour, Sidney de la Rue, and Cecil B. Lyon," 27 January 1948, Washington, D.C., USNA, RG 59, 838.00/1-2748. We shall see later how the insinuation of communism haunted the Estimé presidency.

65. Wilson, *Red, Black, Blond, and Olive*, 87; Nicholls, *From Dessalines to Duvalier*, 197.

66. Nicholls, *From Dessalines to Duvalier*, 198; See also Duvalier, "Notre response a M. Foisset," in *Les Griots*, 1 April 1949, reprinted in *Œuvres essentielles*, 877–85.

67. Harold Tittmann to Secretary of State, 3 December 1946, Port-au-Prince, USNA, RG 59, 838.00/11-2946; J. Edgar Hoover to Jack Neal, 4 April 1947, Washington, D.C., USNA, RG 59, 838.00/4-1947.

68. *Le Nouvelliste*, 22 May 1947; Paquin, *Haitians*, 104.

69. See, for example, *Le Justicier*, 29 January and 6 February 1948.

70. *Le Nouvelliste*, 2 July 1948.

71. *La République*, 3 July 1948, quoted in *Le Matin*, 7 July 1948; *Les Griots*, 9 July 1948.

72. *Le Matin*, 7 July 1948; Harold Tittmann to Secretary of State, 6 July 1948, Port-au-Prince, USNA, RG 59, 838.00/7-648; Chayet Report, MAE, 149.

73. Paquin, *Haitians*, 97.

74. Robert H. McBride to Secretary of State, 20 July 1948, Port-au-Prince, USNA, RG 59, 838.00/7-2048; unidentified report on the Rémy-Viau Affair, ca. 1948, BHFIC.

75. Price, Memorandum to Walker, Woodward, Daniels, 30 July 1948, Port-au-Prince, USNA, RG 59, 838.00/7-3048.

76. Robert H. McBride to Secretary of State, 20 July 1948, Port-au-Prince, USNA, RG 59, 838.00/7-2048.

77. Chayet report, MAE, 149.

78. Harold Tittmann to Secretary of State, "Weekly Report," 4 August 1948, Port-au-Prince, USNA, RG 59, 838.00/8-448.

79. *Le Matin*, 27 July 1948. The beauty queen's blackness was celebrated in an article that appeared in *Les Griots*, 28 July 1948.

80. *Notre Jeunesse*, 24 June 1949.

81. *Chantiers*, 14 June 1947.

82. *Chantiers*, 16 November 1946.

83. At various instances his name appeared on U.S. embassy lists of Haitian communists and several government tracts circulated around Port-au-Prince identified him as such. See, for example, the list of Haitian communists attached to Orme Wilson to Secretary of State, 21 February 1946, Port-au-Prince, USNA, RG 84, 838.00B/22146.

84. Horatio Mooers to Ambassador, enclosure 1, "Memorandum regarding call at Chancery of Daniel Fignolé," 29 November 1946, Port-au-Prince, USNA, RG 59, 838.00/11-2946.

85. Jack West, "Study of Contemporary Leftist Groups in Haiti," 16, attachment to Harold Tittmann to Secretary of State, 11 June 1948, Port-au-Prince, USNA, RG 59, 838.00B/6-1148.

86. Information on the structure and activities of MOP used in this section comes from a survey of *Chantiers* for the years 1946–1948; Rodrigue Casimir, interview by author, 14 June 2003, Port-au-Prince; Daniel Fignolé and Michel Romain, interview by Robert J. Alexander, 25 June 1948, Port-au-Prince; Alexander Papers, RU; and a description of the party based on surveillance information by one of the leading officers in the Haitian Army. See "Memorandum of Conversation Between the Ambassador and Colonel Levelt," attachment to Harold Tittmann to Secretary of State, 29 June 1948, Port-au-Prince, USNA, RG 59, 838.00B/6-2948.

87. Rodrigue Casimir, interview by author, 14 June 2003, Port-au-Prince.

88. *Chantiers*, 10 January 1948.

89. See the address of Carmen Fignolé in *La Famille*, 26 December 1948.

90. The speech held at the inauguration ceremony of the flag was reprinted in a lavish and colorful edition of *Chantiers* celebrating the two-year anniversary of the party. See *Chantiers-Édition Extraordinaire*, 13 May 1948.

91. On the meaning of the colors in the Dessalines flag see Nicholls, *From Dessalines to Duvalier*, 235.

92. Ibid., 15. Bois Caïman was the vodou ceremony that launched the 1791 slave revolt.

93. For a discussion on MOP's exaggeration of its membership, see Harold Tittmann to Secretary of State, 3 July 1948, Port-au-Prince, USNA, RG 59, 838.00B/7-348. See also Lundahl, "Rise and Fall of Haitian Labour."

94. This figure is based on information in Lundahl, "Rise and Fall of Haitian Labour," 96; Nicholls, *From Dessalines to Duvalier*, 189; and Robert H. McBride to Secretary of State, "General Comments on Developments in Haitian Labor Movement," 14 January 1948, Port-au-Prince, USNA, RG 59, 838.504/1-1448.

95. Fignolé, *Contribution à l'histoire*, 180, n. 110.

96. *Le Matin*, 22 October 1947; Harold Tittmann to Secretary of State, 6 November 1947, Port-au-Prince, USNA, RG 59, 838.504/11-647.

97. *Le Matin*, 24 October 1947; Harold Tittmann to Secretary of State, 6 November 1947, Port-au-Prince, USNA, RG 59, 838.504/11-647; "Petit guide ou résumé de L'essentiel de la législation du Travail," in Premier Congrès du Travail, 1949, BHFIC; Hector, *Syndicalisme et Socialisme*, 78.

98. See Harold Tittmann to Secretary of State, "Labor Troubles at the Plantation Dolphin," 24 July 1947, Port-au-Prince, USNA, RG 59, 838.504/7-2447; Harold Tittmann to Secretary of State, 6 November 1947, Port-au-Prince, USNA, RG 59, 838.504/11-647.

99. *Le Matin*, 30 October 1947.

100. Ibid. Hector, *Syndicalisme et Socialisme*, 80, suggests that Fignolé's decision to launch the strike may not have entirely been a result of megalomania or dissatisfaction with the law but was a poor and ill-conceived attempt to force the government to take measures against SOT's rival unions associated with the FTH. Fignolé's intention, Hector maintains, was to offer a "coup pour coup" that would result in the forced dismantling of the PSP. For the government, however, it was clear that repression of the socialists (who in any event had denounced the strike) would only strengthen MOP and increase Fignolé's presence. If the government intended to have any success in the struggle for total control of the unions, it would have to silence Fignolé first.

101. Even after his decision to resign, Fignolé maintained that the strike had no political implications but was organized at the request of fourteen of the stronger unions in the Federation, dissatisfied with low wages and angered by the anti-labor law. See his farewell speech to SOT's General Assembly in Fignolé, *Contribution à l'histoire*, 194–96.

102. Daniel Fignolé and Michel Romain, interview by Robert J. Alexander, 25 June 1948, Port-au-Prince, Alexander Papers, RU.

103. *La Nation*, 4 November 1947.

104. Many of Duvalier's biographers, perhaps influenced by Duvalier's own self-serving legend, wrongly date his split with Fignolé as occurring just after Estimé's election in 1946, when in fact he remained an active member of MOP until the October 1947 strike.

105. The most publicized of these arrests occurred in June 1948 when Fignolé was

incarcerated for a month on circumstantial evidence that he had been distributing antigovernment tracts. See *Le Matin*, 24 June 1948, and *Foi Sociale*, 16 May 1956. Such actions did not deter Fignolé, who a month later incensed Estimé with his strong opposition to the government's handling of the Rémy-Viau murders. On his release, Fignolé sought to gain the U.S. embassy's support against Estimé by sending MOP vice-president Michel Romain to meet with the ambassador, to no avail. Harold Tittmann to Secretary of State, 3 July 1948, Port-au-Prince, USNA, RG 59, 838.00B/7-348. See also Daniel Fignolé, interview by Robert J. Alexander, 23 August 1949, Port-au-Prince, Alexander Papers, RU, and the comments in Alexander, *Presidents*, 193–97.

106. "Memorandum of Conversation Between The Ambassador and Colonel Levelt," attachment to Harold Tittmann to Secretary of State, 29 June 1948, Port-au-Prince, USNA, RG 59, 838.00B/6-2948; Rodrigue Casimir, interview by author, 14 June 2003, Port-au-Prince.

107. See "Déclaration du Bureau Politique du P.C.H," in *Combat*, 15 March 1947.

108. Ibid.

109. Harold Tittmann to Secretary of State, enclosure no. 2 "Communism in Haiti," 2 April 1947, USNA, RG 59, 838.00B/4-247, 1, 2. For a critique of the report, see enclosure no. 1. William Z. Foster, former head of the CPUSA, in *Outline Political History*, 386, makes the exaggerated claim that in 1947 there were over five hundred avowed communists in Haiti.

110. Another principal member of the party, Théodore Baker, the head of the youth arm and core member of *La Ruche*, resigned in December and left rather suddenly for the United States a few days later, where he remained in exile. The last issue of *La Ruche* appeared on 19 December 1946.

111. See the interview with Estimé by the medical students' and their comments in *Le Caducée* (October–November 1946): 5–9.

112. Harold Tittmann to Secretary of State, 7 May 1947, Port-au-Prince, USNA, RG 59, 838.00/5-747. A copy of the tract is attached to H. Mooers to Secretary of State, 2 April 1947, Port-au-Prince, and USNA, RG 59, 838.00B/4-247. See also Luc, "Sur la diffusion," 98.

113. On anticommunism in Cuba, see de La Fuente, *A Nation for All*, 235–37.

114. *Combat*, 26 April 1947. Emphasis included.

115. Hector, *Syndicalisme et socialisme en Haïti*, 58. Hector also correctly mentions that the PCH was heavily influenced by the phenomenon of Browderism, a tactic developed by Earl Browder, general secretary of the CPUSA, who advocated that the Communist Party reform its strategies in order to better integrate into national politics. On Browder's views see, for example, Starobin, *American Communism in Crisis*, 50–80.

116. *Le Matin*, 17 February 1948. An earlier anticommunist law was passed in March 1947 but was not enforced.

117. Ibid.

118. *L'Action*, 8 March 1948; Harold Tittmann to Secretary of State, 12 March 1948, Port-au-Prince, USNA, RG 84, 838.00B/3-1248.

119. Ibid.

120. Robert H. McBride to Secretary of State, 25 February 1948, Port-au-Prince, USNA, RG 59, 838.00B/2-2548.

121. For a fine discussion of these patterns in Latin America, see the introduction to Bethell and Roxborough, *Latin America*, 1–33. See also the essays in Rock, *Latin America in the 1940s*.

122. Robert Bazile, interview by author, 22 June 2000, Washington, D.C.

123. "Communist Potential—Haiti," n.d., Confidential File, Truman Papers, Box 42, HSTL.

124. See for example the article by Stuart Morrisson in the *Miami Herald*, 16 September 1947, which blatantly labels the social policies of the regime as communist. For the *authentique* response to this attack see "Une Lettre de Roger Dorsinville à M. Stuart Morrisson," *Le Nouvelliste*, 3 October 1946; Noé Fourcand, interview by author, 14 July 1999, Pétionville.

125. *New York Times*, 2 May 1947. The NAACP worked with the Haitian government to change public opinion in the United States toward Haiti. See Dumarsais Estimé to Walter White, 26 January 1949, Port-au-Prince, Box A295, NAACP Papers, LC; Peter Hilton to Walter White, 17 January 1949, Box A297, NAACP Papers, LC; and the article "Charge: Haitian Leftist Purge to get U.S. Loan," in *Chicago Defender*, 17 May 1947.

126. See, for example, William DeCourcy to Secretary of State, "Possible Renescence [*sic*] of Communist Party," 15 January 1949, Port-au-Prince, USNA, RG 59, 838.00B/1-1549, and *Les Griots*, 11 November 1949.

127. For example, when simultaneous riots broke out in marketplaces in Croix des Bossales, Pétionville, Cap Haïtien, and Gonaïves in early May 1948, which by all accounts appear to have been spontaneous protests against the high cost of living, Estimé told U.S. Ambassador Tittmann that it was a communist "try-out" for a larger demonstration. See Harold Tittmann to Secretary of State, 4 May 1948, Port-au-Prince, USNA, RG 84, 838.00B/-, and John Romelein to Harold Tittmann, 5 May 1948, Port-au-Prince, USNA, RG 84, 838.00B/-. U.S. authorities, it should be noted, recognized the transparency of Estimé's attempt to use communists as scapegoats to disguise the country's economic woes.

128. See, for example, *La Nation*, 4 February 1948.

129. Some of these unions deserted to MOP after the dissolution of the PCH.

130. Hector, *Syndicalisme et Socialisme*, 48; *La Nation*, 7 October 1948; Roger F. Leonard, interview by Robert J. Alexander, 30 August 1949, Port-au-Prince, Alexander Papers, RU; Max D. Sam, interview by author, 17 May 2000, Pétionville.

131. Doubout and Joly, *Notes sur le développement*, 18.

132. Max D. Sam, interview by author, 17 May 2001, Pétionville; Andrée Roumer-Innocent, interview by author, 2 May 2001, Port-au-Prince.

133. René Victor, interview by Robert J. Alexander, 24 June 1948, Port-au-Prince, Alexander Papers, RU; Hector, *Syndicalisme et Socialisme*, 76.

134. André Cameau, Victor Vabre, and Edouard Benodin, interview by Robert J. Alexander, 24 June 1948, Port-au-Prince, Alexander Papers, RU.

135. Milien Josué, interview by Robert J. Alexander, 21 August 1949, Port-au-Prince, Alexander Papers, RU; Robert H. McBride to Secretary of State, "General Comments on Developments in Haitian Labor Movement," 14 January 1948, Port-au-Prince, USNA, RG 59, 838.504/1-1448.

136. Milien Josué, interview by Robert J. Alexander, 21 August 1949, Port-au-Prince, Alexander Papers, RU; Alexander, *Presidents*, 456.

137. DeCourcy to Hauch, Walker, Woodward, and Hale, "Present Status of Leftist groups in Haiti," June 8, 1949, RG 59, USNA, 838.00/6-849.

138. Roger F. Leonard, interview by Robert J. Alexander, 30 August 1949, Port-au-Prince, Alexander Papers, RU.

139. Corvington, *Port-au-Prince au cours des ans*, 6:240.

140. *L'Action*, 3 May 1948.

141. Dumas-Pierre, "La Garde d'Haïti," 17.

142. Paul Laraque, interview by author, 5 July 2000, New York City.

143. Max D. Sam, interview by author, 7 May 2001, Pétionville.

144. See, for example, the editorials "Politique" in *La Nation*, 23, 26, 29, and 30 April 1948. See also Nicholls, *From Dessalines to Duvalier*, 200–203.

145. Charlier, "Rapport," 305.

146. Ibid.

147. Roger F. Leonard, interview by Robert J. Alexander, 30 August 1949, Port-au-Prince, Alexander Papers, RU.

148. Max D. Sam, interview by author, 17 May 2001, Pétionville.

149. Charlier, "Rapport," 308.

150. Lespès's articles appeared in *Le Nouvelliste* during March 1948. Based on these articles, which criticized the failure of banana nationalization, Estimé created a Banana Monopoly Office and both men accepted his offer to be directors. The office, however, existed in name only.

151. Max D. Sam, interview by author, 17 May 2000, Pétionville. The acceptance of this post stimulated harsh criticism by Fignolé, who argued that it was evidence of the socialists' support for the Estimé government. See *Chantiers*, 13 October 1947. For the PSP's rejoinder, see *La Nation*, 15 October 1947. See also Daniel Fignolé, interview by Robert J. Alexander, 23 August 1949, Port-au-Prince, Alexander Papers, RU.

152. René Victor, interview by Robert J. Alexander, 24 June 1948, Port-au-Prince, Alexander Papers, RU.

153. Harold Tittmann to Secretary of State, "Policies of the Popular Socialist Party," 16 December 1947, Port-au-Prince, USNA, RG 59, 838.00/12-1647.

154. Jack West, "Study of Contemporary Leftist Groups in Haiti," 4, 12, attachment to Harold Tittmann to Secretary of State, 11 June 1948, Port-au-Prince, USNA, RG 59, 838.00B/6-1148.

155. Ibid., 13.

156. Robert Bazile, interview by author, 22 June 2000, Washington, D.C.

157. Harold Tittmann to Secretary of State, Enclosure E. L. Tanner to Harold Tittmann, "Memorandum of Conversation," 26 May 1947, Port-au-Prince, USNA, RG 59, 838.00/5-2647.

158. Harold Tittmann to Secretary of State, Enclosure E. L. Tanner to Harold Tittmann, "Memorandum of Conversation," 26 May 1947, Port-au-Prince, RG 59, 838.00/5-2647. In this report, based on a conversation with Magloire during an informal social gathering at the residence of a prominent member of the bourgeoisie, Magloire revealed

that he had attempted to maneuver toward the presidency in 1946 but desisted once he recognized the problem a military regime would cause for the U.S. government's promotion of democracy in the island; thus he decided against it and used his influence and power to get Estimé elected.

159. One unsubstantiated rumor that received much currency was that Magloire handed in his resignation to Estimé in order to challenge him as a civilian in September, a move that Estimé refused. For a report on the rumors see, for example, DeCourcy to Secretary of State, "Joint Weekly Report," 12 September 1949, Port-au-Prince, USNA, RG 59, 838.00/(W)/9-849.

160. A full and sometimes contradictory account of Roland's role in the 1946 legislative elections is given in Roland, *La naufrage d'une nation*, 241–58.

161. Robert Bazile, interview by author, 22 June 2000, Washington, D.C.; Paul Laraque, interview by author, 5 July 2000, New York City.

162. See the tract "Haitiens!" attached to Officer in charge of American Mission to Secretary of State, 12 September 1949, Ciudad Trujillo, USNA, RG 59, 838.00/9-1249.

163. William DeCourcy to Secretary of State, 17 May 1949, Port-au-Prince, USNA, RG 59, 838.00/5-1749.

164. Paul Cassagnol, interview by Robert J. Alexander, 29 August 1949, Port-au-Prince, Alexander Papers, RU.

165. Ameringer, *Democratic Left in Exile*, 104.

166. *La Nation*, 9 February 1949. See also William DeCourcy to Secretary of State, "Re: Public Reaction to Developments in Roland Plot," 11 February 1949, Port-au-Prince, USNA, RG 59, 838.00/2-1149.

167. William DeCourcy to Secretary of State, 12 January 1949, Port-au-Prince, USNA, RG 59, 838.00/1-1249.

168. William DeCourcy to Secretary of State, 26 September 1949, Port-au-Prince, USNA, RG 59, 838.001/9-2649; DeCourcy to Secretary of State, 12 January 1949, Port-au-Prince, USNA, RG 59, 838.00/1-1249; "Affaires d'Haïti, 1950–1990," Mangonès Collection, BHPSE.

169. William DeCourcy to Secretary of State, 15 November 1949, Port-au-Prince, USNA, RG 59, 838.00/11-1849; Alexander, *Presidents*, 190–91.

170. Daniel Fignolé, interview by Robert J. Alexander, 23 August 1949, Alexander Papers, RU.

171. William DeCourcy to Secretary of State, 13 November 1949, Port-au-Prince, USNA, RG 84, 838.00/11-1349.

172. William DeCourcy to Secretary of State, "Joint Weekly Report," 18 November 1949, Port-au-Prince, USNA, RG 59, 838.00(W)/11-1849, 3.

173. The pamphlet is included in Ralph H. Ackerman to Secretary of State, 22 December 1949, Ciudad Trujillo, USNA, RG 59, 838.00/12-2249.

174. DeCourcy to Secretary of State, "Joint Weekly Report," 23 December 1949, Port-au-Prince, USNA, RG 59, 838.00(W)/12-2349.

175. On the report's findings, which were described by the U.S. State Department as "no white wash," see *FRUS, 1950*, 7:522. John H. Burns to Secretary of State, "Joint Weekly Report," 13 January 1950, Port-au-Prince, USNA, RG 59, 738.00/1-1350; *Weekly*

Review, 22 March 1950, 12–15, WHCF, Box 59, HSTL; Ameringer, *Democratic Left in Exile*, 106–10; Plummer, *Haiti and the United States*, 160.

176. *Life*, 13 March 1950, 107.

177. See Pan-American Union, *Foreign Trade of Haiti, 1945–1950*.

178. Robert H. McBride to Secretary of State, 4 August 1948, Port-au-Prince, USNA, RG 59, 838.00/8-448.

179. Wilson, *Red, Black, Blond, and Olive*, 92.

180. Peter Hilton to Walter White, 24 May 1949, New York, Box A295, folder 2, NAACP Papers, LC.

181. For critiques by government officials see, for example, *L'Action*, 23 September 1948; Robert H. McBride to Secretary of State, 27 September 1948, USNA, RG 59, 838.607PORT-AU-PRINCE/9-2748, and Louis Decatrel, interview by Robert J. Alexander, 31 August 1949, Port-au-Prince, Alexander Papers, RU.

182. The Bicentennial Exposition was likened to Christophe's imposing citadel in the north of Haiti, in a critical report on Estimé's economic record by U.S. ambassador William DeCourcy. DeCourcy noted Estimé's "ruthlessness" in completing the Exposition, a "white elephant" undertaken at an "exaggerated cost to the Haitian people." See William DeCourcy to Secretary of State, "Evidence of Instability in the Haitian Government," 20 December 1948, Port-au-Prince, USNA, RG, 59, 838.00/12-2048.

183. William DeCourcy to Secretary of State, 25 May 1950, Port-au-Prince, USNA, RG 59, 738.00/5-2550.

184. Jack West, "Study of Contemporary Leftist Groups in Haiti," 17, attachment to Harold Tittmann to Secretary of State, 11 June 1948, Port-au-Prince, USNA, RG 59, 838.00B/6-1148.

185. *Le Matin*, 19 April 1950.

186. See the descriptions of the investigations in *Le Matin*, 3 May 1950; Noé Fourcand, interview by author, 14 July 1999, Pétionville.

187. *La République*, 3 May 1950. Similar attacks were made in *Le Soir*, 3 May 1950. To clear his name, Déjoie visited the U.S. chargé d'affaires and showed proof that a recent loan he received for the expansion of his essential oils project from which much of his financial independence derived were acquired from U.S. sources and not, as Estimists had rumored, from Trujillo. This was not the first time the government sought to force the troublesome Déjoie out of the Senate by implicating him with Trujillo's malfeasance. A year earlier, a terrified Déjoie consulted the U.S. embassy about asylum after being followed by Estimé operatives and wrongly accused of being a Roland supporter. See "Memorandum of Conversation between McBride and Senator Déjoie," Port-au-Prince, USNA, RG 59, 350/ASYLUM.

188. William DeCourcy to Secretary of State, 12 May 1950, Port-au-Prince, USNA, RG 59, 738.00/5-1250.

189. For comments on Estimé's appeals to the U.S. embassy, see John H. Burns to Secretary of State, "Deterioration in Strength of President Estimé's Position," 5 May 1950, Port-au-Prince, USNA, RG 59, 738.00/5-550.

190. John H. Burns to Secretary of State, 28 April 1950, Port-au-Prince, USNA, RG 59, 738.00/4-2850.

191. Robert Bazile, interview by author, 22 June 2000, Washington, D.C.

192. Chauvet, *Victime de 1946*; Pierre, *Témoignages*, 27.

193. *Le Matin*, 8 May 1950; William DeCourcy to Secretary of State, 12 May 1950, Port-au-Prince, USNA, RG 59, 738.00/5-1250.

194. *Le Matin*, 9 May 1950.

195. Pierre, *Témoignages*, 28.

196. William DeCourcy to Secretary of State, "Final interview with Estimé," 19 May 1950, Port-au-Prince, USNA, RG 59, 738.00/5-1950.

197. Although the junta intervened on the grounds that it was staving off potential anarchy, its actions were nonetheless unconstitutional, as the Senate should have had the responsibility of selecting Estimé's successor. This fact was not lost on Magloire, who was the leading figure in Estimé's overthrow.

198. John H. Burns to Secretary of State, 21 April 1950, Port-au-Prince, USNA, RG 59, 738.00/4-2150; William DeCourcy to Secretary of State, "Final interview with Estimé," 19 May 1950, Port-au-Prince, USNA, RG 59, 738.00/5-1950.

Chapter 5

1. Walter White to Paul Magloire, 9 June 1950, Washington, D.C., attachment to William DeCourcy to Department of State, 16 June 1950, Port-au-Prince, USNA, RG 59, 738.00/6-1650. This letter was a reply to a note written by Magloire to White in which he claimed that Estimé's failure to respect the country's democratic structure had been the reason for the coup. See Paul E. Magloire to Walter White, 2 June 1950, Port-au-Prince, Box A295, folder 4, NAACP Papers, LC. Note in particular White's marginal comments, which included repeated notations such as "proof?" and "have not people the right to say who they wish to rule?" which suggest a dissatisfaction with the way in which the coup was carried out.

2. Paul E. Magloire, interview by Robert J. Alexander, 3 December 1971, New York City, Alexander Papers, RU.

3. See the descriptions in *Le Matin*, 15, 19, 26, 27, 28, 29, and 30 July 1950, and the supplement of 1 August, devoted entirely to promoting Magloire's campaign. See also Bernardin, *Général Paul Eugène Magloire*, 66–67.

4. Bernardin, *Général Paul Eugène Magloire*, 78; Heinl and Heinl, *Written in Blood*, 531; Diederich, *Bon Papa*, 33.

5. Hartt, "Broadcasting in Haiti," chap. 3.

6. See the address of Monsignor Paul Robert, 4 November 1950, reprinted in Bonhomme, *Révolution et contrerévoltuon en Haïti*, 52–53.

7. Nicholls, *From Dessalines to Duvalier*, 193.

8. Herby Widmaïer, interview by author, 8 May 2001, Port-au-Prince; Issa El Saïeh, interview by author, 13 July 1999, Port-au-Prince; *Le Montée*, 6 January 1956; Diederich, *Bon Papa*, 122–68.

9. Paul E. Magloire, interview by Robert J. Alexander, 3 December 1971, New York City, Alexander Papers, RU.

10. Bernardin, *Général Paul Eugène Magloire*, 10. Paul Laraque, interview by author, 5 July 2000, New York City.

11. Bonhomme, *Révolution et contrerévolution*, 13.

12. *Le Nouvelliste*, 14 January 1954.

13. Rabe, *Eisenhower and Latin America*, chap. 5; Zoumaras, "Path to Panamericanism," 4.

14. Robert Amory to H. S. Craig, "Intelligence Support for Implementation of NSC144/1, 'U.S. Objectives and Courses of Action with respect to Latin America,'" 18 March 1953, Operations Coordinating Board Central File Series, NSC Papers, Box 74, DDEL.

15. See "The Machinery for Soviet-Control—Latin America," 20 January 1955, Operations Coordinating Board Central File Series, NSC Papers, Box 72, DDEL.

16. *Port-au-Prince Times*, 13 June 1951, attachment to John H. Burns to Department of State, 14 July 1951, Port-au-Prince, USNA, RG 59, 738.00/7-1451.

17. *Le Matin*, 6 January 1951; Rodrigue Casimir, interview by author, 14 June 2003, Port-au-Prince.

18. Max D. Sam, interview by author, 17 May 2001, Pétionville. See Georges Petit's editorial in *L'Action*, 30 November 1950, for comments on the repression of the PSP members.

19. Max D. Sam, interview by author, 17 May 2001, Pétionville.

20. Hector, *Syndicalisme et socialisme*, 88.

21. Slator C. Blackiston Jr. to American Ambassador, 12 December 1951, Port-au-Prince, USNA, RG 84, 350/POLITICAL AFFAIRS.

22. Andrée Roumer-Innocent, interview by author, 2 May 2001, Port-au-Prince; Hector, *Syndicalisme et socialisme*, 87.

23. Homer Gayne to Hobart Spalding, "Re: Lack of Freedom of the Press in Haiti," 24 November 1951, Port-au-Prince, USNA, RG 59, 738.00/11-2451; Andrée Roumer-Innocent, interview by author, 2 May 2001, Port-au-Prince.

24. This is based on information from Andrée Roumer-Innocent, who married Alexis shortly after his return. Alexis would later help to form the PEP. See Robert S. Folsom to Department of State, 26 June 1952, Port-au-Prince, USNA, RG 59, 738.00/6-2652.

25. Paul Laraque, interview by author, 5 July 2000, New York City.

26. PPLN manifesto quoted in Diederich and Burt, *Papa Doc*, 313.

27. Robert Folsom to Department of State, 11 June 1952, Port-au-Prince, USNA, RG 59, 738.00/6-1152. See also the transcript of the speech of the Minister of Interior Mauclair Zépherin, at the government press conference denouncing Depestre and the Haitian communists, outlined in Robert Folsom to Department of State, 16 June 1952, Port-au-Prince, USNA, RG 59, 738.00/6-1652.

28. See Robert Folsom to Department of State, 26 June 1952, Port-au-Prince, USNA, RG 59, 738.00/6-2652.

29. Bordes, *Haïti*, 253.

30. Information on this incident is drawn from *Le Matin*, 22 January 1952; *Le Nouvelliste*, 18, 19, and 21 January 1952; Slater C. Blackiston Jr. to Department of State, 22 January 1952, Port-au-Prince, USNA, RG 84, 350/POLITICAL AFFAIRS; Bordes, *Haiti*, 255, 386–88.

31. Slater C. Blackiston Jr. to Department of State, 22 January 1952, Port-au-Prince, USNA, RG 84, 350/POLITICAL AFFAIRS.

32. The resignation statement signed by Romain and two other members was reprinted in *Haïti Journal*, 16 April 1953.

33. *Construction*, 21 November 1951.

34. See, for example, the comments on Fignolé in Robert Folsom to Department of State, 22 January 1953, Port-au-Prince, USNA, RG 59, 738.00/1-2253.

35. See Auguste, *La voix du M.O.P.*, 20. Also Fignolé's own descriptions of his programs, Fignolé, *Mon mandat*.

36. *Construction*, 23 November 1952.

37. Connett to Woodward and Cabot, "Recent Political Disturbances in Haiti," 14 January 1954, Port-au-Prince, USNA, RG 59, 738.00/1-1454.

38. Désinor, *Daniel Fignolé*, 123.

39. Details on this are taken from the statement of Fignolé's wife, Carmen, attached to Robert Folsom to Department of State, 18 January 1954, Port-au-Prince, USNA, RG 59, 738.00/1-1854, and Paul Laraque, interview by author, 5 July 2000, New York City.

40. Doubout and Joly, *Notes sur le développement*, 30.

41. Robert Y. Brown to Department of State, 26 January 1951, Kingston, USNA, RG 59, 738.11/1-2651.

42. Dumarsais Estimé to Julio J. Pierre Audain, "Lettre de Estimé," 7 August 1951, Kingston, typescript, BHFIC.

43. On Estimé's year in exile in Jamaica, where Jamaican and Haitian officials constantly watched him, see the discussion in Dunham, *Island Possessed*, 52–57. On his exile in general see Estimé, *Dumarsais Estimé*, chap. 4. The State Department's staunch support of Magloire over Estimé is revealed in Dean Acheson to William DeCourcy, 4 October 1952, Washington, D.C., USNA, RG 59, 738.00/10-452.

44. Dumarsais Estimé to Harvey R. Wellman, 12 May 1953, New York City, USNA, RG 59, 738.00/5-1253; Wellman to Estimé, 13 May 1953, New York City, USNA, RG 59, 738.00/5-1353; "Memorandum of Conversation between Estimé, Wellman, and Connett," 27 January 1953, USNA, RG 59, 738.00/1-2753. For Estimé's apprehensions about going to the United States, see Estimé to Walter White, 24 July 1950, Paris, Box A295, folder 4, NAACP Papers, LC.

45. American Ambassador to C. G. Follansbee, 15 June 1951, Port-au-Prince, USNA, RG 59, 350/POLITICAL AFFAIRS.

46. John H. Burns to Secretary or State, 29 May 1951, Port-au-Prince, USNA, RG 59, 738.00/5-2951; John H. Burns to Department of State, 16 June 1951, USNA, RG 84, 738.00/0-1651; *Le Matin*, 30 June 1951; Dorsinville, *Marche arrière*, 45.

47. For an account of this period from a member of the army who regularly attended the meetings, see Pierre, *Témoignages*, 42.

48. Ibid.

49. Ibid., 41.

50. Trouillot, *Haiti: State against Nation*, 149.

51. Nicholls, *From Dessalines to Duvalier*, xv.

52. Plummer, *Haiti and the United States*, 143. Writers who share this view include Hartt, "Broadcasting in Haiti," chap. 3, who sympathetically argues that under Magloire Haitians "enjoyed the highest level of prosperity in Haiti's history as an independent nation." Also see Rotberg, *Haiti: The Politics of Squalor* 180–81; Averill, *Day for the Hunter*,

70; Manigat, *Haiti of the Sixties*, 40; and Bernardin, *Général Paul Eugène Magloire*, 119–32, 137–40, 145–48, 153–58, 177–84, passim. Compare Trouillot, *Haiti: State against Nation*, 139–43, whose emphasis on the relationship between the "economic crisis" and socio-political issues in the fifties has influenced the analysis in this section. Gérald Pierre-Charles, writing from a dependency framework, first pointed to the problems in the economic structure during the fifties, in *La economía haitana*. See also Dupuy, *Haiti in the World Economy*, 153–55, and the interviews in *Les chemins de la mémoire: Haiti avant Duvalier*.

53. Bernardin, *Général Paul Eugène Magloire*, v.

54. Plummer, *Haiti and the United States*, 167.

55. The realization of this owed much to the ardor of the NAACP and Walter White in particular, who began to push for the film to be made and premiered in Haiti from as early as 1947. See Walter White to Dumarsais Estimé, 12 January 1947, Box A295, NAACP Papers, LC.

56. Lacombe, "Le tourisme en Haïti," 4. See also Goldberg, "Commercial Folklore and Voodoo in Haiti," 144, and Polyné, "Modernizing the Race," 79–84.

57. These figures are based on estimates taken from Pérez, *On Becoming Cuban*, 167; Schroeder, *Cuba*, 462; Taylor, *To Hell with Paradise*, 160; *Les étapes d'un relèvement*, 83; *Guide économique de la république d'Haïti*, 68; and Lacombe, "Le tourisme en Haïti," 4.

58. There were, of course, exceptions such as the previously noted anti-yaws program and the construction of a rural hospital, the Albert Schweitzer Hospital, in Deschapelles.

59. For details on the Five Year Plan see Lundahl, *Peasants and Poverty*, 307–8.

60. Paul E. Magloire, interview by Robert J. Alexander, 3 December 1971, New York City, Alexander Papers, RU; *Les étapes d'un relèvement*, 144.

61. *Haitian Economy in 1954*, 2. For a discussion on ISI developments elsewhere in Latin America and the Caribbean see, for example, Bethell, *Latin America*, and Mandle, *Patterns of Caribbean Development*.

62. *Haitian Economy in 1954*, 5.

63. "An Economic Program for the Americas: Report of the International Review Advisory Board, 1954," 7, Bohan Papers, Box 1, HSTL.

64. Moral, *Le paysan haïtienne*; Trouillot, *Haiti: State against Nation*, 141.

65. Dupuy, *Haiti in the World Economy*, 155.

66. Rabe, *Eisenhower and Latin America*, 95.

67. Dupuy, *Haiti in the World Economy*, 156; Pierre-Charles, *La economía haitiana*, 151. See also the article, "Haiti retrenches after poor year," in *New York Times*, 5 January 1957.

68. John Foster Dulles, "Memorandum for the President, 'United States Assistance to Haiti since Hurricane Hazel,'" 1 November 1954, Ann Whitman File, Dulles-Hector Series, Box 4, DDEL; *Les étapes d'un relèvement*, 23–28.

69. *Les étapes d'un relèvement*, 145.

70. Lundahl, *Peasants and Poverty*, 629. Lundahl also points out that during this period outmigration to other islands such as Cuba and the Dominican Republic also expanded tremendously.

71. See the tables in Hector, *Syndicalisme et socialisme*, 190–91.

72. *UNESCO Statistical Yearbook*, 17; *Les étapes d'un relèvement*, 109.

73. These figures are taken from Dupuy, *Haiti in the World Economy*, 154.

74. *L'Arène*, 28 April 1956.

75. Roger Baldwin to Robert Murphy, 17 May 1954, Washington, USNA, RG 59, 738.00/5-1754.

76. *Time*, 22 February 1954, 46.

77. "Memorandum from the director of the Office of Middle American Affairs (Newbegin) to the Assistant Secretary of State for Inter-American Affairs (Holland)," 5 January 1955, Washington, D.C., *FRUS, 1955–57*, 6:931–32.

78. Milton Barrall to Department of State, 7 February 1955, Port-au-Prince, USNA, RG 59, 738.00/2-755. For Fignolé's preelection comments, see *Indépendance*, 13 December 1954.

79. Désinor, *Daniel Fignolé*, 116.

80. Milton Barrall to Department of State, 7 January 1955, Port-au-Prince, USNA, RG 59, 738.00/1-755.

81. Trouillot, *Haiti: State against Nation*, 142–43.

82. "Memorandum of a Conversation," 3 December 1956, Washington, D.C., *FRUS, 1955–57*, 6:947.

83. *L'Arène*, 28 April 1956.

84. See the bulletins attached to Milton Barrall to Department of State, 22 May 1956, Port-au-Prince, USNA, RG 59, 738.00/5-2256.

85. See the reports in *L'Arène*, 30 May 1956; *Le Montée*, 26 May 1956; *Indépendance*, 23 May 1956; Milton Barrall to Department of State, 22 May 1956, Port-au-Prince, USNA, RG 59, 738.00/5-2256.

86. Ibid.; *New York Times*, 23 May 1956; *Le Matin*, 22 May 1956.

87. This expression, used to refer to the nonviolent resistance of the student leaders, comes from Dorsinville, *Marche arrière*, 45.

88. Milton Barrall to Department of State, 23 May 1956, Port-au-Prince, USNA, RG 59, 738.00/5-2256.

89. See "Declaration-Louis Déjoie and François Duvalier," 6 December 1956, typescript, Mangonès Collection, BHPSE.

90. See the bulletin of the Parti Progressiste National, attached to Milton Barrall to Department of State, 8 June 1956, Port-au-Prince, 738.00/6-856.

91. *Le Matin*, 15 November 1957. See also *Le Matin*, 1 July 1957; Zéphir, "Dictator Duvalier orders the torture of journalist Yvonne Hakime Rimpel," in *Haitian Women*, 18. The year 1956 was a turning point in the Haitian women's movement. Since 1952, in fact, at least two feminist papers appeared in Port-au-Prince, *La Voix des Femmes*, the organ of the Ligue Feminin d'action Sociale, and *Escale*. For discussion on the developments during this period see also Bouchereau, *Haïti et ses femmes*, and Chancy, *Framing Silence*, 42–43.

92. See the reports in the regional papers, *Le Rampart* (Les Cayes), 12 October and 9 and 23 November 1956, and *Ralliement* (Gonaïves), 19 November 1956. For reactions to Duvalier's declaration to run, see, for example, the editorial in Fignolé's *Indépendance*, 13 September 1956.

93. J. Paul Barringer to Department of State, 21 November 1956, Port-au-Prince, USNA, RG 59, 738.00/11-2156; J. Paul Barringer to Department of State, "Memorandum of meeting with Col. Levelt," 21 November 1956, USNA, RG 59, 738.00/11-2156.

94. Diederich and Burt, *Papa Doc*, 77.

95. "Memorandum of Conversation, Mauclair Zépherin, Rubottom, Neal and Phillipe," 11 December 1956, Washington, D.C., USNA, RG 59, 738.00/12-1156.

96. Dwight D. Eisenhower, OF, Box 186, 11 December 1956, DDEL; editor's note, *FRUS, 1955–57*, 6:948.

97. Extensive discussion of the election is commonplace in works on Duvalier and his regime. The better accounts include Abbott, *Haiti*, 62–68; Trouillot, *Haiti: State against Nation*, 144–56. A full and enlightening account of the events is offered in Désinor, *L'affaire Jumelle*. A provocative analysis is found in Bellegarde-Smith's article, "Class Struggle." Relevant documents are collected in Bonhomme, *Révolution et contrerévolution en Haïti*, and Célestin, *Compilations pour l'histoire*. See also Duvalier, *Souvenirs d'une campagne* and *Œuvres essentielles*, for a thorough collection of his speeches and photographs during his campaign. For interviews with the candidates and insights on the social context of the period, see Diederich, *The Prize*, 1–109.

98. Trouillot, *Haiti: State against Nation*, 145.

99. Bellegarde-Smith, "Class Struggle," 116.

100. See, for example, *Indépendance*, 17 December 1956.

101. J. Paul Barringer to Department of State, 26 March 1957, Port-au-Prince, USNA, RG 59, 738.00/3-2657.

102. See, for example, the article "Duvalier est un dictature," in *Foi Sociale*, 7 January 1957.

103. Taken from the tract, "TIM TIM BOIS SECHE," Mangonès Collection, BHPSE. The term *"Captain' en bas Caban'"* is a double entendre, referring to both a bedpan and Duvalier's years in hiding. "Duvalier preferred to hide, trembling under his bed waiting until *kansonfè* fell. Haitians don't like cowards . . . and they say this man can be president? Ladies and Gentlemen, No! No! No!"

104. *Mopisme Intégral*, 10 May 1957.

105. See the tract "Daniel Fignolé-Hier. Quand il etait communiste communisant," Mangonès Collection, BHPSE.

106. Quotes taken from tract "Le pays haïtien," 4 January 1957, Mangonès Collection, BHPSE.

107. Manigat, *Haiti of the Sixties*, 43.

108. Taken from a tract labeled "Duvalier," Mangonès Collection, BHPSE.

109. See the discussion in Doubout and Joly, *Notes sur le développement* 32–33, and Hector, *Syndicalisme et socialisme*, 94–95.

110. Max D. Sam, interview by author, 17 May 2001, Pétionville.

111. "PPLN-Analysis of the Haitian Situation," quoted in Diedrich and Burt, *Papa Doc*, 333.

112. Depestre, *Bonjour et adieu à la négritude*, 205. Alexis's role in the campaign was the cause of much controversy and further weakened the collective efforts of the Marxist Left. Andrée Roumer-Innocent, interview by author, 2 May 2001, Port-au-Prince.

113. Déjoie and his supporters argued that despite his aristocratic background he was not a representative of the extreme right, but rather a social reformer concerned more with production than vain promises. Louis Déjoie, interview by Robert J. Alexander, 29 October 1958, New York City, Alexander Papers, RU.

114. Bonhomme, *Révolution et contrérevolution*, 197–210.

115. *Haïti Sun*, 31 March 1957; *Le Matin*, 31 March 1957.

116. J. Paul Barringer to Secretary of State, 25 April 1957, Port-au-Prince, USNA, RG 59, 738.00/4-257.

117. "Procès Verbal," 15 April 1957, typescript, Mangonès Collection, BHPSE.

118. The original speech appears in *La Nouvelle Haïti*, 9 May 1957, Mangonès Collection, BHPSE. For a full English translation, see Rotberg, *Haiti: The Politics of Squalor*, 191.

119. *New York Times*, 16 May 1957.

120. Harold Aron to Joseph Montillor, 16 April 1957, Washington, D.C., USNA, RG 59, 738.00/4-1657; Christian A. Herter, "Memorandum for the President," 2 May 1957, Office of the Staff Secretary Records, White House Office Files, Box 2, DDEL.

121. Gerald Drew to Secretary of State, 14 May 1957, Port-au-Prince, USNA, RG 59, 738.00/5-1457.

122. *Le Matin*, 20 May 1957.

123. "A nos frères de Casernes Dessalines, Déclaration Bureau Politique Louis Déjoie," 22–23 May 1957, Mangonès Collection, BHPSE.

124. For details of this battle, the closest the country came to a civil war during the election, see Noel, *Les responsables des vêpres*, and Pierre, *Témoinages*, 81–92.

125. Bonhomme, *Révolution et contrévolution en Haïti*, 335.

126. The description of Fignolé's inauguration used in this paragraph is based on video footage of the event entitled "Événements 1946 à 1957," Video no. 707, Video Collection, BHPSE, and the description in *Mopisme Integral*, 31 May 1957.

127. "Memorandum from the Acting Assistant Secretary of State for Inter-American Affairs (Rubottom) to the Under Secretary of State (Herter)," 15 May 1957, Washington, D.C., *FRUS, 1955–57*, 6:953.

128. *New York Times*, 6, 9, and 12 June 1957.

129. See, for example, the lead article "Chaos in a Caribbean Hotspot," *Life*, 23 June 1957.

130. Memorandum, "Discussion at the 325th Meeting of the National Security Council, May 27, 1957," 28 May 1957, Ann Whitman File, NSC Series, Box 8, DDEL.

131. Ibid.

132. "Memorandum of Conversation, Didier Raguenet to Julian Fromer," 29 May 1957, Washington, D.C., USNA, RG 59, 5-2957.

133. "Memorandum of Conversation, R. T. Davis, Julian Fromer, and Allan Stewart," 31 May 1957, Washington, D.C., USNA, RG 59, 738.00/5-3157. For a lengthy discussion of the implications of the Fignolé government to U.S. interests in Haiti, see also "Memorandum of Conversation, with Rubottom, Frank Cusumano, Elmer Loughlin, and Ernest Gutierrez," 10 June 1957, Washington, D.C., 738.00/6-1057.

134. George H. Alexander to Department of State, "Views of President Daniel Fignolé on Political Parties," 13 June 1957, Port-au-Prince, USNA, RG 59, 738.00/6-1357.

135. See the surprisingly superficial commentary on Magloire's resignation in *Pittsburgh Courier*, 22 December 1956, and the discussion of U.S. black attitudes to political developments elsewhere in the diaspora during the civil rights era in Von Eschen, *Race against Empire*, 164–65.

136. Laguerre, *Military and Society in Haiti*, 96.

137. See Hobart Spalding to Secretary of State, 12 June 1957, Port-au-Prince, USNA, RG 59, 738.00/6-1257.

138. Pierre, *Témoignages*, 106–7.

139. *Le Matin*, 15 June 1957; *New York Times*, 15 June 1957.

140. Daniel Fignolé to Antonio Kébreau, 29 June 1957, Mangonès Collection, BHPSE; Daniel Fignolé, interview by Robert J. Alexander, 19 June 1957, New York City, Alexander Papers, RU.

141. Daniel Fignolé, interview by Robert J. Alexander, 5 May 1959, New York City, Alexander Papers, RU; Daniel Fignolé to Dwight D. Eisenhower, 22 June 1957, New York, USNA, RG 59, 738.00/6-2257; "Memorandum of Conversation—Elizabeth Schermeron and Julian P. Fromer, Re: Daniel Fignolé," 24 June 1957, Washington, D.C., USNA, RG 59, 738.00/6-2457. From New York, where Magloire, Fignolé, and several other exiled political leaders remained during the rest of the campaign, a series of alliances were formed among former enemies, all with the aim of preventing Duvalier's election. A richly detailed account of the activities of the exiled leaders is given by one of Jumelle's partisans who worked closely both with Fignolé and Magloire in New York. See Paquin, *Haitians*, chaps. 20–21; See also the article, "Presidents in Exile," in *Ebony* (n.d.), Vertical File—Haiti, SCRBC.

142. In a conversation with a U.S. embassy official five days before the event, Minister Jean Dauphin, a Duvalier supporter, confessed that a move was afoot to offer Fignolé the presidency. See "Memorandum of Conversation, Jean Dauphin and Julian Fromer," 20 May 1957, Port-au-Prince, USNA, RG 59, 738.00/5-2057. This evidence suggests that Cantave had agreed with the plan in advance but did not anticipate the move by Déjoie to exploit the political cleavages within the army.

143. See Carleton Beals, "Haiti under the Gun—The Peace of Death," *Nation*, 6 July 1957. See also Gerald Drew to Secretary of State, 16 June 1957, Port-au-Prince, USNA, RG 59, 738.00/6-1657, and *Time*, 24 June 1957.

144. John Foster Dulles, "Memorandum to the President, Re-Recognition of the New Government of Haiti," 25 July 1957, Washington, D.C., Box 9, Dulles-Hector Series, Dulles, Papers, DDEL.

145. Pierre, *Témoignages*, 120.

146. *New York Times*, 3, 4, and 7 September 1957.

147. Pierre, *Témoignages*, 116.

148. Bellegarde-Smith, "Class Struggle," 122. This view repeats an older argument made by Rémy Bastien, who claimed that "it was the opinion of the United States Department of State that Haiti needed a middle-class, middle-of-the-road reformer." See Courlander and Bastien, *Religion and Politics in Haiti*, 55, and Manigat, *Haiti of the Sixties*, 43.

149. See the comments on Jumelle, whose actions were described as "communist tactics" in J. Paul Barringer to Secretary of State, 9 February 1957, Port-au-Prince, USNA, RG 59, 738.00/2-957, and J. Paul Barringer to Secretary of State, 12 February 1957, Port-au-Prince, USNA, RG 59, 738.00/2-1257. Exiled Fignolists frequently wrote letters to the State Department in which they called Duvalier the "communist leader." Anonymous to R. R. Rubottom, 16 August 1957, New York, USNA, RG 59, 738.00/8-1657.

150. "Letter from the Ambassador in Haiti (Drew) to the Director of the Office of Middle American Affairs (Wieland), Port-au-Prince, July 18, 1957," *FRUS, 1955–57*, 6:959.

151. Ibid., 960.

152. See "Memorandum of Conversation between Chargé d'Affaires and Mr. Eric Tippenhauer," 24 April 1957, Port-au-Prince, USNA, RG 59, 738.00/4-2557. Local criticism of Duvalier's link with the business community is the substance of the tract "Le Voyage de Duvalier au Cap ou le triomphe des dollars de O. J. Brandt," Mangonès Collection, BHPSE. See also Pierre, *Témoignages*, 116, which mentions regular meetings Duvalier held with members of the bourgeoisie. See also Paquin, *Haitians*, 151–52, who suggests that Duvalier managed to win without accepting support from *milat* businesspeople.

153. Duvalier, *Souvenir d'une campagne*, 206, 210.

154. For the U.S. embassy's report of the election see "Charges of Fraud in Haitian Elections of September 22, 1957," Virgil P. Randolph III to Department of State, 24 October 1957, Port-au-Prince, USNA, RG 59, 738.00/10-1457.

155. J. Paul Barringer to Secretary of State, 20 September 1957, Port-au-Prince, USNA, RG 59, 738.00/9-2057.

156. Virgil Randolph III to Department of State, 14 October 1957, Port-au-Prince, USNA, RG 59, 738.00/10-1457; Nicholls, *From Dessalines to Duvalier*, 209; Heinl and Heinl, *Written in Blood*, 548.

Conclusion

1. Virgil Randolph III to Secretary of State, 17 December 1957, Port-au-Prince, USNA, RG 59, 738.00/12-1757. The proposal and the debate over it are also recounted in Nicholls, *From Dessalines to Duvalier*, 235.

2. A staggering number of militants from the fifties and early sixties were murdered on Duvalier's orders. For a compelling examination of the severity of the terror and its effect on progressive leaders in Haiti, see Pierre-Charles, *Haïti: jamais, jamais plus*.

3. See, for example, Hector, "Charisme."

4. Von Eschen, *Race against Empire*, 5.

5. On this era in Cuban history see, for example, Whitney, *State and Revolution*, and Farber, *Origins*.

6. For example, political contests and the rise in radicalism in Jamaica from independence through the end of the 1970s feature echoes of the process in Haiti decades earlier. The history of radical politics in Jamaica is treated well in Gray, *Radicalism and Social Change in Jamaica*, which has influenced my approach to the study of Caribbean radicalism. See also Fraser, *Ambivalent Anti-Colonialism*; Stone and Brown, *Perspectives on Jamaica*; Lewis, *Walter Rodney's Intellectual and Political Thought*; and Meeks, *Radical Caribbean*. On Trinidad, see, for example, Ryan, *Race and Nationalism*.

BIBLIOGRAPHY

Archives and Manuscript Collections

Archives Nationales d'Haïti, Port-au-Prince
  Correspondance Département de L'interior
  Correspondance Général
  Correspondance Générale Expédiée
  Correspondance Ministère de la Justice
Bibliothèque Haïtienne des Frères de L'Instruction Chrétienne, Port-au-Prince
  "Album des candidats à la deputation et candidats au Sénat," 2 vols., 1946
  Comité Central du Parti Communiste, "L'Analyse schématique 32–34," 1934,
    typescript
  Dumarsais Estimé, "Lettre de Estimé," 7 August 1951, Kingston, typescript
  "Premier Congrès National du Travail, Avril 1949," typescript
  Unidentified report on the Rémy-Viau affair, ca. 1948
Bibliothèque Haïtienne des Pères du Saint-Esprit, Port-au-Prince
  Événements 1946 à 1957, video no. 707, Video Collection
  Edmond Mangonès Collection
Dwight D. Eisenhower Library and Museum, Abilene, Kans.
  John Foster Dulles Papers
  Dennis Fitzgerald Papers
  National Security Council Papers
  President's Official File
  President's Personal File
  President's Secretary's File
  White House Office Files
  Ann Whitman File
Franklin D. Roosevelt Library and Museum, Hyde Park, N.Y.
  President's Official File
  President's Personal File
  President's Secretary File
  Samuel I. Rosenman Papers
  Charles Taussig Papers
  War Production Board Records
  Sumner Welles Papers
Harry S. Truman Library and Museum, Independence, Mo.
  Dean Acheson Papers
  Assistant Secretaries of State for Economic Affairs Files

Merwin L. Bohan Papers
Official File
President's Personal File
President's Secretary's File
Harry S. Truman Papers
White House Central Files
Library of Congress, Manuscript Division, Washington, D.C.
Samuel Guy Inman Papers
Rayford Logan Diaries
National Association for the Advancement of Colored People Papers
Ministère des Affaires Étrangères, Archives Diplomatiques, Quai d'Orsay, Paris
Maurice Chayet Report, 30 April 1950
Moorland-Spingarn Research Center, Howard University, Washington, D.C.
Haitian Collection
Layle Lane Papers
Rayford Logan Papers
Schomburg Center for Research in Black Culture, New York Public Library, New York
Maurice Dartigue Papers
Kurt Fisher Collection
Melville Herskovits Papers
Miscellaneous Papers on Haiti
Vertical File on Haiti
Special Collections, University of Florida, Gainesville
Frank Crumbie Papers
Haitiana Collection
Special Collections and University Archives, Rutgers University, New Brunswick, N.J.
Robert J. Alexander Papers, Interview Collection, 1947–94, microfilm, IDC
Publishers, reel 8
U.S. National Archives II, College Park, Md.
Record Group 40 (Department of Commerce, Division of Negro Affairs)
Record Group 59 (Department of State Decimal File, Lot Files, and Inspection
Reports)
Record Group 60 (Department of Justice)
Record Group 84 (Department of State, Consular Posts)
Record Group 165 (War Department)
Record Group 218 (Joint Chiefs of Staff)
Records of the Department of State relating to Internal Affairs of Haiti, 1930–1939.
Washington, D.C.: National Archives and Records Service, 1982. Microfilm
Publication M-1246.
*Records of the U.S. Department of State relating to Political Relations between the United
States and Latin America and Caribbean States, 1930–1944.* Wilmington, Del.:
Scholarly Resources, 1988, roll 87.

Newspapers and Periodicals

L'Action, 1946–48

L'Action Nationale, 1933–42

L'Action Radicale, 1941

L'Action Sociale, 1946

L'Arène, 1956

L'Assaut, 1934–39

Aya Bombé, 1946–1948

Le Caducée, 1945–49

Cahiers d'Haïti, 1943–45

Chantiers, 1942–49

Chicago Defender, 1946–50

Classe Moyen et Masse, 1946

Combat, 1946–47

Conjonction, various years

Construction, 1951–54

Le Courrier, 1942

Daily Gleaner, 1946, 1953

Les Débats, 1946

Demain, 1946

L'Élan, 1942

Escale, 1954

La Famille, 1948

Flambeau, 1946–48

Foi Sociale, 1957

Les Griots, 1938–40, 1946–49

Haïti Herald, 1956

Haïti Journal, 1933–46

Haïti Sun, 1953–57

Indépendance, 1957

Le Justicier, 1948

Life, 1957

Listín Diario, 1937, 1942, 1944, 1949

Le Matin, 1933–57

Miami Herald, 1946–48

Mopisme Integral, 1957

La Nation, 1943–44, 1946–50

The Nation, 1946, 1950, 1957

New Amsterdam News, 1942–48

New York Times, 1940–57

Notre Jeunesse, 1948–49

La Nouvelle Ruche, 1946

Le Nouvelliste, 1934–57

Opportunity, 1934
La Phalange, 1934–50
Pittsburgh Courier, 1942–50
Ralliement, 1957
Le Rampart, 1957
Rasoir, 1946
La Relève, 1935–40
La République, 1946
Le Réveil, 1939–44, 1946
La Ruche, 1946
Le Soir, 1942
Sud-Ouest, 1942
Time, 1954
Trinidad Guardian, 1946
La Voix des Femmes
La Voix des Jeunes, 1946
Washington Afro-American, 1946

Interviews
By Robert J. Alexander

In Robert J. Alexander Papers, Special Collections and University Archives, Rutgers University, New Brunswick, N.J.

Bellegarde, Dantès, 30 August 1949, Port-au-Prince
Cameau, André, Victor Vabre, and Edouard Benodin, 24 June 1948, Port-au-Prince
Cassagnol, Paul, 29 August 1949, Port-au-Prince
Catraight, Georges, 27 August 1949, Cap Haitien
Colimon, Dantès, 7 January 1951, New Brunswick, N.J.
Decatrel, Louis, 31 August, 1949, Port-au-Prince
Déjoie, Louis, 29 October 1958, New York
Estimé, Dumarsais, 25 June 1948, Port-au-Prince
Fignolé, Daniel, 23 August 1949, Port-au-Prince
——, 19 June 1957, New York
——, 5 May 1959, New York
Fignolé, Daniel, and Michel Romain, 25 June 1948, Port-au-Prince
Josué, Milien, 21 August 1949, Port-au-Prince
Legendre, Franck, 23 June 1948, Port-au-Prince
Leonard, Roger F., 30 August 1949, Port-au-Prince
Magloire, Paul E., 3 December 1971, New York
McQueen, J. W., 24 August 1949, Port-au-Prince
Ramponeau, Georges, 22 August 1949, Port-au-Prince
St. Cyr, Raynol, 1 September 1949, Port-au-Prince
St. Lôt, Emile, 23 June 1960, Philadelphia

Tardieu, Edouard A., and Jacques A. Désinor, 25 June 1948, Port-au-Prince
Victor, René, 24 June 1948, Port-au-Prince

By the Author

Bazile, Robert, 22 June 2000, Washington, D.C.
Bloncourt, Gérald, 18 June 2001, Paris
Casimir, Rodrigue, 14 June 2003, Port-au-Prince
De Pradines Morse, Emerante, 23 July 1999, Pélerin, Haiti
El Saïeh, Issa, 13 July 1999, Port-au-Prince
Fourcand, Noé, 14 July 1999, Pétionville, Haiti
Honorat, Lamartinière, 9 May 2001, Port-au-Prince
Laraque, Paul, 5 July 2000, New York
Lescot, Roger, 16 June 2003, Laboule, Haiti
Pressoir, Raymond, 17 and 20 June, 2000, Bethesda, Md.
Roumer-Innocent, Andrée, 2 May 2001, Port-au-Prince
Sam, Max D., 7 and 17 May 2001, Pétionville, Haiti
Widmaïer, Herby, 8 May 2001, Port-au-Prince

Audio-Visual Sources

Jazz des Jeunes. *Super Jazz des Jeunes*. Ibo Records ILP 113. n.d.
Les chemins de la mémoire: Haïti avant Duvalier. 52 minutes. CIDIHCA, 2002.

Unpublished Private Sources

Fennell, Thomas A. Various correspondence, 1939–1943.
Lescot, Élie. "Confidences intimes," 10 June 1962, typescript.
———. Letter to Pius XII, 27 February 1942.
St. Jean, Ronald. Manuscript on the history of the Haitian labor movement.

Published Primary Sources and Government Documents

Au service d'une cause-souvenirs d'une campagne: Collection "La République." Port-au-Prince: Imprimerie de L'État, 1948.
British Documents on Foreign Affairs, 1936. Washington, D.C.: University Press of America, 1992.
British Documents on Foreign Affairs, October 1937–1938. Washington, D.C.: University Press of America, 1992.
Bulletin du Bureau d'Ethnologie—Rapport 1949. Port-au-Prince: Imprimerie de L'Etat, 1949.
Bulletin trimesteriel de statistique, 27. Port-au-Prince: Institut Haïtien de Statistique, December 1957.
Les étapes d'un relèvement. Port-au-Prince: Imprimerie de L'État, 1956.

Groupe D'Amis. *Realisations.* 21 April 1950.

Guide économique de la république d'Haïti. Port-au-Prince: Institut Haïtien de Statistique, 1964. 2nd ed., 1977.

Haïti: Banque Nationale de la République d'Haïti, Rapport annuel du département fiscal. October 1941–September 1952. Port-au-Prince: Imprimerie de L'État, 1942–52.

Haïti: Rapport annuel du representat fiscal. October 1933–September 1940. Port-au-Prince: Imprimerie de L'État, 1934–40.

Haiti of 1936. Port-au-Prince: Goodwill, 1936.

The Haitian Economy in 1954: A Description of the Economy and Finances of the Republic of Haiti with Particular Reference to its current Program of Economic Development. Port-au-Prince: Imprimerie de L'État, 1954.

Livre bleu d'Haïti, 1946–1949. Port-au-Prince: Imprimerie de L'État, 1950.

Manifeste de la Réaction Démocratique. Port-au-Prince: Imprimerie Haïtienne, 1934.

Pan-American Union. *Foreign Trade of Haiti, 1945–1950, Bulletin no. 1.* Washington, D.C.: Pan-American Union, 1954.

UNESCO Statistical Yearbook. Washington, D.C.: UNESCO, 1968.

U.S. Department of State. *Foreign Relations of the United States, 1941–1957.* Washington, D.C.: Government Printing Office, 1962–87.

Secondary Sources

Abbott, Elizabeth. *Haiti: The Duvaliers and Their Legacy.* New York: McGraw-Hill, 1988.

Alexander, Raymond P. "Haiti's Bid for Freedom." *Nation,* 4 May 1946, 534–35.

Alexander, Robert J. *Communism in Latin America.* New Brunswick, N.J.: Rutgers University Press, 1957.

———. *Presidents of Central America, Mexico, Cuba, and Hispaniola: Conversations and Correspondence.* Westport, Conn.: Praeger, 1995.

Alexis, Jacques Stephen. *Les arbes musiciens.* Port-au-Prince: Éditions Fardin, 1986 [1957].

———. *Compère général soleil.* Paris: Garimand, 1955.

———. *General Sun, My Brother.* Trans. Carrol F. Coates. Charlottesville: University Press of Virginia, 1999.

———. "Les grand problèmes d'humanité générale." *Le Caducée* 18 (January 1945): 9–13.

Allahar, Anton L., ed. *Caribbean Charisma: Reflections on Leadership, Legitimacy, and Populist Politics.* Kingston: Ian Randle Publishers, 2001.

Ameringer, Charles. *The Democratic Left in Exile: The Antidictatorial Struggle in the Caribbean, 1945–1959.* Coral Gables, Fla.: University of Miami Press, 1974.

Andic, Suphan. "Haiti: An Economic Overview." *Caribbean Studies* 18, nos. 1–2 (1978): 115–29.

Anglade, Georges. *L'espace haïtien.* Québec: Les presses de l'Univerité du Québec, 1974.

Aquino, Miguel. *Holocaust in the Caribbean: The Slaughter of 25,000 Haitians by Trujillo in One Week.* Waterbury, Conn.: Emancipation Press, 1997.

Auguste, Joseph. *La voix du M.O.P.: Daniel Fignolé ou le sens d'une lutte.* Port-au-Prince: Éditions Delta, 1989.

Auguste, Michel Héctor, Sabine Manigat, and Jean L. Dominique. *Haití: la lucha por la democracia (clase obrera, partidos y sindicatos)*. Puebla: Universidad Autónoma, 1986.

Averill, Gage. *A Day for the Hunter, A Day for the Prey: Popular Music and Power in Haiti*. Chicago: University of Chicago Press, 1997.

———. "Haitian Dance Bands, 1915–1970: Class, Race, and Authenticity." *Latin American Music Review* 10, no. 2 (1989): 203–35.

Aziabu, Yao E. "Black Activism and American Foreign Policy: From South Africa to Haiti." Ph.D. diss., Duke University, 1997.

Baguidy, Joseph D. *Dynamique d'une revolution: 1946 à Haïti*. Berne: Éditions Coloroffset, 1972.

Bastien, Rémy, and Harold Courlander. *Religion and Politics in Haiti*. Washington, D.C.: Institute of Cross-Cultural Research, 1966.

Béhague, Gerard H., ed. *Music and Black Ethnicity: The Caribbean and South America*. New Brunswick, N.J.: Transaction Publishers, 1994.

Bellegarde, Dantès. *Dessalines a parlé*. Port-au-Prince: Société d'Editions et de Librairie, 1948.

———. *Haïtie et ses problèmes*. Montréal: Bernard Valiquette, 1943.

———. *Histoire du peuple haïtien, 1492–1952*. Port-au-Prince, 1953.

———. *La Nation Haïtienne*. Paris: J. De Gigord, 1938.

Bellegarde-Smith, Patrick. "Class Struggle in Contemporary Haitian Politics: An Interpretive Study of the Campaign of 1957." *Journal of Caribbean Studies* 2, no. 1 (Spring 1981): 109–27.

———. *Haiti: The Breached Citadel*. Rev. and updated ed. Toronto: Canadian Scholar's Press, 2004.

———. "Haitian Social Thought in the Nineteenth Century: Class Formation and Westernization." *Caribbean Studies* 20, no. 1 (March 1980): 5–33.

———. *In the Shadow of Powers: Dantès Bellegarde in Haitian Social Thought*. Atlantic Highlands, N.J.: Humanities Press International, 1985.

Benjamin, George J. *Contribution à l'histoire diplomatique et contemporaine*. Port-au-Prince: Imprimerie de L'État, 1951.

Bernardin, Raymond. *Général Paul Eugène Magloire: Un biographie politique*. Montréal: Éditions du CIDIHCA, 2000.

Bethell, Leslie, ed. *Latin America: Economy and Society since 1930*. Cambridge: Cambridge University Press, 1998.

Bethell, Leslie, and Ian Roxborough, eds. *Latin America Between the Second World War and the Cold War, 1944–1948*. Cambridge: Cambridge University Press, 1992.

Blanchet, Jules. *Idéologies et transformations sociales*. Port-au-Prince: Panorama, 1955.

Bloncourt, Gérald. *Yeto ou le palmier des neiges*. Port-au-Prince: Henri Deschamps, 1991.

Bloncourt, Gérald, and Michael Löwy. *Messagers de la Tempête: André Breton et la Révolution Janvier 1946 en Haïti*. Paris: Le Temps des Cerises, 2007.

Bogues, Anthony. *Caliban's Freedom: The Early Political Thought of C.L.R. James*. London: Pluto Press, 1997.

Bolland, O. Nigel. *On the March: Labour Rebellions in the British Caribbean, 1934–1939*. Kingston: Ian Randle Publishers, 1995.

Bonhomme, Colbert. *Révolution et contrérevolution en Haïti*. Port-au-Prince: Imprimerie de L'État, 1957.

Bordes, Ary. *Haïti: la santé de la république, 1934–1957*. Port-au-Prince: Henri Deschamps, 1997.

Bouchereau, Madeleine G. *Haïti et ses femmes: une etude d'évolution culturelle*. Port-au-Prince: Imprimerie Les Presses Libres, 1957.

Brisson, Monique. "Jalons de notre legislation ouvriere de 1946–1951." *Rond Point* 7 (May 1963): 5–8.

Brutus, Jacques B. "Aperçu historique du mouvement syndical en Haïti." *Rond Point* 7 (May 1963): 2–4.

Brutus, Jacques B., and Monique Brisson. "Le syndicalisme haïtien hier et aujourd'hui." *Rond Point* 7 (May 1963): 59–76.

Calixte, D. P. *Haiti: The Calvary of a Soldier*. New York: Wendell Malliet, 1939.

Célestin, Clément. *Compilations pour l'histoire*. 9 vols. Port-au-Prince: Imprimerie Théodore, 1958–60.

Césaire, Aimé. *Cahier d'un retour au pays natal (Return to my native land)*. Trans. Emile Snyder. Paris: Présence Africaine, 1971.

Chancy, Myriam J. A. *Framing Silence: Revolutionary Novels by Haitian Women*. New Brunswick, N.J.: Rutgers University Press, 1997.

Charlier, Étienne D. *Aperçu sur la formation historique de la nation haïtienne*. Port-au-Prince: Les Presses Libre, 1954.

——. "Rapport du Parti Socialiste Populaire présénté par le Secrétaire général, Étienne D. Charlier." In *Pouvoir noir en Haïti: L' Explosion de 1946*, 283–312. Montreal: CIDIHCA, 1988.

Chauvet, Lucien. *Victime de 1946—Je Vote 1946*. Port-au-Prince, 1956.

Cobb, Martha K. *Harlem, Haiti, and Havana: A Comparative Critical Study of Langston Hughes, Jacques Roumain, and Nicolás Guillén*. Washington, D.C.: Three Continents Press, 1979.

Cohen, Warren I., ed. *The Cambridge History of American Foreign Relations*. 4 vols. Cambridge: Cambridge University Press, 1993.

Collectif du Cinquantenaire. *Haïti, 7–11 Janvier 1946*. Paris: la Flèche du temps, 1998.

Collectif Paroles. *Trente ans de pouvoir noir en Haïti: l'explosion de 1946: bilans et perspectives, 1946–1976*. Lasalle, Quebèc: Collectif Paroles, 1976.

Comhaire, Jean L. "The Haitian 'Chef de Section.'" *American Anthropologist* 57, no. 3 (June 1955): 620–24.

Corvington, Georges. *Port-au-Prince au cours des ans*. 6 vols. Port-au-Prince: Henri Deschamps, 1970–92.

Coulange, Jean. "Indigénisme et musique en Haïti." *Conjonction* 211 (April–June 1993): 59–76.

Courlander, Harold. *Haiti Singing*. Chapel Hill: University of North Carolina Press, 1939.

——. "Not in the Cables: Massacre in Santo Domingo." *New Republic*, 24 November 1937, 67.

Daniels, Douglas Henry. Review of Gage Averill, *A Day for the Hunter, A Day for the Prey: Popular Music and Power in Haiti*, and Gerdès Fleurant, *Dancing Spirits: Rhythms and*

Rituals of Haitian Vodun, the Rada Rite. *Journal of Haitian Studies* 7, no. 1 (Spring 2001): 156–61.

Danticat, Edwidge. *The Farming of Bones*. New York: Soho Press, 1998.

Dash, J. Michael. "Blazing Mirrors: The Crisis of the Haitian Intellectual." In *Intellectuals in the Twentieth-Century Caribbean*, vol. 2 of *Unity in Variety: The Hispanic and Francophone Caribbean*, ed. Alistair Hennessy, 175–85. London: Macmillan, 1992.

———. *Haiti and the United States: National Stereotypes and the Literary Imagination*. London: Palgrave Macmillan, 1997.

———. *Jacques Stephen Alexis*. Toronto: Black Images, 1975.

———. "*Le Je de l'autre*: Surrealist Ethnographers and the Francophone Caribbean." *L'Esprit Créateur* 47, no. 1 (Spring 2007): 84–95.

———. *Literature and Ideology in Haiti*. Totowa, N.J.: Barnes and Noble, 1981.

De La Fuente, Alejandro. *A Nation for All: Race, Inequality, and Politics in Twentieth Century Cuba*. Chapel Hill: University of North Carolina Press, 2001.

Delince, Kern. *Armée et politique en Haïti*. Paris: Éditions L'Harmattan, 1979.

De Matteis, Arthur. *Le massacre de 1937 ou une succession immobilière internationale*. Port-au-Prince: L'Imprimerie II, 1987.

Depestre, René. *Bonjour et adieu à la négritude*. Paris: Éditions Robert Laffont, 1980.

———. *Étincelles*. Port-au-Prince: Imprimerie de L'État, 1945.

———. *The Festival of the Greasy Pole*. Trans. Carrol F. Coates. Charlottesville: University Press of Virginia, 1990.

———. "Pierre Mabille: une aventure de la connaissance." *Conjonction* 202 (April–June 1997): 9–16.

———. "La Révolution de 1946 est pour demain." In *Pouvoir noir en Haïti: L' Explosion de 1946*, 57–94. Montreal: CIDIHCA, 1988.

Derby, Lauren. "Haitians, Magic, and Money: *Raza* and Society in the Haitian-Dominican Borderlands, 1900–1937." *Comparative Studies of Society and History* 36, no. 3 (July 1994): 488–526.

Derby, Lauren, and Richard Lee Turits. "Historias de terror y los terrores de la historia: la matanza haitiana de 1937 en la República Dominicana." *Estudios Sociales* 26, no. 92 (April–June 1993): 65–76.

Désinor, Carlo A. *L'affaire Jumelle*. Port-au-Prince: L'Imprimeur II, 1986.

———. *Daniel Fignolé: un espoir vain*. Port-au-Prince: L'Imprimeur II, 1986.

Diederich, Bernard. *Haiti's Bon Papa*. Philadelphia: Xlibris Publishers, 2007.

———. *The Prize*. New York: iUniverse, Inc., 2007.

Diederich, Bernard, and Al Burt. *Papa Doc and the Tonton Macoutes*. Port-au-Prince: Henri Deschamps, 1986.

Dorsinville, Roger. "Les 'Authentiques' et le cercle enchanté." In *Pouvoir noir en Haïti: L'Explosion de 1946*, 155–82. Montreal: CIDIHCA, 1988.

———. *Lettre aux hommes claires*. In *Pouvoir noir en Haïti: L' Explosion de 1946*, 183–89. Montreal: CIDIHCA, 1988.

———. *Marche arrière*. Quebec: Collectif Paroles, 1986.

———. "1946 ou le délire opportuniste." *Pouvoir noir en Haïti: L'Explosion de 1946*, 35–56. Montreal: CIDIHCA, 1988.

Doubout, Jean-Jacques, and Ulrick Joly. *Notes sur le développement du mouvement syndicale en Haïti*. Port-au-Prince: Imprimerie Abécé, 1974.

Dumas-Pierre, Antonin. "La Garde d'Haïti et la conjoncture de 1946." *Présence Haïtienne* 4 (November–December 1975): 15–25.

Dunham, Katherine. *Island Possessed*. Chicago: University of Chicago Press, 1994.

Dupuy, Alex. *Haiti in the World Economy: Class, Race, and Underdevelopment since 1700*. Boulder, Colo.: Westview Press, 1989.

Duvalier, François. *Œuvres essentielles*. Vol. 2. Port-au-Prince: Imprimerie de L'État, 1964.

———. *Souvenirs d'un campagne, Septembre 1956–Septembre 1957*. Port-au-Prince: Imprimerie Theodore, 1958.

Dymanche, Lyséas. *La puissance du Colonel Paul E. Magloire*. Port-au-Prince: Imprimerie du Commerce, 1950.

Efron, Edith. "The 'New' Movement in Haiti." *Caribbean Quarterly* 4 (January 1955): 14–31.

Estimé, Lucienne H. *Dumarsais Estimé: dialogue avec mes souvenirs*. Port-au-Prince: Éditions mémoire, 2001.

Farber, Samuel. *The Origins of the Cuban Revolution Reconsidered*. Chapel Hill: University of North Carolina Press, 2006.

Fennell, Thomas A. "Haiti Makes Rubber History." *Agriculture in the Americas* (July 1941): 7–11.

Fiehrer, Thomas. "Political Violence in the Periphery: The Haitian Massacre of 1937." *Race and Class* 32, no. 4 (October–December 1990): 1–20.

Fignolé, Daniel. *Contribution à l'histoire du mouvement syndicale en Haïti (Tome I: Janvier 1946–Novembre 1947)*. Port-au-Prince: Imprimerie Eben-Ezer, 1954.

———. *Mon mandat*. 2 vols. Port-au-Prince: La Gazette du Palais, 1954.

———. *Soixante-cinq jours au ministère de l'éducation nationale—première partie*. Port-au-Prince: Imprimerie M.O.P., 1952.

Fletcher, Henry Prather. "Quo Vadis Haiti?" *Foreign Affairs* 8, nos. 1/4 (1929/1930): 533–48.

Foster, Charles R., and Albert Valdman, eds. *Haiti—Today and Tomorrow: An Interdisciplinary Study*. Lanham, Md.: University Press of America, 1984.

Fowler, Carolyn. *A Knot in the Thread: The Life and Work of Jacques Roumain*. Washington, D.C.: Howard University Press, 1980.

Fraser, Cary. *Ambivalent Anti-Colonialism: The United States and the Genesis of West Indian Independence, 1940–1964*. Westport, Conn.: Greenwood Press, 1994.

Gaillard, Roger. *Les Blancs débarquent*. 7 vols. Port-au-Prince: Imprimerie Le Natal, 1973–1983.

———. *La destinée de Carl Brouard*. Port-au-Prince: Henri Deschamps, 1984.

———. "In Memoriam: André Breton et nous." *Conjonction* 103 (December 1966): 5–10.

———. "Je vous salue Mabille." *Conjonction* 202 (April–June 1997): 35.

———. *L'univers romanesque de Jacques Roumain*. Port-au-Prince: Henri Deschamps, 1966.

Gayot, Gérard G. *Clergé indigène*. Port-au-Prince: Imprimerie de L'État, 1956.

Georges-Jacob, Kleber. *L'Ethnie Haïtienne*. Port-au-Prince: Imprimerie de L'État, 1941.

Gerus, Jean-Claude. "The Effects of the Cold War on U.S.-Haiti Relations." *Journal of Caribbean Studies* 10 (Winter 1993–Spring 1994): 54–62.

Giles, A. Hubert. "War and the Trade Orientation of Haiti." *Southern Economic Journal* 13 (June 1947): 266–84.

Gindine, Yvette. "The Magic of Black History: Images of Haiti." *Caribbean Review* 6, no. 4 (1974): 25–30.

Goldberg, Alan Bruce. "Commercial Folklore and Voodoo in Haiti: International Tourism and the Sale of Culture." Ph.D. diss., Indiana University, 1981.

Gray, Obika. *Radicalism and Social Change in Jamaica, 1960–1972.* Knoxville: University of Tennessee Press, 1991.

Green, David. *The Containment of Latin America: A History of the Myths and Realities of the Good Neighbor Policy.* Chicago: Quadrangle Books, 1971.

Greene, Anne. *The Catholic Church in Haiti: Political and Social Change.* East Lansing: Michigan State University Press, 1993.

Gruening, Ernest. "The Withdrawal from Haiti." *Foreign Affairs* 12, 1/4 (1933/1934): 677–79.

Guéry, Fortuna. *Témoignages.* Port-au-Prince: Henri Deschamps, 1950.

Guillén, Nicolás. *Prosa de prisa: Crónicas.* Havana: Universidad Central de las Villas, 1962.

Gunther, John. "Hispaniola." *Foreign Affairs* 19, no. 1/4 (1940/1941): 764–77.

Haiti of 1936. Port-au-Prince: Goodwill, 1936.

Haitian Women Between Repression and Democracy. Port-au-Prince: ENFOFANM, 1995.

Hart, Richard. *Towards Decolonisation: Political, Labour, and Economic Development in Jamaica, 1938–1945.* Kingston: Canoe Press, 1999.

Hartt, David N. "Broadcasting in Haiti, Its History, Penetration, Social Role and Perspective." Ph.D. diss., Florida State University, 1977; rev., 1993.

Hector, Michel. "Charisme et mouvements populaires en Haïti." *Revue de la Société Haïtienne d'Histoire et de Géographie* 50, no. 180 (March–June 1994): 7–75.

———. *Crises et mouvements populaires en Haïti.* Montreal: Éditions du CIDIHCA, 2001.

———. "Solidarité et luttes politiques en Haïti: l'action internationale de Joseph Jolibois Fils, 1927–1936." *Revue de la Société Haïtienne d'Histoire et de Géographie* 49, no. 176 (June 1993): 29–33.

———. *Syndicalisme et socialisme en Haïti: 1932–1970.* Port-au-Prince: Henri Deschamps, 1989.

Heinl, Robert Debs, and Nancy Gordon Heinl. *Written in Blood: The Story of the Haitian People, 1492–1995.* Revised and expanded by Michael Heinl. Lanham, Md.: University Press of America, 1996.

Hicks, Albert C. *Blood in the Streets: The Life and Rule of Trujillo.* New York: Creative Age Press Inc, 1946.

Hill, Donald. *Calypso Callaloo: Early Carnival Music in Trinidad.* Gainesville: University Press of Florida, 1993.

Hudicourt, Max L. *Haiti Faces Tomorrow's Peace.* Trans. Anita Dlyn Weinstein. New York: L'Association Démocratique Haïtienne, 1945.

———. "Jim Crow Menaces Haiti." *Crisis* 51 (November 1944): 354–64.

Hull, Cordell. *The Memoirs of Cordell Hull.* Vol. 1. New York: Macmillan, 1948.

Hunt, Michael. *Ideology and U.S. Foreign Policy.* New Haven, Conn.: Yale University Press, 1987.

Hurbon, Laënnec. "American Fantasy and Haitian Vodou." In *Sacred Arts of Haitian Vodou,* ed. Donald J. Cosentino, 181–97. Los Angeles: Fowler Museum of Cultural History, 1995.

James, Winston. *Holding Aloft the Banner of Ethiopia: Caribbean Radicalism in Early Twentieth-Century America.* London: Verso Press, 1998.

Janken, Kenneth Robert. *Rayford W. Logan and the Dilemma of the African-American Intellectual.* Amherst: University of Massachusetts Press, 1993.

Jean-Baptiste, Fitz. "Étude thématique et bibliographique de la presse haïtienne de 1946–1950." M.A. thesis, Université de L'État d'Haïti École Normale Supérieure, 1999.

Jeanty, Edner A., and O. Carl Brown. *Paròl granmoun: Haitian Popular Wisdom.* Petionville: La Presse Evangelique, 1996.

Joachim, Benoît. *Les racines du sous-developpement en Haïti.* Port-au-Prince: Henri Deschamps, 1979.

Jones, Kenneth Lester. *The Harley Harris Bartlett Diaries (1926–1959).* Ann Arbor: K. L. Jones, 1975.

Kaussen, Valérie Mae. "Romancing the Peasant: History and Revolution in the Modern Haitian Novel (Maurice Casséus, Jacques Roumain, Marie Chauvet)." Ph.D. diss., University of California, Santa Cruz, 2000.

Kirby, John. *Black Americans in the Roosevelt Era: Liberalism and Race.* Knoxville: University of Tennessee Press, 1980.

Knight, Franklin. *The Caribbean: The Genesis of a Fragmented Nationalism.* Oxford: Oxford University Press, 1978.

Kornweibel, Theodore Jr. *"Seeing Red": Federal Campaigns Against Black Militancy, 1919–1925.* Bloomington: Indiana University Press, 1998.

Labelle, Micheline. "La force opérante de l'idéologie de couleur en 1946." In *Pouvoir noir en Haïti: L' Explosion de 1946,* 133–54. Montreal: CIDIHCA, 1988.

———. *Idéologie de couleur et classes sociales en Haïti.* Montreal: Presses de L'Université de Montreal, 1978.

Lacombe, Robert. "Le tourisme en Haïti." *Association France-Haïti Bulletin Périodique,* nos. 5–6 (June–December 1958).

Laguerre, Michel S. *The Complete Haitiana: A Bibliographic Guide to the Scholarly Literature, 1900–1980.* 2 vols. Millwood, N.Y.: Kraus International Publications, 1982.

———. *The Military and Society in Haiti.* Knoxville: University of Tennessee Press, 1993.

———. *Voodoo and Politics in Haiti.* New York: St. Martin's Press, 1989.

Laraque, Paul. "André Breton en Haïti." *Nouvelle Optique* 1, no. 2 (1971): 126–38.

Largey, Michael D. "Haiti and the French Caribbean." In *Caribbean Currents: Caribbean Music from Rumba to Reggae,* ed. Peter Manuel, 56–72. Philadelphia: Temple University Press, 1995.

———. *Vodou Nation: Haitian Art Music and Cultural Nationalism.* Chicago: University of Chicago Press, 2006.

Latortue, François. *Le droit du travail en Haïti.* Port-au-Prince: Les Presses Libres, 1961.

Lawless, Robert. *Haiti: A Research Handbook*. New York: Garland Publishing, 1990.

Le Roy, Félix Morisseau. *Natif-Natal: un conte en vers*. Port-au-Prince: Éditions Haïtiennes, 1948.

Lescot, Élie. *Avant l'oubli: christianisme et paganisme en Haïti et autres lieux*. Port-au-Prince: Henri Deschamps, 1974.

Lewis, Gordon K. *Main Currents in Caribbean Thought: The Historical Evolution of Caribbean Society in Its Ideological Aspects, 1492–1900*. Baltimore: Johns Hopkins University Press, 1983.

Lewis, Rupert Charles. *Walter Rodney's Intellectual and Political Thought*. Detroit: Wayne State University, 1998.

Leyburn, James G. *The Haitian People*. New Haven, Conn.: Yale University Press, 1941.

Lobb, John. "Caste and Class in Haiti." *American Journal of Sociology* 46 (1940): 23–34.

Logan, Rayford W. *The Diplomatic Relations of the United States with Haiti, 1776–1891*. Chapel Hill: University of North Carolina, 1941.

——. *Haiti and the Dominican Republic*. New York: Oxford University Press, 1968.

——. "The International Status of the Negro." *Journal of Negro History* 18, no. 1 (January 1933): 33–38.

Lowenthal, Ira P., and Drexel G. Woodson. *Catalogue de la collection Mangonès, Pétionville, Haiti*. New Haven, Conn.: Antilles Research Program, Yale University, 1974.

Luc, Jean. "Sur la diffusion du Marxisme en Haïti." *Nouvelle Optique* 2, no. 6 (1972): 89–104.

Lundahl, Mats. "Economies of Colour." *Axess Magazine* 5, no. 9 (2007), <http://www.axess.se/english/2007/09/theme—lundahl.php.htm>. 20 April 2008.

——. *The Haitian Economy: Man, Land, and Markets*. New York: St. Martin's Press, 1983.

——. *Peasants and Poverty: A Study of Haiti*. New York: St. Martin's Press, 1979.

——. "The Rise and Fall of the Haitian Labour Movement." In *Labour in the Caribbbean: From Emancipation to Independence*, ed. Malcolm Cross and Gad Heuman, 88–119. London: Macmillan, 1988.

McCrocklin, James H. *Garde d'Haïti, 1915–1934: Twenty Years of Organization and Training by United States Marine Corps*. Annapolis, Md.: Naval Institute, 1956.

McLeod, Marc C. "Undesirable Aliens: Race, Ethnicity, and Nationalism in the Comparison of Haitian and British West Indian Immigrant Workers in Cuba, 1912–1939." *Journal of Social History* 31, no. 3 (Spring 1998): 599–623.

Magloire, Jean. *Dumarsais Estimé: esquisse de sa vie politique*. Port-au-Prince: Imprimerie de L'État, 1950.

Malek, R. Michael. "Dominican Republic's General Rafael Trujillo and the Haitian Massacre of 1937: A Case of Subversion in Inter-Caribbean Relations." *SECOLAS Annals* 11 (March 1980): 137–55.

Mandle, Jay R. *Patterns of Caribbean Development: An Interpretive Essay on Economic Change*. New York: Gordon and Breach Science Publishers, 1982.

Manigat, Leslie F. *Ethnicité, nationalisme, et politique: le cas de Haïti*. New York: Éditions connaissance Diffusion d'Haïti, 1975.

——. *Haiti of the Sixties, Object of International Concern: A Tentative Global Analysis of the Potentially Explosive Situation of a Crisis Country in the Caribbean*. Washington, D.C.: Washington Center for Foreign Policy Research, 1964.

Mathurin, Augustin. *Bicentenaire de la fondation de Port-au-Prince*. Port-au-Prince: Imprimerie des Antilles, 1975.

Meeks, Brian. *Radical Caribbean: From Black Power to Abu Bakr*. Kingston: University of the West Indies Press, 1996.

Métreux, Alfred. *Voodoo in Haiti*. Trans. Hugo Charteris. 1959. Reprint, New York: Schocken Books, 1972.

Michel, Georges. *Charlemagne Péralte and the First American Occupation of Haiti*. Trans. Douglas Henry Daniels. Dubuque, Ia.: Kendall-Hunt Publishing, 1996.

Mintz, Sidney W. "Can Haiti Change?" *Foreign Affairs* 74, no. 1 (January/February 1995): 62–78.

———. *Caribbean Transformations*. New York: Columbia University Press, 1989.

Moral, Paul. *Le paysan haïtien*. Port-au-Prince: Éditions Fardin, 1961.

Nemours, Alfred. *Les présidents Lescot et Trujillo*. Port-au-Prince: Imprimerie de l'État, 1942.

Neptune, Harvey R. *Caliban and the Yankees: Trinidad and the United States Occupation*. Chapel Hill: University of North Carolina Press, 2007.

Nicholls, David. "Biology and Politics in Haiti." *Race* 13, no. 2 (1971): 203–14.

———. *From Dessalines to Duvalier: Race, Colour, and National Independence in Haiti*. 1979. Reprint, New Brunswick, N.J.: Rutgers University Press, 1996.

———. "Ideology and Protest in Haiti, 1930–1946." *Journal of Contemporary History* 9, no. 4 (1974): 3–26.

Noel, Ascencio A. *Les responsables des vêpres du 25 Mai*. Port-au-Prince, 1957.

Oriol, Jacques. "In Memoriam: Lorimer Denis." *Bulletin de la Bureau d'Ethnologie*. Port-au-Prince: Imprimerie de L'État, 1957.

Pamphile, Leon D. *Haitians and African Americans: A Heritage of Tragedy and Hope*. Gainesville: University Press of Florida, 2001.

Paquin, Lyonel. *The Haitians—Class and Color Politics*. New York: Multi-Type, 1983.

Péan, Leslie. "Unité et conjoncture politique en Haïti: L'Union patriotique haïtienne 1920–1930." *Collectif Paroles* 13 (August–September 1981): 29–33.

Pérez, Louis A. Jr. *Cuba Between Reform and Revolution*. New York: Oxford University Press, 1995.

———. *On Becoming Cuban: Identity, Nationality, and Culture*. Chapel Hill: University of North Carolina Press, 1999.

Peters, Carl Edward. *Lumiére sur le humfort*. Port-au-Prince: Chéraquit, 1941.

Phareaux, Lallier C. *La vie contemporaine*. Port-au-Prince: Imprimerie de L'État, 1953.

Phifer, Juliette. "Public Education in Haiti since 1934, a Survey of Education in the Republic of Haiti." Ph.D. diss., York University, 1948.

Pierre, Pressoir. *Témoignages: 1946–1976, l'espérance déçue*. Port-au-Prince: Henri Deschamps, 1987.

Pierre-Charles, Gérard. *La economía haitiana y su vía de desarrollo*. Mexico: Cuadernos Americanos, 1965.

———. *Haití: la crisis ininterrumpida*. Havana: Casa de las Americas, 1979.

———. *Haïti: jamais, jamais plus!: les violations des droits de l'homme à l'époque des Duvalier*. Port-au-Prince: CRESFED, 2000.

Plummer, Brenda Gayle. "Black and White in the Caribbean: Haitian-American Relations, 1902–1934." Ph.D. diss., Cornell University, 1981.

———. *Haiti and the Great Powers, 1902–1915*. Baton Rouge: Louisiana State University Press, 1988.

———. *Haiti and the United States: The Psychological Moment*. Athens: University of Georgia Press, 1992.

———. "Race, Nationality, and Trade in the Caribbean: The Syrians in Haiti, 1903–1934." *International History Review* 3 (October 1981): 517–39.

———. *Rising Wind: Black Americans and U.S. Foreign Affairs, 1935–1960*. Chapel Hill: University of North Carolina Press, 1996.

Polizzotti, Mark. *Revolution of the Mind: The Life of André Breton*. New York: Farrar, Strauss, and Giroux, 1995.

Polyné, Millery. "Modernizing the Race: Political and Cultural Engagements Between Haitians and African Americans, 1930–1964." Ph.D diss., University of Michigan, 2003.

Post, Ken. *Arise Ye Starvelings: The Jamaican Labor Rebellion of 1938 and its Aftermath*. The Hague: Martinus Nijhoff, 1978.

———. *Strike the Iron: A Colony at War: Jamaica, 1939–1945*. 2 vols. Atlantic Highlands, N.J.: Humanities Press, 1981.

Posy, Bonnard. "Jacmel 1946." *Conjonction* 202 (April–June 1997): 59–66.

Pouvoir noir en Haïti: L' Explosion de 1946. Montreal: CIDIHCA, 1988.

Preeg, Ernest H. *The Haitian Dilemma: A Case Study in Demographics, Development, and U.S. Foreign Policy*. Washington, D.C.: The Center for Strategic & International Studies, 1996.

Price-Mars, Jean. "Classe ou caste? Étude sur 'The Haitian People' (Le peuple haïtien de James G. Leyburn)." *Revue de la Société d'Histoire et de Géographie d'Haïti* 13, no. 46 (1942): 1–50.

———. *So Spoke the Uncle (Ainsi parla l'oncle)*. Trans. Magdaline W. Shannon. Washington, D.C.: Three Continents Press, 1983.

Rabe, Stephen G. *Eisenhower and Latin America: The Foreign Policy of Anticommunism*. Chapel Hill: University of North Carolina Press, 1988.

Ramsey, Kate. "Without One Ritual Note: Folklore Performance and the Haitian State, 1935–1946." *Radical History Review* 84 (Fall 2002): 7–42.

Renda, Mary A. *Taking Haiti: Military Occupation and the Culture of U.S. Imperialism, 1915–1940*. Chapel Hill: University of North Carolina Press, 2001.

Rey-Charlier, Ghislaine. "Note d'introduction." In *Pouvoir noir en Haïti: L'Explosion de 1946*, 279–83. Montreal: CIDIHCA, 1988.

Rigaud, Milo. *Sténio Vincent: révélé par la justice et par l'opinion publique*. Port-au-Prince: Henri Deschamps, 1957.

Robinson, Cedric J. *Black Marxism: The Making of the Black Radical Tradition*. Chapel Hill: University of North Carolina Press, 2000.

Rock, David, ed. *Latin America in the 1940s: War and Postwar Transitions*. Berkeley: University of California Press, 1994.

Rodman, Selden. *Haiti: The Black Republic*. New York: Devin-Adair, 1961.

——. *The Miracle of Haitian Art*. New York: Doubleday, 1974.

——. *Renaissance in Haiti: Popular Painters in the Black Republic*. New York: Pellegrini and Cudahy, 1948.

Roland, Astrel. *Le naufrage d'une nation, ou, les dessous ténébreux de l'affaire Roland-Estimé-Magloire en Haïti, 1949–1950*. Quebec: Imprimerie Laprairie, 1984.

Roorda, Eric Paul. *The Dictator Next Door: The Good Neighbor Policy and the Trujillo Regime in the Dominican Republic, 1930–1945*. Durham, N.C.: Duke University Press, 1998.

——. "Genocide Next Door: The Good Neighbor Policy, the Trujillo Regime and the Haitian Massacre of 1937." *Diplomatic History* 20, 3 (Summer 1996): 301–20.

Rotberg, Robert I. *Haiti: The Politics of Squalor*. Boston: Houghton Mifflin, 1971.

——. ed. *Haiti Renewed: Political and Economic Prospects*. Washington, D.C.: Brookings Institution Press, 1997.

Roumain, Jacques. "Haiti: A Dictatorship—Lessons and Results." *Negro Worker* (May 1937): 14–19.

——. *Masters of the Dew*. Trans. Langston Hughes and Mercer Cook. London: Heinemann, 1978.

——. *Le sacrifice du tambour-assoto*. Port-au-Prince: Imprimerie de L'État, 1943.

Ryan, Selwyn D. *Race and Nationalism in Trinidad and Tobago: A Study of Decolonization in a Multiracial Society*. Toronto: University of Toronto Press, 1972.

Sagás, Ernesto. *Race and Politics in the Dominican Republic*. Gainesville: University of Florida Press, 2000.

Savaille, Rulhière. *La grève de 29: la première grève des étudiants haïtiennes, 31 Octobre, 1929*. Port-au-Prince: Ateliers Fardin, 1979.

Schmidt, Hans. *The United States Occupation of Haiti, 1915–1934*. New Brunswick, N.J.: Rutgers University Press, 1995.

Schroeder, Susan. *Cuba: A Handbook of Historical Statistics*. Boston: G. K. Hall, 1982.

Seza, Mari Dyevela. "Koudèy sou istwa mouvman fanm nan-an Ayiti." *Jounal Bon Nouvèl* (March 1999): 8–10.

Shannon, Magdaline W. *Jean Price-Mars, the Haitian Elite, and the American Occupation*. New York: St. Martin's Press, 1996.

——. "The U.S. Commission for the Study and Review of Conditions in Haiti and Its Relationship to President Hoover's Latin American Policy." *Caribbean Studies* 15, no. 4 (January 1976): 53–71.

Sheller, Mimi. *Democracy after Slavery: Black Publics and Peasant Radicalism in Haiti and Jamaica*. Gainesville: University Press of Florida, 2000.

Simpson, George E. "Haiti's Social Structure." *American Sociological Review* 6, no. 5 (October 1941): 640–49.

——. "Haitian Politics." *Social Forces* 20, no. 4 (May 1942): 487–91.

Singham, Archibald W. *The Hero and the Crowd in a Colonial Polity*. New Haven, Conn.: Yale University Press, 1968.

Saint Armand, Edris. *Essai d'explication de "Dialogues de mes lampes."* Port-au-Prince: Imprimerie de L'État, 1942.

"Un siècle de constitutions haïtiennes, 1883–1983." *Le Petit Samedi Soir* 598 (April 1985).

Smith, Matthew J. *"From Dessalines to Duvalier* Revisited: A Quarter Century Retrospective." *Journal of Haitian Studies* 13, no. 1 (Spring 2007): 27–39.

Starobin, Joseph R. *American Communism in Crisis, 1943–1957.* Berkeley: University of California Press, 1972.

Stone, Carl, and Aggrey Brown, eds. *Perspectives on Jamaica in the Seventies.* Kingston: Jamaica Publishing House, 1981.

Taylor, Frank Fonda. *To Hell With Paradise: A History of the Jamaican Tourist Industry.* Pittsburgh: University of Pittsburgh Press, 1993.

Tèt kole ti peyizan ayisyen. *Dosye Chef Seksyon: Chef Seksyon—Yon system ki merite Elimine.* Lawrence: University of Kansas Institute of Haitian Studies Occasional Papers, June 1995.

Trouillot, Hénock. *Dimensions et limites de Jacques Roumain.* Port-au-Prince: Éditions Fardin, 1975.

Trouillot, Michel-Rolph. "Culture, Color, and Politics in Haiti." In *Race,* ed. Steven Gregory and Roger Sanjek, 146–74. New Brunswick, N.J.: Rutgers University Press, 1994.

———. "Jeux de mots, jeux de class: les mouvances de l'indigénisme." *Conjonction* 197 (1993): 29–48.

———. *Haiti: State against Nation.* New York: Monthly Review Press, 1990.

Turits, Richard Lee. *Foundations of Despotism: Peasants, the Trujillo Regime, and Modernity in Dominican History.* Stanford: Stanford University Press, 2003.

———. "A World Destroyed, A Nation Imposed: The 1937 Haitian Massacre in the Dominican Republic." *Hispanic American Historical Review* 82, no. 3 (November 2002): 589–635.

Vega, Bernardo. *Trujillo y Haití.* Vol. 1 (1930–1937). Santo Domingo: Fundación Cultural Dominicana, 1988.

Verna, Chantalle Francesca. "Haiti's 'Second Independence' and the Promise of Pan-American Co-operation, 1934–1956." Ph.D diss., Michigan State University, 2005.

Vincent, Sténio. *Efforts et résultats.* Port-au-Prince: Imprimerie de L'État, 1938.

———. *En posant les jalons.* 5 vols. Port-au-Prince: Imprimerie de L'État, 1939–45.

Von Eschen, Penny M. *Race against Empire: Black Americans and Anticolonialism, 1937–1957.* Ithaca, N.Y.: Cornell University Press, 1997.

Watkins, Mark H. "The Social Role of Color in Haiti—Some Facts and Impressions." *Monthly Summary of Events and Trends in Race Relations* 3, no. 8 (March 1946): 250–51.

Weil, Thomas E. *Haiti: A Country Study.* Washington, D.C.: Foreign Area Studies, American University, 1982.

Weston, Rubin Francis. *Racism in U.S. Imperialism: The Influence of Racial Assumptions on American Foreign Policy, 1893–1946.* Columbia: University of South Carolina Press, 1972.

Whitney, Robert. *State and Revolution in Cuba: Mass Mobilization and Political Change, 1920–1940.* Chapel Hill: University of North Carolina Press, 2001.

Wiarda, Howard J. *Dictatorship and Development: The Methods of Control in Trujillo's Dominican Republic.* Gainesville: University of Florida Press, 1970.

Wilson, Edmund. *Red, Black, Blond, and Olive: Studies in Four Civilizations: Zuñi, Haiti, Soviet Russia, Israel*. New York: Oxford University Press, 1956.

Wingfield, Roland, and Vernon A. Parention. "Class Structure and Class Conflict in Haitian Society." *Social Forces* 43, no. 3 (March 1965): 338–47.

Wood, Bryce. *The Making of the Good Neighbor Policy*. New York: Columbia University Press, 1961.

Zoumaras, Thomas. "The Path to Panamericanism: Eisenhower's Foreign Economic Policy Toward Latin America." Ph.D. diss., University of Connecticut, 1987.

Note: Page numbers in *italics* refer to illustrations.

Acau, Jean-Jacques, 198 (n. 6)

Action, L', 131

Action National, L', 24

Action Radicale, L', 41

Adelina (empress), 40

ADEM. *See* Association des Étudiants en Médecine, Pharmacie et Art Dentaire

African Diaspora, 193

African heritage: Griots on, 24–27, 37; in Magloire's presidency, 152; romanticization of, 8

African political systems, 25–27

Agriculture: under Magloire, 164–66; rubber cultivation in, 43–47, *45*

Agriculture, U.S. Department of, 44

Aid, U.S., 113–15, 166

Ainsi parla l'oncle (Price-Mars), 8–9

Air Force, 178

Air travel, 107–8

Alexander, Raymond Pace, 82

Alexander, Robert, 134

Alexis, Jacques Stephen, 73–79, *81*; in 1946 elections, 89, 93; in 1957 elections, 175; death of, 187; education of, 127; on imperialism, 93; in labor movement, 88; under Magloire, 156; Marxism of, 73; in medical school, 73; on *noirisme*, 87; in revolution of 1946, 71, 76–79; in *La Ruche*, 75

Alexis, Nord, 153

Alexis, Stephen, 73

Alliance Démocratique, 174

Alphonse, Fénélon, 152

American Civil Liberties Union, 55

Americanization, 50, 53

Amicale club, L', 58, 83

Analyse schématique, L', 19–21, 200 (n. 31)

Anarchy, 17, 177

"Anciens jeunes" (song), 60

Anticolonialism: of Griots, 25–26; in Jamaica, 194; of Parti Communiste Haïtien, 93

Anticommunism, Haitian, 16–23; under Estimé, 129–31, 141; under Magloire, 152, 154–55; repeal of, 99; under Vincent, 16–17, 20–23

Anticommunism, U.S.: effects on radical movements, 3–4, 189; and Fignolé's presidency, 179–80; rise of Marxism and, 15, 18; and support for Magloire, 154–55

Anti-Haitianism: in Dominican Republic, 29–30, 203–4 (n. 83)

Anti-Imperialist League of Mexico, 21

Anti-liberalism, 26–27

Arab-Haitians, 4, 223 (n. 11)

Arbenz, Jacobo, 154–55, 180

Arbes musiciens, Les (Alexis), 187

Archival sources, 2, 3

Aristide, Jean-Bertrand, 193, 195

Armand, Durcé, 35, 36, 42, 67

Armand, Pierre, 178

Armée d'Haïti, 137, 145

Armour, Norman, 115, 117

Army: in 1957 elections, 176–85; and Fignolé's presidency, 180–81. *See also* Armée d'Haïti; Garde d'Haïti; Military rule

Arts: black consciousness in, 59–61, 106–7, 192

Assaut, L', 24

Association Démocratique Haïtienne, 55

Association des Étudiants en Médecine, Pharmacie et Art Dentaire (ADEM), 73, 157

Atlantic Charter, 54

Auguste, Tancrède, 15

Augustin, Rémy, 49

Authenticity: cultural and racial, 25

Authentiques: and economic policy, 113; Fignolé's criticism of, 121–22; under Magloire, 159–61; meaning of, 108–9; versus *milat* elite, 117–21; *noirisme* of, 109; origins of term, 224 (n. 26); and second term for Estimé, 140

Authoritarianism, 29, 140

Averill, Gage, 60

Baguidy, Joseph, 110

Baker, Théodore, 74–77, *81*, 85, 93, 229 (n. 110)

Balaguer, Joaquín, 31

Banana industry, 29, 47, 115–16

Bank, national, 114, 179

Barbot, Clément, 167

Bartlett, Harley Harris, 44

Bastien, Rémy, 210 (n. 50), 241 (n. 148)

Batista, Fulgencio, 30, 156

Bauduy, Marcel, 53

Bauxite, 165

Bazile, Robert, 67, 103, 137

Beals, Carleton, 182

Beaubrun, Théodore, 83

Beaufils, George, 75, *81*

Beaulieu, Christian, 16, 19, 36, 51, 56, 199 (n. 8), 212 (n. 89)

Beauvoir, Vilfort (foreign minister), 143

Béhague, Gérard, 60

Bellegarde, Dantès, 27, 61, 82, 151

Bellegarde-Smith, Patrick, 172, 183

Bernardin, Raymond, 163

Bicentennial Exposition (1949–50), 107, 141, 143–44

Big Stick policy, 28

Black Americans: on Fignolé's presidency, 180; influence of Haiti on, 193; on Lescot regime, 55; on revolution of 1946, 82; Roumain supported by, 21; on Vincent dictatorship, 36; during World War II, 57

Black consciousness: and anti-superstition campaign, 48; in arts, 59–61, 106–7, 192; under Estimé, 104–8; government promotion of, 106–7; under Lescot, 40, 56–61; under Magloire, 152; opportunity for change through, 2. *See also* Color and color divisions

Black Haitians. *See* Intellectuals, Haitian; Middle-class blacks; Non-elite blacks

Black Jacobins, The (James), 57–58

Black market, 118

Black nationalism. See *Noirisme*

Black power: *authentiques* and, 109; contradictory nature of, 116–17; equilibrium through, 105–6; *Les Griots* on, 105; *milat* elite challenged by, 105, 109; nationalization of, 104–8

Black presidents: meaning of, 105–6; need for, 41, 207 (n. 3)

Black supremacy, 121

Blanchet, Jules, 56, 86, 99, 135

Blanchet, Lina Mathion, 59

Bloncourt, Gérald, *81*; in *Combat*, 85; in exile, 85; radicalism of, 74; in revolution of 1946, 76–79, 82–83; in *La Ruche*, 75

Bloncourt, Tony, 74

Blum, Léon, 63, 122

Bontemps, Arna, 57

Borders, 29–30, 34, 203–4 (n. 83)

Bordes, Léon "Ti-Roi," 145–46, 160

Borno, Louis, 35, 40, 110

Bourgeoisie. *See* Elite

Bourjolly, Fritz, 22

Bourjolly, H., 90

Boyer, Jean-Pierre, 29

Bradley, Francine, 36–37

Brandt, O. J., 47, 118

Breton, André, 75–76, 77, 82

Brierre, Jean, 56, 78, 81

Britain, 128
Brouard, Carl, 24–28
Browder, Earl, 229 (n. 115)
Bureau d'Ethnologie, 106–7

Cacao, 166
Caco resistance, 7, 10
Caducée, Le, 73
Cagoulards (masked thugs), 185
Cahiers d'Haïti, 56
Calixte, Démosthènes P., 35, 95–97, 206
    (n. 114), 221 (n. 131)
Camille, Roussan, 56
Cantave, Léon, 176, 178
Caribbean: black intellectuals of, 57–58;
    patterns of resistance in, 194
Caribe, El, 142
Casernes Dessalines, 178
Casimir, Lumane, 106, 223 (n. 13)
Casimir, Rodrigue, 123
Casinos, 143–44
Cassagnol, Paul, 139
Caste system, 5
Castro, Fidel, 187, 194
Catholic church: anti-superstition cam-
    paign by, 47–50, 69; and Estimé's
    presidency, 117–18; on Magloire's elec-
    tion, 152; Parti Socialiste Populaire on,
    135
Cator, Sylvio, 81–82
CDN. *See* Comité de Défense Nationale
CEG. *See* Conseil Exécutif Gouvernement
CEM. *See* Conseil Exécutif Militaire
Cement, 165
Cénacle D'Études, Le, 58
Censorship, 156, 182
Centre, Le, 17–18
Centre d'Art, 59, 74, 108
Césaire, Aimé, 57, 75
Chamber of Deputies: Estimé in, 110–11;
    Lescot in, 40; on Lescot's presidency,
    41
Chantiers, 63–66, 94, 105, 127, 142
Charlier, Étienne, *131;* in 1946 elections,
    89, 98; in 1950 elections, 142; during

Lescot regime, 51–53; Magloire's
    repression and, 155; Marxism of, 19,
    86–87; in Parti Socialiste Populaire,
    86–87, 134
Charlier, Philippe, 97, 137
Chauffeurs, 159, 167, 174
Chauvet, Lucien, 146
Chef de section, 67
Chenet, Gérald, 74, 75, 76, *81*
Christophe, Henri, 144, 233 (n. 182)
Civil war: 1957 threat of, 177–79
Class, social: in 1957 elections, 169, 173–
    74; color linked with, 4–7, 105; in
    Marxism, 20; of *milat,* 4, 198 (n. 6).
    See also Elite; Middle-class blacks;
    Workers
Classe Moyen et Masse, 88
Club Intrepid, 73
Club Mopiste, 123, 127
Clubs de dimanche, 58, 63
CMG. *See* Conseil Militaire de
    Gouvernement
Coffee cultivation, 47, 143, 164–67
Cold war, 104, 130, 155
Collège Odéide, 93
Colonialism. *See* Anticolonialism; Occu-
    pation of Haiti by U.S.
Color and color divisions: in 1946 elec-
    tions, 92–93; in 1957 elections, 169,
    173–74; in armed forces, 67; class in,
    105; class linked with, 4–7, 105;
    Estimé on, 6–7, 111; Fignolé on, 65; in
    Lescot regime, 39–40, 42; in Marxism,
    20, 127–28; Parti Communiste Haït-
    ien on, 87; Parti Socialiste Populaire
    on, 87, 134–35; politicians' avoidance
    of issue of, 43; politics of, 4–7; versus
    race, 4; scholarly focus on, 4–7, 193;
    social functions of, 5–6
Color prejudice: Estimé and, 119–20, 135;
    Lescot and, 42–43, 58
Combat, 83–85, *84*
Comité de Défense Nationale (CDN),
    90–91
Comité de la Grève, 78

Comité Démocratique Féminin, 79–80
Communism. *See* Anticommunism, Haitian; Anticommunism, U.S.; Marxism
Communist Party of Haiti: attempts to establish, 16, 19. *See also* Parti Communiste Haïtien
Communist Party of the United States (CPUSA), 16, 17, 51, 85, 218 (n. 61)
Communitarianism, African, 26
Conference of International Workers Organizations, 54
Congress, U.S., 46
Conjonction, 73
Conseil Exécutif Gouvernement (CEG), 176–78
Conseil Exécutif Militaire (CEM), 80–83; on 1946 elections, 81, 82, 89, 90; coup plots against, 96; establishment of, 80; on labor movement, 88; Lescot's resignation obtained by, 80–81; on Marxists, 85; opposition to, 90–91; U.S. recognition of, 82
Conseil Militaire de Gouvernement (CMG), 182–85
Conservatism: of Magloire, 152; political parties of, 83
Constant, Dorléans Juste, 19
Constitution: of 1805, 1; of 1932, 21–22, 94, 97; 1942 suspension of, 43; 1944 revision of, 54; of 1946, 96–97, 115, 140, 144
Construction, 158
Continental, Le, 44
Cook, Mercer, 82
Corps d'aviation, 66
Corruption: in armed forces, 66–67; and black power, 116–17; under Estimé, 110–11, 147–48; under Magloire, 166–67
Corvée work system, 7
Coulanges, Ernst, 174
CPUSA. *See* Communist Party of the United States
Cri des nègres, le, 21
Cryptostegia vine, 43–44

Cuba: deportation of workers from, 30; on Parti Communiste Haïtien, 84, 85, 218 (n. 60); patterns of resistance in, 194; revolution in, 187, 194; Roumain in, 51; Socialist Party of, 87; tourism in, 164
Cultural difference, 57
Cultural nationalism, 8–9, 108
Culture, French, 8, 24–27
Culture, Haitian: in Bicentennial Exposition, 107; black consciousness in, 58, 192; contemporary, 192–93; Estimé's promotion of, 106–8; during Lescot regime, 58–61; political, 3, 191–92; U.S. interest in, 107–8

Dajabón, 30, 31
Dalencour, François, 27, 83
Dalencourt, Lelio, 104
Damien strike (1929), 9, 14, 15, 76
Dams, 164, 166
Dance movement, 59–61
Dartigue, Maurice, 44–46, 73
Dash, Michael, 53
Daumec, Lucien, 175
David, Jean, 96, 97, 142, 161, 162, 224 (n. 25)
Davis, Roy Tasco, 177, 180
Debt, national: under Estimé, 113–15; under Magloire, 165
DeCourcy, William, 147, 233 (n. 182)
De Gobineau, Arthur, 24, 25
Déjean, Joseph, 63, 109, 146
Déjoie, Louis: in 1957 elections, 169–78, 181–85; in constitutional debates, 96; Estimé opposed by, 144–45, 233 (n. 187); in exile, 187; Fignolé's criticism of, 100; Magloire opposed by, 169, 170; U.S. support for, 183
Demain, 86, 92
Demesmin, Castel, 97, 146
Democracy: first attempt to create, 104; under Magloire, 158, 170
Denis, Lorimer: on 1946 elections, 95, 98; at Bureau d'Ethnologie, 106–7; on

Catholic church, 117; in *Chantiers*, 66; on equilibrium through black power, 105; Estimé supported by, 105; in *Griots*, 23–28; in *Les Griots*, 104–5; during Magloire regime, 161; in MOP, 104; in Parti Populaire Nationale, 83

Depestre, René, 74–77; in 1946 elections, 89, 219 (n. 84); and 1957 elections, 175; education of, 127; under Magloire, 156; in revolution of 1946, 76–77; in *La Ruche*, 75, 76

De Pradines, Kandjo, 59

De Pradines Morse, Emerante, 59, 77

Derby, Lauren, 203 (n. 83)

Désinor, Clovis, 83

Desulmé, Thomas, 97

Diaquoi, Louis, 16, 23–24, 26

Dictatorships: Breton on, 76; of Magloire, 161–62; U.S. nonintervention and, 29; of Vincent, 36–37

Djazz. See Music

Dominican Republic: anti-Haitianism in, 29–30, 203–4 (n. 83); borders of, 29–30, 34, 203–4 (n. 83); Haitian occupation of, 29; in massacre of 1937, 29–33; opposition to Estimé in, 138–39, 142–43; in World War II, 43. *See also* Foreign relations, Dominican-Haitian

Dominique, Jean, 132, 192

Dorsinville, Roger: in 1946 elections, 92, 98; as *authentique*, 109, 224 (n. 26); Estimé supported by, 111; on Fignolé's speeches, 100; during Magloire regime, 160; on revolution of 1946, 71

Drew, Gerald, 177, 183

Drought, 46, 116

Dulles, Allen, 180

Dunham, Katherine, 59, 110

Dupuy, Jean, 142

Duval, Amilcar, 41

Duvalier, François "Papa Doc" (president, 1957–71), *184*; in 1946 elections, 94–95, 97–98; in 1957 elections, 149, 171–85; on Catholic church, 117; in *Chantiers*, 66; conflict leading to regime of,

1, 7; on equilibrium through black power, 105–6; as Estimé's successor, 161, 184; Estimé supported by, 105; Fignolé's split with, 127, 228 (n. 104); in *Griots*, 24–28; in *Les Griots*, 104–5; groundwork for election of, 161, 162; in labor ministry, 127; legacy of, 194; during Magloire regime, 161, 162, 167; in Magloire's fall, 170; on Marxism, 27, 202 (n. 69); in MOP, 94–95, 104, 122, 127; in Parti Populaire Nationale, 83; as president for life, 187; on revolution of 1791–1804, 25; on revolution of 1946, 184; rise of, 161, 162; scholarly assessments of, 2; start of presidency, 187; U.S. education of, 28; U.S. support for, 183–84

Duvalier, Jean-Claude, 192, 194

Duvigneaud, Frédéric, 35, 41

École Normale Supérieure, L', 112

Economic aid, U.S., 113–15, 166

Economic control: by Haitian elite, 13; by U.S., 29, 113–14

Economic decline: under Magloire, 163–68

Economic policy: of Estimé, 113–16, 135, 143–44; of Lescot, 43–47, 69, 113; of Magloire, 163–68

Education: Estimé's reform of, 112; Fignolé as minister of, 99, 112; Fignolé on need for reform of, 64; under Magloire, 157; Marxism in, 72–74; MOP work on, 123, 127; and resistance to occupation, 7–8

Efron, Edith, 107

Eisenhower, Dwight D., 154, 180

Elections, legislative: of 1941, 53, 54; of 1944, 54; of 1946, 81, 82, 89–98; of 1950, 140–45, 149; of 1955, 167; suspension of, 54

Elections, presidential: of 1930, 9; of 1936, 13, 21–22, 201 (n. 38); of 1941, 37, 40–42, 68, 110–11; of 1946, 72, 89–98, 104, 231–32 (n. 158); of 1950,

150–52, 157–58; of 1952, 140; of 1957, 150, 168–84

Elite: color politics and, 4–7; in economy, 13; educational access and, 8; end of rule by, 72, 105, 108–9; during Estimé's presidency, 117–21; Fignolé's critique of, 64–65; and Griots, 25–28; interest in folklore, 58–59, 213–14 (n. 104); and Lescot's presidency, 41, 42; Magloire's relations with, 152–53; as *milat*, 4, 198 (n. 6); during occupation, 7–8; radicals' impact on, 191; on Vincent dictatorship, 37–38; during World War II, 47. *See also Milat* elite

El Saïeh, Issa, 223 (n. 11)

Embassy, French, 79

Embassy, U.S.: on 1946 elections, 90; on 1957 elections, 174, 178, 183, 185; on Duvalier regime, 187; on Magloire regime, 170, 172; on Parti Communiste Haïtien, 85; in revolution of 1946, 77, 78

Equilibrium: through black power, 105–6; Magloire on, 152, 167

Estimé, Dumarsais (president, 1946–50), 11, 97–148, *111*, 189–90; in 1941 elections, 110–11; 1946 election of, 72, 90–92, 97–98, 219 (n. 84); anticommunism of, 129–31, 141; armed forces under, 136–38; background of, 110; on banana industry, 115–16; and black consciousness, 104–8; black intellectuals in administration of, 108–9; as break from elite rule, 72, 105, 108; career of, 110–11; coalition cabinet of, 98–101; color politics of, 6–7, 111, 135; corruption under, 116–17, 147–48; coup plots against, 100, 136–47; death of, 160, 161; Duvalier as successor to, 161, 184; economic policy of, 113–16, 135, 143–44; in exile, 159–60; fall of, 140–48, 149–50; Fignolé's opposition to, 121–27, 228–29 (n. 105); inaugural speech of, 111–12; labor movement under, 112–13, 124–27; leadership style of, 110–11; legacy of, 107, 110; on Lescot's presidency, 41, 111; during Magloire's regime, 159–61; Marxism under, 127–36; national debt under, 113–15; nationalist myth regarding, 110, 224–25 (n. 31); popularity of, 103–4, 112, 136; reactions to election of, 97–98; reasons for failure of, 147–48; reforms by, 112; resignation of, 147; scholarly assessments of, 110; second term sought by, 140–45; and tourism, 106–8, 143–44

Estimé, Lucienne Hertelou, 161

Ethiopia, 26

Ethnological schools, 52

Étincelles (Depestre), 74

European political systems, 25–27

Export-Import Bank, 44, 46, 113

Exposition, Bicentennial (1949–50), 107, 141, 143–44

Famille, La, 123

FBI, 87

FDU. *See* Front Démocratique Unifié

Fédération des Travailleurs Haïtien (FTH), 126, 132–33

Fédération Haïtien des Travailleurs (FHT), 133

Fennell, Thomas A., 44–46

Fethière, Antonio, 22

FHT. *See* Fédération Haïtien des Travailleurs

Fieherer, Thomas, 32

Fignolé, Carmen, 123

Fignolé, Daniel, 64, 125; in 1946 elections, 89–91, 93–98; in 1950 elections, 141, 142, 157–58; in 1955 elections, 167; in 1957 elections, 173–79; Aristide compared to, 193; background of, 63; coup against, 181–83; death of, 192; Duvalier's split with, 127, 228 (n. 104); as education minister, 99, 112; Estimé opposed by, 121–27, 228–29 (n. 105); in Estimé's coalition cabinet, 99–101, 121, 122; in exile, 181, 187; in Front

Révolutionnaire Haïtien, 85–86, 88;
influence and popularity of, 63, 65, 86,
122, 190, 215 (n. 125); in labor movement, 63, 65–66, 88, 125–27, 228
(n. 100); legacy of, 190, 193; Magloire
criticized by, 157, 158–59, 167;
Magloire supported by, 151–52, 157–
58; on Marxism, 65, 122; in MOP, 93–
95, 121–23; *noirisme* of, 63–66, 189; in
Parti Populaire Nationale, 83, 88–89;
protests against removal of, 181–82; as
provisional president, 179–81; return
to Haiti, 192; U.S. influence on, 189
Fignolé, J. N., 63
Fignolé, Job, 63
Films, U.S., 48, 164
Five Year Plan: of 1945, 46–47; of 1951,
164
Flag: Haitian, 10, *10*, 187, 194; MOP, 123–
24, *125*; U.S., 10, *10*
Flambeau, 83, 104
Foi Sociale, 179, 182
Foisset, Père, 117
Folklore, Haitian: in dance, 59; elite interest in, 58–59, 213–14 (n. 104); government support for, 106–7; Roumain's
study of, 52; shift in attitudes toward,
58
Folsom, Robert S., 70
Fombrun, Charles, 90, 142
Fombrun, Marcel, 142
Forbes commission, 9
Foreign policy, U.S.: anticommunism in,
154–55; Big Stick policy, 28; cold war
in, 104, 130, 155; Good Neighbor Policy, 28–29, 33, 37; and Magloire
regime, 154–55; nonintervention, 28–
29; and Vincent regime, 28, 36–37
Foreign relations, Dominican-Haitian:
under Estimé, 138–39; under Lescot,
68–69; under Magloire, 152; massacre
of 1937 in, 29–33
Foreign relations, U.S.-Haitian: under
Estimé, 113–15, 130–31, 145; under
Lescot, 44, 69, 208–9 (n. 23); under

Magloire, 152, 154–55, 160; under Vin-
cent, 13–14, 29
Fouché, Luc, 151
Fourcand, Noé, 109–10, 114
France: Haitian students in, 127, 156;
négritude movement in, 57; political
system of, 25–27; surrealism in, 75;
trade with, 165; in World War II, 73–74
François, Saturnin, 19
French clergy, 47–50, 117–18
French culture, 8, 24–27
French resistance, 73–74
FRH. *See* Front Révolutionnaire Haïtien
From Dessalines to Duvalier (Nicholls), 5
Front Démocratique, 141
Front Démocratique Unifié (FDU), 80
Front Révolutionnaire Haïtien (FRH),
85–86, 88
FTH. *See* Fédération des Travailleurs
Haïtien

Gabriel, Mesmin, 63
Gaillard, Roger, 127, 156
Garde d'Haïti: Bazile as head of, 103; con-
flict in, 67–68; corruption in, 66–67;
coup plots in, 67–68, 96; under
Estimé, 136–38; under Lescot, 42, 50,
51–52, 66–69; Marxism and, 15; and
massacre of 1937, 32, 34–35, 40; pol-
iticization of, 40; in revolution of
1946, 77–80; size of, 66; socialism in,
67, 77; strengthening of, in 1930s, 13;
under Vincent, 14, 34–36; in World
War II, 43. *See also* Military rule
Gardes côtes, 66
Genocide. *See* Massacre of 1937
Glaneur, Le, 91–92
Gómez, Fernando, 68
Good Neighbor Policy, 28–29, 33, 37
Gouverneurs de la Rosée (Roumain), 55, 74
Grande Parti National Démocratique, 158
Great Britain, 128
Greene, Anne, 108
Griots, 23–28; on African heritage, 24–
27, 37; *authentiques* influenced by, 109;

in *Chantiers*, 66; dissolution of, 28, 58; on French culture, 24–27; Marxism rejected by, 26–27; on *milat* elite, 25–27; and *négritude* movement, 56–57; *noirisme* of, 25–28; origins of, 23–24; on race, 24–25

Griots, Les, 24, 28, 104–5, 161

Guatemala, 155, 179

Guichard, Paulette, 120

Guillén, Nicolás, 51, 53

Haiti, borders of, 29–30, 34, 203–4 (n. 83)

Haitian American Sugar Company (HASCO), 18, 88

Haitian Labor Union, 33

Haitian People, The (Leyburn), 5

Haitian Revolutionary Committee, 169

Haitian revolution of 1791–1804, 25

Haitian revolution of 1946, 11, 71–83, 189; CEM in, 80–83; Duvalier on, 184; effects of, 71–72; fragmentation of, 2; Lescot's response to, 79–81; Marxists in, 72–83; political parties after, 83–89; spread of, 80; start of, 76–80; as turning point, 2; U.S. response to, 82

Haïti Démocratique, 158–59

Haiti Faces Tomorrow's Peace (Hudicourt), 55

Harlem Renaissance, 8

HASCO. *See* Haitian American Sugar Company

Hazel, Hurricane (1954), 165–66

Hector, Michel, 84, 129, 228 (n. 100)

Heinl, Nancy, 88, 110

Heinl, Robert, 88, 110

Henriquez, Alphonse, 119, 129–30, 141, 145, 151, 158

Herskovits, Melville, 48, 55

Hertelou, Lucienne, 92

Heure d'Art Haïtien, L' (performance), 58–59

Hevea trees, 44, 45

Hispaniola: borders of, 29–30, 34, 203–4 (n. 83)

Holly, Arthur, 24

Honorat, Lamartinière, 104

Hoover, Herbert, 9, 28

Hudicourt, Max, *18*; in 1946 elections, 89, 90, 91–92; accused of coup plot, 18; in constitutional debates, 96, 97; death of, 133–34; Estimé opposed by, 91–92; in exile, 36, 51, 55; Fignolé's criticism of, 100; legacy of, 23; during Lescot regime, 51–56; on Lescot's election, 42; on Marxism, 17–19; on national debt, 113; in Parti Socialiste Populaire, 86; on race, 39; return to Haiti, 51, 86; socialism of, 53, 86; trial and imprisonment of, 18–19; against Vincent dictatorship, 36

Hughes, Langston, 21, 57

Hull, Cordell, 36, 37, 54

Hurricane Hazel (1954), 165–66

Hurston, Zora Neale, 57

Identity, national, 4, 59

Imperialism. *See* Anticolonialism; Occupation of Haiti by U.S.

Import Substitution Industrialization (ISI), 165

Income tax, 118

Independence: anniversaries of, 1, *14*, 167; Second Independence, 1, 26

Indigénisme, 57, 106–7

Institut d'Ethnolgie, 52

Institut Français, 73

Institut Mopique, 123

Intellectual Haitian-Dominican Congress, 30

Intellectuals, Caribbean, 57–58

Intellectuals, Haitian: in Estimé administration, 108–9; as Griots, 23–28; during Lescot regime, 58–61; as ruling elite, 108–9; surrealism influencing, 75

Intellectuals, U.S., 21, 55, 57. *See also* Black Americans

Inter-American Congress on Demography, First, 55

Inter-American Peace Commission, 139

International Institute of Afro-American
Studies, 55
Interviews, 3
ISI. *See* Import Substitution
Industrialization
Italy, 26

Jacob, Kléber Georges, 63, 104
Jamaica: anticolonialism in, 194; Estimé
in, 159–60; tourism in, 164
James, C. L. R., 57–58
January revolt of 1946. *See* Haitian revolution of 1946
Janvier, Louis Joseph, 25, 63
Jazz, 59–60
Jazz des Jeunes, 60, 61, 106, 223 (n. 11)
Jazz Saïeh, 106, 223 (n. 11)
Jean-Baptiste, Nemours, 152
Jean-Claude, Martha, 59
Jeannot, Yves, 92
Jeanty, Luc, 106
Jeanty, Occide, 60
Jérémie, 45
Jeunesse Progressiste de Port-au-Prince
(JPP), 132, 156
Jewish refugees, 43
Johnson, James Weldon, 36
Jolibois *fils*, Joseph, 21, 22, 33, 61, 201
(n. 39)
Joly, Ulrick, 159
Joseph, Albert, 132
Josué, Millien, 133
JPP. *See* Jeunesse Progressiste de Port-au-
Prince
Jumelle, Clément: in 1957 elections, 171,
173, 176, 179, 181, 185; death of, 187;
in Estimé administration, 112; in
Magloire administration, 157
Junta. *See* Military rule
Juste Constant, Felix Dorléans, 84–85, 89,
92–93, 128
Justicier, Le, 119

Kansonfèrisme (iron pants), 154, 162
Kébreau, Antonio, 178, 181, 182, 185, 187

Kompa-dirèk music, 152
Korean War, 154
Korne kabrit, 43–44
"Kote moun-yo" (song), 106, 223 (n. 11)

Labor, Ministry of, 112, 126, 127
Labor movement: in 1946 elections, 94; in
1957 elections, 174; development of,
61, 192; establishment of, 2; under
Estimé, 112–13, 124–27; Fignolé in,
63, 65–66, 88, 125–27; legalization of,
88; under Lescot, 61–66; under
Magloire, 159; *noirisme* in, 61–66;
Parti Communiste Haïtien in, 61, 62,
88; Parti Socialiste Populaire in, 132–
33; political parties of, 94; union
membership in, 124–25; under Vincent, 61; during World War II, 61–66.
See also Workers
Lacroix, Abel, 42
Lacroix, Franck, 141
Lafontant, Marc, 51
Lam, Wilfredo, 75
Lamy, Amilcar, 63
Land acquisition: for rubber cultivation,
44–46
Lanoix, Franck, 120, 151
Laraque, Ernest, 119
Laraque, Gustave, 153
Laraque, Henri, 89, 91
Laraque, Paul, 67, 75
Lavaud, Franck, 80, 81, 90, *111*, 137, 146–
47
Legendre, Franck, 22
Léger, Georges, 30, 32, 83
Léger, Love, 66, 109, 146
Legislature: 1935 dissolution of, 21, 33;
1946 constitutional debates in, 96–97;
1946 dissolution of, 81; anticommunism in, 129–30; conflict between
milat elite and *authentiques* in, 119;
and Estimé's reelection, 140–45. *See
also* Chamber of Deputies; Elections,
legislative; Senate, Haitian
Le Gouâze, Monsignor, 50

Leonard, Roger, 134–35
Le Roy, Felix Morisseau, 103
Lescot, Élie (president, 1941–45), 11, 39–
    70, 188; 1941 election of, 40–42, 68;
    anticommunism of, 17; and anti-
    superstition campaign, 47–50, 69;
    career of, 40–41; and Catholic church,
    49–50; color divisions under, 39–40,
    42; consolidation of power by, 42;
    coup plots against, 67–68; economic
    policy of, 43–47, 69, 113; education
    under, 73; end of regime, 40, 70, 71,
    80–81; Estimé on, 41, 111; extension
    of term, 54–55; as foreign minister, 14,
    40–41; Garde under, 42, 50, 51–52,
    66–69; as ideal successor to Vincent,
    38, 41; as interior minister, 17, 40; and
    labor movement, 61–66; Marxism
    under, 51–56, 72–83; and massacre of
    1937, 33; reaction to revolution, 79–
    81; rubber project of, 43–46, 45; start
    of revolution against, 76–80; Trujillo's
    relations with, 40, 41, 68–69; U.S.
    relations with, 44, 69, 208–9 (n. 23);
    World War II involvement of, 43
Lescot, Gérard, 42
Lescot, Roger, 42
Lespès, Anthony: in 1950 elections, 142;
    economic plan of, 135; in Estimé's
    coalition cabinet, 99; Lescot's meeting
    with, 56; Magloire's repression and,
    155; Marxism of, 19, 86–87; in Parti
    Socialiste Populaire, 86–87, 134
Levelt, Antoine, 80, 81, 90, 111, 137, 146–
    47, 172, 220 (n. 88)
Lewis, Gordon, 4
Leyburn, James, 4–5
Liberalism: noirisme against, 26–27
Liberal Party, 4, 83
Life magazine, 143
Light-skinned Haitians: terms for, 198
    (n. 6). See also Milat
Ligue Anti-Imperialiste, 19
Ligue d'Action Social et Démocratique,
    85

Ligue de Défense des Libertés Publiques,
    158–59
Ligue de la Jeunesse Patriote Haïtienne, 9
Ligue Feminin d'Action Sociale, 200
    (n. 21)
Lind, Omar, 17, 18
Listín Diario, 31, 49
Literacy programs, 123
Literature: censorship of, 156; nationalist,
    8–9
Locke, Alain, 55
Logan, Rayford, 57, 82, 96, 114, 193, 213
    (n. 97)
Lycée Pétion, 52, 63, 78, 110
Lydia Bailey (film), 164

Mabille, Pierre, 73–74, 77, 79, 82
Magloire, Félix, 61
Magloire, Franck, 76
Magloire, Jean, 49
Magloire, Paul Eugène (president, 1950–
    56), 11–12, 111, 149–72, 154; in 1946
    elections, 90, 96, 219 (n. 84), 231–32
    (n. 158); in 1950 elections, 150–52;
    anticommunism of, 152, 154–55; in
    banana industry, 116; in CEM, 81; con-
    solidation of military rule by, 150–53;
    economic decline under, 163–68; elite
    relations with, 152–53; and Estimé's
    reelection, 142, 144, 145; Estimé sup-
    ported by, 111; in exile, 187; fall of,
    169–72; family of, 153, 161; governing
    style of, 154, 161–62; opposition
    repressed by, 153–63; political aspira-
    tions of, 90, 151, 231–32 (n. 158); pop-
    ularity of, 137–38, 170; resignation of,
    172; in revolution of 1946, 81; rise of,
    67, 153; scholarly assessments of, 161–
    62; start of presidency, 149, 152–53; as
    threat to Estimé, 137–38, 145–47, 222
    (n. 135); U.S. relations with, 152, 154–
    55, 160
Magloire St. Aude, Clément, 24, 75
Manifeste de la Réaction Démocratique, 13
Mao Zedong, 122

Marcelin, Phito, 19

Marchand, Lucien, 78

Margron, Gaston, 113

Marines, U.S. *See* Occupation of Haiti by U.S.

Martelly, Gérard, 85

Martial law: after 1946 elections, 91, 96; during 1957 elections, 178; under Vincent, 17

Marxism, 14–23; in 1946 elections, 89–91; in 1957 elections, 174–75; as anarchy, 17; under Duvalier, 187; under Estimé, 127–36; Fignolé on, 65, 122; fragmentation of, 51–52, 53, 72; Griots' rejection of, 26–27; growth of movement, 15, 19, 72, 74; and Hudicourt, 17–19; influence in 1930s, 23; international assessment of, 128; under Lescot, 51–56, 72–83; Magloire's repression of, 155–57, 162; and massacre of 1937, 34; and nationalism, 17; political parties of, 83–88; repeal of legislation against, 99; in revolution of 1946, 72–83; of Roumain, 15–22; and socialism, 52, 86–87; surrealism and, 75–76; U.S. fears of, 15, 18, 85, 154; under Vincent, 14–23; during World War II, 40, 51–56. *See also specific political parties*

Massacre of 1937, 29–33, 34, 204 (n. 90); legacy of, 37, 40; protests after, 33–35, 188, 205 (n. 107)

Massacre of 1957, 182

Matin, Le, 41, 76, 100, 154

Mayer, Frederick, 34, 37

McCarthyism. *See* Anticommunism, U.S.

Media. *See* Press coverage

Medical university: during Magloire regime, 157; Marxism at, 72–74; in revolution, 77–78

Memory, national, 194–95

Menard, Max, 71, 75, 78, 85

Merceron, A. N., 53, 54

Mercier, Roger, 85, 129

Mexico, 53, 55

Middle-class blacks: as *authentiques,* 109; in conflict with *milat* elite, 117–21; educational access of, 7; education of, 112; emergence of, 5; on Fignolé's presidency, 180; Griots on, 23; in labor movement, 62; in Magloire's presidency, 152; *noirisme* among, 40, 106–7; during occupation, 188; role of, 5

Milat: use and meaning of term, 198 (n. 6)

Milat elite: versus *authentiques,* 117–21; black power challenging, 105, 109; end of rule by, 72, 105, 108–9; during Estimé's presidency, 117–21; Fignolé's criticism of, 121–22; Griots on, 25–27; on *noirisme,* 27; political parties of, 83; in politics of color, 4

Military rule, 149–85; in 1957 elections, 168–84; consolidation of, 150–53; economic decline during, 163–68; repression of opposition in, 153–63. *See also* Magloire, Paul Eugène

Minimum wage laws, 113, 166

Miss Haiti beauty pageant, 120

Montasse, Gérald, 75, 129

Montecristi, 31

Mooers, Horatio, 122

MOP. *See* Mouvement Ouvrier Paysan

Mouvement, Le, 41

Mouvement Organisation du Pays, 179

Mouvement Ouvrier Paysan (MOP): in 1950 elections, 141; anticommunism of, 122; establishment of, 93–94; Estimé opposed by, 121–27; evolution of, 122–23; flag of, 123–24, 125; fragmentation of, 104, 127, 158; literacy program of, 123; under Magloire regime, 155, 157–58; *noirisme* of, 124; reform of, 179; repression of, 126–27, 155; revival of, 141

Mulâtre: use of term, 198 (n. 6)

Mulatto: use of term, 198 (n. 6)

Musée Panthéon, 194

Music, 59–61; black consciousness in, 106–8; during Magloire's presidency,

152; *rasin* movement in, 193; vodou, 60, 106–8, 152, 223 (n. 11)

Mussolini, Benito, 26

NAACP, 36, 108, 180, 193

"Natif Natal" (song), 60, 103

Nation, La, 53–55; on 1946 elections, 91; closure of, 55, 56, 68, 142; on coups, 67–68; establishment of, 53–54; during Estimé regime, 131, 132; and Fédération des Travailleurs Haïtien, 132; and Hudicourt's death, 134; influence of, 54; and Parti Socialiste Populaire, 86, 131

Nation, The, 182

National Archives, 112

National Bank, 114, 179

National identity, 4, 59

Nationalism: cultural, 8–9, 108; in music, 60; opportunity for change through, 2

Nationalist movement: fragmentation of, in 1930s, 14–15; and Marxism, 17; origins in occupation, 7–10, 188; Roumain's critique of, 19–20

Nationalization: of banana industry, 115–16; of black power, 104–8

National Labor Bureau, 132–33

National Medical School, 73–74, 77–78, 157

National Party, 4

National Security Council, U.S. (NSC), 180

National unity: Magloire's rhetoric of, 151–52

Nazism, 27

Négritude movement, 56–57, 75

Negro Worker, 22

Nepotism, 42

New York Times, 130–31

Nicholls, David, 5, 6, 23, 25, 105, 162, 210 (n. 51)

Nightclubs, 152

Nixon, Richard, 180

Noirisme: in 1946 elections, 91, 92–93, 104; anti-liberalism of, 26–27; of

authentiques, 109; authoritarianism in, 140; versus Catholic church, 117; corruption and, 116–17; critics of, 27; divisions within, 104, 121, 136; under Estimé, 104–8; of Fignolé, 63–66, 189; in Front Révolutionnaire Haïtien, 86; of Griots, 25–28; in labor movement, 61–66; Lescot's use of, 42–43; during Magloire regime, 161, 162, 170; of MOP, 124; Parti Communiste Haïtien on, 87; Parti Socialiste Populaire on, 87, 134–35; political incorporation of, 104; political parties of, 83, 86; racism in, 27; rise of, 2; spread of, to non-elite, 40, 106–7; U.S. influence on, 189; during World War II, 40, 56–61

Non-elite blacks: educational access of, 7; *noirisme* among, 40, 106–7. *See also* Middle-class blacks

Nonintervention policy, U.S., 28–29

Norweb, R. Henry, 31

Noticias de Hoy, 51

Notre Jeunesse, 123

Nouvelle Ronde, La, 8

Nouvelle Ruche, La, 85

Nouvelliste, Le, 41, 50, 53, 119, 154

NSC. *See* National Security Council, U.S.

Numa, Edgar Néré, 89, 92, 97, 98, 142

OAS. *See* Organization of American States

Occupation of Dominican Republic by Haiti (1822–42), 29

Occupation of Haiti by U.S. (1915–34): debt accrued during, 113–15; end of, 1, 9–10, *10*, 13; Forbes commission on, 9; Marxism and, 18; origins of nationalist movement in, 7–10, 188; resistance to, 1, 7–10; scholarship on, 2; start of, 7

Orchestre Saïeh, 60

Organization of American States (OAS), 143

Ortega Frier, Julio, 30, 31

Ortiz, Fernando, 55

Padmore, George, 57
Paintings, 59
Palace Guard, 35, 42
Pan-African Conference of 1941, 59
Pan-American Airlines, 107–8
Pan-Americanism, 28, 44
Paquin, Lyonel, 119
Parti Communiste Haïtien (PCH): in 1946 elections, 89, 91, 92–93; on color divisions, 87; establishment of, 19; under Estimé, 127–31; fragmentation of, 51–52, 128–29; in Front Révolutionnaire Haïtien, 85–86; Juste Constant in, 84–85; in labor movement, 61, 62, 88; leadership changes in, 127–28; against Lescot regime, 51–52; on massacre of 1937, 34; versus other communist groups, 84, 85; program of, 19–21, 84, 200 (n. 31); revival after revolution of 1946, 83–88; Roumain's influence on, 22, 51–52, 56, 84; against Vincent dictatorship, 36
Parti Communiste Manchousite, 88
Parti Démocratique Populaire de la Jeunesse Haïtienne (PDPJH), 85, 86, 95
Parti d'Entente Populaire, 187
Partido Socialista Popular (PSP): Cuban, 87, 218 (n. 60)
Partie Révolutionnaire Haïtienne, 33
Parti Libéral Socialiste, 83
Parti Ouvrier Progressiste Haïtien (POPH), 129, 131
Parti Populaire de Libération Nationale (PPLN), 156, 157, 174–75
Parti Populaire Démocratique, 36
Parti Populaire Nationale (PPN), 83, 85, 88–89, 90
Parti Populaire Social Chrétien (PPSC), 83, 141, 142
Parti Socialiste Haïtien (PSH), 88, 90, 92
Parti Socialiste Populaire (PSP), 86–88; in 1946 elections, 89, 98; in 1950 elections, 141, 142; on color divisions, 87, 134–35; dissolution of, 142; establishment of, 86–87; under Estimé, 131–

36; in Estimé's coalition cabinet, 98–101; after Hudicourt's death, 133–34; in labor movement, 88; Magloire's repression of, 155–56; organizational experience in, 87; philosophy of, 87, 134; on Roland's opposition, 140; U.S. concerns about, 135–36
Paul, Edmond, 4
Paulino, Anselmo, 138
PCH. See Parti Communiste Haïtien
PDPJH. See Parti Démocratique Populaire de la Jeunesse Haïtienne
Peasants: art of, 59; in banana industry, 115–16; Griots on incorporation of, 25; rubber project's impact on, 45–46
Peguerro, H., 18
Pennet, Max, 78
Péralte, Charlemagne, 7, 10
Peters, Carl Edward, 50
Peters, DeWitt, 59
Petit, Georges, 9, 19, 21, 22, 52, 95–96, 131, 134
Petit Impartial, Le, 9, 15, 24
Peuple, Le, 62
Phalange, La, 49
Pierre-Louis, Bignon, 89, 97
Pierre-Louis, Joseph Nemours, 173, 175
Pierre-Louis, Rossini, 129, 134, 142, 151, 155, 158–59
Pierre-Paul, Antoine, 33
Pittsburgh Courier, 82, 104, 114
Plummer, Brenda Gayle, 163–64
Poetry, 74
Police forces: corruption in, 67; in revolution of 1946, 77; secret police under Magloire, 154
Political conflict: color consciousness in, 6; origins of, 1–2
Political culture: radicals' transformation of, 3, 191–92
Political parties: conservative, 83; under Magloire, 170; rise of, 2, 83–89. See also specific parties
Political systems: African versus European, 25–27

Politics: impact of radical movements on, 3, 190–94; incorporation of *noirisme* in, 104

POPH. *See* Parti Ouvrier Progressiste Haïtien

Port-au-Prince: Bicentennial Exposition in, 107; Cator as mayor of, 81–82; demographic shift in, 61–62, 166; Griots in, 23–24; massacre of 1957 in, 182; resistance to occupation in, 7–8; in revolution of 1946, 78; tourism in, 107–8; workers in, 61–62, 113

Port-au-Prince Times, 155

Postoccupation era (1934–57): gaps in scholarship on, 1–3; promise of, 2

PPLN. *See* Parti Populaire de Libération Nationale

PPN. *See* Parti Populaire Nationale

PPSC. *See* Parti Populaire Social Chrétien

Presidents: black, 41, 105–6, 207 (n. 3); provisional, 173, 175–76, 179–81. *See also* Elections, presidential; *specific presidents*

Press coverage: of 1946 elections, 89–90; of anti-superstition campaign, 49; of Bicentennial Exposition, 143; censorship of, 156, 182; of coup plots, 67–68; of Lescot's election, 41; Magloire's repression of, 154; of Marxists, 18, 22; of massacre of 1937, 31–33; of massacre of 1957, 182; on national debt, 113–14; after revolution of 1946, 83; of revolution of 1946, 77, 78, 82. *See also specific publications*

Pressoir, Raymond, 75, 76

Price-Mars, Jean: and coup against Lescot, 67; cultural nationalism of, 8–9; in Estimé's coalition cabinet, 99; and Fignolé, 63; and Griots, 23, 24, 27; during Lescot regime, 52; on Lescot's presidency, 41; on national debt, 113; on *noirisme*, 27; on vodou, 8, 48, 58

Problème des classes à travers l'histoire d'Haïti, Le (Duvalier and Denis), 66, 105

Prosper, Marcaisse, 137, 145, 147, 167

Protestant groups, U.S., 48–49

Protests: after 1946 elections, 91; against Duvalier regime, 192; in Estimé regime, 131, 145–46, 230 (n. 127); against Fignolé's removal, 181–82; against Magloire regime, 169–70; after massacre of 1937, 33–35, 188, 205 (n. 107); in revolution of 1946, 76–79; against Vincent dictatorship, 36. *See also* Strikes

Provisional government of 1957, 173–76, 179–81

PSH. *See* Parti Socialiste Haïtien

PSP. *See* Partido Socialista Popular; Parti Socialiste Populaire

Public works, 112

Puerto Rican Agricultural Company, 46

Race: versus color, 4; Griots on, 24–25; in national identity, 4; politicians' celebration of, 43

Racism: of Estimé, 110; in *noirisme*, 27

Radical movements, 188–95; allegiances among, 3, 6, 189; anticommunism's effects on, 3–4, 189; changes within, 3; coalition of, after revolution of 1946, 85–86; emergence of, 3, 7; fragmentation of, 6, 121, 188–90; ideological foundations of, 191; impact of, 3, 190–94; lack of scholarship on, 1, 2; origins of, during occupation, 7–10; political culture transformed by, 3; rivalries among, 3. *See also specific groups*

Radio: Duvalier's addresses on, 176, 177; expansion of, 60–61; Fignolé's addresses on, 99–100; Magloire's use of, 152; opposition to Estimé on, 139; after revolution of 1946, 83; in revolution of 1946, 79, 81

Ramponeau, Georges, 108

Ramsey, Kate, 48

Randolph, Virgil, III, 187

Rasin movement, 193

Réaction Démocratique, La (RD), 17–18, 19, 34, 36
Red Cross, 53
Refugees, 43
Regards, 34
Reinbold and Company, 47
Religion: peasant, 8; Protestant, 48–49. *See also* Catholic church
Rémy, Jean, 109, 119–21
Rémy, Tristan, 16
République, La, 104, 119, 145
Resistance: patterns of, in Caribbean, 194; to U.S. occupation, 1, 7–10; during World War II, 40, 74
Réveil, Le, 22, 55, 63, 65
Revolution. *See* Haitian revolution of 1946
Revue Indigène, La, 8–9
Rex Theater, 58–59, 76, 77
Reynaud, F. Burr, 83
Reynolds Mining Corporation, 165
Rigaud, Georges, 53; in 1946 elections, 89, 92; in 1957 elections, 174; economic plan of, 135; in Estimé's coalition cabinet, 99–100, 222 (n. 135); Fignolé's criticism of, 99–100; and Hudicourt's death, 134; under Kébreau, 183; on national debt, 113; in Parti Socialiste Populaire, 134; in revolution of 1946, 80
Road building, 165
Rodman, Selden, 59
Rodríguez Lora, Sebastián, 143
Roland, Astrel, 138–40, 142
Roosevelt, Franklin D.: and Fignolé, 63; foreign policy of, 28–29; on massacre of 1937, 32–33; and Vincent dictatorship, 36; in World War II, 43
Rosemond, Henri, 55
Rotberg, Robert, 110
Roumain, Jacques, 15–22, *18*; accused of coup plots, 17, 20–21, 51, 199 (n. 7); on anti-superstition campaign, 50; background of, 15–16; beliefs of, 15–16, 18–19; and CPUSA, 16, 17; death of, 55–56; in exile, 22, 51; *Gouverneurs*

de la Rosée, 55, 74; Griots and, 27; legacy of, 23, 74, 190; during Lescot regime, 51–56; Marxist critique of society by, 19–20; on massacre of 1937, 34–35; nationalism of, 8, 9; on nationalist movement, 19–20; presidential pardon of, 22; return to Haiti, 51; in *La Revue Indigène*, 8, 9; surveillance of, 51; trials and imprisonment of, 18–19, 20–22; on vodou, 58; writings of, 52, 211 (n. 69)
Roumain, Michel, 36, 51, 56, 135, 158
Roumain, Nicole, 79–80
Roumer, Andrée, 132
Roumer, Emile, 56
Rouzier, Gontran, 77, 118
Rubber cultivation, 43–47, *45*
Rubber Development Corporation, 46
Ruche, La, 71, 75–76, 80, *81*, 85
Rural areas: anti-superstition campaign in, 48–49; Estimé's development projects in, 112; police corruption in, 67; Protestantism in, 49

Sadors, Jean (pseudonym), 65–66
St. Armand, Edris, 74; in 1946 elections, 89, 91; Estimé opposed by, 129; in Fédération des Travailleurs Haïtien, 132; in labor movement, 132, 133; in Parti Communiste Haïtien, 83–85, 128; in Parti Socialiste Populaire, 131
St. Lôt, Emile: in 1946 elections, 93; in 1957 elections, 179; L'Amicale club of, 58, 83; as *authentique*, 109; in constitutional debates, 96, 97; Estimé opposed by, 144, 147; Estimé supported by, 111; in Front Révolutionnaire Haïtien, 85; in labor ministry, 112, 126; on Marxists, 99
Sajous, Marcellus, 19
Salgado, Pierre, 157
Salomon, Lysius, 7, 26, 58, 88
Salomon, René, 58, 88, 89, 90
Sam, Justin, 53, 86–87
Sam, Max D., *131*; in 1946 elections, 89,

91, 92; background of, 53; in Estimé's administration, 99, 100, 135; on Estimé's color politics, 135; Lescot's meeting with, 56; Magloire's repression and, 155; in Parti Socialiste Populaire, 86–87; in revolution of 1946, 77

Sam, T. A. Simon, 53

SCISP. *See* Service Coopératif Inter-Américain de la Santé Publique

Séïde, Marc, 109, 160

Séjour, André, 104

Selassie, Haile, 26

Senate, Haitian, 21–22, 36

Separation of powers, 21–22

Service Coopératif Inter-Américain de la Santé Publique (SCISP), 161

SHADA. *See* Société Haïtiano-Américaine de Développement Agricole

Silvani, Monsignor, 49

Social class. *See* Class, social

Socialism: and communism, 52, 86–87; in Estimé's coalition cabinet, 98–100; in Garde, 67, 77; during Lescot regime, 52, 53; and *noirisme*, 87, 88; political parties of, 86–87; in revolution of 1946, 77; U.S. pressure on, 189. *See also specific political parties*

Société Haïtiano-Américaine de Développement Agricole (SHADA), 44–47, 45, 50, 93

Society: functions of color in, 5–6; under Lescot, 58; Marxist critique of, 19–20, 23

Soir, Le, 49

SOT. *See* Syndicats d'Ouvriers et Travailleurs

Soulouque, Faustin (emperor), 29, 40

Soviet Union: cold war with, 104, 130, 155; and Parti Communiste Haïtien, 128. *See also* Anticommunism, Haitian; Anticommunism, U.S.

Standard Fruit and Steamship Company, 29, 115–16

State Department, U.S.: in 1957 elections, 183; on economic aid, 115; and Lescot

regime, 46, 47; and Magloire regime, 160, 172; opposition to Estimé and, 139; on rubber cultivation, 46; and Vincent dictatorship, 36–37

Sterlin, Fernand, 132, 133

Strauss, Lévi, 75

Strikes: and 1950 elections, 141; during 1957 elections, 175–76; under Estimé, 125–27, 228 (n. 100); legalization of, 88; under Magloire, 157, 159, 167, 169–70; during occupation, 9, 14, 15, 76; after revolution of 1946, 88; in revolution of 1946, 76–79. *See also* Protests

Students: under Magloire, 156–57, 169–70; in revolution of 1946, 76–79

Suffrage: universal male, 151; women's, 171

Sugarworkers, 30

Suicide: of Hudicourt, 133–34

Superstition: Catholic campaign against, 47–50, 69

Supreme Court, 172, 173

Surrealism, 75–76, 77

Surveillance: of Parti Socialiste Populaire, 87; of Roumain, 51; of students, 78

Sylvain, Franck, 176, 177

Syndicats d'Ouvriers et Travailleurs (SOT), 124–26

Tardieu, Edouard, 83

Tax, income, 118

Teacher education, 112

Théâtre du Verdure, 107

Thezan, Emmanuel, 224 (n. 25)

Thezan, S., 33

Time magazine, 167

Ti-Roro, 106

Tittmann, Harold, 115

Tonton Makout, 187

Totalitarianism, 162

Tourism: development of, 59, 107–8; Estimé's promotion of, 106–8, 143–44; under Magloire, 163–64

Tourism, Department of, 107

Trade: with France, 165; with U.S., 13, 29

Tricinquantenaire (1954), 167

Trinidad, 194

Trois D, Les, 23–24

Trouillot, Michel-Rolph, 5–6, 69, 162, 172

Trujillo Molina, Rafael Leonidas, 29–33; in 1957 elections, 183; Calixte's relationship with, 96; Lescot's alliance with, 40, 41; Lescot's conflict with, 68–69; Magloire's relationship with, 152; in massacre of 1937, 29–33; and opposition to Estimé, 139, 142–43; U.S. nonintervention in rise of, 29; in World War II, 43

Truman, Harry, 145

Turits, Richard, 204 (n. 90)

Union Démocratique Haïtien, 83

Union des Indépendants, 141, 142

Unions. *See* Labor movement

United Fruit, 47, 115–16

United States: in 1946 elections, 93; in 1957 elections, 174, 177, 178, 183–84, 185; Duvalier's education in, 28; economic control by, 29, 113–14; on Fignolé's presidency, 179–80; Fignolé's understanding of, 122; Hudicourt's exile in, 55; on Kébreau junta, 182; on Lescot's election, 41–42; on massacre of 1937, 30–33; recognition of regimes by, 82, 180, 182; vodou stereotypes in, 48; in World War II, 43. *See also* Anti-communism, U.S.; Foreign policy, U.S.; Foreign relations, U.S.-Haitian; Occupation of Haiti by U.S.

University of Haiti, 72

University of Michigan, 28

Vabre, Victor, 133

Viau, Alfred: in 1957 elections, 173; death of son of, 119–20; Estimé opposed by, 138–39, 142

Viau, Gérard, 119–21

Victor, René, 132

Vieux, Antonio, 51, 160

Vigie, 22

Vincent, Sténio Joseph (president, 1934–41), 10–11, 13–38, 14, 188; 1930 election of, 9; 1936 election of, 13, 21–22, 201 (n. 38); anticommunism of, 16–17, 20–23; coup plots against, 20–21, 33, 35–36; dictatorship established by, 36–37; in end of U.S. occupation, 1, 9–10; Griots and, 23–28; and labor movement, 61; leadership style of, 13–14; Lescot under, 17, 33, 40; Marxism under, 14–23; and massacre of 1937, 29–33, 37; resignation of, 37; on second independence, 1, 26; superstition laws of, 48; U.S. relations with, 13–14, 29

Violence: in 1957 elections, 169, 177–78, 182; Duvalier's use of, 185, 187; Magloire's use of, 153, 169–70

Vocational schools, 8, 13

Vodou: Catholic campaign against, 47–50; defenders of, 8, 25, 28, 58; elite interest in, 214 (n. 104); Estimé government's support for, 106–7, 117; in Magloire's presidency, 152; in music, 60, 106–8, 152, 223 (n. 11); *noirisme* on, 27; shifts in attitudes toward, 58–59, 152; stereotypes of, in U.S., 48

Voltes, Georges, 91

Von Eschen, Penny, 193

Vulcain, Francis, 155

Washington Afro-American, 82

Weltfish, Regina, 55

West, Jack, 82–83, 122, 136

White, J. C., 41, 207–8 (n. 6)

White, Walter, 36, 57, 108, 150, 180, 193, 234 (n. 1)

White Haitians: Jewish refugees and, 43; in Lescot's administration, 42

Widmaïer, Ricardo, 60

Williams, R. P., 15

Wilson, Orme, 80, 98

Woolley, Stephen, 137

Women's League, 171

Women's movement: in 1957 elections, 171, 238 (n. 91); origins of, 200 (n. 21); in revolution of 1946, 79–80

Women's Union, 171

Workers: in 1946 elections, 91, 94; in 1957 elections, 174, 175; and Dominican–Haitian relations, 30; under Estimé, 112–13; Estimé supported by, 103; in Front Révolutionnaire Haïtien, 85; population of, 62, 62; in Port-au-Prince, 61–62, 113; in radical political parties, 85–86; in revolution of 1946, 78, 80. *See also* Labor movement

World War II, 39–70; anti-superstition campaign in, 47–50; black conscious- ness in, 40, 56–61; cooperation with U.S. in, 43–44; economic policy during, 43–47; French resistance in, 73–74; Haitian entry into, 43; labor movement in, 61–66; Marxism in, 40, 51–56; *noirisme* in, 40, 56–61; refugees from, 43; rubber cultivation in, 43–46

Woulo konmpresè (steamroller), 86, 89, 96, 99–100, 178

Writers: Griot, 24–28; Marxist, 15–16, 74–75; nationalist, 8–9; *négritude*, 57. *See also specific publications and writers*

Zamor, Saint-Juste, 19